Nostalgia
   Isn't What It
Used to Be

SIMONE SIGNORET

Nostalgia Isn't What It Used to Be

PENGUIN BOOKS

Penguin Books Ltd, Harmondsworth,
Middlesex, England
Penguin Books, 625 Madison Avenue,
New York, New York 10022, U.S.A.
Penguin Books Australia Ltd, Ringwood,
Victoria, Australia
Penguin Books Canada Limited, 2801 John Street,
Markham, Ontario, Canada L3R 1B4
Penguin Books (N.Z.) Ltd, 182–190 Wairau Road,
Auckland 10, New Zealand

First published in France under the title
La Nostalgie n'est plus ce qu'elle était
by Éditions du Seuil 1976
This English translation first published
in the United States of America by
Harper & Row, Publishers, Inc., 1978
First published in Canada by Fitzhenry &
Whiteside Limited 1978
Published in Penguin Books by arrangement with
Harper & Row, Publishers, Inc., 1979

LIBRARY OF CONGRESS CATALOGING IN PUBLICATION DATA
Signoret, Simone, 1921–
Nostalgia isn't what it used to be.
Translation of La nostalgie n'est plus ce qu'elle était.
Includes index.
1. Signoret, Simone, 1921– 2. Actors—France
—Biography. I. Title.
PN2638.S47A3413 1979 791.43′028′0924 [B] 78-27395
ISBN 0 14 00.5181 3

Printed in the United States of America by
Offset Paperback Mfrs., Inc., Dallas, Pennsylvania
Set in Garamond

Contents

Preface

OF course, it all began with a taped conversation which lasted six days.

Of course, it was giving in to a fashion, publishing one's "memoirs."

Of course, I had said no; no, no, no, for years.

Of course, finally I said yes. Well, I said, "Yes, maybe," without a contractual obligation. I would talk, I would answer Maurice Pons's questions, and then we'd see what it looked like. If it looked like something, we'd go to it—that is, we'd have it printed and it would become an object called a "book," if you're not too fussy about what the word "book" really means.

At the end of those six days I found myself dispossessed of most of my memories and the owner of a flowering, and consequently deflowered, memoir. I *felt* it, but I didn't *know* it yet.

After I'd read the transcript of my endless conversation on tape, I decided to stop the whole thing. Until then it hadn't cost a penny, not for me and not for the publisher.

It was unreadable. Listenable, perhaps; listenable and

seeable if there had been a camera as well as a tape recorder, to show the hands, the eyes, the hesitations, the evasions, and the silences.

But for someone who loves books it was unreadable. For me, unreadable.

So those six hundred typed pages became a dossier, and that dossier was stashed away on the highest shelf of a closet so it would sleep far from my eyes. Which it did for a year.

In the middle of one lazy afternoon, I suddenly took out a notebook and started writing about my mother and the hairdressers in Neuilly-sur-Seine. I just wanted to see whether things would look different if one wrote them on paper rather than speaking them into a microphone.

It was like pulling out one stitch in a sleeve—suddenly the whole sweater began to unravel.

So every day I sat down in front of that blank paper, without ever consulting the dossier of my nonstop interview (except for Chapter 14, as you'll see if you stay with me).

At first I felt my way timidly, as does any beginner who is learning alone. I did my underwater diving slowly, to bring up the corals and the flotsam that lie at the bottom of one's memory.

Without the interview, the idea would never have occurred to me.

Without that interrogation I would never have found myself in a state to interrogate myself, after the fact. In silence and in solitude.

SIMONE SIGNORET

Nostalgia
Isn't What It
Used to Be

Chapter 1

IT took me a long time to make up my mind to commit my memories to paper. My memories aren't my exclusive property. They are life. I'm convinced that we are all fashioned by one another, and when you start telling the story of your life, you're telling the story of others. Even the options we decide on throughout our existence are always caused by someone else; a chance encounter, or perhaps because you'd like to be esteemed by certain people. Not many, in fact. I'm well aware that the thing I call my conscience is, in reality, what some half-dozen people consider me to be. Not necessarily those I see often—and people who have no idea they are my conscience. But I know they're watching me! In my mind they are men. All of them. It's very odd: I don't really feel the female eye penetrating me. Nor are these men necessarily people I've been emotionally involved with.

I was born in 1921 in Wiesbaden, in the Rhineland, during the French occupation. When my parents returned to France, I was two years old. So I don't remember that period . . . just what my father did.

My father was the son of a Polish Jew, a diamond merchant, whom I never knew. His mother was an Austrian Jewess whom I never liked very much, probably because she never really accepted my mother. In a Jewish family the worst thing a son could do was to marry a non-Jew. And that is just what my father did. He was born in France, in Saint-Gratien. He belonged to the generation that did a three-year period of military service; then four years of war, followed by three years in France's army of occupation in Germany. He was trained as a lawyer, but he worked for an advertising agency. It was called La Maison Damour, and the boss's name was Étienne Damour. I fondly imagined a man with such a name to be a very tall and handsome man; I met him one day and was a little disappointed. However, he can't have been a complete fool, since at one time or another he employed people like the Prévert brothers; Grimaud, the film cartoonist; Aurenche, the screenwriter; film director Marcel Carné; and a photographer named Zuber.

Maison Damour published a review entitled *Vendre (Sales)*, and on its cover was a profile of an open-mouthed head topped by a Phrygian bonnet—the French liberty cap—which looked to me like the zinc cowls that cap Parisian chimneys. So, as far as I was concerned, my father worked with a deity named Damour and wrote for a paper that looked like a chimney cowl.

One day—I must have been about five—my father came home around noon in tears. Our apartment was on the fourth floor, and there was no elevator. Usually my father announced his arrival by whistling Siegfried's motif, which was always the family's rallying call. That day he came up slowly, silently, step by step, and collapsed crying on the landing. Damour was dead.

My mother was born in Paris, the daughter of a modest milliner from Valenciennes and an obscure painter from Marseilles.

All of my early childhood was spent in the Parisian suburb of Neuilly-sur-Seine. A small apartment on the Rue

Jacques-Dulud, the Neuilly zoo, the market, and a Singer sewing machine were my world. "Come see the little spool go round," my mother would say whenever she changed the bobbin. She made me cute little dresses cut from Rodier leftovers bought in the Neuilly market.

The Neuilly market looms large in my memories of an only child. Especially the one on the Avenue de Neuilly. One day I got lost, and when my mother found me, I was sitting on top of a pyramid of potatoes chez Camille, smiling, confident, quite sure she would find me. I wasn't at all frightened. She was—very!

At the Neuilly market my nose was just about level with the fascinating wares displayed. My favorite booth was that of the milk-and-cheese man; the great half wheels of stacked Gruyère separated us. He couldn't see me because I was too tiny; this allowed me to explore the deep holes in the cheese, which were rapidly transformed into grottoes while my mother waited for her chunk of Isigny butter to be weighed.

Besides the Rodier fabrics and potatoes from Camille's, my mother bought a lot chez Charlot. Charlot was a kind of colossus who bellowed abusively at clients and whose very beautiful wife wore a leather bandolier slung over her shoulder, just like a streetcar conductor. Her lips were painted almost black. There were no trestle tables chez Charlot, everything was piled on the ground—and consisted of leftover merchandise from well-known shoe and leatherware manufacturers. I remember vividly some evening slippers, one pair in gold lamé and the other in silver lamé. They were useless to my mother—she was hardly a socialite—but she bought them anyway, and I'd borrow them for playing at being a lady. She stuffed the toes with newspaper, and I would parade around my room, trailing a draped curtain behind me, when I was recuperating from whooping cough or measles.

Every year, for one month, the market was occupied by—or rather shared its space with—the fairground folk from the Fête de Neuilly. In the mornings there'd be the "superperceptive" fortune-tellers, in bathrobes and curlers, cleaning up in front of their caravans and behind the market gardeners' stands. There was Mademoiselle Thérésa, the fat lady, who weighed in at two hundred kilos without her blue satin cape with its fake ermine collar, without her paste tiara and the throne on which she sat to present herself to the audience, which was invited to touch one of the enormous powdered thighs she disclosed beneath her cape. One day, no doubt a school-free Thursday, when I was sent out with the young Breton maid to ride on the merry-go-round, she simply couldn't resist the temptation of sharing with me her delight in approaching such an outstanding curiosity as Mademoiselle Thérésa. This same young Breton was soon to leave us for good because of a certain Saturday night at the fairground. Much later I learned that all the Paris pimps hung around the Fête de Neuilly to replenish their annual supplies.

Among the other vivid images of that time is my mother's reflection in a mirror—or rather in many different mirrors—and here is the reason. At the time, my hair was cut in a pageboy style, rather like Joan of Arc, and my mother took me to have it cut in barbershops. In the plural. We must have gone through half a dozen of them between my fifth and sixth years. We would arrive; I would be set on a pile of telephone directories between two customers being shaved and trimmed; my mother would make sure the cotton wool wedged between my neck and the big wrap was quite clean—which would upset the artist to whom she gave her instructions—and then she would sit down and smile reassuringly at me in the mirror. She would pick up the available reading matter; without fail there'd be something called *Le Rire* or *Le Sourire*—smutty and very French, a kind of equivalent of *Playboy*. She would leaf through the magazine with an air of disgust, and then replace it ostentatiously on the little table she had removed it from.

As long as our artist was busy with my fringe and locks,

14

all would go well, except for the clippings that would fall into my eyes and on my nose, which he would flick off with a kind of shaving brush. But come the moment to do the back: Two hard, expert fingers pushed my head forward. I could no longer see my mother's face, but I knew I'd hear this phrase—it never varied: "May I ask you, monsieur, to kindly pass your instrument through a flame," at precisely the moment he would start clicking his clippers preparatory to an attack on the back of my neck. A sudden pause in the snipping. My head still down, I saw nothing. And then the artist would reply along these lines: "Madame, this salon is run with the greatest care." My mother would get up and approach the two flaming little jets of gas on either side of the mirror, and she would begin to launch forth on a condensed lecture on human hygiene, from which it would emerge that I was but a child, that frequently adults are carriers of grievous germs, and that in any case the gas jets had not been installed merely for decorative purposes. All this would be delivered with exquisite politeness. Then she would sit down again. The artist thereupon singed his instrument, with a smirk at his two colleagues which never escaped my attention. He would rub up the back of my neck, and then there would be no sound except the click of the still warm clippers on my neck. When it was all over, no little massage was proposed, no lotion or free soap samples, he would just peel off the big wrapper. We paid and left, and as soon as we were outside, my mother would say: "Well, we'll never set foot in there again!"

I was an only child, and overprotected. I never had a cat because a little neighbor had her eye put out by hers. I never was allowed a pair of roller skates because one of my mother's cousins fractured his skull on the edge of a sidewalk in Arles in 1911. But I had canaries and goldfish. When they died, the fact would be hidden from me, and they would be replaced the same night by live ones, which were not always the same size or color.

One summer, in Le Pouliguen, on the Atlantic coast, we became shrimp saviors. I had caught three shrimps and a little crab. That evening we put a pailful of sea water on the bedroom mantel in our *pension de famille;* and my mother settled down in bed with a book. She was not one of those ladies who put their children to bed and then go out dancing. I began to cry, and explained that I wanted to put my three shrimps and the crab back into the sea. She dressed me again in my rompers, and we took the pail and emptied the contents into the harbor. I was blissfully happy . . . and she was too. Ever since I told this story to Suzanne Flon, between a matinee and an evening performance, I get postcards from ports around the world carrying a message that goes: "My great-great-great-great-great-grandmother owes her life to you. Signed, A Grateful Shrimp."

I was an only child, and only children, especially, are included in the conversation. One day I was terrified that Madame Albertine, who came from Puteaux for two hours a week to do our cleaning, would never come back, since she had "disappeared."* When I was six, they explained intelligently such incomprehensible words as "trainfulof-Americanplenipotentiaries" and "SaccoVanzetti." One May evening in 1927, my mother, closing my bedroom shutters, suddenly exclaimed, "There he is!" An airplane droned overhead—it was Lindbergh. One morning that same year, she said, "They've arrived." It was Nungesser and Coli. They told me the story of Siegfried and they told me the story of Achilles, and it seemed to me that these two failures of invulnerability were peculiarly similar. I scared myself with Gustave Doré illustrations for Andersen's tales, which a family friend had the weird idea of offering me when I was seven. Crime was never mentioned in front of me. Juicy items in newspapers were censored as far as I was concerned; so that later, by way of reaction, I became terribly inquisitive about affairs like that of Violette Nozières, and still today I'm an incomparable quiz kid in this domain.

*"*Albertine disparu,*" as in Proust, who was discussed in my house.

My first school was a chic little place called the Cours Lafayette, which among other advantages was located very near the Rue Jacques-Dulud, where we lived. My only memories of the kindergarten class in the Cours Lafayette are of little royal-blue chairs, a classmate whose car and chauffeur awaited her after school, and the boy in the chair next to mine, who would slip his hand into my bloomers, murmuring, "If you say anything, you'll go to jail because my father is a member of Parliament." He was red-haired, and he slipped out of my life, if that's the correct expression, at the age of six.

I began my proper schooling at the Lycée Pasteur, which was coed. In my class there were five or six girls and about twenty boys. We would line up to a drum beaten by Monsieur Félix. My teacher was named Madame Arrighi, and the principal's name was Monsieur Champagne—it really was! He was young, he had a handlebar mustache, and he came very often to visit Madame Arrighi while we labored over our first subtractions. During recreation time we played war games: The boys would divide into two sides, and we girls were forced to play the spies. Not nurses—spies. We were invariably caught by one side or the other and cruelly punished for our indefensible activities; we would be rolled in the gravel in the courtyard of the imitation Louis XIII building that is the Lycée Pasteur of Neuilly-sur-Seine.

There were two gang leaders. One was David—he was small—and the other was my personal torturer, Malissard. He would take it out on my little gray felt hat with the black velvet ribbon. He even went so far as to roll it in the muddy gravel one rainy day. I had always hidden the Malissard persecution from my mother. But that day she caught him at it while she was waiting for me behind the gate. She threatened to box his ears; Malissard, blushing violently, swore that he would never do it again—and my life became hell during every recreation period thereafter. Outside school hours, this well-brought-up little boy would pass my mother with a respectful bow. And she would congratulate herself for having stepped in at the right moment.

There is an enormous fleet of enormous trucks crisscrossing all of France with "Malissard" emblazoned on their flanks; in fact, to be accurate, they say "Malissard and Son." For years, without even knowing whether my Malissard could be that son, whenever one of those trucks rumbled by it would act upon me like a reversed time machine. I would even imagine a Malissard son the commander of this armada of the highways: part admiral, part buccaneer, cruel and breezy as I knew he could be.

One day in 1954, at the Saint-Maurice studios, between takes of *Les Diaboliques*, the uniformed gatekeeper very respectfully brought me a visiting card on which was written: "Jacques Malissard, certain that you no longer remember him, presents his respects and would very much like to bring you his greetings, if you would be kind enough to authorize his entry onto the set."

And so I met this grown-up Malissard, who spent a half hour with me in that incomprehensible and magical place which is a movie set. He wanted me to explain everything to him, and all I talked about was my felt hat, Madame Arrighi, Monsieur Félix and his drum, and Monsieur Champagne, who had become a radio star. I asked him to tell me about trucks, and he blushed—he had become shy.

I graduated brilliantly from the tenth class to the ninth. Our new teacher, Mademoiselle Hendrix, didn't like me: I was not in her catechism class, which she gave outside school hours. It wasn't exactly that she made snide comments, but she had a way of calling her flock of little lambs after a grammar class which, retrospectively, sends chills down my spine.

Thus, Mademoiselle Hendrix didn't like me. But my mother adored geography. And that was why I produced for our geography class the most splendid imaginable illustrations of our handsome hexagonal country. Our coasts, whether north or west or south, went from a brilliantly dark midocean color to the palest watery blue;

our Vosges, our Alps, and our Pyrenees went from sepia and sienna to the creamiest white; our splendid rivers began at sky-blue sources to throw themselves into jade-green estuaries. The contours of my masterpieces were irreproachable: Not a cape, not a bay, not a peninsula was missing. Once the outline had been traced on a paper previously used for wrapping our butter in, washed and carefully ironed, my mother would set to work with great gusto. Obviously Mademoiselle Hendrix, who had her personal reasons for not liking me, could not like my mother's masterpieces, which I innocently brought in as my own homework. So she would play a game with good marks: She would put two stars on my desk, walk a few steps down the aisle, come back, reflect lengthily, and take one back. She never asked me whether I had help at home; I think she wanted above all to punish my mother for my lack of religious education by awarding her only one star when what she really deserved was the class prize for excellence.

One day, on Saint Charlemagne's day, a company of actors—which I believed for ages after was the Comédie Française—came to our school. They played *Le Malade Imaginaire* in our echoing covered courtyard. All the actors spoke in a manner that seemed to me so unnatural that the notion of naturalness in the theater remained foreign to my personal mythology for a long time. Since I had seen professional actors speak, and especially laugh, like that, that must be the way it was supposed to be. A great many people, unhappily, never revise this kind of early judgment.

My paternal grandmother sometimes took me out on Sundays, ostensibly to "get a breath of fresh air." I can't remember our ever taking air other than that which exists inside a movie house. I remember distinctly that we saw *The Jazz Singer* (which I never saw again, so this is not a superimposition of memory). When the hero's mother died and her young daughter-in-law was inconsolable, my grandmother gave me to understand what a splendid thing it was to see a family in which the daughter-in-law and mother-in-law loved each other so much. (I got the message.)

Of course, there was the zoo, with caged lions—that was before those ridiculous concrete rocks were built for them—and they made me cry. The seals, on the other hand, seemed to me to be happy; at least they had their water, and kilos of fish thrown to them by a keeper who addressed them only in German.

Once I was taken to the little merry-go-round at the Rond-Point of the Champs Élysées. At that time my mother was going to Annales, to a series of lectures, and she would come back in a very Proustian state. I seem to remember her standing in a reverie in front of the *chalet de nécessités*.* I, seated on my little wooden horse, my stick in hand, missed the rings each time we went around. I looked across at my mother, who smiled. There were some little geniuses who triumphantly finished their turn on the merry-go-round with their sticks as beringed as the fingers of Gypsies; and their mothers were proud and happy. Mine consoled me without the least hint of bitterness or shame. It would have to be an intellectual attraction like Proust to lure us so far from home, because with the exception of some visits to my maternal grandparents in the Ternes area, and to Uncle Marcel and Aunt Irène on the Square Lamartine, my mother and I rarely went beyond Neuilly.

Uncle Marcel and Aunt Irène, whose story I won't enter into in detail, were the only rich—very rich—members of the Kaminker-Signoret family. I no longer remember exactly how Uncle Marcel and Aunt Irène came to be related to us, but I do remember that until my seventh year, at about five o'clock on some Sunday afternoons we would take a taxi—and my mother never failed to say we could just as well go by bus—to No. 7 bis Square Lamartine. The taxi would stop in front of a varnished bottle-green entrance that transformed the ground floor

*Public rest room.

of a big apartment building into a kind of private house. There, answering our ring, would be Rémy, the faithful servant disguised as a kind of valet in a striped vest, who would take our coats. He would call me "Mademoiselle Kiki" (that was my nickname at the time), which was a change from the "Hi, sweetie" of our Madame Albertine from Puteaux. We would pass first through a kind of circular hall, then came an enormous salon containing a grand piano, and finally a smaller salon. After the smaller salon came my Aunt Irène's room, decorated in the style of Marie Antoinette, all draped in blue and containing an upholstered dressing table with an oval mirror, around which hung necklaces of pink, gray, and black pearls. Beyond this I could see a bathroom, which seemed gigantic, with enormous bowlfuls of soap hooked around the bathtub. After that came my Uncle Marcel's room, all done in mahogany. I was to rediscover exactly the same design in the first grand English hotel I stayed at, where eventually success was to lead me in London. It was rather like a cabin on one of the big ocean-going liners, only ten times as big. My uncle's bathroom, done in marble, copper, and mahogany, had an effect that was virile, serious, and functional, which impressed me. Finally, a corridor led to what was called the "boudoir," a room made for intimacy which looked out on a small interior court. The floor of that court was made of a kind of glass like that in the bottom of a bottle, which filtered the electric light from a basement that had been arranged as an ultramodern guest apartment. Little orange trees in pots lived on this glass surface, and a trompe l'oeil row of painted trellises on the far wall presented the optical illusion of a long corridor leading to a park. I must say, all this cheered up that gray wall, which, although it was in the elegant sixteenth arrondissement, was still only a blank wall. A corridor then curved back to the circular hall, where a door at the right opened on a dining room entirely covered with Aubusson tapestries. It was enough to take away your appetite; not all that petit point, patiently carried out by all those seventeenth-century embroiderers, but because of the subject: the hunt.

Aunt Irène and Uncle Marcel's home was Versailles, Malmaison, the Louvre, and Bagatelle all rolled into one, with Le Corbusier in the basement for dessert. Only once did I ever penetrate as far as the pantry and kitchen. These were presided over by a lady named Maria, and I never could find out whether she was Rémy's wife or not, which bothered me because I thought Rémy was very handsome and Maria was too fat. Though I was only the poor relation, I was still part of a distinguished family, still a young lady of the château.

The weekly ceremony usually took place in the little salon. Uncle Marcel had a white beard and he smelled of violets, which came from sucking little violet drops. He would take me on his knees and tell me that he loved me very much, in a French ever so slightly tinged with an Austrian accent. He wore what was then called a smoking jacket, made of black velvet and closed with frogs and loops. Aunt Irène wore diamond earrings with a pendant at the end, which changed, according to the season, from rubies to sapphires and from pearls to emeralds. Her clothes were made of very fine wool, and I remember them as dusty rose, beige, pale blue, or white. She was small, slim, beautiful, and haughty. She never took me on her knees. Then there were the habitués of the house, one named Princess Ismet, I believe, and a bishop who, as was explained to me, had converted Uncle Marcel and Aunt Irène to Catholicism. There were lots of Oriental carpets, and a parquet floor in the grand salon that was the color of honey. There were great round blue boxes, crisscrossed with black, marked "Chez Boissier, Confiseur," on the side tables. There were silver teapots, silver sugar bowls, and cups with little claws instead of bases. There were silver sugar tongs, and spoons so small that their only use was stirring sugar in tiny cups. The conversation darted from one subject to another, and I understood very little of it. I was bored. And so was Uncle Marcel; he would bounce me on his knees to the sound of a quavery tune that must have originated far back in his memory. His memory of when he was a young, poor Austrian Jew, now that he was an old, rich, newly French Catholic. I think he had made a fortune on the stock market.

Then came an equivocal time, between seven-fifteen and seven-thirty, when my mother was murmuring that we must go home. Not that one actually smelled cooking, but there was a discreet tinkle of silverware to be heard from the dining room. Finally, we would put on our coats without having been asked to stay for dinner. True, my young age and the seriousness of my studies indicated an early bedtime....

(I wanted to describe the Square Lamartine because about fifteen years ago Irwin Shaw, who had just settled in France, gave a party at his Paris apartment, 7 bis Square Lamartine. Thirty-five years later, the only thing that had really changed was that the boudoir had become a children's room. Much more cheerful.)

At our apartment, Rue Jacques-Dulud, on the fourth floor, there was a small corridor, then a dining room and two other rooms: mine and that of my parents, which doubled as a living room; there was a large kitchen and a tiny washroom. Recently installed in the washroom was an object that fascinated me, particularly on account of the precautions demanded. It looked like a wooden bureau topped with a slab of marble; into it was set a porcelain basin that tilted backward and dumped its contents below. The water for this contraption had to be brought in pitchers and poured into a tank behind the mirror. This false bureau, which looked like a dressing table, was topped by a single spigot. It ran hot, tepid, or cold according to the hour one turned it on. When it ran, everything was fine; you had "running water," the boast of all the "for rent" signs attached outside half the houses in Neuilly at that time. When the spigot didn't work, things weren't so good, but when the whole thing ran over, they were very bad. What I mean is, the magic and mystery of

23

this object would be dissipated when the pail, craftily concealed in the base of the false bureau, had not been emptied in time. This sometimes happened on a Sunday evening, which would end the day in rather picturesque fashion. Then my father would help my mother sponge water off the turquoise-and-yellow linoleum, which was beginning to warp in large waves.

What my father loved on Sundays was the Square Lamartine. As soon as the weather was nice, my father, who never took walks, would go out with me at around eleven-thirty and we would promenade up the elegant Allée des Acacias and down the Avenue du Bois. The people we met were extremely well dressed; my father would greet those he knew and others he thought knew him. On the Avenue du Bois he would raise his hat in salutation to a pink marble palace, but his explanations concerning Boni de Castellane are dimmer in my memory than those of my mother concerning Sacco and Vanzetti. My mother never joined us on our snobbish promenades. While we were out she would clean the house and prepare our Sunday chicken with rice. We were supposed to bring home the cake from chez Chavy, pastry cook and baker; she was no longer altogether welcome there since she had requested the salesgirl to refrain from licking her thumb to pick up the tissue paper that wrapped our daily bread. I hope I have been Proustian and pretentious enough; the reference to Boni de Castellane surely did not escape you.

Sunday afternoon was, for my father, a long intermission between the walk along the Allée des Acacias and the Avenue du Bois, and that kind of dip into worldliness he anticipated when he hailed the taxi that was to take us to the Square Lamartine. During the morning episode I was the cute little girl dressed in Rodier leftovers made on her mother's sewing machine; then there was that vulgar moment of buying the cake, even though in any novel dealing with the French bourgeoisie this is seen as a Sunday morning ritual, and finally we would leave to go to the world that filled his dreams. I forgot to say that while Uncle Marcel amused himself at being bored along with me, my father wasn't bored for a second, and visibly did not bore his audience—except my mother, who was no longer impressed. She would sit there, silent, beautiful, well-dressed for the occasion by her own hand, wondering what she was doing there among the boxes from Boissier, the sugar tongs, and the Aubusson tapestries far away in the dining room. Maybe she was thinking about what she would cook for my supper; or maybe she was thinking about the book that she had really read, and about which everyone was talking without having cracked the cover; or maybe she was thinking that she must remember to empty the pail in the washroom; or maybe she was thinking about her parents, who still had no electricity at home.

Sometimes on Thursday afternoons we would walk from Rue Jacques-Dulud to the Avenue des Ternes, where my mother's parents lived. We would walk along the Avenue de Neuilly, primly passing Luna Park with its scenic railway and the squeals of fake distress echoing over its palisades. I knew about Luna Park and its amusement arcades, and I knew that those arcades were not for a child my age. We would turn left off the Avenue de la Grande Armée into a small street whose name I never knew but which I called the street of the Japanese, because of a small hotel that seemed to be inhabited only by Japanese. When we arrived at the Saint-Ferdinand crossroads, I would make my mother tell me once again about her first communion in the Église Saint-Ferninand, and from there we would walk to 49 Avenue des Ternes.

Though 49 Avenue des Ternes had a façade that was impressive, my grandparents' apartment did not look out on the avenue—it faced the small inner courtyard. My grandfather had never got over having left the South of France, and he went on painting sunsets on the Mediterranean in his little studio in the Rue Émile-Allez, in the seventeenth arrondissement. His clientele consisted mainly of Greek shipowners from Marseilles, with names such as Photopoulos and Graphotopoulos. They bought his sunsets for their drawing rooms in Marseilles.

I have a memory of sometimes sleeping in this tiny apartment, which seemed always to smell of coffee and kerosene. I was put to sleep on a couch in the "salon," among flickering shadows produced by the oil lamp and surrounded by sculptures made by one of my grandfather's classmates at the École des Beaux-Arts. His name was Roux; he had won a Prix de Rome and was a "success." My grandfather was anything but a "success." "Of course, it's only the charlatans who succeed," my grandmother would murmur. Among those charlatans was one named Picasso. Whenever as a little girl I heard the name Picasso, it was always "that charlatan Picasso."

So you see, almost nothing happened in my childhood until I was nine years old, and that Christmas they gave me a baby brother. All that year when we talked about Christmas presents in the lycée, there were those who wanted a silver fountain pen or a leather satchel or a bicycle, but I wanted "a little brother or a little sister." My parents had promised. They hadn't given me a dog or a cat or roller skates, so if they didn't give me a little brother or a little sister, it would have been a betrayal. My very intelligent parents made a sparkling gift of what in other families can induce those well-known "displacement traumas" that have provoked stacks of literature I haven't read. It was all very simple: If I was a good girl, I would get a little brother for Christmas. I was, and I did.

My mother missed the mark by three days. Alain was born on the twenty-eighth of December. When I finally saw him, what amazed me most was that he already had nails and hair and eyes, a nose and ears, and a voice. He was all swaddled up and looked like a doll in his crib. I had been sent to spend the vacation with my Aunt Rosa and my Uncle Georges, whose history I will spare you (although you should know that my Aunt Rosa, a young woman from Arles, a war widow and my mother's second cousin, met

Uncle Georges, a young Belgian in the Allied occupation army of the Rhineland, in Wiesbaden—it really could be a very interesting chapter). This lighthearted note no doubt is to help me forget that this baby died in 1958. His appearance was the first really great event in my life.

Twenty months after the birth of Alain, Jean-Pierre came. I have never understood or tried to understand why my father and mother, who had waited nine years before having a second child, then had two, one right after the other. However it happened, the result was that one little girl felt the fullest surge of maternal love of which she was capable at that time. So it was that at nine I entered into the age of responsibility.

My mother was eight and three-quarters months pregnant with my second brother, and we had decided to spend the summer in Paris. When I say "we," I mean my mother and I. When he stopped working at Damour's, my father began to travel more and more, since he had become an interpreter at big international conferences. In fact, I believe he invented simultaneous translation. I can still remember one evening in 1934 when he came home in the evening exhausted, having translated Hitler's first big speech in Nuremberg "live" for the French radio network.

All of a sudden, on the eve of the Catholic holiday on August 15, my mother decided that we didn't look well and it was really too hot in Paris. The next morning we took the train to La Baule. We hadn't reserved a room, and we traveled with a huge trunk filled with woolens (one never knows) and our shrimp nets from the year before. We also had an enormous amount of hand baggage. We registered the trunk, and then, with our hand baggage and our victuals, we marched into a third-class carriage. To eat in the dining car was unhealthy, and it would have been unthinkable to prepare sandwiches at home—they would have gone limp during the trip. Instead we brought a package of butter, slices of ham, bread, the knife for the bread.... That made a whole lot of packages, without counting a twenty-month-old infant who might at any moment honor us with a saturated diaper. For travel, we always wore our oldest clothes; trains are so filthy. And yet, as we stood on the platform, I saw elegant ladies wearing beige and brown, carrying alligator handbags and fashion magazines. Because of this childhood image, when I started earning my livelihood, I took great care with my traveling ensembles. (Today thoughts like this never cross my mind.)

We arrived in La Baule and found a room in a *pension de famille*. The next day my mother went out to look for a gynecologist and a clinic, both of which she found in the elegant quarter of La Baule. And everything went off in the most natural way possible. One night my mother woke me up, saying, "Darling, I think it's the moment." I got up, went downstairs, telephoned the clinic; then I woke the landlady of the pension, we phoned for a taxi, and when it arrived, put my mother in it. The next morning I took my little brother to the clinic, and we discovered another little brother in his cradle.

I was eleven years old. The whole time my mother was in the hospital I alone was in charge of my brother Alain. I dressed him, I took him to the beach, I took him to the clinic, I gave him his food, and all that seemed absolutely natural to me. People looked at me with an air of surprise, and I couldn't understand why.

My father wasn't with us very much. He came from time to time and brought presents. Things were going from bad to worse between my parents. I was on my mother's side completely. We kept moving, and the apartments kept getting bigger and bigger, but we seemed increasingly like "displaced persons." Our last apartment was on the corner of the Rue d'Orléans and the Avenue du Roule, in one of those imposing buildings they constructed around 1900, complete with hydraulic elevator, beveled mirrors, and a terribly distinguished concierge, who treated us with contempt. We lived in that immense apartment, but we never put up any wallpaper; we lived surrounded by the sizing, which was a pretty salmon color—it was a bit like living in the lining of a piece of clothing. We were living in salmon! There had once been a beige carpet, but the previous tenants had removed it when they left, and all that remained was a leftover in a storeroom. Overhead hung naked light bulbs. Next week we'd get around to shades. . . .

In buildings like that, with a superb main stairway and a steep service staircase, the families retain the same servants for a lifetime, and so we were rather badly thought of. In our family, maids would stay about three weeks and then leave, generally without giving notice. In the beginning, my mother always thought they were marvelous, "hard-working and devoted," as it would say in the references, but at the end of three weeks they would begin to be disappointing. And then on the fourth Monday they were no longer there. I would know right away, when I came home from school for lunch, by the time it took my mother to open the door.

I was going to a private secondary school, for at that time there was no lycée for older girls in Neuilly. But my school was just across the street from the lycée for boys, the Lycée Pasteur, where I had spent my first school years, and the girls continued to see the boys they had known when they were small. I would bring home a lot of girl friends, but I was often embarrassed, because my mother was very fussy. On rainy days, for example, she would ask the girls to remove their boots, saying, "It's very unhealthy to keep your boots on in the house; it makes for humid feet." My friends found my house much livelier and more amusing than their own orderly homes. On Thursdays I was often invited to an over-organized tea. At my house you went into the kitchen to prepare your own slices of bread and butter and jam. The things that most embarrassed me seemed to them the most fun.

My school and the Lycée Pasteur were both really the same establishment. We had the same teachers. We had Daniel-Rops, Georges Magnane, Gabriel Chevalier, and later Sartre. Philosophy is the only class I didn't have in

Neuilly. But the boys I knew had Sartre as their teacher. The first day he arrived, when they saw getting out of a taxi a little man whose eyes protruded slightly, it produced schoolboy laughter. He was wearing a brown camel's-hair coat and a navy turtleneck sweater, most unusual for that time. He had already written *La Nausée*, which was published the first year he taught at our lycée. At first the boys thought he was off his rocker. They were the offspring of the typical Neuilly middle class: vice-presidents of engineering firms; that sort of caliber. Gradually Sartre captivated them completely—they all wanted to get a Ph.D. in philosophy.

Those were the prewar years when the all-important things were happening in Germany. But Hitler became a reality in my life only when little German-Jewish girls started arriving at our school. When people say, "We really didn't know what was happening in Germany," I always wonder how they managed to blindfold their eyes and stuff their ears. Periodically, German Jews would come to stay at the house. Strangely enough, it was never my father who brought in these refugees. It was always my mother, who was much more indignant than he was, at least so far as the Jewish question was concerned. I remember some of the girls who would help my mother with the housework. One of them, who was especially beautiful and touching, was named Lotte. We never lost track of her. A few of them would stay with us for a few days before traveling on. They would talk a great deal, but in German. I remember a group of which half left for America, the other half for Palestine. This division seems to resemble what happened at the end of the last century during the great Diaspora, when some went off to the sweatshops of New York and others went to battle mosquitoes on the shores of Lake Tiberias.

My mother's not being Jewish may have made her more sensitive on the subject. In any case, she seldom reacted as others did. At about that time, she noticed one day that a toothbrush she had just bought herself said "made in

Japan." We returned to the store and there faced the owner, who wore a Basque beret and was probably a Croix de Feu* militant. Very politely, my mother said, "I would like to exchange this toothbrush. You see, it's made in Japan." "So?" "Well, you see, monsieur, the Japanese have just signed an agreement with the Germans and Italians, and so any Japanese merchandise, even a little toothbrush, becomes armaments for Japan, Italy, and Germany. Fascist countries." I wished the ground would open and swallow me up. The man replied, "So you want a French toothbrush, is that it?" "No, I'm not a chauvinist. No, all I want is a toothbrush that is not German, Italian, or Japanese." We went home with a toothbrush that was made in England. My mother considered her day to have been well spent, and today I agree with her. But at twelve or thirteen one gets terribly embarrassed.

I was never really conscious of the fact that my father was Jewish and that a personal bond united me with those refugees. The things I heard about went on elsewhere; they couldn't happen in France. Nor can I rightfully say that I was ever awakened to a Jewish consciousness. I had never been personally faced with anti-Semitism. My father was the archetype of the assimilated Jew, and I was brought up as an agnostic.

My school was not religious. The Catholic school in Neuilly was run by a Madame Daniélou, the mother of a cardinal. The girls who went there wore uniforms and took walks in file along the streets of Neuilly. They looked down on us, but we didn't care at all. We met a few of them in music school, the Cours Martenot.

The Cours Martenot was run by two sisters, Madeleine and Geneviève, in a private house on the Rue Saint Pierre. They had invented a very attractive method, with musical games and finger exercises that I still know how to do. They had a younger brother who had been in the signal corps during the war. We sometimes saw him racing

*A French neofascist movement in the thirties.

through the garden like a madman, wearing a white smock. He worked in a shed at the end of the garden, from which emanated terrible sounds: transfigured human voices, strange noises. He was working on an invention, which finally saw the light of day: It was called Martenot waves. Suddenly the Cours Martenot was famous.

On Thursdays one would meet the girls from the religious school. I cannot remember feeling deprived when they had their solemn first communion at the Église Saint-Pierre. Maybe I was a bit envious of their white dresses and veils, to say nothing of the watches or the fountain pens they would get as presents. But I cannot remember experiencing a mystical vacuum. Once, the mother of one of my friends invited me to their country house, where she explained to me that one must pray. I do remember saying a few prayers, but the experience never led anywhere.

On the other hand, I already had the beginnings of a political consciousness. Once again, Mother was the cause. When one can return a Japanese toothbrush to the store, one has understood what is going on in the world, even though the attitude is sentimental. My mother always had a photograph of Briand nailed up over her bed. Also, she had been part of an "occupying army" in Germany, and she had hated it. As far back as I can remember, she'd told me stories about how she had lived in a huge house in Wiesbaden, and how enormous quantities of food arrived for the French occupants. The German family who owned the house lived in the attic and had nothing to eat. My mother would bring milk to the German children. As a tiny child I was trained to hate occupation, so when France was in its turn occupied, I already had an experience to fall back on.

My mother practiced a kind of quixotic pacifism, which she most certainly inculcated in me. My father, however, eager to assimilate completely, didn't really wish to stick his neck out. I don't mean that he was reactionary; he was simply far from the left. The newspapers he brought home were *Gringoire* and *Candide*.*

To give you an idea of the atmosphere, let me tell you something that happened at the time of the Popular Front.† My other grandmother, my mother's mother, came from Valenciennes. Her maiden name was Dubois, but she liked to remind people that she was a Dubois de Poncelet, and that one of her grandfathers had been guillotined during the Revolution. She talked a great deal about this, but she never mentioned her father, who, I think, was a butcher. She had been a milliner, and she had met my grandfather, a painter named Signoret, when she was very young. He was tall and handsome. He was from Marseilles, the son of the chorusmaster of the Marseilles opera. My grandmother, who liked to chat with people sitting on the benches along the elegant avenues of Neuilly, always managed to drop into the conversation a phrase like "My husband, a great artist. . . ." Her captive audience would generally assume that she was the wife of Gabriel Signoret, a well-known actor, a misunderstanding she never bothered to clarify.

After my grandfather's death, my grandmother had come to live with us. She was then a tiny old lady with white hair. She once had been to America, before her marriage, to visit a cousin from Valenciennes who had made his fortune there. (He'd run away from home because of some misdemeanor or other—who knows?) She told me stories about New York in the 1890s. And also stories with Indians in them: how her cousin had put barrels of liquor all around his property, and when the Indians came during the night to drink "firewater," her Valenciennes cousin would catch them! Almost certainly untrue, but my grandmother reeled out her stories by the

*Right-wing politico-literary weeklies.
†A general election in 1936 overwhelmingly voted in a government of the left, with Léon Blum at its head.

yard. She also tinkled around on the piano and sang ditties from operettas: "*Un grand singe d'Amérique, qui régnait à Piombino...*" ("There was once a big monkey from America who ruled in Piombino..."); "*De Madame Angot je suis la fille...*" ("I am the daughter of Madame Angot..."). I thought she was slightly round the bend, and her stories bored me. Today, of course, I would give anything to be able to hear them again.

At the time of the Popular Front there was a parade along the Avenue du Roule. We were then living on the sixth floor of that luxury building. And as my mother was terrified that my little brothers might fall some sixty feet below, she had had a fine-mesh chicken wire put over the balcony, which crisscrossed the sky but was invisible from the street. The day of the parade, my grandmother went onto the balcony to watch. Since she was so tiny, she held on to the mesh with one hand, so that from below all that could be seen was a white-haired little old lady, her clenched fist incessantly raised, on top of this luxury building. The people below began to hurl insults. Most of them were militants in the right-wing Action Française, boys from the lycée. I looked up and saw my grandmother! I ascended as quickly as I could go in the elevator and removed her from the balcony....

In *L'Enfance d'un Chef*, Sartre mentions the boys who sold *Action Française*° at the entrance of the Saint-Pierre de Neuilly church. I remember vividly one handsome boy who was a member of our gang, and the day he sold the famous issue with the headline "France under the Heel of the Jew."† That time I recall clearly having a visceral Judaic reaction. It was before Sartre came to the Lycée Pasteur.

Sartre managed to rearrange the mental furniture in some of those boys. There were some who were receptive. He would take them to a bistro, which was the first time a

---

°A newspaper virulently in favor of the monarchy in the thirties.
† Léon Blum.

teacher dared do that. He would lend them books. He introduced them to the great American novelists: Hemingway, Dos Passos, Steinbeck, Faulkner. And since these boys were my friends, his teaching boomeranged onto me.

In our group of boys and girls there were already Chris Marker, Jacques Besse, and the son of Daladier, among others. We would meet at noon, after school, on the Avenue du Roule, in front of a little newspaper store called the Sabot Bleu. We never went to a café; that wasn't done at the time. Also, we weren't allowed to cross the street. There was a boys' side of the sidewalk and a girls' side. So our meeting place was the Sabot Bleu, and from there we walked and we talked. One of the main subjects of conversation was Charles Trenet. All the boys, imitating the singer's style, had bought blue shirts, white ties, and hats. Trenet was terribly important. Then there was the Hot Club. The first Django Reinhardt concerts were being played at the Maison de la Chimie. We talked about the books we thought were important: *Poussière*, *Sparkenbroke*....

I hardly ever went out. I saw the great films of that time only much later, at the Cinémathèque, when they had become classics. I can count the films I saw during my childhood and adolescence on the fingers of one hand. They were of great importance to me. For example, *Little Women*. The only horror film I have ever seen in my life I saw the day before I took my baccalaureate exam. That day we went boating on the lake in the Bois, and then we went to the movies "to relax." It was a terrifying thing called *Love from a Stranger* with Basil Rathbone, which I can still conjure up if I want to scare myself. I also saw *Three Comrades*, and sobbed at the end. When I was twelve, I saw Fritz Lang's *M*. We had asked at the box office, "Is this film for us, madame?" and she had replied, "Yes, yes, go right in; it'll teach you to be careful."

The only cinema we went to in Paris was the Ermitage, because they had deep upholstered armchairs. We would buy seven-franc tickets and then move over to the more comfortable seats, which cost ten. Afterward we would go to Pam Pam, where they served fruit juices, and we'd listen to Charlie Kunitz.

We went to the theater very little. Just to the Comédie Française and to the Atelier. I once saw *Hunger* by Knut Hamsun. As a curtain raiser, they played Laforgue's *Hamlet*, with Roger Blin, whom I had seen in a movie called *Entrée des Artistes*, and I thought he was superb. I saw Dullin's *Julius Caesar*, with Marchat playing Mark Antony—beautifully, I thought—and Jean Marais as a Gaul. In this play we learned the Roman handshake, which went up to the forearm, and it so impressed us that the entire lycée adopted it.

The International Exhibition of 1937 was in full swing. Like everyone else, I went to see it. But before that there was the horrible, abominable Colonial Exhibition, to which, I'm sorry to say, I was taken—by the lycée, I believe. I saw the temple of Angkor Wat and was given a little ring made of elephant hair—the French colonial empire, for heaven's sake!

What I remember best about the International Exhibition is the Russian pavilion. There was a series of huge empty frames; the pictures had been hastily removed because they showed generals who had just been liquidated. I remember the German pavilion because there was an elevator boy of fabulous beauty—the very prototype of the young Nazi. We went up and down and up and down in the elevator to gaze at this young man. There were two Spanish pavilions. In the Republican pavilion was Picasso's *Guernica* and a basin full of mercury into which people threw coins. I can still see it clearly now, and hear our French teacher, who did a fine job of explaining *Guernica*. Until that time, most of what I knew about the Spanish Civil War came from the cartoons in *Gringoire* and *Candide*. I need hardly add that in our group which met at Sabot Bleu no one ever talked about volunteering for one side or the other. But eight hundred kilometers away, in Marseilles, the adolescent Montand had his ears full of talk about imminent departures for the Spanish front, not all of which actually took place.

For the group that met at the Sabot Bleu, departure meant the long summer vacation. For several years we had been going to Saint-Gildas-de-Rhuis, in Brittany. The Bretons would rent their houses for the summer and stay with their cousins. The inventory of furnishings would inevitably include six Japanese egg cups and a Tonkinese bowl brought home by a sailor son.

The summer residents were mostly families from Nantes, Vannes, and Rennes, who had splendid vacation houses in the region. The finest house belonged to the Messmers; there was a Messmer boat at anchor in the port, and very likely in the church there were Messmer pews. From behind the fences I greatly admired the swings installed in those splendid gardens, which is why, much later, after Montand and I had bought the house in Autheuil, one of the first things I did—long before I got around to more serious things—was to order a swing and ancillary gear from the carpenter. I said to my daughter, "You're going to have a swing," and she answered, "Oh?" Really!

My father made only rare appearances at Saint-Gildas; the good old family atmosphere that prevailed on its beach had very little appeal for him. One splendid sunny day in September 1938, the postman brought us a telegram, sent from Munich, which said: "The peace has been saved. Papa." It impressed the postman that my father had been a member of that famous delegation of imbeciles.

A year later, without a telegram from my father announcing the event, the bell at the top of the Saint-Gildas church spire began to toll. It was war.

Chapter 2

IT was war. The young family fathers eligible for the draft left immediately. Some of them had only just arrived; the working-class men savoring their new rights to annual paid vacations acquired under Popular Front legislation. They'd just had time to catch their first sunburns before they went to join their units. Their families followed. But we didn't hasten back to Paris. We stayed on, encouraged to do so by my father, who recognized an unhoped-for opportunity to be alone in Paris. He explained to us that life in the city would be impossible, dangerous, even murderous, and my mother, who remembered the Big Bertha shellings, agreed not to go back.

So we stayed on at Saint-Gildas, leaving our rented house at the agreed time, around the middle of September, after completing the abominable inventory. We moved into a huge house, rented for next to nothing because it was out of season. We completed a new inventory, after which my mother, my little brothers, and I settled into our winter quarters in the brisk air beside the Atlantic. The little ones went to the village primary school, where they caught their first lice, and I was enrolled in the lycée in Vannes, in the final, philosophy year.

At first I lived with a family in Vannes, and then I moved to the house of "Aunt Claire," a friend of my mother's. Her children, Éliane and Jean, were friends of mine from infancy; we were all a bit squeezed, but I was very happy in that house. I had a friend named Alain, whose father was a pharmacist named Resnais. And there was Louis Monnier—but that story would take too long to tell. As much time as to tell stories about Uncle Georges and Aunt Rosa. . . .

There were twelve of us in the philosophy class: girls from Vannes and a few evacuees, but I was the only Parisian. Our history teacher was a marvelous woman named Madame Samuel. The curriculum was very exciting because we were in the process of living it. It began, as I remember, with the Russian Revolution in 1917, included the beginnings of fascism in Italy and Germany, and ended with the current period. Madame Samuel taught with fire and passion.

Science classes were held in the lycée's annex, which was next door to a very odd house. Every Wednesday we would see strange-looking women going in. They were the ladies of the Vannes bordello, whose mandatory weekly medical visits coincided exactly with our natural-history lab period. The girls from the secondary school, who were not allowed to go out without a hat—I bought a beret, which I crammed down to eye level—came and went at exactly the same time as the girls from the bordello.

In the beginning I didn't understand. At that time I was completely innocent. The tiny bits of worldly education I picked up came from the provincial daughters of the Breton bourgeoisie. I heard my first dirty jokes and smutty stories in Vannes. There had been none in Neuilly. And I was so naïve that everything had to be explained.

One day Madame Samuel left us; she had been transferred in the middle of the year. I was very sad; I missed her terribly. And then, many years later....

Many years later, in 1947—I had already made two or three films—I was asked by two young writer friends, Claude Roy and Jacques-Francis Rolland, to come and tend their stand at the National Committee of Writers sale. This took place at the Maison de la Pensée Française, whose king—whose uncontested high priest—was Aragon. Absolutely everybody was there—from Aragon to Mauriac. It was a time of high hope and solidarity. The sale was due to begin at two, but we had been asked to be there at half-past one to help set up the display of books. The hall was filled with posters hanging from the ceiling, bearing the names of authors, and among them I noticed one of Lucie Aubrac, a woman who had become very well known around the time of the Liberation. It was the middle of the war, she was pregnant, and her husband, a member of the Resistance, was arrested, along with Jean Moulin, by the Gestapo. She went immediately to Gestapo headquarters in Lyons, which was run by Barbie,* and there she put on a most extraordinary show: "I know about that man you've arrested—as far as I'm concerned you can shoot him right away. But you should know that he's a bastard who raped me and got me pregnant. All I want is that he marry me, forcibly if need be, so that my child will have a name. After that you can do what you want with him." And they fell for that trick! Since the marriage could not take place in prison, the Gestapo laid on transport, and the Resistance attacked the police truck right in the center of Lyons. And that's how Lucie Aubrac managed her husband's escape!

When I noted the poster, I said to myself: "I want to see what that woman looks like." I turned it around and—I'm sure you're ahead of me—there was Madame Samuel.

But to get back to the lycée in Vannes, the war, and my baccalaureate: Till the end of May it was life as usual. The

*Barbie is living today in Bolivia.

men from the tank corps took over the terraces of the crêperies and went on reconnaissance missions around the girls' lycée. I also discovered with delight that all the subjects hitherto considered forbidden became, at the end of my final year, subjects for essays. I read for the first time *La Condition Humaine* and *Les Thibaults*. Every Saturday I caught the chuffing little train for Saint-Gildas.

Then suddenly in May things happened very fast. It was the fall of France, which meant a wave of refugees arriving in all sorts of trains, coming, it seemed, from everywhere. The people of the region did not fall all over themselves to put them up. I took many of them to Saint-Gildas. My mother welcomed them into our big house, at first with good humor. Later this could turn to impatience when she would discover that the poor victims were often anti-Semitic, racist, or even fascist.

It was June when the Germans arrived in Saint-Gildas. On horseback! They were fantastic—tall, tanned, Wagnerian. (Which brings to mind my father: By that time we were sure it would be a long time before we heard my father whistle Siegfried's motif again. We had had no news from him for ages; the last message had come from somewhere near Bordeaux. We felt, without having proof, that he had left for England.) The day after the "fall of Saint-Gildas," there was a knock on the kitchen door and I found myself face to face with a German officer and a soldier. I called my mother. She looked at them for what seemed a long time and then said, "Who are you, messieurs?" They stood there a moment, perplexed. "We are members of the German army." It was a scene out of Barrès. "And what do you want?" my mother asked. "We would like to inquire, madame, if we might lodge here without disturbing you." They tramped through the entire house, which pleased them, and decided to send us four soldiers. That same evening we were duly delivered three peasants from Hanover who spoke only dialect, and a gentleman farmer named Schroeder, also from Hanover, whom my mother instantly terrorized.

The three bumpkins had never seen the ocean. In the morning they were terrified because, at ebb tide, they thought the ocean had disappeared. . . . My mother assigned them chores; she sent them off to fetch water and feed the rabbits. She made them wipe their feet before they entered the house. Having brushed up on the German she had acquired in Wiesbaden and refreshed with the German-Jewish refugees, my mother issued housekeeping and farming orders in her little domain. Apart from that, we lied. "Where is your papa?" asked the Germans. We had no idea; he had disappeared in the upheaval. "And Kaminker—a Breton name, *nein*?" Yes, yes, it sounded like a Breton name. Schroeder, in particular, was very fond of me, while showing all due respect. After playing Barrès, we were in the middle of a tale by Vercors.

Our house was on the coast, with the sea at the end of the garden and an island a little way out. One day Schroeder asked my mother what the island was, and she replied, "It's Birmingham." He pursued it no further. He was a man of culture; he knew that the ocean rose and fell. Another day, when I was in the garden with my brothers, he came out on the flagstones carrying something that looked like a little jewel case. He opened it, took out a monocle, and placed it in his eye. The monocle fell out; he bent down and picked up the pieces. A quick look, to see if I had seen. I had seen. He smiled, sadly, desperately, and went back into the house. This attempt to appear aristocratic, this sad failure of the panoply of the perfect Prussian—I knew I should have laughed, but somehow I just couldn't.

One day they obviously got their orders—vacation over—and they disappeared. I think they were part of the wave of German troops that were to be the English invasion force, and which the English repelled by bombarding the sea. The French hospitals at the time were full of burned German troops, and I've always believed that Schroeder was one of them. Before he left he told us all about himself. He tried to show us his trophies: his SA insignia, a couple of Jewish stars. Things were becoming "gross," as my daughter would say—well, as she would have said last year....

The departure of our four horsemen from Hanover marked the end of our relative comfort. Later Saint-Gildas was invaded by a company of motorcyclists from Berlin. From four, we went to twelve in the house. They were led by a man named Link, who was very sharp and quite devious and who knew how to get information in the village. One day, in the kitchen, he smiled and said, "I know your father is a Jew, and that he's in England."

His little investigation had turned up some kindly Breton separatists who couldn't bear Parisians, Jews, or the English, and who were happy to provide Link with information.

We realized the cushy period was over for the Kaminker family. The Germans gave us twenty-four hours to find other lodgings, and my mother decided, "We're going back to Paris."

I just had time to pass my philosophy baccalaureate in our occupied lycée in Vannes. My three-hour final exam was punctuated by the tramping of boots on the sidewalk and the noise of departing cars. There was no oral part to the exam and so the results were posted very quickly; I passed. I had chosen a fine subject for my essay: "Define the connections between passion and will." It would not be long before I would find these connections in reality.

So the Kaminker family moved into the deserted Paris of 1940—into a splendid deserted building. Its only remaining inhabitant was the concierge, and she was still just as distinguished, and even more disagreeable. At last she had a perfectly valid pretext: The rent had not been paid for months, a fact we did not know. We hadn't a centime to bless ourselves with, and the glow on our faces, tanned from a year of fresh Breton air, was superficial. The outlook was far from rosy. But the weather was still fine, and we repossessed our seven salmon-colored rooms and our sunny balcony. My little brothers found the toys they had left behind a year earlier. We were back home, but without admitting it to ourselves, we knew we were really DPs now.

I immediately went out to look for work. I found my first job with the help of my former teacher of Latin and literature, Philippe Vantieghem. Vantieghem has left an indelible impression on all the girls who were his students at the Neuilly secondary school. He was as handsome as Melvyn Douglas, he arrived in a Rosengart car, and the label inside his overcoat, when he hung it on the classroom peg, said "Lanvin." During class he would fidget elegantly with a silver pencil. He would look at one of the plainest girls in the class and say, "Mademoiselle, speak to me of love [long pause] . . . in Racine." The tales of his successive widowerhoods, due to the suicides of his wives, bowled us over. The boys at the Lycée Pasteur hated him. Whatever his virtues and vices, it was to him I turned to help me find a job. Vantieghem immediately got me some tutoring lessons in Latin and English. These lessons account for my false reputation as a "language teacher," a designation that still haunts me in some of the old film biographies.

Between repetitions of "What is pink? . . . The rose is pink," I scanned the want ads. One afternoon I presented myself in Les Halles, the central Paris market, answering an ad that said "Storekeeper." I was shown into a dingy room where some old men and an old woman were scribbling away on little mahogany desks lighted by green opaline lampshades. Years later I was to buy some of these lampshades in the Village Suisse antique market at a very high price, but that day they seemed to me the height of desolation. The horror must have shown on my face; I didn't get the job. It both mortified and relieved me.

Little by little, the boys and girls from my class and from the Sabot Bleu returned. Some were enrolled at the Sorbonne, others at the Cours du Louvre. We still saw one another. Their parents tended to be kind to me, curious about our fate and anxious about our future—masked with a touch of prudence which never escaped me. Obliquely they would ask after my father. In Saint-Gildas I had already developed the moving response: "We don't know; he's disappeared." This seemed to finish off all questions. At that time people never said whether or not they listened to the BBC's broadcasts—they didn't know yet whether you were supposed to boast about it or not. At that time Pétain was still a perfect symbol of reassurance for the good French bourgeois. It was autumn 1940, and the good people who had shared the world of my adolescence had none of my reasons for terror and anguish. Their lives continued much as before, by which I don't mean to say that they were bad. They were waiting. The others, those who might have shared my feelings, simply weren't there. They hadn't come back. At that time it was mostly the inhabitants of the fourth arrondissement, the Jewish section, who had resumed their old habit of fear. These people were where they had always been, for the good reason that they had never left. But the fourth arrondissement is far from Neuilly-sur-Seine, and I knew no one there. Where we lived, there were kids whose fathers were in officers' prisoner-of-war camps, and good news of them was beginning to trickle out. In the windows of some stores one suddenly saw displayed 1914–18 army citations meant to indicate that the owner was a good Frenchman even though his name was Levy. A little while later those citations were replaced by a sign saying "Jewish Store"— but we weren't there yet.... In short, the general atmosphere hovered over everything, but nothing was as yet official.

One day I saw an ad in the paper that was to be of prime importance to my life: "The Harcourt Studio* requires attractive young girls who speak languages for its sales force." "Languages" was an oblique way of saying "German." The only word in the ad that caught my attention was "Harcourt."

When I was sixteen and came out of the movie theater

*France's most famous photographers of stars at the time.

where *Port Arthur*, with Danielle Darrieux made up as a Japanese, was playing, I went home, planted myself in front of my mirror, and pulled my eyelids up toward my temples with my fingers. I bit my upper lip with my lower teeth to accentuate a cupid's bow, and saw Darrieux looking back at me. Simone Simon was my twin sister, and Annabella was my stand-in. So you see, for a girl my age who knew nothing of the cinema, the Harcourt Studio rang out like Hollywood.

I wouldn't have admitted it to a soul, not even to myself, but that ad evoked the stories I had read in the rare movie magazines that came my way—stories that told of some salesgirl or schoolgirl or secretary who had been "discovered" in the street or behind a counter by a famous director who just happened to be walking by. All this has nothing to do with what is called a vocation. I was like all those other little girls dazzled by the movies; the "great stars" were inaccessible, but there, at Harcourt-Hollywood, as I walked around in my salesgirl outfit, someone would come along and suddenly say, "Mademoiselle, would you like to be in the movies?" We all know that it never happens like that, and we all know also that we once thought it did. When Montand was fifteen, he walked up and down a certain street in Marseilles where Warners, Fox, and Paramount had their regional offices. He was waiting to be discovered. No one discovered him. . . . So, as far as the ad was concerned, let me admit to you that for a moment I entertained that secret thought, fleetingly and with a touch of shame. But what was concrete and serious was that someone was offering work, a way to daily bread, and immediately. The trick was getting hired.

At that moment I remembered a friend in my class named Rosita, whom we called Zizi. She had left just before the end of one school year, saying, "I'm going to get into the movies!" At the time, I would have cut my tongue out rather than admit that I would have loved to do the same thing, so like all the other little bourgeoises I laughed and shrugged and went back to my Virgil. Zizi actually appeared in three small roles, which we all went to see at the Chézy. Since none of us had the slightest notion of the cinema, we couldn't tell the difference between a small role and a walk-on, so we shrugged again. Then, suddenly, Zizi became Corinne—Corinne Luchaire in *Prisons sans Barreaux*. The newspapers were calling her the revelation of the year, and it was true. So we all went together to the Champs Élysées to see. We no longer shrugged. We were deeply impressed.

Of course, she and I no longer saw each other. But one evening she appeared like the good fairy. There was a party given jointly by the Lycée Pasteur and my secondary school, and there she was, an alumna. She was wearing a dark blue velvet dress, very low cut, with tiny satin straps, and a white fox cape. She embraced me and then she looked at my dress, which was white muslin, but from a pattern in *Marie-Claire*, and she said, "What a pretty dress—who made it?" "My mother." "You're so lucky; I have to go and buy things from the couturiers." She drank a glass of bubbly and then left with the three tall boys she had brought with her and who were obviously devoted enough to go with her while she did her good deed. She had made her appearance with grace and charity. Before she left, she kissed me again and said, "Good-bye. Call me." That was in June 1938.

And I did call her, but not until September 1940. The phone was answered by Françoise Luchaire, her mother. No, Zizi wasn't there, she was in the unoccupied zone. . . . A recommendation to Harcourt? . . . Why be a salesgirl when one has a baccalaureate? . . . And my father—where was my father? . . . Yes, of course. . . . If you're looking for work, I'll make an appointment for you with Jean. You must go to see him at the *Petit Parisien*; he's editor in chief there, you know. He knew you when you were a child. He's starting a new paper; I'm sure he'll find something for you. . . . Which is how, without professional qualifications, without knowing how to type, and without Jean Luchaire's asking me "Where is your father?" I found myself the next day in the offices of the *Petit Parisien*. I was hired at 1,400 francs a month as the assistant to the personal secretary of the future director of the big collaborationist newspaper that was to be called *Le Nouveau Temps*. I went home to the Avenue du Roule and announced to my mother and my little brothers that I had found a job. So there it was; I was just nineteen years old, but I was the head of a family who was going to bring 1,400 francs a month into the house. Still, today, I can hear the noise of that first pay envelope, tinkling with coins, when, a month later, I slapped it proudly onto the kitchen table. After Barrès and Vercors, we were in the middle of Zola.

The paper was about to be launched. Luchaire was still in his office in the *Petit Parisien*, but he was looking for new offices. In fact, my first job started on a Sunday morning. I found myself with my boss, who had told me to bring along a pencil and paper, in an immense apartment on the first floor of 32 Rue du Louvre. There we met an elderly gentleman named Seligmann (if I remember rightly), who with dignity and sadness said that he was ready to sell his place, which until then had been one of the biggest trimmings houses in France. He had seen the light; he preferred selling his business before the Commissioner for Jewish Affairs got his hands on it. He took us around. All along the walls of most of the rooms were a multitude of narrow little drawers containing miles of silken pompons and trims and cords, awaiting their new destiny. He spoke very little, and Luchaire not much more. Negotiations were rapid and courteous—obviously Luchaire had the means. Then the old gentleman left. Luchaire and I did the tour again; this time we were the proprietors. I followed him with my little notebook in hand while he said, "Take it down—that'll be my office. That's the waiting room—take it down." Silently I took down what he said. We were a very odd couple: the kid and the collaborator who was already booked for the firing squad.

All at once, after having christened one of the rooms "the editorial room—take it down," he continued in the same tone, without looking at me: "You'll be seeing your father again; don't worry about it." (He spoke to me with the familiar *tu*—he had known me since I was a child.)

That same day he took me to see O. P. Gilbert, whom he had asked to be editor in chief. I didn't understand why he had taken me with him, since he never asked me to take any notes. However, during the next two hours I quickly understood that I was in the process of learning a great deal. First of all, I learned that O. P. Gilbert was a wonderful man, and then it quickly became obvious to me that my boss wasn't being taken terribly seriously by his future editor in chief, who seemed to be expressing grave doubts about the lack of bias of what would be written in *Le Nouveau Temps*. Until recently there had been an austere financial evening paper named *Le Temps*, which had not appeared since the arrival of the Germans; the name *Le Nouveau Temps* played cleverly on a misapprehension that was quite useful to those who considered themselves the new order—and still it encompassed an attempt to pick up the old readers of *Le Temps*. So you see, although I wasn't taking notes, I wasn't wasting my time. It soon became evident from their conversation that O. P. Gilbert, who had been a colleague of Luchaire's at the time of the Franco-German rapprochement (that time so dear to my mother—remember Briand's photo) was not ready under any circumstances to become editor in chief of a fascist newspaper. "What do you think I am?" replied Luchaire, howling with laughter. Gilbert twiddled with a lock of his white hair that barely concealed a war scar. I knew that if he said yes, I would have a father on the newspaper. He did say yes, and he did become my father during the two or three months that preceded a falling out between the two men—which was already foreshadowed that first day.

The paper's first issue was seized. The heirs of *Le Temps* did not appreciate having their name linked with *nouveau*. *Le Nouveau Temps* was requested to change its name to *Les Nouveaux Temps*, which wasn't the same thing at all and was much more in keeping with the new order. All this comes to mind today, but at the time it didn't have much effect on me; I even think I didn't understand. Since I really didn't know how to do very much, they installed me in a corner of Madame Baudouin's office; she was personal secretary to Luchaire and my immediate superior. I had a telephone and an old typewriter on which to learn—I learned very fast, and if today I still know how to do a clean letter, I owe it to Madame Baudouin. I was a kind of glorified office girl. I was sent on errands, such as buying flowers for the famous Zarah Leander when she passed through Paris. I was a filter for telephone calls, announcing the caller's name loudly so that Madame Baudouin could decide whether the call should be put through to the boss. Every morning I heard the voice of Counselor Achenbach, who has become so well known lately. I heard the voice of Abetz or his wife, who had been Luchaire's secretary in the thirties before she became the wife of the ambassador to Germany. (She would simply say, "Please tell him Suzanne is on the phone.") Every day, too, there was a call from "the office of the President"; it took me a little while to understand that was Laval. Above all, there were embarrassed voices that said, "Tell him Maurice...SDN in 1935...he'll understand"; or "I'm a friend of his sister's...." This would make it even clearer; Luchaire's sister was married to a Jewish doctor.

Geographically speaking, my little corner was a very privileged place. I sat in a cubbyhole right in front of Luchaire's office. His office was luxurious; he had bookshelves built, which were filled with a collection called "Masque." There was a well-furnished washroom and a huge couch. He saw a lot of people in the afternoons. I watched a whole raft of ladies pass rapidly through that padded doorway during the winter of 1940; some because their husbands were prisoners and they wanted them back (one even returned with her husband a few weeks later to say thank you), and others because they needed a quick permit for some commercial enterprise. Occasionally there were men and women who were so nervous before they went through the door that I knew their affairs would not be discussed on the big couch. These Luchaire would accompany to the threshold when they came out, patting them on the shoulder and saying that he would look into the matter.

He told the truth; he did do them favors. I watched a lot of people go by who didn't realize that I was looking at them, who may have glimpsed me in passing and who wonder today where they saw me for the first time. But I saw very few of these same people do anything at all for Luchaire when he was condemned to a death that he probably deserved. The only appeal for mercy filed at his trial was the one I forced my father to send when he came back in 1945. But I am ahead of my story. For the moment, I'm still wearing my schoolgirl clothes; I have a well-brought-up little black chignon on my head and heavy family responsibilities that both terrify me and fill me with pride. Madame Baudouin was very kind to me; she called me "Petit." It's a funny thing—in my whole life only she and, years later, Montand have called me "Petit."

All the people who worked on the paper were very kind to me. They were producing something that rapidly became disgusting, but they were all very nice. In the beginning, they followed the sober tone of the old *Temps* when they wrote their anglophobic, anti-Semitic pieces; at the same time they were being very nice to the little Kaminker girl, whose father was in London. By then they all knew. They knew because one day Luchaire called me into his office, sat me down, and said solemnly: "I have good news for you. I know where your father is [long pause]. In London, and he's speaking on the radio." I must have said, "Oh, my God!" I was probably overplaying like crazy; then Luchaire went on: "That's why you're better off here than elsewhere." So my "Papa's disappeared" act wouldn't work anymore. Well, it simplified things. With the exception of one or two bastards, whose names I won't give because I'm not one who takes pleasure in such things—and especially not when people have paid for their misdeeds—I can't remember anyone who really believed what they wrote in *Les Nouveaux Temps*. You might say those were the worst bastards, which wouldn't be far from the truth.

My favorite jobs on the paper were to be sent to buy very expensive bouquets of flowers at the luxury florists on the Place de la Madeleine, or to Maxim's or l'Aiglon or the Fête Foraine with the table settings for a "benefit for our dear prisoners"; and sometimes Madame Baudouin sent me out to the editorial room with something or other—probably when she wanted to take a phone call she preferred me not to hear. That's where I met Henri Jeanson for the first time. He had come to talk with his old friend O. P. Gilbert about how it was impossible for one of them to remain as editor in chief of *Aujourd'hui* and the other of *Les Nouveaux Temps*. There, too, I met a very handsome man named Claude Blanchard, who said, "What should I tell your father tomorrow?" He had just come clandestinely from London and was going back clandestinely the next day. And because, peace or war, Parisians remained Parisians, in the winding corridor between the director's office and the editorial room somebody with a sense of humor on the paper had propped up in a corner two fishing rods, called *gaules*, whose sole purpose was to make people say in passing, "Well, well, *deux gaules....*"

I would arrive holding a piece of paper that was generally of supreme unimportance, and all the guys would ask for news of what was happening "there," as if "there"—the director's office—were a hundred miles away. Their tone would contain a certain contempt for their paymaster, which only half pleased me. I had a chaste crush on A. M. Julien, the music critic, who came only once a week to deliver his piece, and whom I considered superb—above all because he had played Julien in *Gilles et Julien*, and he'd conserved his droopy forelock, which had been his stage makeup during his splendid past. The men probably had designs on me, but they remained respectful.

Maybe it was because I was young, or maybe it was because of my family responsibilities, about which everyone knew; in any case, no one tried to take advantage of the situation. I was very pretty at the time, but however "new" the times, they were quite different from today. And I was filled with the dread of yet another responsibility—I already had two children to feed, as well as a mother.

The cold was terrible that first winter of the occupation, so the family huddled together in a minimum of space. We lived mostly in the kitchen and in the dining room, which we had made into a kind of dormitory for all four of us. My brothers went to school and I brought in the paycheck. When my mother was served with a summons to pay up, I took out the three remaining Oriental carpets and sold them to a bogus marquis whom I had met at the newspaper. My mother cooked mangel-wurzels, and we listened to the BBC. We were never sure whether or not it was my father, although we believed we recognized his voice. We celebrated Christmas, the four of us, with a bunch of cheap little things I had bought in an inexpensive store in the Rue du Louvre. I spent a hundred francs in all, before taking the métro home. The gifts ranged from decals to a Game of Goose, and we put up a tiny folding Christmas tree made of far too green paper.

As they had cut off our telephone, whenever I had to work overtime I would send a *pneumatique** to my mother, perfectly typed, so that she would be proud of my progress. This would generally be on the day of one of the benefits; they would begin with a cocktail in the *Nouveaux Temps* offices. Luchaire's lady guests would arrive in skunk coats and very tall hats, wearing the first cork-soled shoes I had seen. I would be asked to take charge of the telephone, not because strategic news was expected, but to note guests who were going to arrive late. My friend Zizi

---

*A message, typed on special thin paper, sent by pneumatic tube to the post office closest to its destination and hand delivered from there.

was invited to all these parties, and she never failed to remember a kiss for her poor friend relegated to her cubbyhole. She was always superbly dressed by Fath—I remember especially a black-and-white-striped satin dress that was stunning. Forgive me if I'm overusing literary references, but on those evenings we were playing Delly!°

I sent the *pneumatique* to my mother so that she wouldn't worry, but she worried all the time, poor woman, and for good reason. My work on the newspaper both dismayed and reassured her. She budgeted the 1,400 francs a month with much talent, and it was necessary! She and I had calculated that I needed fourteen francs a day for my métro fare and my lunch chez André, across the street from the paper. I don't know whether André listened to his clients' conversations, but if he did, he must have had a great deal to tell in 1945. . . . She worried that a summons evicting us from the apartment would arrive at any moment; she had had my little brothers baptized Protestant, which the nice Pastor Ebershold had done, antedating the certificates. She worried about me, about my youth and the temptations that surely would besiege me. There she was wrong; I was very, very good, for the reason I have already mentioned: I was scared stiff of pregnancy.

Such was life in Neuilly. I continued to see my friends on Sundays, but I was no longer really with them. I was working, they were studying or pretending to, and a few of the girls were getting married. If a few of my ex-classmates felt a twinge of resistance, I was unaware of it at the time. Perhaps the political stance of my newspaper made me suspect; it's possible but improbable. In any case, nothing was ever said.

I stayed at *Les Nouveaux Temps* for eight months, from September 1940 to June 1941. My time there ended when I moved from the right bank of the Seine to the left bank and entered the world of the Café Flore.

°Soap-opera classics of the thirties.

Chapter 3

ONE evening in March 1941, instead of taking the métro at the Louvre for Neuilly, I walked across the footbridge of the Institute and up the Rue Bonaparte, and pushed open the door of the Café Flore—because I had an appointment with a boy there. It never occurred to me that by opening that door I was entering a world that would change the rest of my life.

Actually, I could just as well have begun my story with these words: "The person I am today was born one evening in March 1941 on a banquette in the Café Flore, Boulevard Saint-Germain, Paris, sixth arrondissement." The kid from Neuilly, erstwhile office girl for the collaborators, unknowingly was now crossing her third frontier, where at last I would find the world to which I really belonged, and which I had been unconsciously seeking for a long time. It sounds a bit pompous, told like that; it becomes less heavy if I tell you that as I sat down on that historic banquette I knocked over the celluloid bell that protected the macaroons (without coconuts) that were on the table.

I had a date with a boy. Two days previously I had been

to see *La Main Passe* at the Théâtre des Mathurins, thanks to one of those complimentary tickets that Madame Baudouin sometimes produced the day before an opening. I was all alone and very intimidated. Intimidated by being at an opening, and embarrassed to be there alone. During the intermission, in the theater's little foyer, I was reading my program for the fifth time, surrounded by people who seemed very much at ease and who were talking very loudly. But on the steps leading to the dress circle was a quiet trio who were looking at me. They were a very handsome young man, a very beautiful young woman, and Roger Blin, who had impressed me so much at the Théâtre l'Atelier. They were looking at me: the girl kindly, the young man gravely, and Roger Blin . . . hardly at all.

During the last act the girl watched the play, and Blin did too, but the young man watched me, and I must have been looking at him, since I knew he was looking at me. Afterward, on the sidewalk of the Rue des Mathurins, the girl said loudly, "Good night. See you tomorrow." The young man came toward me and said simply, "Where are you going?"

I said, "Home." And he said, "Come on, let's go have a drink," and I went with him. Today, after thirty-four years of a friendship punctuated by intermittent storms and arguments, generally of an ideological nature, when someone asks us where we met, Claude Jaeger generally says, "On the sidewalk on the Rue des Mathurins." That first night not only did I follow him into the bistro next to the Gare Saint-Lazare, but because he had a good face, and above all a trustworthy face, I told him everything. Everything. That my father was in London, that I was half Jewish, that my mother and little brothers depended on me; about *Les Nouveaux Temps* and my 1,400 francs a month. He listened. Then he accompanied me to the last métro from Saint-Lazare to Neuilly, and during that late-night trip home I had time enough to make a thorough survey of the inexcusable folly I had just committed. I was wrong to worry; what follows proves my point.

So, after I had knocked over the bell covering the wartime macaroons and excused myself to the furious *patron* (it was a long time later before I could call him "Paul" and "*tu*"), I looked around. The Flore was filled, full of people with faces and clothes one saw neither in Neuilly nor on the Rue du Louvre. Whether they were very young, less young, or elderly, they all looked alike. They were a family; I was the new girl. We were in a café, but the conversations weren't noisy; the tone was serious. The lighting was dim, and there were books and magazines among the beer glasses; they all seemed to know one another, and there wasn't a single German. Yet one heard foreign accents. The men wore turtleneck sweaters and corduroy jackets under grimy raincoats, and their hair was a bit too long. The women wore no makeup; in fact, there were very few of them. Nobody was fashionable—they were their own fashion.

The beautiful young woman who had said loudly, "Good night. See you tomorrow," was at one of the tables. She smiled at me, she smiled at the new girl, and all the more so since she knew how the new girl had gotten there. She came over to sit with us; I suppose she wanted to know more about her pal's discovery. Her name was Sonia, Sonia Mossé. She was terribly nice, and I never saw her without her smile during the months that followed—until the day I no longer saw her at all because one morning the Gestapo came and took her and her sister to Drancy. They never came back. I've told you her family name, Mossé, but that evening I would have been incapable of telling you the full names of any of the people I met. People passed our table, stretching out a hand and saying Fabian, or Roger, or Nina; I was discovering a society in which one didn't necessarily use one's family name. It was a society in which the actors said they were actors even if they were unknown or out of work, a society composed in large part of painters and sculptors without galleries. I was completely "displaced"—and yet I had just found my place in the world. In fairy tales, the pumpkin carriages take you to

Maxim's; but there are others that take you to the Flore, to princes who are handsome, intelligent, gifted, generous, funny, and poor. How lucky I've been!

I wasn't entirely aware of it that evening, yet surely I suspected it. I was intimidated, impressed, shocked, and fascinated. I came back the next day. And the next. And the next. At first I came to meet Claude. Soon I came for the Flore. Our idyll turned quickly into companionship. I wasn't ready and I was scared. He was very kind, very much in love with another girl, and very good at a deep, penetrating look that still works with the ladies today. So things rapidly became simple between us. We liked each other a lot and we talked. He was much, much older than I was—he was twenty-four. He protected me, and somewhat lackadaisically he plugged for the state auditors exam, while he dreamed of becoming a film director.

Soon everything seemed bizarre and contradictory. A sane, balanced girl can't spend her evenings on the banquettes of the Café Flore among people wanted by the police—some of them Jewish, many of them Communists or Trotskyites, Italian antifascists, Spanish Republicans, bums, jokers, penniless poets, sharers of food ration tickets, ambulatory guitarists, genial jacks-of-all-trades, temporary no-goods—when she has spent her day taking messages from Abetz to Jean Luchaire, or helping Madame Baudouin complete the invitation list for a benefit. By which I mean to say that I had found my proper place on the imitation-leather banquettes of the Café Flore, but the people of the Flore, who condemned any sign of collaboration, were beginning to object because I was working where I did. My double life on the Rue du Louvre and the Café Flore was no longer possible.

So after about three months, fortified by what I thought I had learned at the Flore in conversations with actors and assistant directors and authors, all generally jobless, I asked Luchaire for an interview, and told him that I could no longer stay on the paper, and was going. He said, "What are you going to do?" And so I bluffed. I answered, "The movies." He smiled. So I took the bit in my teeth, probably to impress my new friends who were not there to see me. "In any case, I've got to leave. You see, monsieur, you're all going to end up in front of a firing squad."

He laughed. He said, "Good luck," and kissed my cheek. As I was leaving, he said, "If you need anything, you know where to find me." He was flabby, weak, corrupt, handsome, and generous, and at the time, with my new intransigence, I would have said a coward. But I can't say that, knowing how he died. It was indeed in front of a firing squad, a cigarette between his lips, shouting, *"Vive la France!"* It was a completely anachronistic thing to do for the internationalist he pretended he was. Still, it must have been difficult to go through with the gesture when one has just refused the blindfold and is probably close to collapsing, faced with a bunch of kids who have been ordered to fire at you. And who fire.

I just said that I was bluffing when I told Luchaire that I was going to make movies. Actually, it was no longer just a bluff. I had broken the taboo. The secret, asleep inside me, was now wide awake. I wanted to act. I was willing to admit it; I was no longer ashamed of it. Before that, with my slumbering secret, here is the way my mind worked: Everyone wants to act, just as everyone wants to be beautiful, rich, and loved. But you don't admit these things; it's not proper. Still, today, I have a great deal of trouble believing people who say they never dreamed of being actors in their youth. I generally decide they're liars—in some cases I'm probably right. So I was no longer bluffing. I wasn't fooling my mother, either—I couldn't. Since my discovery of my new world, my homecomings had grown later and later, and my language had changed. From a distance—she never set foot in the Café Flore—she followed the changes in her daughter. When I talked to her, I avoided the word "café"; judging from the way I talked, the Flore was a place halfway between a workers' cafeteria and a cenacle where "fantastic," "madly interesting" people met. Even my vocabulary had changed: I was simultaneously enthusiastic and evasive when she would ask me just why all these people were so "fantastic" and "madly interesting." I would accentuate their nonconformity, pointing out how similar it was to her own at the time of the Japanese toothbrush incident, which delighted her. But I knew quite well she would have detested this café where everybody used the familiar *tu* and *toi* to everybody else.

Since I talked less and less about what happened at the newspaper and more and more about what I had learned at the Flore during the hour I spent there before I came home, she was hardly surprised when I announced my decision to leave the newspaper and "become an artist." In fact, she was really marvelous. Despite the troubles she saw ahead, she thought it was worth a try, and she never tried to discourage me. That was really quite an achievement; my leaving *Les Nouveaux Temps* meant the end of our monthly security. But it was also a kind of rehabilitation. She told me that she had full confidence in me. Which meant, of course, that she had confidence in the way in which she had brought me up. And she was right. Although I didn't "turn out" right away, in any case I didn't turn out badly ... which she knew, and which she told me. And that is how, in the space of two days, I settled my problems with my family and my boss and became a potential actress and a full-time "Floriste."

And "potential actress" is the correct term. To be perfectly honest, while I savored my first real taste of freedom, I didn't do much except hang around the Flore, providing myself with good excuses for hanging around there. I changed my habits. Instead of dropping in after work before going home to Neuilly, I started doing what most of the others did—that is to say, I lived there. That meant arriving around noon, then going off for lunch at Rémy's in the Rue des Beaux-Arts, or Chéramy's in the Rue Jacob, with meal tickets and often on credit, or else to the Petit Saint-Benoît, with tickets and without credit. At about two we'd return to the Flore for an ersatz wartime coffee with saccharine. From three-thirty on we'd walk around the area, discovering the beauties of the Place Furstenberg, or the Rue Chat-Qui-Pêche, or the Cour de Rohan, or we would lean on the wall of the Quai des Grands-Augustins and contemplate the Quai des Orfèvres. Punctually at six we would reappear at the Flore to meet those we had left at three-thirty, if they hadn't come on the walk with us. One would order a lemonade, one only, which would last till dinnertime. On the next to last métro I would return to Neuilly, feeling guilty for the day's total lack of productiveness. I would tell my mother a slightly different version when relating the day's events. I was wrong to feel guilty; I was in the process of learning everything in one fell swoop. Now I had time.

Roger Blin, Fabien Loris, Raymond Bussière, Leduc, Decomble, Mouloudji and Crolla, Frankeur: These are the names that rise in my memory when I think of that spring of 1941—you see I'm not giving you the names of stars. There were no stars in that place, but all these people could tell you all about the "October Group" or recite "The Battle of Fontenoy" for you in hushed tones, because in 1934 they had acted for the workers in the factories. Or they could tell you about *Numance* or *Tableau des Merveilles*, which their pal Jean-Louis Barrault had put on in an attic in the Rue des Grands-Augustins. They could hum "I'm Fifteen, You're Fifteen, Together That Makes Thirty...." They talked about the "shellshuckers," who hadn't yet come back. They were their friends Jean Rougeul and Sylvain Itkine, who had started a little "candy" factory in Marseilles, where the basic ingredients were the shells of almonds and other nuts. The factory functioned with the help of a few other refugees from the Flore, while they waited for hypothetical visas to Portugal or Mexico. They spoke so vividly about their friends that when one of them—tired of waiting for his visa, disgusted by an almond paste made of shells, and unable to bear exile any longer—

pushed open the door of the Café Flore after having traveled more or less secretly from the unoccupied zone, I, the new girl, knew who he was before he had even introduced himself. I never had the opportunity to meet Itkine; he never reappeared. After the war I saw *La Grande Illusion* again, and it was difficult to imagine that the timid little man who explained to Jean Gabin that "this is a fourteenth-century door" (Gabin-Maréchal couldn't have cared less anyway) was the same man who had died in a cellar of the Gestapo under torture without revealing a single name.

All the people I've just mentioned were poor. They worked very little; sometimes they even refused to work. Roger Blin, for example. They asked him to do over, with a different actor, the scenes he had done with Marcel Dalio in *Entrée des Artistes*, so they could reissue the film without the Jew Dalio in it. An old "friend" of Dalio's instantly agreed to replace his old friend. But since Blin categorically refused the deal, the remake couldn't be done. I was learning.

The person I learned most about was Jacques, who was never there. I became intimately acquainted with their laughter, affection, vacations, courageous incidents, parties—all including Jacques. Prévert, of course, is the Jacques I'm going on about. I had not been *Drôle de Drame* or *Quai des Brumes* or *Le Crime de Monsieur Lange*, but before I ever met him, which was to happen in 1942, I thought like him, I spoke like him, I laughed at the same things he did, I had long since memorized him by heart from all those who loved him.

All this is what I meant when I said that hanging around the Flore wasn't a waste of time. Then, too, you might suddenly find yourself seated between Picasso and Dora Maar, because they knew Jaeger a little and had invited you both to lunch because you were young, attractive, nice, vulnerable, insolent, and extraordinarily impressed by them. So that suddenly you were saying to yourself:

"My God, I'm eating with the 'charlatan'!" Or you'd be sent out to buy a tube of yellow number something-or-other for Soutine, who didn't dare go into the art-supply store where he'd always bought colors for fear of being denounced by the owner, whom he'd known for years. You bought the wrong yellow and were bawled out by a man whose paintings you had never seen but who you discovered after his death was a great painter. You laughed till you cried with a Swiss-Italian sculptor with kinky hair and a cane, whose face was a patchwork of the most beautiful lines caused by humor, anguish, and kindness you'd ever seen; you collapsed laughing when he told a story about a very rich lady who was so ugly that every day he made the bust he was doing of her smaller in order to attenuate her ugliness. You went to dinner at the Quatre Vents with him, his brother Diego, and Jaeger on the charge account of the same lady, who was in the process of becoming the shrunken head of a Jivaro. Twenty-five years later, in a sumptuous New York penthouse, you'll again laugh till you cry when you see the same work, which is about the size of a package of Marlboros, clutched in the lacquered hand of a very chic lady who is in the process of telling you that she has bought this Giacometti for a fortune because it is one of the rare works from that "depressive period" when the artist saw everything small. A memorable moment in your education comes the day you hear the "charlatan" repeat for you the answer he gave the Germans the day they asked him about *Guernica:* "Did you do this?" and he replied: "No, you did!" And you howl laughing because he's telling you himself; it's not something you will read years later in a solemn book about the occupation. And then one morning in June 1941, while Léo Marjane sang "Oh, he was handsome, he was tall, my lover of the fête Saint-Jean" on the radio, on the other side of Europe everything changed. During the night the USSR had been attacked, which meant the end of the pact. Speaking of the pact, I never understood what it meant in 1939. Maybe if Madame

Samuel had stayed the whole year at the lycée she would have made it clear to us. The photograph of the famous Ribbentrop-Molotov handshake didn't impress me half so much as the "splendid fur bonnets of the plucky little Finnish army" in '39, "the Lottas."

As far as the material side of life went, we still had a little money left over from the sale of the Oriental carpets to the bogus marquis, and I had sold a few books the family considered rare, which were not as rare as we had thought, but things were beginning to be tight at home. We saved a few things that the Bazaines, friends of my parents, had put away for us before our things were seized and sold at auction; and following due legal procedures we were evicted from our apartment by the police commissioner of Neuilly. My mother courageously accepted employment as a seamstress in charge of linens in a hospital in Valréas in the unoccupied zone, where they would lodge her and my little brothers. She tucked the two small boys under her arm and left, for once with a minimum of parcels. One of them, however, contained a stuffed toy elephant dressed in a gray wool sweater—in which she had hidden an old revolver of my father's that she had refused to hand in to the police in 1940. She hadn't the slightest intention of using it, but just as one does not buy a toothbrush from the enemy, one does not surrender one's arms. . . .

I was sad that they were going, and at the same time I was relieved. Sad because it was the first time the four of us would be separated, and relieved because I would no longer have to embellish the story of what I had done with my day (I purposely say "embellish" rather than "lie") as I had embellished my first contact with my profession, my first day's filming, my first day as an extra.

Thanks to a very nice lady who had recommended me to one of her friends who was an assistant cameraman, one day I got a call sheet from the Studio Saint-Maurice. It ran something like this:

Please be at the studio Saint-Maurice promptly at 8 A.M. Scene: an elegant bar. Costume: spring furs. Role: Supplementary artist. Fee: 120 francs. Film: *Le Prince Charmant*. Signed: Harispuru Production Office.

I took my métro at Neuilly, kissing my mother and my little brothers as they saw their big sister off to be in the movies. At the Château de Vincennes, the end of the line, I caught the wood-fueled bus to Saint-Maurice, where I asked the way to the studio. And at exactly eight o'clock I was standing in front of the gentleman who had signed "Production Office," who now asked me to show him my work permit. I told him I had forgotten it. . . . At the time, to be an extra—I mean a "supplementary artist"—you had to have a card issued by the propaganda staff of the German army which proved you were indisputably Aryan. He seemed to believe my tale, but he did notice a total absence of the "spring furs" requested in the call sheet. He said, "We'll put you in back; you don't need makeup—you won't show. Go to Set A." So I went to Set A and spent the day seated at a table at the back of the "elegant bar" that was a background for the love scene between Renée Faure and Jimmy Gaillard, the stars of the picture.

I was very disappointed that I hadn't been made up; I was as silly and childish as that! The other extra they put at my table as a fiancé, husband, or cousin—even if you were barely visible at the back, an elegant bar at that time could not include lone women—was surprised to meet me for the first time. He was a professional, a real one—he surely had a work permit—and he decided to educate me. He gazed sadly at my winter/spring/autumn suit that I had dragged from Vannes to the Rue du Louvre to the Flore to the Studio Saint-Maurice, and said, "You know, without a wardrobe you'll get nowhere." He had everything: hunting outfit, white dinner jacket, Prince of Wales checked suit. From time to time a tall, very handsome young man said, "Let's have some quiet now. The supplementary artists— when you see my hand signal, start clapping." Since my purported husband, cousin, or fiancé obeyed these orders very seriously, I too applauded things I hadn't seen; the reverse-angle shot would be filmed after the handsome young man said: "The supplementary actors have half an hour's break." At the end of the day's work I learned that we were to film the "matching" shots and were on early call for the next morning—"same time, same costume."

In the métro that took me back to Neuilly that evening without a stop at the Flore, I was trying to figure out how I would tell the family what my first day in the movies had really been like. I hadn't cared for it at all, and I didn't know how to describe it. So I probably embellished— that's what I meant a little while ago.

I suspect that there isn't an actor alive who was able to truthfully answer his family's questions after his first day's activity in his future profession. However stupid, incoherent, disappointing, and mechanical my first day in the back of that "elegant bar" had been, with an extra who had nothing in common with my pals of the October Group and still less with my mother, delicate reader of Proust that she was, it had nonetheless been my first day on a set—and I couldn't describe it honestly. Had I been honest, I would have said, "It's too stupid—I just can't do that." But instead of saying that, I embellished. I think I said that I was very tired and that I had to get up early the next morning because I had been asked to come back—which gave an impression that I played such an important part in the action of *Le Prince Charmant* that it would be impossible for them to continue without my presence. In reality, I despised myself for being an object that applauded nothing and got 120 francs for it. I despised myself for going back there the next day, and I despised myself for not telling the truth. Take it as you will.

What I had done above all was to embellish the situation by omission. I had understood quite clearly that first day that "forgetting" my work permit was a game I couldn't go on playing indefinitely. One of two things would happen: Either I would have to deal with someone who would take

the risk of closing his eyes and pretend to believe me—
which was, believe me, a form of resistance—or I would
have to deal with bastards who would prevent me from
working—which for them was a form of collaboration—
for the renascence of the French film industry!

I never did try to get a permit. According to the new
laws, I was only half Jewish, but I did not have the
baptismal certificate necessary for crossing over the line to
be on the right side of the law. I do believe that I was
sprinkled, in Wiesbaden, by the chaplain of the army of
occupation (surely in order to please my Signoret-Dubois
de Poncelet grandmother), but in 1921 no one would have
believed that this certificate would one day be an
important testimonial for my future, so no one had
bothered to keep that piece of paper.

I could have asked the good Pastor Ebershold to
baptize me Protestant at the same time he did my little
brothers—he surely would have done it. I didn't ask him. It
was stupid, certainly it wasn't clever, and above all, it
wasn't rational. I might also have asked Luchaire to fix
things for me. I could have. He would doubtless have been
very efficient, and been happy to do so. I had been too
close to the ways of the world in my little cubbyhole at *Les
Nouveaux Temps* not to know all about that. But when I
try to put myself back inside the skin of the girl I was at the
time, I'm incapable of explaining my attitude. My call to
the studio had been sent to me in the name of Signoret. I
had dropped Kaminker, which was not Breton enough for
real connoisseurs. I did go in for a certain hypocrisy.
"You're related to Gabriel Signoret?" "An uncle . . ."
repeating my grandmother's game on the Neuilly benches.
But at the same time, I was walking around with my real
identity card in the name of Kaminker.

I wasn't innocent; it was a game. It wasn't heroic,
because it didn't help anyone. It was only useful to me in
relation to an established order that I categorically
rejected. It was in no way related to some solidarity with
the Jewish community I had never known. And in any case,

I was determined to play this game all alone, without a witness for the future failures I had already sniffed out that first day on the set.

I had understood that, professionally, I had begun on a slalom course which you could always enter; you could even avoid the bumps and make it past the poles, but you could never make it across the finish line. Because to make it across the finish line you had to have that work permit. I'm lingering so long on the importance of that piece of paper because I want to point out to today's kids who are trying to break into the cinema that for four long years, in France, the barriers erected were not those of the exhibitors, directors, distributors, or producers, but simply a bunch of cops who—without any consideration for potential talent—referred only to arbitrary German law. I'll try not to ramble on about it, but it'll be difficult. Because each time, during those four years, that I was on to a good "break," I never landed anything except a job as an extra or a "silhouette" or one of those little roles not mentioned in the credits.

A "silhouette" is a speaking extra. It's just below a "small part." It's a sentence or two in a crowd scene: "It's hot today," or "Garçon, I'd like to pay." The camera follows the main actor and pans across the table where you're sitting. But in concrete terms, a silhouette means three times an extra's pay, at the end of the day. I'm not a pro at shop stories, but here I can't resist telling you about the famous producer who, combining his duties as producer-director-accountant, replied to an extra who had just told him that his paycheck should be 500 francs, not 120, because he had spoken in a scene, "Well, then, you missed a splendid opportunity to shut up."

I lived—survived—thanks to the silhouettes. At the end of my second day as an extra in the "elegant bar," the script girl, who had noticed me—and in passing I just want to say that it's always more beneficial to be noticed by the script girl than spotted by the producer—said to me, "Monsieur Boyer is making another film immediately. We'll give you a silhouette." That's the way things happen in the movies, if you're not too dumb, if you behave yourself, and if people notice that you're interested in what's going on. By the second day the clientele of the elegant bar had been reduced to two or three "matching" extras, who were consequently more closely integrated into the action. We were no longer sent off to play in the courtyard while the grownups worked. So I watched, and began to understand much more about what was happening. I was learning. And it must have shown on my face, which is how I got my first part as a silhouette.

It was a film called *Boléro*, with Arletty as the star. I had one sentence, spoken as I went up the staircase of the *maison de couture* on a day I was "Milliner's apprentice, silhouette, 500 francs." The sentence was: "Madame, the Countess d'Arménise awaits you in the salon." I got out my sentence at breakneck speed. They thought I was funny. It was all the funnier because I didn't know that Arménise was the name of the chief cameraman, and that I was part of an "in" gag I didn't suspect. They told me I was very good, which delighted me. My "forgotten" work permit had been swallowed without hesitation. As for my salary, compared with the 1,400 francs a month on the newspaper, it was colossal. All this went on at the Studio Pathé on the Rue Francoeur. And since they had thought I was funny, they recommended to the Pathé directors that I be sent to a school they had just established called the Cours Pathé, run by Solange Sicard.

Solange Sicard was a very nice woman. She had played a bit with Jouvet, she limped as a result of an attack of polio, she had never been successful and wasn't embittered by it; she was a good teacher, insofar as acting can ever be taught. She didn't teach me what to do, but she did teach me what never to do. Emphasizing verbs, for example. One should never say, "I *hate* you"; one should say, "I hate you." It seems like a very small thing, but it's very important. She immediately classified me as a comic, because of a defect in my pronunciation that makes me hiss on *ch* and *j*. My classmates were Suzanne Flon, Jacques Dynam, Andrée Clément, André Valmy, Jacques Dufilho, Liliane Bert, and Hermantier.

We worked twice a week. During the time I was there I managed to really perfect only one scene to the point where it was playable for eventual auditions with directors in search of new talent, and that was a scene from the second act of *La Femme en Blanc*, by Marcel Achard, which I played with Dynam. At that time it never occurred to me that acting might be something other than knowing your text by heart and reeling it off exactly as had been indicated by the teacher. In a funny way I was in exactly the same state of mind as I had been on Saint Charlemagne's Day at the Lycée Pasteur.

The ambitious project launched by Pathé had the aim of creating a talent pool like that of the big American firms and, of course, UFA in Nazi Germany. If you worked hard, you were supposed to be rewarded with a contract for a sum I have forgotten, which was supposed to assure you of a small regular salary, but above all, of jobs in the Pathé productions. I don't suppose I was very good in *La Femme en Blanc*, for the reasons mentioned above, but since we were all in the same boat, I was probably no worse than the others.

I was fired by Pathé because of my participation in a pseudo-medical short called, if I remember rightly, *Comment Vaincre sa Timidité*, in which I played the untimid friend of Liliane Bert, who was the poor timid girl who could do nothing right. The whole thing took two days to make in a car of the métro, and probably ran seven minutes on the screen. The censors must have been extremely vigilant, because very soon the people at Pathé let me know that I should have told them about my "situation," and that I must understand that in view of my "situation" there could be no question of a contract, nor could I even continue attending the Cours Pathé.

But Madame Sicard gave private tuition at her own house. I went, and she never charged me a sou. There again, I met my friends, some of whom had in the meantime landed the famous contract with its small salary. I will now tell you about the saddest and most depressing failure I had during that period, and then we'll go on to the good things. Louis Daquin had done screen tests with me for a part in *Le Voyageur de la Toussaint*. We were six girls and seven boys. None of the other girls was retained, and I was giving all seven boys their cues. Apparently I had gotten the part, and everyone on the set at the end of the day considered that I had been hired. And despite all I knew by now about films, I thought so too. There's no law against dreaming. But Louis wasn't authorized to hire me, so he told me my hair style wasn't right. He was miserably unhappy and yet he still didn't dare tell me: "Listen, you don't have the paper; I can't take you." Those things just weren't said aloud. So I was given a very nice small part in *Le Voyageur de la Toussaint*. And it was really very decent of him to have taken the trouble.

Before beginning on what I've already called the good things, I want to say a word about the small parts, because later I might forget. It's very hard to play a small part in films. It's different in the theater; if you play Rosencrantz in *Hamlet*, you're still part of a company, and you've lived through the weeks of rehearsal, the coffee breaks, and the stage fright of a first night. In films, it's the opposite. For example, if your part is "the cousin," your call sheet will read: "Role: cousin. Sequences: wedding dinner and the opening of the will." From the moment your call sheet arrives, you're dreaming about this cousin you're going to be for a day or two of your life, without knowing anything about her. Is she a poor cousin? Is she flirtatious? Is she a cousin of the bridegroom, in which case maybe she's in love with the bridegroom? Or is she a greedy cousin who will be very disappointed when the will is opened? In short, you're dreaming of something you know nothing about, since you haven't read the script. You arrive at the studio, and the dresser for the production—who is not the dresser for the stars—greets you and says, "Who are you?

71

Oh, yes, the cousin. Room Four." "Oh, yes, the cousin; come for your makeup, mademoiselle." The chief makeup man doesn't have time for you because he's busy with the star; he gives a few instructions to his either very young or very old assistant, who fusses with your face a bit while the great man is painting with great care the face of a lady whom you don't immediately recognize because the makeup job has just begun and her hair is still in curlers. Maybe he stops work for an instant in order to glance at what is being done with you. You're dying of fright, so you say nothing; they're all talking about yesterday's dailies, about that outdoor scene that was so funny when the cow came ambling into frame. More actors arrive; they're all part of the family and they know perfectly well whose father or lover they are, and here comes yesterday's scene with that cow again.... In the meantime, you're wondering whose arms you're going to throw yourself into, squealing, "Oh, Julian, I'm so happy about your marriage! I told you it would happen, I told you...." Or, "Poor Aunt Jeanne, she loved you so much." Those are the two speeches they sent you by *pneumatique*, and you know them *really*, but *really*, by heart. In a little while you're going to say them to somebody to whom you've never said "*tu*," with whom you've never eaten in the cafeteria, who doesn't know your name, and who's just asked the makeup man whether you've been hired to be the waitress or the cousin; after which the head makeup man, consulting his list, announces that you're the cousin. They expect you to "be in the skin" of your character (which is wrong; it's your skin that becomes an envelope around someone else), to be a member of a family that is doubly strange to you. You haven't the slightest reason to be pleased by this marriage, you have no idea what the gentleman has done to bring it about, and as for Aunt Jeanne, you haven't a clue as to who she was. Later your cousin is seated in his chair while they're adjusting the lights on his stand-in, who generally is another extra with whom you've worked on another film, and who, consequently, says "*tu*" to you....

That's what a small part is all about. I didn't have many of them during those four years. And after 1944 I didn't get them anymore. The films I make today are full of small parts, and although it may not be apparent, I empathize with those actors' worries; I know their anguish, their frights, and their blunders. It's not such a good idea to arrive in the makeup room with a fat philosophical tome that you plunk down on the makeup table to prove that you're really quite above the cinema—while all the time you're scared stiff and desperately want to be in movies. That's the kind of thing that irritates the mountebanks who haven't studied philosophy, and it brings out a superior smile in the intellectuals who have become mountebanks—they know that you don't have to be an idiot to be an actor. You see, I know what I'm talking about; I did it once, the number with the fat tome. You don't do that kind of thing twice. But now, really, let's proceed to the good things . . . the miracles.

When everything on the road ahead is blocked, the miracle is survival. And since one survives thanks to others, the miracle is meeting them. It's a miracle to be engaged for the entire filming of *Visiteurs du Soir* because there's a man named Sabas at the Flore who sent you to see Marcel Carné, the emperor of the cinema, and Carné hires you to be one of the four *dames du château*, which means that you will be in every scene: the dances, the banquet, the hunt; you'll have your costume made to measure and be made up. (At last!) Of course, you're still an extra, but you have a kind of identity in the action, which takes place under the eyes of the inhabitants of the château. It's a miracle when you're part of a group that's taken to the South of France and gets only a cursory check at the line of demarcation. And perhaps the greatest miracle of all is that Carné keeps you for the duration of the film. For those three months I was one of the few survivors among the extras. Carné dismissed people after each scene: He would line us all up and review us like a colonel, saying, "You're finished . . . you're finished . . . you're finished. . . ." But he kept me.

73

Only three of us remained for the whole film: Arsénio Fregnac, Madeleine Rousset, and me. Carné kept us because he liked us and because we made him laugh. During all the location scenes, even when I wasn't in them, I hung around and watched. For the first time in my life I was shoulder to shoulder with stars! I didn't miss one. And they weren't just anybody: Arletty, Jules Berry, Ledoux, Marcel Herrand.

We were living in Vence. The extras lodged in a pension called Ma Solitude, near the railroad tracks, and the stars lived in the Grand Hotel on the square, surrounded by plane trees, which have since been cut down. In order to earn a little more money I had said I could ride a horse like nobody's business.

Apart from two or three friends who had taken the job in order to get across to the unoccupied zone, most of the cast was made up of professional extras, the people with the complete wardrobes. Arsénio was really very funny. The three of us were inseparable, and Madeleine and I profited from the advantages of his success. Arletty, Ledoux, and Herrand were particularly nice to us. There, too, a miracle took place; in Paris there would have been no possibility of relations between extras and stars, but there was in this little town in the provinces, and in the Verdon Pass, where we risked our lives on the backs of the horses lent to us by the police troopers. We ate very badly on location, which was the fault not of Paulvé, the producer, but of one of the unit production managers, who was pinching pennies, which, needless to say, didn't drop onto our paper plates, but into his pocket. It was not unlike the opening shots of *Potemkin*, the day the pots of beans were dumped into a field near Tourettes because the lords and ladies of the château had found cockroaches in them. One Sunday Jacques Le Breton, the sound engineer, invited Arsénio, Madeleine, and me to drive down by bus to Saint-Paul-de-Vence. We gazed at the façade of the famous Colombe d'Or, but we didn't dare go in. We ate across the street.

One day a new assistant arrived. He was very gentle, very timid, and very courteous to the extras, and we were very insolent and impolite to him. He was an Italian, and he represented the interests of Scalera, the coproducers of the film. His name was Michelangelo Antonioni. When we returned to Paris, to film the banquet and the ball, among the extras were Alain Resnais, Chaumette, who was a "speaking page," and Jean Carmet, a school friend. Carmet worked regularly with Herrand and Marchat, and that is how I soon found myself hired by the Théâtre des Mathurins as a woman of the people of Thebes in a very bad version of *Oedipus*, which was called *Dieu Est Innocent*. I was no longer a dame du château with a salary of 200 francs a day on horseback and 170 francs on foot. The salary of "a woman of the people of Thebes" was fifteen francs a day, but I was delighted to be in the theater. Marchat was Oedipus; Balachova was Jocasta; Jandeline was Antigone; Claude Magnier was Eteocles or Polynices, as was Erno Crisa; the abominable Vandéric was Tiresias, and Daniel Gélin was Haemon. Playing a woman of the people of Thebes consisted of chanting, along with a handful of other actors—given the tiny stage of the Mathurins and the equally tiny budget—sentences the longest of which was: "Jocasta, the Queen Jocasta, is dead...oh...oh...oh...." My fellow tragedians who chanted with me were named Jean-Marc Thibault, Christian Duvaleix, Yvette Étiévant, Gilles Quéant, Jean Carmet (who also had a sea chanty), and Arsénio, whom Herrand had picked up at the same time as he did me. Since Oedipus isn't a terribly cheerful story, the stage was always in semitotal darkness, and a phonograph, hidden in a corridor, kept playing a record called "Crowd Noises," which was supposed to amplify our lamentations and make the audience believe that there were two thousand gathered in the Rue des Mathurins and we were but a delegation. One day a distracted stagehand mistakenly played the other side of the record, which was called "Airplane Noises." Except for the first night, and perhaps the second or third, I cannot remember a single performance where the plebs of Thebes didn't come onstage for their lamentations without collapsing in laughter. We would be overcome by the giggles in the wings five minutes before we were to go on, we'd be fighting them the whole time we were onstage, and we'd finally crack up as soon as we came off. Onstage we would take up splendid Greek stances; we would cover our eyes with our forearms and lower our heads to show grief and humiliation—and we would split our sides laughing!

One day I found myself directly in Marchat's line of sight. It was just after he'd put out his eyes, and he saw me; in fact, he saw only me. All the others were laughing, but it was me he saw. As he was trying very hard to be believable in this crushing part—very badly written by a gentleman who had lots of money and who had underwritten this play which Herrand and Marchat had put on only to enable them to stage Synge's *Deirdre of the Sorrows* afterward—I quite understand that he was furious. So they fired me, which did annoy me a bit. I left with my rented Greek sandals. They were black and had laces of real leather, and they were reported to have been worn by Gabin in Duvivier's *Golgotha*—he had very small feet.

I was unhappy to lose my job, but still I was very gay: Two weeks into rehearsal I had begun my life as a woman; I was living with Daniel Gélin on the fifth floor of a little hotel in the Rue Monsieur-le-Prince. We were exactly the same age, and we loved each other very much. We listened to *Daphnis and Chloe* and Bing Crosby records. We went to the Flore very little; it scared Gélin at the time. We walked a lot, and we would plant ourselves in a métro entrance when we heard the boots of the German patrol and it was just midnight. He was a great pal of the whores who inhabited the other floors of the hotel. And they in turn were very nice to me; they would loan me their shoes on the days I had auditions, and they would be very sad if I didn't get the part.

Since Daniel and I were exactly the same age, I was too

old for him. That was when I met Marcel Duhamel. He liked me very much. And since he liked me very much, he shared his joy when a postcard from Germaine arrived from the unoccupied zone. I loved Germaine from a distance, without knowing her and without jealousy. She was the beloved of this man of forty who introduced me to surrealism and gave me his translation drafts of Henry Miller to read; who put Fletcher Henderson and Red Nichols on the phonograph as soon as he woke up; who told me about the Moscow trip of the October Group in 1934; who once again told me all about Germaine and covered me with a tenderness and an incestuous paternal protection which I surely needed. All this with hardly a sou between us. It was great.

Chapter 4

PIERROT Prévert was the first of the Préverts to come back to Paris. He came with a scenario by Jacques called *Adieu Léonard,* which was the biggest find for the paperless persons in the Flore.

Its stars were Charles Trenet, very unhappy at being an actor, Pierre Brasseur, and Carette. The feminine lead was Jacqueline Bouvier (who was to become Jacqueline Pagnol), very beautiful, charming, and funny. There was a whole host of small parts, all those unusual minor roles that Jacques loved so: Blin was a Gypsy, along with Vitsoris, a Greek Trotskyite in hiding. I was a Gypsy. My hair was curly and I wore a very beautiful dress. I didn't say a word; I made baskets. Mouloudji was a chimney sweep. Robert Scipion, not yet the inventor of the *Nouvel Observateur* crossword puzzles, was an assistant and a planter of Caïffa. He ran by, calling, "Caïffa! Caïffa!" There was also a girl from the October Group whose name I have forgotten: She was Jewish, her husband was in a concentration camp, she had left her kids behind in Paris in order to do the film on location and earn a little money. She cried all the time.

We had an assistant cameraman called Maréchal. Half of his face was superbly handsome; the other half was completely blown away. Beauty and horror. It was a souvenir from Spain. He had been the hero of one of the episodes in Malraux's *L'Espoir (Man's Hope)*.

The film was made in Dax, in the southwest. The weather was beautiful, we were working—it was a breather. Above all, it was the Café Flore on holiday. What luck to be young, with those people, and in that production where there wasn't the slightest discrimination between actors, extras, technicians, and stars. Brasseur and Carette supplied a nonstop stream of stories. Carette would begin one; Brasseur would seem to be laughing wholeheartedly, but in reality he was already preparing the next. Trenet was the only one among us who had any money. He would buy the hams cured in the region and we would all throw ourselves upon them greedily. Witta, the script girl, was irritated because Trenet said "tranway" with an *n* when she wanted him to say "tramway." We would all gather around him, sitting in the grass, and on the spur of the moment he'd compose songs. He would improvise about ten a day, which he would forget immediately. There was also a Gypsy—a real one—a cousin of Django's, of course, whom we called Camembert, and who played the guitar. As soon as Trenet started humming a tune, Camembert would join him on the guitar. What with Brasseur's and Carette's stories, Jacqueline Bouvier's humor, and Camembert and Trenet's concerts, we were entertained by a constant show.

We all took the train back to Paris. I was in the same compartment as Carette, his wife, Ninette, and Maréchal. Half an hour out of Dax, the train stopped in the middle of some fields. German police. Papers. Carette took out his identity card and Ninette took out hers. The Fritzes looked at Maréchal: A war hero commands respect; they clicked their heels and gave him back his card. My card still said Kaminker. The two guys carried a kind of dictionary, and they started going down their lists to see whether "Kaminker" was on them. There was a long silence, very long; it seemed to me to go on forever. Ninette and Carette looked out at the landscape. Maréchal's eyes never left me; he stared, he held my hand with his eyes. . . . The Fritzes pulled out a second dictionary. Finally, they closed it, gave me back my card, and left. We never said a word; we didn't even say "Ooh." Maréchal smiled at me; I smiled at him.

Months went by, and then one day I learned the story of Maréchal, who had suddenly disappeared from the film world. He had joined the maquis and he died in the Vercors region, so I was told. It was because of an English parachutist in hiding there, who was not careful enough. They were both caught by the Germans and shot on the spot. The Germans went to the nearest village and said, "There are two corpses up there. Go bury them." The farmers buried the two corpses and wrote "a blond man" on the tomb of the Englishman and "a dark man" on Maréchal's. Legend has it that one day two women who didn't know each other met at the grave and discovered that they had both been in Maréchal's life. That silent Maréchal who never said a word.

When I arrived from Dax at the Gare d'Austerlitz, someone was waiting for me on the platform. The films have used meetings in train stations so much that they have become a total cliché. If these sequences have been repeated so often, it's because they make very telling images. It is quite moving, in films, to experience the shyness and reticence and clumsiness of a man and a woman meeting after three weeks of separation, when their love affair had begun only three days before the woman's departure, and for three weeks each has asked himself whether the other was as deeply involved. It plays well in a film, but it's still better in real life. We had both spent three weeks thinking about each other, Yves Allégret and I, and that was how we began a story that was to last six years.

We were married for only one year, the last one, from 1948 to 1949. It was an attempt at normalization, which didn't make much sense, because the best part, lived in the midst of enormous difficulties, was over. And this best part was that we loved each other enormously, and we drifted along willy-nilly, and then in the end we both surfaced, he as a director and I as an actress, after the Liberation.

When we met he was already a director, but the only film to prove it had been accidentally burned in the processing lab. For the Champs Élysées film people he was still just Marc's brother, the assistant. But at the Flore he was Yves. He had been a member of the October Group, and he had made a very good short called *Prix et Profits, ou l'Histoire d'une Pomme de Terre (Price and Profits, or the Story of a Potato)*. He had also been one of the four or five young men who had served as Trotsky's secretaries during his Barbizon period. His family did not view him kindly. They didn't view me at all. The one exception was my sweet Nadine Vogel, who was Marc's wife at the time, and whose sister, Marie-Claude Vaillant-Couturier, had just been sent to Auschwitz. The only relations I ever had with the Allégret family were the times we ate cans of pâté de fois gras in our little room in the Hotel Saint-Yves. They had been filched that day from an Allégret sister's reserve on the third floor of the superb seventeenth-century building right opposite the Café Flore's terrace. Allégret would leave me seated in front of a cup of saccharined coffee, saying, "I'll go see how they are," and would cross the Boulevard Saint-Germain. He would reappear ten minutes later, pull a can of something edible out of his pocket, and put it right back, saying, "They're fine."

I would be pleased that they were fine because I like people to be fine even when I don't know them. I didn't know them; they didn't know me. We were all very discreet. Their discretion remained exemplary. Neither the birth in 1945 of my first child nor his death at the age of nine days, nor the birth of Catherine in 1946, ever caused them to lay aside their natural discretion.

I must hasten to add that if discretion was practiced on that side of the Boulevard Saint-Germain, it was less prevalent in the district town hall. The day I thought Catherine was old enough to know that her beginnings had been under the heading "Born of an unknown father," I told her just what I am about to tell you. In 1946 peace reigned, but restrictions continued. One morning, around my sixth month of pregnancy, I left cheerfully for the town hall on the Place Saint-Sulpice to get the supplementary milk and butter coupons that my "interesting condition" entitled me to. As I passed the police precinct on the ground floor of the building, I thought back to that evening in March 1944 when Allégret and I had been caught in a police raid and had spent a few hours inside. I thought to myself: What luck—what luck that all that's finished! I was really feeling pleased with life. I was wearing a plaid coat cut from a blanket that Marcel Duhamel had swapped for an ersatz fur blanket in 1942. It was still rendering loyal service. On the third floor of that building was a huge room containing ladies enthroned behind a counter separated by sort of wire-mesh ticket booths. The ladies were in charge of distributing the coupons. They wore hats; they were the guardians of the treasure and doled out charity. We, the ladies with big bellies, lined up in front of the booths, each trying to guess how many months separated the others from their respective deliveries. When my turn came, the patronizing lady said, "Show me your family identity card." "I don't have a family card." "Well, then, we'll put down 'unwed mother,'" she bellowed for the benefit of the group. Since I hadn't been left in the lurch and I wasn't neurotic, I repeated, "Yes, an unwed mother," with a smile that said: "and young, and happy—and you can get stuffed, you old hag." During the months that followed, the thing became a joke. She would easily spot me because of my plaid coat, which I made sure of wearing each time, and before it was even my turn she would thunder, "Well, still no family card?" And I would reply, "Nope! still an unwed mother." At my eighth month I asked for my wool and layette coupons. My request seemed to be very troublesome. She consulted another of the benefactors, and they huddled together over a pile of files. Finally, she handed out a few precious tickets. My next stop was the Rue Saint-Sulpice, where a wool shop nestled between two religious-book stores. The elderly haberdasher looked at the tickets and then at my belly and disappeared to the rear of the store, where she remained a long while before coming back with some skeins of wool—khaki colored. A great deal of khaki wool had been sold during the war so the ladies could knit balaclavas and other comforters for our dear prisoners, but the war must have been too short to exhaust the stocks of khaki wool. I thanked the lady, retrieved my tickets, and went back up the three flights of stairs in the town hall. There I gave the patronizing lady her coupons, saying, "I don't know whether I'm going to have a boy or a girl. I would like some blue, pink, or white wool. But in any case, I don't intend to start dressing the baby like a soldier." And with this sparkling exit line I waltzed out of the town hall of the sixth arrondissement.

I didn't set foot in the place again until some years later, when, accompanied by Montand, I went to see my daughter Catherine being handed a prize for hard work and progress during her first year of kindergarten.

Since there are no bad guys in my story, Catherine understood why she was "born of an unknown father." When I met Allégret he was married and had a child. He had been separated from his wife for two years, he loved me and I loved him, and I wasn't bothered by matters of legal respectability. I never asked him to get a divorce. The law then stipulated that a married man could not legally recognize a child born out of wedlock if he already had a child from his marriage. Catherine not only understood, but she rather liked my story, which is also hers.

I have been as good a mother as I know how to be. I've not been the mother mine was for me. I haven't been the kind of mother who wakes her child every morning and puts it to sleep every evening. I couldn't do that and continue my profession. When I said that I was more of a mother for my brothers than I was for my child, that is the honest truth.

When I was away from home, I had the exceptional good fortune of having the help of wonderful women whom I loved because they loved my child and my child loved them. It has never occurred to me to be jealous of them. And I had the wonderful good luck that my sister-in-law Elvire was always a second mother for Catherine, and she still is today. But Catherine never had a mollycoddling mother except for her first twenty-one days, when I nursed her. How warm it was, that little head on my forearm. The milk she gobbled every three hours could cause panic; the gram of weight lost since yesterday's weighing time caused terror; and the safety pins that might open undid me. I was melted by those movements of the small lips that I thought were her first smiles until a young pediatrician, Raymond Mande, explained that they were probably the effects of a touch of colic.... Typical experiences, I'm sure.

I allowed myself to enjoy this contemplative and animal condition for a short time only. It was as though Catherine's arrival had brought about the thing I had hoped for so long; one morning I prepared a few emergency bottles and then left to make a test for the first big part of my career. I believed naïvely that I could fit in this test between two feedings. I had borrowed a lovely dress from a friend, and it became all sticky with the milk that should have been going down the throat of my beautiful child. When I returned home five or six hours later, Catherine had already downed her first bottle, which is how the whole thing was settled for her and for me.

At twenty-one days, Catherine inherited a mother who was no longer the same, a different woman from the one who had nursed her the day before. When a bunch of strangers hire you to play an important part in a film for which they've done a lot of serious casting and you've been selected from among ten others, you stop being a real mother. You have become a professional. And your infant

84

becomes an actor's child. If its parents have any kind of sense of dignity, they spare it those interviews in the nursery that generally take place on Sunday morning when the actress suddenly busies herself with her child after a week of work. She is busy in the nursery, but probably all the time she's thinking about the scene that's coming up on Monday, and she's slightly worried about the break in her concentration that Sunday means. She's busy in the nursery, but she keeps an eye on her script. She looks at her child and discovers the changes that took place while she was absent during the week. She wonders whether maybe she isn't missing something. But on Monday she's delighted to rejoin her temporary family, and she no longer wonders about anything.

Catherine is my daughter and the daughter of Allégret, but at the age of three she also became Montand's daughter. She has babbled on the knees of Gérard Philipe, she's had Mercurochrome put on her scrapes by Jacques Becker, and she's had help with her homework from Clouzot. She knows nothing about years of failure and worry and fear. She was born into this world, and consequently she never had to go through a period like Harcourt-Hollywood. When she in her turn started in this profession, for which she is fabulously gifted, the handicaps she had were the opposite of those met by others, those who come from a different world. It is difficult and unfair to be the child of actors; just ask Romy Schneider or Jane Fonda—or ask Catherine herself.... But that's quite a time skip from the skein of khaki wool. Probably caused by my hurry to get to June 6, 1944....

By which I don't mean to say that nothing happened during the last months of the occupation. So much happened that I could fill the next four hundred pages and still not be finished. During those last months, every day was an adventure. It would begin when you woke up and not end until you awakened the next day, if indeed in the meantime you managed to make it home. Everybody lived like that. Which includes the collaborators, who sensed the end of their good times coming with the German downfall. Warning signs were in the air. Police raids were increasingly frequent. Anybody at all could be picked up for no heroic reason—just like that, by accident. All the men of STO° age had more-or-less faked papers. Almost everyone was in an irregular situation. Some of those well-intentioned and orderly families who during the first years of the occupation had explained how much they appreciated this new order, very "correct," which France so badly needed, now suddenly discovered the Germans were brutes because their own beloved sons had been picked up at the entrance of the École des Sciences Politiques, with the two ends of the Rue Saint-Guillaume blocked off by French police trucks to facilitate this maneuver. (And it happened that these were sometimes the mothers of those mothers who in May 1968, as they swabbed the swollen faces and blinded eyes of their own sons, discovered in their turn that the French police, who they thought were there only to take care of traffic, were also capable of brutality. But of course, there is a difference of degree.)

One began to see faces in the street that one hadn't seen for years. Some people thought it was easier to go to ground in the big city. So they left the villages in which they had been living under false names for months. They would suddenly discover that the grocer who had ingratiated himself with the militia was growing craftier, that he would spell out the false name on the ration card in a strange, suspicious manner. Unless, of course, he was the other kind, with whom suddenly butter wouldn't melt in his mouth as he pointed out how very conciliatory and understanding he had been all these months. Both these attitudes seemed dangerous and were apt to land you in the trap. The end was in the air, and people suddenly felt panic that they might not live to see the end simply because they

°Service Travail Obligatoire, a Vichy-instituted law that provided the Germans with a massive labor force.

had gone out to fetch a loaf of bread. I can imagine what it must have been like for the heroes, the real ones.

I lived among many of them, those heroes. But at the time I didn't know that they were. We must be clear about what is meant by "resistance." I would be a liar if I told you that I was part of the Resistance. In my vocabulary, resistants are only those who truly acted, and with full consciousness of what they were doing. I did not perform a single really heroic act. I did no harm, which in itself is not so bad. As I look back on it now, I realize that I often got involved. . . . I was given things to do about which I didn't know all the facts and couldn't see the outcome. I've mentioned "Aunt Claire," with whom I lived in Vannes from 1939 to 1940. In June 1941 her son Jean, my friend, was arrested by the Germans in Nantes, where he was a student. Aunt Claire asked me to come to Vannes, but on the way she asked me to stop in Nantes and pick up two suitcases in a hotel. I thought the two suitcases contained Jean's books and personal effects, but when I arrived in Vannes and we opened the suitcases, one was full of papers and the other full of ammunition. Had I known that I was carrying around munitions, I might have qualified as a heroine. But I did it innocently, which, in retrospect, is frightening enough. We wrapped up that ammunition into small packages and threw them in the Rabine, an arm of the sea that stretches into the old city of Vannes. Aunt Claire died in Ravensbrück. I didn't. It could have happened, but it would have been accidental.

One day when Allégret and I were walking along the Quai Voltaire, we met Jean Painlevé, wearing a Basque beret. He muttered, without stopping, "Hello—you haven't seen me." Later we discovered that he was one of the heads of the Resistance that was centered in the Musée de l'Homme.

One evening Jaeger decided at a quarter to twelve that he was too tired to go home, even though he lived nearby, and we put up a folding bed, no questions asked, which we discovered empty at seven in the morning, with a note pinned to it that said: "Thank you, good luck, see you soon." Later, after the war, we found out that he had been a colonel in the FTP° and in charge of the region that included the whole western portion of France.

Nor does it particularly mean anything that one day we skipped out of a hotel-restaurant whose owner was a collaborator, leaving behind a whacking big bill.

And on the evening of the sixth of June, D-day, we took a train to the country, far from Paris, which was called "joining the maquis"—but that, too, really carries no weight.

I was a member of a kind of personal maquis, an Allégret maquis. There was a big house in Charmes-la-Grande in Haute-Marne, called La Sapinière, which had been empty for years. All six children of Pastor Allégret had spent their vacations there during the twenties. The house contained odds and ends, haunting reminders of those long-ago vacations. I never knew Pastor Allégret; he died long before my time. I think I would have liked him; surely he would have been less discreet as far as I was concerned than the family on the Boulevard Saint-Germain. The house I knew was empty, but still one sensed that its previous master had been generous and kind. In any case, the entire village thought of him as the best of men. The "maquisards" of that time were Serge Reggiani, Janine Darcey, Allégret, and I. Serge had retained his Italian nationality and was thus classified as a deserter; Allégret was wanted by the STO; Janine was with Serge; and I was with Allégret. Later our maquis grew to nine people.

But it would take far too long to go into the details of this story (forgive me, Danièle, Daniel, Serge, Janine, Monsieur and Madame Reggiani; and forgive me, Reggiani dog). Daniel Gélin was wanted for STO service, and Danièle had newly acquired the name Delorme with

°Frances Tireurs Partisans, a Communist-organized branch of the Resistance.

forged papers. Her mother, imprisoned for many months at Compiègne, had been deported to the Ravensbrück camp; her father was in London. Danièle was little more than a kid. I was her senior in years. Even today I'm still the elder. She's no longer a child, but that gap will never be filled. Her knowledge and wisdom astonish me. And for thirty-three years our bond has remained unbroken.

We hadn't a sou among us. We ate a lot of greenery gone wild that continued to grow in what had once been the kitchen garden. The farmers of the region considered the friends of their pastor's son rather weird. Allégret, Gélin, and Serge would go out on their bikes to try and round up some food. They would do this by engaging in lengthy conversations with farmers who were mainly interested in finding out who the ladies were. They had never seen them before, and who was that gentleman with the Italian accent they had met at the tobacconist's? "So you're here on vacation, Monsieur Yves? ..." They sometimes brought back eggs, and once they came with enough flour so that Madame Reggiani could make an anti-Mussolini pasta.

We listened to the radio. We found an old atlas and we drew the outlines of the USSR over the map of Russia. We tried to figure out the reconquered towns whose names had changed. When it came to the western front, things were easier; we knew Saint-Lô and Caen and Évreux. We lived through the liberation of Paris by radio at Charmes-la-Grande. We laughed and cried and kissed each other and were furious to have missed it. We were overcome when we heard the bells of Notre Dame. We nearly had a minor tragedy because of the *Marseillaise* of Rouget de Lisle. The radio played it over and over; it was the day for it if ever there was one. But Serge couldn't stand the *Marseillaise*. When he was small, every time he had heard it it was sung by a gang of bastards who taunted him for being a "macaroni." But the rest of us had suddenly become true-blue French, and we liked our *Marseillaise* and we even liked to sing it, emphasizing the revolutionary meaning of the first verse. (As everyone is aware, nobody knows the second verse.) So that superb day ended with a tinge of bitterness. Bitterness caused also by the fact that although the great bells of Notre Dame had tolled, the chimes of the little church of Charmes-la-Grande announced the hours and half hours but remained resolutely silent as far as any patriotic announcement was concerned. The Germans were still there.

In order to follow the vagaries of the Second World War we needed not an atlas but a road map of the district. A battle was raging at Chaumont, a few kilometers away. We could hear the cannon. In the next village the Germans had improvised a little massacre before leaving. We were beginning to wonder whether we wouldn't have done better not to join this maquis. People were much better off in Paris. They had their Free French arm bands and the Paris police, who no longer frightened anybody (they had even been awarded a Legion of Honor).

One morning the boys went out in search of food and information. The girls were cleaning house. All of a sudden, shaking my dustcloth out a second-story window, I saw a strange-looking vehicle describing a sort of figure eight before it disappeared. Then I heard a low mechanical growl. The three of us ran down to the road, where we could hide behind the trees and observe. The strange vehicle was there. It was the first jeep I'd ever seen. But the growl came from a column of tanks. It was raining; it must have been about eleven in the morning. All the guys were sitting around eating the same thing, a kind of orange-colored pâté. They were handsome, tanned, not a bit Wagnerian. There were Gary Coopers, Paul Munis, Spencer Tracys, John Garfields, and Donald Ducks. They laughed a lot. Then, from among the peasants, they saw three androgynous creatures dressed like boys come forward, speaking English.

Serge had cut our hair very short. And in the attic of the old house we had found some American surplus from the First World War. We even had laced boots—we were far ahead of the fashion. We must have seemed like apparitions in the middle of the road in that tiny village. They behaved like my mother four years before, but this was an occasion for playing something by Hemingway. They said, "Who are you? Are you peasants or what?" We took four of them up to the house. We launched ourselves into what we thought was worldly small talk, waiting for the boys to come back so we could show off our trophies. They returned with their bikes stuffed into the back of a Dodge, also bringing back four soldiers they had met en route. We talked about all the things we had been denied for four years. Was Louis Armstrong still alive? Yes, but Carole Lombard was dead, and so was Gershwin. *Gone with the Wind* and *The Great Dictator*—were they good movies? So Clark Gable was a colonel! "What's that orange pâté you're eating?" "K rations. You want some?" Yes, we did. K rations were to play the same role as trinkets used to do in countries that had gold ore. With the difference that here they were exchanged against nothing—or exchanged in return for the admiration on the faces of the indigenous population at the sight of this ingenious waterproof, fireproof package about the size of a carton of cigarettes, which contained all that was necessary to nourish, please, comfort, refresh, and fortify. With the exception of the pack of five cigarettes and the little package of toilet paper, everything—pâté, cheese, powdered lemon juice, chocolate, hard candies, and chewing gum—had written on it the exact amount of vitamins and calories necessary for the sustenance of an American citizen. The makers of this pâté, cheese, fruit juice, hard candy, and chewing gum wanted their "boys" to realize how important they were to the war effort. Their names were emblazoned on the packages.

We were delighted to see once more the red, white, and green circle of the Lucky Strike package. We were enchanted by lemonade made without lemons and coffee made without a coffee grinder that nonetheless was real, not ersatz, coffee. Gary Cooper was a minister in civilian life; he noticed the lectern in the dining room immediately.

Donald Duck was a Communist and he believed naïvely that he would always be able to proclaim this fact. He had been to Moscow, and Allégret had too. Which year? No, he had gone later. Madame Reggiani mixed up her thank yous and *danke schöns* as she handed out glasses of champagne....

They camped near us for several days. As soon as they could, they came to the house, because we spoke English and because we were funny and because we knew their music and their culture. The day they left they gave us gifts. But their presents weren't all trinkets: They gave us a five-ton Citroën truck they had hauled all the way from Saint-Lô, but which they had decided they didn't like—they still preferred their Dodge. They gave us two BMW motorcycles they had pinched from the Germans but which no longer amused them. They left these things on our lawn, saying, "You're wonderful people," and they wrote down their names and addresses and invited us all to New York and Pittsburgh and Milwaukee. Then they left.

They left, and for a while the others came back: We were caught in the Arnhem pocket. The battle for Arnhem was in full swing. We were sandwiched between the Allied and German armies. We stuck the truck and the motorcycles in a barn. We would go off and contemplate them; we didn't touch them. And finally the others left for good. Then, for two or three days, we lived without friends and without enemies—except for one, a poor fifteen- or sixteen-year-old kid who hid in the woods. He got riddled with shot by a local commando; they had gotten together twenty or so guys to shoot him down and drag him into the town hall as a trophy. He died in his oversize uniform like a little dog.

Then the Americans came back. They were not the same but they were the same. This time it was the real thing. Charmes-la-Grande was liberated, and our spire pealed liberation. All the French flags that had been hastily folded up the week before now floated proudly from the windows of the small-game hunters. And then the mayor entered into our lives.

Gary Cooper, Donald Duck, and their friends, in leaving us their presents, had explained that the only thing they couldn't give us without incurring reprisals was gasoline. But gasoline was what we needed. We had decided to return to Paris in the truck. We had begun to make a van of it. When the new American contingent arrived, we attracted them to the house with cultural fireworks. We urged them to park their jeeps outside the kitchen door. We talked to them about Dos Passos and Mae West in the dining room. Then the boys would excuse themselves for a moment, and in a flaming hurry they would suck out a few drops of Texas gold with rubber tubes carefully prepared in advance. After filling a few empty wine bottles, they would rinse out their mouths and then come back and sit down quietly. After a few days of this game we still didn't have enough gas to make it to Paris, but we did have enough to start, or in any case to get the truck out of the barn.

Because they were gay and playful, the boys couldn't resist the temptation to go and race their motorcycles on the road a bit—they just wanted to see how they worked. They worked very well. They worked so well that the whole district knew about them, and the mayor came in his official capacity to reclaim our pretty toys, which he called "spoils of war," adding for good measure that one really shouldn't be a thief when one is the minister's son. He never was willing to believe our story of the presents. We often wondered what Haute Marnais provincial buttocks straddled our Teutonic motorcycles, and where our truck—that splendid product of the French proletarian assembly line that was once on its way to becoming the chariot of Thespis—was carrying its beets.

So, deprived of transportation, the maquis of La Sapinière decided to go home as best they could. The Reggianis went their way; Allégret, Danièle and Daniel, and I went ours. I was very pregnant with the little boy who was to die after nine days. I planted myself by the side of the road, sticking my stomach out as far as it went. When a gentleman stopped, I signaled to the others, who had retired to a respectful distance. The gentleman was a good sport. He laughed—and he took all four of us all the way to Paris.

So that was the end of that. It has taken a long time to tell it all, 1940–44. It seemed like twenty years.

That was the end of it for us. But it wasn't finished for those who were in the camps. And it wasn't finished for the soldiers. And it was just beginning for the collaborators. And it had been finished a long time for those who had died.

One summery winter day in California in 1959, Montand suddenly said, "You know, really, we're survivors." We were at the table. The waiter had just put down water glasses filled with ice. The tinkle of ice is a background noise to all American meals, and especially in Beverly Hills, where there are no city sounds. All you hear is a rustling. Someone had been talking about Simon Biouvouare *Mandareens*; it would make a fine film, especially that American love story.... As for the rest, all those French occupation stories are so complicated.... We tried to explain politely that Simone de Beauvoir's *Les Mandarins* was set after the occupation. Were we sure? Yes, we were quite sure. On that side of the world one could confuse wartime with the time that followed. For them, "Hey, hi, hey, ho," the German marching chant, was something they had seen in a war film; it would never be an army marching down the Champs Élysées. But the rest of us—from Brest to the suburbs of Leningrad—we were all escapees from a common disaster. When Montand said, "We're survivors," he didn't mean just the two of us. The English are survivors of German bombing raids, but they never heard that Teutonic "Hey, hi, hey, ho" stomping down the Strand. And the Americans, leaving aside the

Indians and the blacks, are neither escapees nor survivors. That's their good fortune.

As soon as we returned from our private maquis we met real maquisards. Colonel Claude Jaeger commissioned from the ex-"insubordinate" Yves Allégret a documentary about the liberation of Le Mans by the FTP. France was not yet entirely liberated; there were pockets of Germans left all along the Atlantic, and Tillon's FTP force did not consider itself demobilized. They still had their arms—the few arms that had been parachuted to them. It is not for me, since I'm not a Communist, to tell the story, which is in reality history, of the notorious fact that toward the end of the war the Communist maquis no longer got the goods they'd been promised. The arms they expected were parachuted far from the planned zones. About four years ago, in front of our log fire, André Dewavrin, known during the war as Colonel Passy, and Jorge Semprun, ex-FTP, courteously went through that old sore again. The conversation lasted for three hours and began with Semprun's sentence: "Well, Colonel, we're still waiting for those Sten guns...." The rest of us—Florence and Jean-Pierre Melville, Chris Marker, Madame Dewavrin, Colette Semprun, Montand, and I—just listened, open-mouthed.

But let me return to Le Mans. The FTP took us everywhere: to farmers who had hidden them deep in the woods, where one could still see fresh traces of their campsites, to dropping zones they had often staked out for nothing. They talked endlessly, and it was fascinating. There was one man who never said anything, and he always looked sad. The others were very kind to him, but they never let him get a step away. Finally, I asked them who he was. "He's one of us, but he was captured and he talked under torture. He managed to send us a message that he had talked. As we're afraid somebody might try to shoot him, we cart him around with us all the time." The documentary I mentioned earlier, for which I was the script girl—the entire crew was five people—was never finished. Allégret caught diphtheria, which is quite remarkable when one is forty years old. We went back to Paris, where I had my baby and lost him due to monstrous negligence in a clinic that cost the earth (the cost of living has gone up since then).

Allégret and I had always lived in hotels or in little furnished apartments. The last of them, the one we had left to go to La Sapinière, was at 7 Rue du Dragon. The rent was almost nothing, but there was a good reason for that. It was the "letter box"—a standard safety precaution—for one of the biggest Resistance networks. The Gestapo came twice to search. They found us, but we were not what they were looking for. The new tenants provided a safe cover for the letter box, but they weren't in on the secret. Jacques Sigurd told us all about it after the Liberation. He was part of the network, and at one point he had tried to dissuade us from living at 7 Rue du Dragon, but as he'd refused to explain anything, we'd sent him off with a flea in his ear. When I think that it was in this trap that we'd cheerfully put up a camp bed for Claude Jaeger, who wasn't allowed to sleep in the same place two nights running. . . .

After the Liberation we went on living in cheap rented flats. We lived up and down the Rue Vaneau: 54, 52, and finally a little apartment in 56. That was the first place that was really our own, with chairs that belonged to us.

As for my professional life, it was at about this time that I played my last small part. It was a film called *Le Couple Idéal*, directed by Rouleau. I played an idiot housemaid who got sent out to see whether the obelisk in the Place de la Concorde had been removed. In the summer of 1945 I finally got my first interesting part, short but prominent, in a film of Allégret's called *Les Démons de l'Aube*. While making *Les Démons de l'Aube* I also made Catherine. The film opened a week before her birth. Then came my "milky" tests for *Macadam*. That did it; I was off and running. Things picked up: It didn't occur to me then that one could make a film without a firm contract for the next one. In *Macadam* I learned a great deal from Jacques Feyder, Françoise Rosay, and Paul Meurisse. I made

Fantômas, in which Marcel Herrand was my father. I went to London to make *Against the Wind*, which didn't bowl over either the English or the French, but which gave me my first contact with the English film world, where I was to have my greatest opportunity in 1958.

My English was good enough for the film. However, it occurs to me now that I've entirely forgotten to tell you about my summer in Sussex—it must have been in 1937. I went to stay with a gentleman-farmer type of family. They were charming people, but not entirely honest. I was the classic paying guest. In three months I was supposed to gain complete mastery of the language of Shakespeare, as we jokingly say in French, though what in fact we mean is to get to grips with the finer complexities of everyday spoken English—not Elizabethan. (Regarding the great bard himself, Will Shakespeare, we'll get to that little item in due course!) At the end of a week I was doing quite well. My "opposite number" was named Audrey; we were both exactly the same age. However, she behaved as if she were eight years old and spoke only to her pony, Pixie. Her parents were great chatterboxes, which made me talkative too. Then another young French girl turned up, whose parents had worked their fingers to the bone to send her over to learn English. I had a week's head start. Whenever she wanted to say something, she would ask me not only to say it for her but to translate the reply as well. She returned to France no better off linguistically; I went back doubly bilingual. Then Audrey came to the Avenue du Roule to learn French. At the end of a week she couldn't bear the separation from Pixie. As she wept in English, I consoled her in English. She, too, left exactly as she'd arrived, and that is how, ten years later, I was hired to act in English in an English film. In any case, I was busy unlearning the teachings of Solange Sicard. I suddenly realized that in order to be understood you had to emphasize the verbs. "I hate you" has to be spoken "I *hate* you," unless it's more important that it's *you* that I hate rather than another, in which case it is "I hate *you*." Unless, of course, it's of prime

97

importance that *I* hate you, really me. All this may seem murky, but any French actor who has been in an Anglo-American film and has been coached will understand me. English is an economical language; the tonic accent expresses the thought or feeling.

While I was cultivating my tonic accent at the Ealing studios, Allégret and Jacques Sigurd were preparing a splendid present for me. *Dédée d'Anvers* was very important for me. While making it, I never realized that I was being given a cream puff. Nor did I have any sense of the great publicity it could cause, since that kind of thing wasn't practiced then. Today, any unknown girl given a film that important, which meets with such critical and commercial acclaim, would be on the cover of every magazine. (Which would probably be dangerous for her.)

Sacha Gordine produced *Dédée d'Anvers*. He was always looking for four and a half francs in order to make five. But he loved the cinema. He wanted to make a film with me because I was a potential box-office attraction due to my success in *Macadam*. I acted in *Macadam* because the role of the whore was up for grabs; if there had been a laboratory assistant or a nun, I would have tried to hook the laboratory assistant or the nun. As it happened, I was good as the whore. Not as good as I thought I was: I saw it again recently, and let me tell you, what I did there was not extraordinary. But I was a new face, and that's always interesting.

Sacha Gordine had an instinct for commercial success. He offered me this part in a good old melodrama. Allégret and Sigurd got to work and they wrote a very good script with super parts for Bernard Blier, Dalio, Marcel Pagliero, and Marken, and a corker for me. We all laughed a lot. The film was enormously successful, which allowed Sigurd and Allégret to make a film with Gérard Philipe, *Une Si Jolie Petite Plage*, a project they had cherished for a long time, which didn't make a penny and is a little masterpiece. From then on I didn't stop working.

Becoming the star of a successful film didn't change the way I considered my job. What changed was that I could have said to myself: "Well, that's it. I've made it." But there's an odd quirk inside that didn't change with "success"—and it still hasn't. I think: It worked this time. I put it over on them. I made them believe I could do it. But one of these days they're going to discover the fakery. They're going to find out I'm only an amateur.... Still, today, when I begin a film in a part that has been offered to me and some of the fee has been paid upon signing the contract, I give you my word of honor that on the first day, during the first minutes when I become the character and she takes on my voice and face and walks with my feet, I think: Maybe what I'm doing isn't at all what they expected.... And I feel like saying, "If this isn't it, we'll stop. I'll give you your money back." This is what happens in my mind on the first day of every film. Now it's almost a routine; I know I'll have to go through that each time, and perhaps more and more. It's almost moral fraud to pretend you can play this or that part because of all the ones you have already played, when each time it's a different thing.

In any case, what the success of *Dédée d'Anvers* brought me was an understanding that I was in the process of being catalogued as a whore, and that from then on I'd have two, three, four years of them. What I didn't realize— I didn't even suspect it—was that if people had liked Dédée so much, it was because of the misfortunes of the poor girl, so kind and generous, who was basically a victim of society. If I had understood this, I would have spent my time playing sympathetic characters—and would have deprived myself of great pleasure. I understood all this so little that I naïvely took on Dora in *Manèges*—that monster, that bitch, that liar, that real whore without a sidewalk and without a pimp—written by Sigurd and Allégret. The audience didn't really like this very fine film; it upset them. And they detested me. I don't mean the critics; I mean the people in the street. Once more there were Blier, Marken, Villard, horses, and I. We laughed a lot while the film was being made. But we had come a long way since the Mathurins; the director couldn't fire us.

Before *Manèges*, I made a film directed by Maurice

Tourneur called *L'Impasse des Deux Anges*, with Paul Meurisse, in which Danièle Delorme played her first small part and Marcel Herrand was my rich lover. I went to Zurich to participate in a Swiss-American thing called *Four Days Leave*, which American insomniacs can still sometimes see on the late late show. Alex, supreme hairdresser of the stars, star himself, who had once been kind enough to do my hair during the terrible silhouette time and who naturally became my personal hairdresser (and remains my pal), was in on the Zurich deal. That was in 1949. We scoured the chocolate shops and the watch shops, and the clothing stores for raincoats and children's coats—he had two and I had Catherine and Gilles. It's odd; I'd almost forgotten that in 1949 we were still amazed by the sight of oranges and clothes to be had without coupons.

Gilles was Allégret's son. He began staying with us in the Rue Vaneau in 1946. When his little sister was born he was eleven. For me, he formed a link with my little brothers (I don't often mention the third brother; he died when he was twenty)—my little brothers, those pseudo Protestants who had been taught Latin by the principal of the Catholic school in Valréas thanks to the efforts of my mother when she was a pseudo linen lady at the hospital. (When I say pseudo linen lady, I don't mean that she did her job badly; I just mean that she played at being the linen lady while nourishing her intellectual life with books.) While they were still in Valréas I went to see them once. It was when I was making *Les Visiteurs*. I slept in a huge whitewashed room, where all three of them lived. It was a little like being back in the Avenue du Roule, but there was sun and there were no Germans—at least not yet. I had the feeling that they were as sheltered there as they could be. But it wasn't very gay. I sent money whenever I could. Thanks to *Les Visiteurs* I sent a lot. I remember that the mother superior, learning that I was there, asked to see me. She had heard that the daughter of the temporary linen lady was an "artist." Yes, I was making a film in Nice. I had come up between takes. Since she had never set foot in a movie house, she thought I was a star, and she wondered what the mother and brothers of a star were doing in her establishment. Then my mother and my little brothers came back to Paris. The boys made up their missing schoolwork with lightning speed. Once they were reprimanded for hiding the photograph of an actress who had played the whore in *Macadam* in their desks. I didn't search my mother's luggage when she came back, but I'm sure that the little elephant with the revolver hidden in it was still there.

In 1945, after five years' absence, my father reappeared. He was in uniform. His paths had taken him from London to Accra, from Accra to New York, and from New York back to London. He found his pretty child pregnant thanks to the labors of a director who had never directed anything and, just to round everything off, was the younger brother of a Colonel Allégret who was my father's direct superior in the chain of command that led to General de Gaulle. Decidedly, I was accumulating my gaffes as far as the Allégret family was concerned. His pretty child, who had been a virgin schoolgirl when he had last seen her, was now an actress without a contract, a future unwed mother, and to top it off, she demanded that he file a deposition in behalf of Luchaire—the same Luchaire, you must remember, who had provided his family with a livelihood for a little while. I've always thought that Claude Blanchard, when he went back to London in 1941, never thought it necessary to explain to my father where he had met me. My father returned to New York, where he trained most of the United Nations simultaneous interpreters. Then he went to Strasbourg, where he did the same for the Council of Europe. He is eminently respected and liked by all who have worked with him. We really missed each other, he and I. Of course, he had the joy of sharing my "triumphs," like my Oscar, but we never shared the bad times.

Chapter 5

I met Yves Montand on the nineteenth of August, 1949, in Saint-Paul-de-Vence at the Colombe d'Or, at about eight-thirty in the evening. It was his evening off during a summer tour. He was with his pianist, Bob Castella, who is still his pianist, and with his guitarist, Henri Crolla, who is no longer his guitarist. Since autumn 1960 he no longer plays the guitar for anyone. He is the only dead person I know who can make people laugh till they cry from wherever he is today, and his friends gather to remember him in tears.

Allégret and I loved the music hall. We had gone to Montand's concerts since he began giving them. But when we went backstage it was to see Crolla, because we were proud of our pal from the Café Flore, whom we had known when he was busking for his daily bread. We didn't dare approach Montand; his dressing room was always bursting at the seams.

By now things were going very well for me. After *Dédée d'Anvers* there were movie-contract propositions for both Allégret and me. We had just finished making

Manèges, and a trip to Hollywood was in the cards for autumn. I had signed a four-year contract with Howard Hughes for one film a year agreeable to us both. At the moment I was on vacation with the children—with Catherine, who was then three, and Gilles, who was fourteen.

Montand, at the time, went to the movies constantly. He had seen everything. Everything except my films. The first film of mine he saw was *Manèges*, and by that time we had been living together for three months. He has always maintained that if he had seen it before he met me, he wouldn't have fallen in love with that bitch.... Oh, the dangers of being identified with one's characters! I'll come back to that subject.

But to return to the meeting in Saint-Paul; Montand came to dinner. And the next day he came to lunch, and in the evening I went down to Nice to hear him sing. And then he came back up to Saint-Paul, and I went down to Cannes to hear him sing. Finally he left with Crolla and Castella to sing somewhere else ... and it was dreadful. That's the way it was. I'm not going to treat you to *True Confessions*. In those four days we had been struck by lightning, and something indiscreet and irreversible had happened.

I say "indiscreet" because this affair was so obvious to its witnesses. The Préverts were there, all the Préverts, the Pigauds were there, the whole family Roux was there, and Gilles was there, and all of them were fond of Allégret, and of Montand, and of me. They were all witnesses, but I didn't want to make them accomplices. So when Allégret came down, I went to wait for him by the side of the road. I didn't want him coming into the bar of La Colombe to be greeted by: "Well, Monsieur Allégret, how was your trip to Paris? The weather's been fine here ..." and so on. I was the first to tell him that something had happened.

I didn't know that it was going to last twenty-eight years, but I knew that something irreversible had happened. At least for me. And I had no intention of playing a scene from a drawing-room comedy. Feydeau is a really terrific playwright: All those pompous imbeciles, those people full of ambition but without talent, those heartless bourgeois idiots—they surely deserve the howls of laughter they inspire in an audience which generally hasn't a clue that it's watching itself live. (So many of the French love the stories they call "ass stories," and they're the same people who tell "pansy stories," accompanied by obscene laughter.) But Saint-Paul wasn't the holy land of broad comedy and no one laughed. I still hadn't realized that we were going to cry as much as we did, but the main thing is that no one laughed.

The person who did the crying was mostly me. Nothing in the world is sadder than to cause hurt to someone for whom one wants only good, and to be incapable of doing the only thing that would fix everything, which is to stop loving the other. It becomes ridiculous to try to hold on to reason. It becomes terrifying to think about that other, who isn't there, who has perhaps forgotten about it all. It is miraculous to get a telephone call from the other end of France. It's killing to walk around pretending that everything's fine and to feel awful all the time. In short, it was as it is for anyone, anyplace in the world, when something like this happens.

I didn't leave Allégret right away. For a few weeks we really tried, all three of us, to heal the wound. It didn't work at all. The summer had ended; we were all back in Paris. In a sophisticated novel, our situation might very well have prompted a chapter entitled "The Idyll on the Ramparts." It was far from being idyllic. It was quite simply passion, with all that goes with it.

I do not know to what extent one is free to choose the things that happen to one. If I had met Montand in a foreign town, far from everyone I knew, or anyone who knew Montand or Allégret, there wouldn't have been witnesses; we wouldn't have lived our story under many eyes, which magnified everything. I think that love stories are like those other commitments in life that one takes on, which are also in the end love stories. Montand gave me an ultimatum. He explained to me that he had had enough of those ladies who filled his afternoons; I'd better pack my bags and come live with him or else there wasn't any point in even telephoning.

He had no wife, but he was married to the music hall and had the kind of attachments I've just mentioned. When he was very young he had had a big affair with Piaf. At twenty-three he was wounded to the quick when Edith no longer wanted him. The day she no longer wanted him was the day he became her professional equal. In the beginning he had been someone to teach. She didn't teach him everything he knew, because there are things no one can teach anyone. One has them or one doesn't. But as soon as he started flying with his own wings, and choosing his own songs, or refusing those she wanted him to sing, Edith left him. As he loved her, and loved to laugh with her—something that came easily and often with Edith—he had been very unhappy for a long time. But that was in the past. He was absolutely free when this affair burst upon him. A passion is a very preoccupying thing. And if you sing a bunch of songs every night, you'd do well to be occupied with that and nothing else. It's very disturbing for your work, passion is.

So I packed up my goods and chattels. They didn't amount to much. I hurt Allégret a great deal, and Gilles. I hurt Catherine less, because she was still very small and she was used to my absences. I upset the habits of my friends. When you change your life, you change the lives of your friends. I was judged, condemned by some and encouraged by others, who didn't share my abiding tenderness for Allégret. It is difficult and cruel, and once again, indiscreet, to "make a new life," as they say. It's all watered by hot tears. The new love has to be very strong to take off in that curious two-seater plane called a new couple. But we did it; against all odds we flew. . . .

These days, when Jean-Christophe Averty, the TV director, comes to the house to see Montand, he still sometimes turns to me and says, "That's a song he sang at the time you were a groupie." Groupies are girls who follow singers and musicians. They are generally young and pretty and without definable occupations; above all, they are perfectly interchangeable. When I became Montand's groupie, he was singing in a nightclub called Baccara which has long since vanished and which was the last nightclub he ever sang in. It was there that I learned about the strong complicity between waiters and performers in a cabaret. There are clients and there are the others. I was one of the others. Montand changed for the show in a kind of glorified plywood closet in the basement kitchen area. The cabaret stage manager had pasted a silver star on the door and tacked up a few bits of material inside. That was the dressing room. That was where Montand warmed up his voice, Crolla warmed up his fingers on the guitar—there where the waiters bellowed out their orders and the chefs screamed at each other. Since I wanted to hear him sing and I couldn't decently park myself at a table every night, I had an arrangement with the barman. I'd hang around in the dressing room underground until Montand was about to begin, and then a waiter would fetch me. In the dark I would slip behind the bar, and there, standing beside the barman, I played groupie. During the applause we would quietly compare "them" with "those" that had been there last night. When they didn't react and call for more songs, they had invariably not called for another round of drinks, either.

After the show we would take Crolla back to his own groupie. She was "Crollette"—really Colette. They had been living at the City Hotel on the Place Dauphine since they were married. (It was near here that one evening during the war, leaning on the parapet of the Quai des Grands-Augustins between Blin and Loris, I had declared pompously, "One day I'm going to live in one of those houses." I'd pointed at the buildings along the Quai des Orfèvres—there are sixteen of them, I think.) After we had dropped off Crolla we would walk around the Île de la Cité and then cross the Seine and go back to Neuilly. Back to the chic part of Neuilly, not the Neuilly of my Sabot Bleu. Still, there was the same trip up the Avenue de Neuilly, the marketplace, and the red traffic light at the Rue d'Orléans, where the Avenue du Roule and my schoolgirl memories begin. It also brought back our expulsion from our apartment and the filming of *Manèges*. ... It was not a good itinerary for a pair of new lovers.

In our elegant little furnished apartment there was a person who ruled and terrified me. I've forgotten her name. She dusted the white piano, cooked a bit, and answered the telephone a lot, announcing to Montand in a stage whisper in front of me, "It's Mademoiselle Ghislaine." Or, "What should I tell Mademoiselle Chantal?" She came to work wearing a hat that she liked to point out was a present from Madame Thing. . . . "Monsieur remembers?" Had I been one of the passing ladies we might perhaps have become very chummy, but living there, I was in the way. In brief: If one is beginning something, one really should start from scratch. And Montand thought so too. So one fine day, a very fine day, a guy came by who, when we asked him the question we were asking everybody at that time—Do you know of an available apartment?—answered, "No, but I know of a shop." Very funny! Where was the shop? Quai des Orfèvres. An hour later, the deed was done. It was a bookshop beside the Restaurant Paul; the bookseller was a friend from the Lycée Pasteur whom I hadn't seen for ten years. There was a kind of mezzanine that was joined to the shop by a narrow staircase. At the back of the shop there was a door that was no longer in use. Behind that, there were two small rooms looking out on the Place Dauphine, in which a rare-book dealer carried out his business. We strolled around the outside and then we offered him a sum for his rooms. He accepted. He made us no present, but we didn't expect him to. His name was Berggruen. He has since become a very well known art dealer. And that was how we found the apartment we called the "caravan," in which we still live today. That was really where it all began. The apartment had everything going for it: We were on both the Quai des Anciens-Orfèvres and the Place Dauphine. It seemed to us right, normal, and ethical.

I went to get Catherine. At that point I stopped being the lady of whom the concierge said, as I passed her lodge, "Well, well, there goes the lady from the second floor who ran away. She's come to see her little girl. . . ." My little girl grew up in that "caravan." She played on the staircase of the Palais de Justice with a gang of other kids—whose specialty was ringing doorbells and scampering away—and slept in a folding bed on the Place Dauphine side. It was exactly as written about in those ladies' magazines when they describe how to economize on space when there isn't much of it. She did her first homework to the sound of Crolla's guitar and Bob's piano and Soudieu's bass; to the drums of Paraboschi and the voice of Montand. She never lived in one of those big apartments with dark corridors, at the end of which, in a nursery, children wait for someone to come and say good night to them. She was lucky to be a girl, or rather I was lucky that I hadn't had a boy. She was four, Montand was twenty-nine; it was inevitable . . . they fell in love. So the "caravan" now contained two groupies.

The little groupie went to school. And I went to the studios less often. I was no longer one of those actresses who couldn't stand the idea of not having signed a contract for another film while still working on the current picture. People said that I was "sacrificing my career." I was sacrificing nothing. I was simply clever enough not to sacrifice my life; and I was clever enough not to say no to good films when they were offered to me. So much for the story of my sacrifice. . . .

I was discovering a whole new world: the music hall. Let them make their *Four Days Leave*, in Zurich and on the banks of the Nile. I was enjoying listening to the new songs people came to offer Montand, and enjoying being initiated into the mysteries and difficulties of this craft about which I knew nothing. Ages before, I had learned to read a script. Now I was learning how to read a song, that little script of some three verses. I learned that a good song should be "round." I learned that the "running order" of songs in a performance and even more so in a recital is as important as the editing of a film. Since my first successes I had always lived among people of my profession, with whom I discussed things on an equal footing. All of a sudden I was living with someone who knew something I didn't know, something I would never know how to do. I was curious, impressed, and, yes, intimidated.

When Montand sings, he arrives at the theater very early. If the curtain goes up at nine, he gets there at seven. But already at six, wherever he may be, he isn't where he is. He's somewhere else, and already he's alone. At first that was quite hard to understand. It was as though he had suddenly left me. He was there, but he had left me. It took a little while before I realized that from six o'clock on, I wasn't supposed to talk. I was supposed to be available, invisible, and especially I wasn't supposed to be elsewhere.

We would arrive at the empty theater. The cleaning women who were dusting would be loudly discussing their private lives, one shouting down from the dress circle, the other in the orchestra stalls. The dressing rooms were in the concrete basement. There was the noise of trickling toilets. That was the only sound in the place. I'm in the process of telling you about the old Théâtre de l'Étoile, where there is now a garage, and in whose corridors I spent more hours than a lot of the people who have sung, danced, or flown on the trapeze there in the course of the years. Because each time Montand was signed up at the Étoile he stayed for six months.

You enter the dressing room. There's the mail. Letters from composers; and many, many letters from women, who never seemed to suspect that the man who at six o'clock left the woman whom at the moment he loves the most in the world couldn't care less what his voice has produced in what these ladies call their hearts. I read all those letters. With a funny mixture of pride and jealousy.

Some of them were very beautiful, as if by a kind of Madame Bovary, pouring out literature. Some were crude, with crude photographs attached. When they talked about his songs, they interested him. The photographs too, sometimes.

Little by little, the corridors would come to life. The musicians would arrive, one after another, knock on our door, come in and crack jokes. They were like the picadors visiting the torero before the beginning of the bullfight. There would be no kill, but there was always the risk of that little death implicit in a bad performance. When the torero began to put on his "suit of lights"—in reality a dark-brown shirt and matching trousers—the groupie-aficionada would feel so out of place, so useless, that even though the picadors and the torero were very fond of her, she would go out and take a turn around the corridors. That's what I meant by "intimidated." It's still true today. When Montand dons his brown stage clothes, he is a solitary man. Although both of us have become what all those years together have made us, it changes nothing at that moment. He's going up on that stage, all alone. It's no accident that Chris Marker called the film he made about Montand *La Solitude du Chanteur de Fond*.

I once had an extraordinary conversation with Jacques Brel. Radio Luxembourg offered him one entire day on the air; he could shape his program any way he wanted. So he went out and taped interviews with a whole lot of people, including me. I understood right away that he had chosen me because I was Montand's wife rather than for what I am myself. He asked me all sorts of questions on lots of different subjects, and then at the end I asked him one question. I asked him: "In your opinion, what should the wife of a man who sings in a music hall be like?" He replied, "There isn't any; she doesn't exist." "Let us say that in an ideal society there is one; what should she be like?" He said something like this: "She should be there before he goes onstage, but she shouldn't be visible; she should be in the audience during the performance; and she should be there at the end, but she should disappear the moment people start arriving in the dressing room; she should go home very fast and prepare dinner and be on the threshold when her guy arrives, saying, 'Bravo, bravo! You were even better than you were yesterday....'" He was right: That woman doesn't exist. And I haven't been that woman. But I have been some facets of that woman. For instance, I didn't go home to cook a meal.... But it was an enriching experience for me to be amazed and intimidated. Anguished for the other, proud of the other. I *chose* to be a groupie; I was not recruited. I had a profession that I chose not to exercise. That's passionate, fascinating, and funny.

We laughed a lot backstage at the Théâtre de l'Étoile once the corrida was over. Montand ditched me at six in the evening, but at eleven-fifteen he would come back to me. He came back to me during the applause: he would thank them courteously, while they screamed, "Another, another!" The curtain would come down, and go up again—and during the brief moment while it was down it was me he would look at, and it was to me he smiled. They would scream, "Another!" for a long time, and then the lights would go on in the theater and there would be a long sighing "Oooh." We would go down to the dressing room and then there would be another bizarre little moment during which I sensed that I would do better to speak only if I was spoken to, and then the relaxation would set in and the fun would start. It would take another hundred pages for me to tell you what the after-the-show atmosphere was like at the Théâtre de l'Étoile. Montand's dressing room would resemble the famous ship's cabin of the Marx Brothers film, because soon everyone seemed to know that our friends who were acting elsewhere would hurry to remove their makeup in order to arrive in time to catch up with yesterday's gag. If you don't believe me, ask José Artur, François Périer, Bernard Blier, Roger Pigaud, Serge Reggiani, and Jacques and Pierre Prévert, among others, who are reliable people and worthy of belief.

111

It didn't frustrate me not to act. I have never been frustrated by not acting during the times I wasn't acting. But on the other hand, when I do act, nothing else interests me. Which means in essence that if I had acted all the time, I would never have been interested in anything or anybody else. There have been times when I have tried to work against this truth, which I did not yet possess. I acted for a few days in Ophuls's *La Ronde*, in the sketch with Reggiani and in the one with Gérard Philipe, where he was so extraordinary, and for which many of the critics insulted him. I acted, but I was clock-watching. I also made *Le Traqué*, a thriller directed by Frank Tuttle. These pictures were made during the Baccara period, and I went to bed at three in the morning and got up at seven; I yawned all day and waited for Montand to fetch me at the studio, knowing he wasn't a bit pleased with his new role as "lover of the actress." I also made something called *Ombres et Lumières*, in which I played a mad pianist who fell a victim to a traumatic shock during a Tchaikovsky concerto—the Russians loved it. In any case, it was the only film of mine they had seen when we went there in 1956. Actually, it was when I *did* make a film that I was frustrated. My heart wasn't in it. My mind was elsewhere.

I was supposed to have gone to America in 1949, on a four-year contract I've already mentioned. After the Liberation the Americans sent talent scouts to Europe, whose mission it was to ship home anyone they thought capable of freshening up the American film world. Each of the big companies had its scout. Their proposition was standard: "A seven-year exclusive contract." In 1948 Montand had signed a contract with Warner Brothers, but later, when he had it carefully translated and reread it, he realized too late that he had just allowed himself to be tied hand and foot for seven long years, during which time he would be a salaried employee forced to do whatever they decided for him, or possibly even worse, to do nothing at all. He broke his contract, Warner sued him, and the whole thing created quite a stir in Paris. Montand sent one telegram to Warner Brothers that became notorious because it cost 30,000 old francs, it was so explicit on all points. For a lot of quite phony reasons, the Montand-Warner episode took on a political and chauvinistic character that was pounced on and exploited. "Montand says no to the Americans and refuses their dollars" was the tone in some of the newspapers. The real reasons were of an artistic nature, for though the cold war had already begun, it had not yet been officially declared. He didn't say no to either the Americans or their dollars; he'd merely told Jack Warner to get stuffed, just as he once had to the owner of the ABC Music Hall in Paris, who'd refused to have the piano tuned.

I, too, had been talent-scouted. *Dédée* had been very good box office in New York, but I had systematically refused to tie myself up for seven years with either Paramount or Metro-Goldwyn-Mayer or, if I remember rightly, with Fox. It wasn't that I was more intelligent than Montand was, but I spoke and read English, and perhaps had better counsel. However, a very big agent called Charlie Feldman was more stubborn that the rest, and one day he came up with what I thought was a reasonable proposition, and I accepted it. In effect it was prodigious. It offered a nonexclusive contract for four films, to be agreed upon by myself and Howard Hughes, and completed within four years. I didn't know much about Howard Hughes. I knew he made airplanes and I knew that he had made films in which actresses had had very good parts. But I never went to Hollywood in the autumn of 1949. Without Montand, I wouldn't have gone as far as from the Porte de Vincennes to the Porte d'Asnières. So America—you can imagine! I offered excuses and promised that I would come later. Mr. Hughes was very patient; he would wait for me. In fact, he had to wait for a very long time. In 1950 Montand and I both signed the Stockholm peace petition. After that, America was for us definitely *out*.

Chapter 6

THE Stockholm petition was a pacifist text issued by the international peace movement to ban nuclear weapons. There were Communists in the peace movement. There were also a great number of non-Communists. There were ministers and priests, upper-class and working-class people, and intellectuals. It was massive refusal of the atomic bomb. When people refused to sign it, the usual question asked was: "So you're *for* the atomic bomb?" They never said yes; they always said they were apolitical. . . . They were lying; because it was taking a political stand simply to avoid getting in wrong with the Americans, who at the time were the only ones to have the bomb and to have used it. It would have been hard to say, "Oh, yes, I like it very much," after you had seen photographs of Hiroshima. So you see, it was difficult not to sign. . . .

The *Figaro* did some research on the people who had signed the Stockholm petition. Some extraordinary answers were provided by those interviewed. The late lamented Maurice Chevalier said something like this: "I never read it; I didn't mean to do it. If I'd read it I wouldn't have signed it." Fernandel said he had signed it "to please the chief cameraman." François Périer came up with the best, the most intelligent and most dignified answer: "You tell me that this text was composed by Communists. That's something I never thought about. I read it and it seemed to me both intelligent and interesting. I am a Christian and I would have preferred that it came from the Vatican. Unfortunately, it was not the Vatican that asked me to sign."

The *Figaro* did not interview us. Neither Montand nor I was a member of the Communist party, though we were in agreement with the majority of its opinions. A great many people believed we were card-carrying Communists. But it was a time when sending a denial to a newspaper that "claimed" you were a Communist—the quotes are intentional—gave the impression of denying an accusation. We didn't think it was wrong to be a Communist. The Communists I had met during the war, when I didn't always know at the time that they were Communists, were people I respected enormously. In 1950, while America waged war in Korea, we were pursuing ours in Vietnam— that is, Indochina. At that time the Communist sailor Henri Martin was in prison in Melun for having refused to point his ship's cannons in a direction he had not foreseen when he had volunteered for service in 1944. That direction was not Japan. The militant Communist Raymonde Dien—she was then nineteen years old—had lain across the railroad tracks in the Saint-Nazaire station to prevent an arms convoy from making its delivery.

At that time it was the Communists, the CGT,° and the UNEF† students who were being blackjacked in the Latin Quarter demonstrations. Old phrases like "insubordinate," "mercenaries," "colonial empire," "villainous laws," "the bread of the workingman," and "Moscow's gold" were

°Confédération Générale du Travail, a trade union.
†Union Nationale des Étudiants de France.

back in fashion, depending upon which newspaper one read. The future promised to be of heroic proportions— and I had just discovered the *plight* of the workingman.

Beginning with my time at the Flore, I had been living in a left milieu and feeling very much at home there, but I had never had any contact with what is called the working class. I really knew it only through what I had read and what people had told me. I was absolutely typical of what is called a "left intellectual," with all that includes of the ridiculous, but also of the generous. Oddly enough, my first meeting with Montand was also my first incursion into the workingman's world, the proletariat, if not the subproletariat. Montand comes from the Florentine countryside, and his childhood was spent among the lumpen proletarians of southern France. He was only two when his antifascist father emigrated. The Livis arrived in France speaking not a word of French, and they settled in La Cabucelle, a suburb of Marseilles that makes Aubervilliers—not the healthiest or most attractive of Parisian suburbs—seem like Neuilly-sur-Seine!

If Reggiani was called a "macaroni" in Paris, Montand was a "babi" in Cabucelle. He was just learning French; at the same time he was picking up a smattering of Armenian, Arabic, Greek, and Spanish from his playmates, whose fathers and mothers were the workmates of his parents. The work they did was the kind that is offered to unskilled foreign laborers. The work was next door to where they lived. The sirens of the gas factory, the gut factory, and the docks were the chronometers of the whole district. When Montand took me there, it was the first time in my life that I sat down at a table among people who all had worked in factories for the major part of their lives. When his friends in the area learned that he was there with his "fiancée," they all came to see. Once the usual comments on the hardships imposed by success and on life in Paris, where the sun never shines, were over . . . it was about their work that they talked. And their work was what Montand no longer did, and what logically he would still have been doing, along with them, if by some bizarre turn of nature (which still remains a mystery to me) he had not understood all by himself, and very early in life, that Fred Astaire was a darn sight more sensational than one realized, that Trenet was poetry, and that there was a poet named Prévert. Whereas I, with my papa who whistled Siegfried's motif and my grandfather with his sunset paintings, with my serious reading and Neuilly and the Café Flore—even though setting out for work on location at the crack of dawn, as it were, briefly misled us actors into identifying ourselves with the working classes, because we'd be passing the entrance to the Renault automobile factory as the workers were herded behind the gates—I began to see things in a different light.

The scene took place when we started living together. The first thing Montand wanted to do was to show me to his family. The fact of being naturalized doesn't make any difference: When one loves a woman one shows her to one's mother and father and friends. That's the way things are still done in Tuscany and in Florence. In other places too.

We realized when we signed the Stockholm petition that this would prevent us from going to the United States. At that time the cold war had just been officially declared. A little while before that, Feldman had sent his colleague Minna Wallis, one of the Hollywood pioneers, who'd been a secretary at the studios when they were little more than glass houses. She fought every foot of the way to try and take me back to America with her. We were on vacation at Saint-Paul, Montand and I, and she saw how we lived together, but as a good talent scout she argued with us for a couple of days, and then she surrendered. She kissed us both. Then she took a day off, during which she explained to us that we were quite right not to allow ourselves to be separated even for a day. She had seen "love stories" like ours by the score which had died because of Hollywood. They would be furious with her when she went back, but it was worth it, we were "wonderful people." Then she left.

After we signed the Stockholm petition, I often thought that she would have been in a far greater mess if she had managed to take me back with her....

I have said that we were not Communists but that we agreed with them on most things. Now I'll tell you why we aren't Communists; or more exactly, why we never joined the party when everyone thought we were already card-carrying members. Everyone thought so except the Communists, at least those who knew how to read the subtle signals in their newspapers, which always referred to us as "our friends Yves Montand and Simone Signoret," just as they later wrote "our friend Gérard Philipe"; then, very shortly afterward, "our friends Yves Montand, Gérard Philipe, Simone Signoret." "Friends" are not "comrades"; still, they are friends. And what is more precious than friends, especially when they don't go around proclaiming that they are not comrades?

We didn't join the party because we were often dismayed by its cultural positions. Montand was no longer a metalworker, but he remembered their strikers' demands. I am not a miner's daughter, but I understood what the miners wanted; in any case, I understood more than I had before. However, our particular area of interest is culture, whether one considers the film and popular songs major or minor arts. In our film clubs we had seen and seen again *Chapayev*, *Maxim's Childhood*, *The Thirteen*, *The Last Night* (I'm not going to walk into a trap by mentioning Potemkin), which had given us some idea of the "Soviet" genius (we carefully avoided calling it Russian). And suddenly, attracted by reviews in *Lettres Françaises* or *L'Ecran Français*, we'd get sidetracked at screenings that ran the usual hour and a half but seemed to last all day, in which there was no trace at all of the Soviet genius, not to speak of the Russian genius. We didn't like it. It worried us. Perhaps we had perverted tastes. And we didn't like the painting either. At least not the sort one was advised to like.

We talked things over with the Communists. They were always patient and understanding. Of course, we couldn't understand! "A song about miners, that's very important." "It's important if it's a good song about miners," Montand would answer. "It's better if it's good," they replied, "but what's important is that it's about miners. . . . Now, 'Luna Park' is fun, but do you really think that these are times for fun? The working class has other fish to fry at the moment than to spend their Saturdays on a scenic railway. . . . 'C'est Si Bon' is charming, of course, but don't you think the beat is very American?" "Yes, it's rather American, but the American beat is very good. After all, the Negroes invented American rhythm." " 'Sanguine, Joli Fruit' is a bit erotic, isn't it?" "You people in the party, don't you ever make love?" "Oh . . . he's so funny!" But when he sang "Quand un Soldat" they were pleased. Yes, that wasn't so bad, singing "Quand un Soldat" (which was banned on the radio) at the Étoile theater in the middle of the Indochina war to a full house in which there were always one or two hotheads looking for a fight, or even a whole rowful of them; not bad. Though there was that day in Mantes-la-Jolie, where some little twerps tarred the posters announcing the recital; not pleasant, that. It was all the less agreeable in that it happened the week of André Gide's death, which was briefly reported in *L'Humanité* with the pithy sentence: "André Gide didn't just die; he was already dead." This caused a stormy session between me and the very people who were responsible for the smearing of Montand's posters. Hemingway had his share, too, of Zhdanovian comment. "It's absolutely shameful to spend one's time and talent on a tale about an old man and a fish when there's so much to be said about McCarthyism." There was something at the base of it: Gide had written *Retouches* and Hemingway was silent; but I had read them both, had read everything they had written, and it seemed to me *L'Humanité* was dealing with the whole thing somewhat lightly. But that was probably my bourgeois origin falsifying my view. . . .

One day at the Porte de Vincennes there was a rally sponsored by the peace movement addressed to all womanhood. Gérard Philipe recited "Liberté," Montand sang "Quand un Soldat," Danièle Delorme did something or other, and I had written a little text (I'm not a very good *diseuse* and I can't sing). It was a kind of salute to all the mothers, fiancées, wives, sisters, daughters, and cousins (that was fashionable at the time) of the world. It included French women, Russian women, Chinese women, Koreans, Vietnamese, Americans. But in the account of it in the next day's *L'Humanité* the Americans had somehow dropped off the list. "It's a printer's error," I was told; more like a bloody hole, it seemed to me. I hadn't read "Amerincas" or "Scarmeina." I hadn't read a damn thing. It was all the sillier, since I had gotten thunderous applause for my Americans. The audience had understood exactly what I was saying.

Montand and I were dismayed by the idea that we would never set foot in America. We'd say to ourselves: "It's a pity. We'll never see Broadway; we'll never watch Fred Astaire dance or meet Henry Fonda; we'll never know what Hollywood is like, or the Golden Gate, or the Brooklyn Bridge; we'll never know all those things the American film world meant for all those people of our generation and our profession." But it remained at this rather superficial level. We had put an X across the idea. Everything had become simple again. There were good guys and bad guys. The bad guys had the atomic bomb, and they wouldn't let you come to their country if you didn't like their bomb. We weren't going to suddenly tell them we liked their bomb in order to get a visa. There remained our memory of our smiling liberators, the splendid spectacle of the Allies—the Russians, English, and French—in Paris in 1945. . . .

The others were the good guys. They were poor, they had lost about twenty million men, their children had died of hunger in besieged cities, the Nazis had shot down their babes as though they were clay pigeons and had had themselves photographed while they did it. Stalingrad had resisted, been burned, and conquered. The Ukrainians had burned their crops in order to stop the enemy; it was surely true: We had seen it in *Why We Are Fighting*. The French Communist party was the party of those who had died before a German firing squad. We thought everything had become simple again. It was an oversimplification.

But still, we never joined the party. We were fiancées but never brides. I won't go into the Stalin years here, those years when people of good faith were deceived, used, and puzzled to a point where they no longer believed in their own natural reactions and thought themselves subversive and counterrevolutionary. There are a lot of good books that deal with the subject. And a lot of less good books too. Those were years of bitterness and cruel confusion. Some of those books were written by ex-militants who lost all on the day they lost their faith. Our great deception came in 1956 with the speech "attributed to Khrushchev." But then Stalin had never seemed like Santa Claus to me. I had kept the bad habits and bad relationships of my Café Flore anarchist-Trotskyite years. But for those who had never doubted, or had never wanted to admit that they doubted, those who had swallowed the "white smocks," the "traitor Tito and his clique," "Claude Bourdet, intelligence agent," "Nizan, police stoolie," "Sartre, sold out to imperialism," and "Marty and Tillon, those police agents"—for them, what Khrushchev then revealed was a dagger to the heart. On the other hand, it was balm to the hearts of those militants who had been excluded from the fold precisely because they had refused to swallow certain grass snakes, which turned out to be pythons. We, the skeptics, had swallowed some things and spat out others. After all, we were at liberty—even to make mistakes. We believed in worthwhile causes; to undertake everything possible to try and save the Rosenbergs was indispensable, as indispensable as treating with contempt those who refused to sign. At the same time we pinned our hopes on things we should never have believed in. To countersign a text that Paul Éluard thought wise to write at the time of the Kalanda trial in Prague, which said: "I have got too much to do with the innocent proclaiming their innocence, to spend time on the guilty asserting their guilt"—that was not necessary; it was so unnecessary that it was really monstrous and criminal. We believed Jaeger, who explained to us that we should sign; but we should have examined it further even when we were urged by someone we respect. That ought not to be sufficient. To say that there were no concentration camps in the Soviet Union, getting our information from *Lettres Françaises*, which was embroiled in a lawsuit with Kravchenko, who had written a book denouncing the camps—that was naïve and stupid.

On the other side, to know that in America the Committee for Un-American Activities hounded people because one day in 1936 they gave fifty cents to someone collecting money for the Spanish Republicans; threw ten Hollywood screenwriters in jail because they refused to cooperate with the committee in denouncing their friends and answering yes or no, they had or hadn't been Communists a single day of their lives; to know that Dashiell Hammett, author of *The Glass Key, The Thin Man*, and *The Maltese Falcon*, was in prison for those very reasons; to know that Lillian Hellman, author of *The Little Foxes*, was unable to work because she had refused to answer Senator McCarthy's questions, saying that the first thing she had been taught as an American citizen was that you didn't sell out your friends—to know all that meant keeping abreast of events, not dealing in secondhand gossip: to hell with the American press and American television, an eye hovering permanently over the "accused" in Washington.

Well, there you are. The cold war. You didn't have to have a party card to know these things. There were the things that one knew, and those one didn't. The things one didn't know were the most horrible. And the truly guilty were those who knew and who hid those facts. As I haven't popped in a literary reference for a long while, I'm allowing myself the luxury of one now. "He who doesn't know is an ignoramus. He who knows and keeps quiet is a scoundrel" (Bertolt Brecht, *Galileo*).

Brecht, too, appeared before the Un-American Activities Committee when in exile in America. A record was made of his interrogation. He was asked some extraordinary questions: "Do you know a certain Kurt Weill? . . . Did you ever talk politics with him?" And this one: "What were your reasons for leaving Germany in 1933?" His answers were of no help to the investigators, and soon afterward, he went back to East Berlin, where other adventures awaited him.

So that's it. That's my explanation for why we were not Communists and why we were not anti-Communists. When I analyze that period now, on a personal level there's quite a lot to say: It was a difficult time, but also remarkably rewarding. It was difficult partly because we were hounded by a *certain* press. Periodically I would be portrayed "selling *L'Humanité-Dimanche* in a mink coat," or, what was worse, "sending out the maid to sell *L'Humanité-Dimanche* while watching from a distance to make sure she does it well." Then there's this one: I had my "worker's blues made by Hermès." That's not quite so stupid because, after all, the jeans worn by all the nicely brought up young girls today are nothing more than American workers' blues.

In another section of the press it was the opposite; we were boycotted. In order not to boycott them in return I'll tell you that it was *Match*. I'd just as soon not go back to the Montand posters blackened with tar, or the stink bombs, or the tear gas in the Théâtre des Célestins in Lyons. Or the provocations, or the threatening letters. As I said, hounding! All the rest—and there was plenty of it—was thoroughly rewarding. Morally, artistically, and—to put things in perspective—financially too. Morally because we weren't uptight within ourselves. We were free. We had the good luck to be French and in Paris. There was no McCarthy or Zhdanov in Paris. Montand sang what he wanted to. And since we don't live in a soap bubble but on a big sphere where there was lots of action going on, that made his choice of songs even tougher, whether they were comic, poetic, or "committed," as the current saying goes.

To live up to the opinions we held meant being watchful on both flanks. Right and left. There had to be nothing in the songs to flatter the reactionaries, and nothing that might fall in meekly with populism or demagoguery. As he does a beautiful job, it worked. And when it works, it brings in bags of bravos and disappointed "Oooh's" after the last curtain call, and it brings in bags of money. The audiences were a mixed crowd. The mass public was already Montand's, since he is by definition a popular singer—and popular singers hail from the plebs, only very occasionally from highbrow circles. It's lovely when ordinary people on bikes whistle the melody of "Saltimbanques," from a poem by Apollinaire, because of a popular singer. The other lot, the elegant contingent—he had them, too; when the stuff's good they don't bear grudges.

This then was the character Clouzot came to see for a part in *The Wages of Fear*. I used the word "character" deliberately; for his Mario, Clouzot wanted the man Montand and the music-hall performer Montand. A music-hall personality is the direct opposite of an actor. It means being oneself, in one's own suit, with a repertory one has chosen oneself, with good musicians one has chosen for oneself, and lighting supervised by oneself—all to ensure that you will amuse, move, enchant, and captivate an audience who come to see *you*.

Montand had already had one acting experience with *Les Portes de la Nuit*. At twenty-three he had replaced Jean Gabin, for whom Jacques Prévert had written this splendid role for a forty-year-old. Neither the friendship nor the talent of Prévert and Carné had been able to make of Montand anything other than a pale reflection of his own personality, not that of the character. He adored going to the movies, but he was determined never to suffer again in front of a camera. He turned down Clouzot's offer. Clouzot dug in his heels. Montand made him promise that if it didn't pan out, he would release him. Clouzot promised. Montand began working on scenes from Anouilh.

124

This went on at Carrère's country inn at La Moutière, where the four of us had set up camp: Georges and Véra Clouzot, Montand and I. In the afternoons Montand would audition in front of Clouzot just like a freshly arrived young provincial student at the Simon drama school. And at around six he would leave for the Théâtre de l'Étoile, where he'd sing to packed houses. It was a good arrangement. I have never seen Clouzot happier than during that time, when he was with the woman he loved, a script that went from good to admirable, and an attentive student who elsewhere was a topnotch winner without Clouzot's having been in any way responsible.

Gabin refused the other part because he thought his audience wouldn't come to see him play a "coward," and Vanel, who hadn't made a film for a long time, was taken on following screen tests for which he bent over backward. That's how he came to do *The Wages* and how he became our friend.

The Wages of Fear was shot entirely on location in the Camargue. I followed in the wake. Véra and I shopped at the antiquated Dames de France department store in Nîmes. We embroidered little jet-glass beads onto espadrilles. We watched the filming, and we swam in the icy river a hundred yards from a notice board warning "Danger, Poliomyelitis," which we only spotted later. We all lived at the Toto Hotel, and Clouzot insisted that Toto himself, the owner, should attend screenings of the dailies. Vanel and Montand bought a pile of cheap dishes at the Prisunic, which they smashed at dinnertime during mock quarrels triggered by remarks like: "I've made a hundred and one films, and no young whippersnapper cabaret-artist bumpkin is going to teach me my job" and "Acting with an old-timer from the silent screen—what a bore!" Plates would fly, and Toto's father, assuming they were hotel property, logged up an inventory of the breakage. The town firemen loaned their hoses and gear for an ambush over the road leading to the location lot; everybody acted fourteen years old. They were making a major movie and I was on a marvelous vacation. I often quarreled with Clouzot, but that was part of the fun. He got a kick out of it. If, perchance, I wasn't aggressive fast enough, he would provoke me. It generally started with "Poor Brasillach...so sensitive, so delicate." "So sensitive and so delicate that he wrote for *Je Suis Partout.*"° That would make the evening.

I just said that I had a marvelous vacation. In fact, it was a prolonged vacation, since I hadn't worked for a year and a half. When Montand had signed up for *The Wages*, I had contracted to do *Casque d'Or* with Jacques Becker. So one summer morning in 1951 I was summoned back to Paris for costume fittings, hair styles, and makeup for the film.

In 1942, at the Café Flore, among the people who were talked about but who weren't there was another Jacques besides Prévert—Jacques Becker. Marc Maurette, who, with Becker, had been one of Jean Renoir's assistants, often said, "Ah, you'll see when Jacques comes back." Jacques came back from being a POW, as the saying went. Maurette had called me for a small part in the first film Becker made on his return from captivity, *Dernier Atout*. Clasping my bit of paper, I appeared at the requested hour at an office on the smart Boulevard Malesherbes. At the far end of a small corridor there was an immense round room, and at the back of this room were four men seated around a desk. They all looked alike. All four sported mustaches, which weren't fashionable then. In much the same way as you never know beforehand into whose arms you are supposed to throw yourself when playing a small part, the Jacques Becker that Maurette had described was indiscernible. There were at least ten meters to cross before reaching the four-headed desk. I crossed them in complete silence. Then someone with a slight stammer said, "Whom have you come to see?" I showed my paper. "I asked you to come?" "Well, Maurette said that...." "What have you been in?" "Nothing." "Well, go to the drama

°Brasillach was executed at the Liberation. *Je Suis Partout* was a vile anti-Semitic paper.

conservatory and when you've got something to show, come back and see me." I recrossed the ten meters of no man's land. I'd hardly reached the door when he said, "Turn around. I suppose you're photogenic." . . . (End of Act I.)

Act II. I'm in Vence with the *Les Visiteurs* cast. It's a drizzly day. Blin and Decomble, who are shooting in *Dernier Atout* in Nice, just down the coast, call me at the boardinghouse, saying, "Come over and spend the day with us in Nice." I get the bus, arrive in Nice, and go to the set, where Becker sees me. "What, you're in Nice and you didn't phone me?" "Why should I have phoned you?" "You're not Gaby?" "No; I'm the girl you sent to the conservatory; I'm not Gaby. I didn't go to the conservatory, but you're a lot nicer to Gaby, who isn't very talented, than you are to someone you don't even know."

Act III. Years passed. Between 1946 and 1949 I'd run into Jacques now and again; things were going well for me and for him too. We were not friends; or rather we weren't yet the friends we'd become after working together. The anecdote concerning our first meeting would be trotted out after the kind of private screenings where we would meet from time to time. It was a good conversation starter (especially if the film hadn't been good) in a neighboring bar where the PR man would gather together a handful of Parisian personalities. All this is leading up to saying that when I signed the contract for *Casque d'Or*, Jacques and I really hardly knew each other.

The subject was superb. A number of people had wanted to make this film. Renoir and Duvivier had thought about it before the war; Allégret had given it serious consideration too. But it was Becker who offered me the part; perhaps in the back of my mind there was a touch of revenge in memory of my visit to the Boulevard Malesherbes production office. Be that as it may, I had signed a contract and was now on my way to Paris.

The morning I was due to leave I had gone along with the *Wages* film unit to Las Piedras, the mock-up location village, thirty kilometers outside Nîmes. At three in the afternoon I began my farewells to everyone, and then Montand escorted me back to the car. I was blubbering. It was the first time we'd be separated in two years. I blubbered all the thirty kilometers back to Nîmes. I packed my bags, blubbering. I wept copiously over the whole Toto family as I bade them good-bye. I got to the station still sobbing, and when the train for Paris pulled to a stop, I gazed at the sleeping car in which my berth had been reserved. I stopped crying. I didn't get into the train. And as it pulled out of the station, for a few brief seconds I had the strongest feeling of freedom I have ever felt in my life.

When the film unit came back to the hotel, I was given the full festive treatment, as if I were the world's greatest heroine. I was sensational! What I'd done was unheard of. My agent, Paulette Dorisse, whom I had telephoned with instructions to make any excuse she wanted but that wild horses wouldn't drag me back to Paris, had never heard anything like it, either. She was furious. Even Clouzot, who was quite capable of killing an actress who dared pull such a trick on him, gave up Brasillach for an evening and drank to the "grand amour." Fiesta reigned at the Toto Hotel.

The next morning I was less at ease. I was waiting for incensed, threatening, or suing phone calls. I telephoned the Toto Hotel from Las Piedras: "Any calls for me?" "No, madame, nothing." Then about nine that evening Toto came to the dinner table, saying, "Monsieur Becker is asking for you on the phone." Everybody reacted with "Ah . . . ah" and "Well . . . well." For the rest of my life I'll see Toto's hand-cranked phone behind the reception desk. Jacques said, "You're quite right. We only live once. A true love is something one tends every day, like a plant." "Thank you, Jacques, you're very kind. I hope I haven't upset your plans too much?" "No, no, not at all. I'm fixing things right away." And he mentioned the names of two actresses who might replace me. . . .

The next morning I got the first train to Paris. And rightly so. I went back to make what is perhaps the finest film I ever made. Jacques was waiting for me at the station, and he took me straight to the hairdresser for a platinum-blond job, announcing that he would collect me at half-past twelve to check that the color was right. After that we'd have lunch, then we would go see about the costumes, after which we'd order the shoes. He arranged such a tight schedule there was no way for me to escape, either physically or morally. Just as the bleaching operation ended, there followed the epilogue to the three-act play I've been talking about. Jacques was looking at the roots of my hair like Louis Pasteur peering through a microscope, when I said, "Aren't you going to say hello to the lady at the next table, Jacques?" "But I don't know her." "Of course you do, Jacques; look again. . . . It's Gaby."

I didn't realize the importance of this film while we were shooting it. One never knows whether what one is doing will turn out to be something exceptional. The hope is always there, but you just can't tell. And Jacques was someone who didn't drape filming with the ceremonial cloak of the humbug miracle-worker. His favorite expression was: "Today we're going to have fun." And it's true; we had lots of fun. He dug up a café-hotel on location in Annet-sur-Marne; we stayed there, he and Annette Wademand, Serge Reggiani and I, and one or two others. Although the bedrooms had no running water, there were superb old-fashioned porcelain basins. At the far end of the kitchen garden were the "conveniences." The rest of the cast had been accommodated in a real hotel. For a day or two we were baffled by this peculiar idea, but once we started wearing our costumes we realized that it was brilliant. Marie and Manda were much better off here than in a conventional grand hotel. And since Jacques loved Marie and Manda, he didn't mind going without a bathroom himself.

I could go on for hours telling you how this film was a labor of love, joy, friendship, and humor. I believe this comes through when one sees it. But I would rather talk about something that happened to me on the professional level. I had come face to face with what is called dissociation, or dual personality. I'd read nothing on this phenomenon. Only fairly recently have I read what Diderot and Stanislavski wrote about actors. Something very strange and disturbing happened to me in *Casque*. We'd already done some three weeks' filming on location. When a whiff of fog was needed, we had fog; when a shaft of sunlight was required, the sun would shine. It was miraculous. And then on a Monday—Mondays are important: getting back into harness again when filming is always difficult after the Sunday break—on a vacant lot, preparations were under way to shoot the scene in which Marie goes off to look for Manda, who works for the cabinetmaker, played by Gaston Modod. She sends the fiacre driver with a message for her lover. Manda steps out of the shop and runs into her on the vacant lot. They go toward a small shack, when Manda's regular sweetheart, played by Loleh Bellon, appears.

It's eight o'clock in the morning. Makeup is done in a bistro rented by the production office, in the midst of the usual Monday morning chatter. "What did you do yesterday?" "I slept." "I went to the movies." Et cetera. In other words, nothing that has anything to do with what we are about to act. After being made up, I go upstairs to the bedroom of the bistro's owner. My usual dresser is sick and her replacement hasn't the faintest idea of costume continuity. She dresses me. She helps me with my corset, hands me the various things I ask for. I had two pairs of boots for the film: one superb pair made of gray suede with black patent leather, and another pair of very ordinary brown leather. My dresser hands me the beauties, at which point I say, "Oh, no, I'm going to wear those this evening." "Why? Are we going to film tonight?" "No! Skip it, it doesn't matter. . . ."

I realized that I was getting dressed in a bistro-owner's bedroom beside a vacant lot in Belleville in the Paris suburbs, to go out in a moment and say to Manda, my friend Serge Reggiani, "Come this evening; I'll wait for you at l'Ange Gabriel...." It wasn't me I was dressing—Montand's wife, Catherine's mother—but Marie, who was already thinking ahead to what she would wear that evening to go out with Manda...a scene we filmed three weeks later at the Billancourt studios, where the l'Ange Gabriel set was in the process of being constructed.

It was very strange. I found that things were happening to me that I had no control over, which seemed to come neither from my mind nor from my will. Consequently I was someone else. Then it hit me and I said, "This must be what they call dissociation! Stacks of stuff have been written about it." I said nothing about it at the time to anyone, but it is the answer to all those naïve questions people often ask you: "How do you manage to cry?" "You must have a fantastic memory to learn all those lines." When it isn't difficult to memorize dialogue—if it's good—because you are speaking words that the character would say in that particular situation. Nor is it hard to cry when you're unhappy; and if my character is unhappy she cries, and I cry.

In the course of exercising my craft, *Casque d'Or* was a turning point. I discovered that basically you know nothing about this craft and that there is nothing to learn. As one ages one needs less and less of its science. There are two schools of thought: There are those actors who explain to you that they know exactly how they're going to do the part; that they're experienced enough to avoid coming a cropper over this and that. And then there is the other method, which is to have no method at all. This is mine. I didn't choose it, nor did I decide that it was a method; it's just the only one that suits me. I feel a real need not to think, not to analyze.

While I'm filming I need someone who's going to think and analyze for me—the director. He's the one who has to pull the whole thing together. This is the only way I can work, and what a luxury it is. One comes offering oneself, as it were, with all that one hopes one is capable of doing—and I'm emphasizing the lack of certainty—and above all, bringing something to a part one hasn't chosen oneself. At this point in my life and my career and my craft, if I read a book where there's a marvelous woman's part, into which I feel I can project myself, I reject it in advance. The idea must come from the outside; someone else must have thought of it for me, must mold it for me; someone who has chosen me, dreamed me—even if it's a nightmare, even if it's to act a monster.

When I saw the final show print for the first time, I felt that Jacques had dreamed a good dream when he had thought of us—Serge, Dauphin, Bussière, and all the rest. And I think he got us to make a masterpiece. Unfortunately, besides me, my husband, one or two good friends, and a handful of anonymous spectators, the ranks of enthusiasts were thin. The film was a total flop. I never keep reviews, so I can't quote them exactly, but *Cahiers*, which may still have been called *La Revue du Cinéma*, panned the vulgarity of both the dialogue and the photographic composition. And Georges Sadoul, the Communist critic, who'd liked it well enough the first time he saw it, and said so, readjusted his aim a week later in *Lettres Françaises*, condemning Becker for having made a film directed against the working class. How could an honest carpenter end up on the scaffold, when it was his duty to take a militant stand within the union instead of being led astray and sympathizing with a bunch of street urchins? The other critics' verdict was: a silent movie lacking plot and suspense. Serge was too willowy; they would have preferred something more masculine (that went for the producers too). Apparently all Manda's surface fragility, which concealed a staggering inner strength, went straight over their heads. Mayo's costumes, so true in their style, left them cold. They were used to those adapted reconstructions, to those hourglass corsets, 1950 style, which render the majority of films made then with a story set in the naughty nineties so unbearable to watch today. Jacques knew! He didn't want us to be in disguise. He didn't want a ragtag-and-bobtail show. Serge, with his mustache, his corduroy pants and black twill jacket, was ahead of his time. He dressed like the kids who read *Libération**° nowadays. More accurately, his costume had been carefully reproduced from the pages of *Le Petit Journal Illustré.†*

The film opened in Brussels before it was shown in Paris. I think it was a publicity scheme. I was in Brussels with Montand, who was giving a recital there. A preview was held for the Belgian press (about a dozen journalists turned up) one morning in an enormous movie house on the Place Broucker. Montand, Crolla, Bob, and I sat in the mezzanine trying to discern the reactions of these first spectators. They shifted from one buttock to the other, talked, yawned. Since the theater owner had very kindly set up a small buffet in the foyer after the projection, they could not help but see me. They looked embarrassed and said nothing. I said, "You didn't like it?" They shook their heads sadly. One man plucked up his courage and said, "It's weak, very weak."

Casque d'Or had its world premiere in Brussels; it played in that city for four days. And for once, Paris followed Brussels, which had set the tone. After *Casque d'Or* Serge went five years without making a film.

Jacques was very sad and didn't understand. He was in love with his film. *Casque d'Or* is a great, simple tribute of the glory of love and friendship. While the film was being made we were all in a state of grace. Jacques was in love with Annette, and his love of love filtered through the images. I was in love with Montand, and Manda reaped the benefits. And since Manda was Serge, it was deliciously incestuous to pretend to a different kind of love, when we had loved each other so much for such a long time. And Jacques loved us all. We had spent eight weeks "having fun" passionately, and now people didn't understand our film.

°An extreme leftist daily.
†A popular picture magazine, now long extinct.

Then rumors trickled in from abroad. In London, *Golden Mary* was hailed as a masterpiece. In Rome, *Casco d'Oro* was making a fortune. In Berlin—I've forgotten what it was called there—it was the same thing. Finally, it was receiving its due. We had not all been victims of a group aberration. We had really and truly made a fine film. *Casque d'Or* brought me my first foreign trophy, the British Film Academy Award, which is the English Oscar. That was in 1952. But it took ten years for *Casque d'Or* to come back to a Paris cinema, and Jacques had died without savoring this joyful moment.

After we made this film, a friendship grew between the three of us that was of the greatest importance for Montand and me. Jacques lived in our house in the country whether we were there or not. There was Annette; then there was Françoise Fabian; they married at Autheuil. In the house there are two rickety lamps that are sacrosanct because Jacques constructed them one rainy day out of two huge bottles—and they were already rickety the day they were made. There is a horrible African object, somewhere halfway between an amphora and a giant coffeepot, brought back from the location of *Ali Baba*—of which Jacques himself said that it would be banned to anyone over eight years old.... And there's a 45-rpm record he discovered, called "A Little Lettuce with a Bit of Mayonnaise," which nearly made the hit parade last winter.

One Sunday in November 1959, Bob called us in Hollywood to tell us that Jacques was dead. That evening, when I went to bed, the little clock he had given me stopped. I never had it repaired. One day it started up again all by itself. Believe me or not, as you will.

In 1973, while I was making *Rude Journée Pour la Reine*, René Allio's film, *Casque* was revived in Paris. Arlette Chosson, who plays the pregnant girl in Allio's film and who is a member of the Vincent and Jourdheuil theatrical company, went to see it with a bunch of her friends. The next day she arrived shattered by the film and said, "It's marvelous! It's absolutely marvelous! It's

Brechtian!" "Why Brechtian?" "Because it's beautiful." "Is everything that's beautiful Brechtian?" "Yes." "Shakespeare is beautiful. Is he Brechtian?" "Yes." I think Jacques would have laughed. We were far from Auguste Renoir and Toulouse-Lautrec, but I think he probably would have liked it.

For the eight weeks it took to make *Casque d'Or* we wrote and telephoned every day, Montand and I. A few times Jacques let me go to Nîmes. I would take the night train on Saturday evening, arrive at dawn, and leave Sunday night to be on the set on time on Monday. Once we missed each other: Montand couldn't reach me on the telephone and I couldn't find him at the Toto Hotel. So he jumped into his car to come and surprise me while I was already in the train for Nîmes. We were very unhappy to be separated, but curiously enough, it didn't mar our work. However, after I had made *Casque d'Or*, I decided to quit my profession, and I announced it to the press.

No one understood. The film's lack of success had not "debased my coin" as it had for Serge, for the unfairest reasons, which I mentioned earlier. I was in demand. And I refused offers. I wanted to be where Montand was. I wanted to be able to go on tour with him and the musicians. I had become a groupie again. And today I would probably be an old ex-groupie, ex-actress, and probably ex-Madame Yves Montand, too, if a small household incident had not exploded in the "caravan" one peaceable day.

Montand is always super in a major crisis. If there's a fire, it's Montand who finds the water. If you're losing blood, it's Montand who knows how to make a tourniquet. He's a man to cope with major occasions. But let's say that for the routine stuff he can at times be a trifle difficult—that is, when he is not downright impossible. On that particular day I was knitting, like a devoted, unobtrusive, and happy wife. He was in rehearsal and it wasn't going exactly as he wanted. That's when he noticed that a small scrap of paper he had put on the piano had disappeared, a bit of paper no one should have touched and on which he had noted something vitally important. All of a sudden it was as though someone had misplaced the Constitution! It was found. It had traveled from the piano to the telephone table. I don't know who was responsible for the awful transfer. He probably did it himself, since his notes were intended for a lyric writer to whom he'd telephoned earlier on. The fact is, abetted by the clicking of my knitting needles, I was getting on my husband's nerves. He stared at me for a second or two before saying, "What are you doing stuck there knitting?" "I'm here because I want to be here. If I weren't here I'd be working." "That's easily said! In order to work, somebody's got to offer you a part."

I hadn't worked for the past eighteen months. That wasn't particularly heroic. I had no material worries. I had refused parts with the serenity of someone who isn't hungry and who doesn't have to worry about paying the rent. It's a luxury. There aren't all that many actresses who have it. Only one refusal had caused a twinge of distress, and that was *Thérèse Raquin*, which the Hakim brothers had offered me. I had accepted verbally on condition that Marcel Carné would be the director. It was while *Casque d'Or* was being made, before my grand decision to give up acting (the Hakims had coproduced *Casque d'Or*). So I had said yes and then later had said no to *Thérèse*, and in the files of the Hakim brothers, as indeed in the very well kept files of Marcel Carné, I was surely classified as "that pain in the ass who doesn't know what she wants."

"In order to work, somebody's got to offer you a part"? Why, I could be in the middle of making *Thérèse!* "They didn't really want you for *Thérèse*. By the way, I hear that X is about to accept." I always fall for this trick. I rose, carefully rolled up my handiwork, aligned the two needles in the ball of wool, and took about a hundred years to reach the telephone. I laboriously looked up the production office's number (I knew it by heart). I was saying to myself: He's going to stop me. He was reading the newspaper. Slowly, very slowly, I dialed the number. I don't play poker, but the big deals Montand tells me about after his poker sessions must be something like what I was doing. I said, "Robert, it's Simone. I've reconsidered. I'd like to do *Thérèse*." I was ready for anything: "It's too late....We're no longer interested....Carné is mad. ...Mademoiselle X has signed a contract...." Though Robert Hakim is not famous for having an angelic voice, he had it that day when he answered, "I'm delighted. Let's sign a contract tomorrow." I hung up. I said to Montand, "You see."

It was touch and go. I was returning from the end of the earth. Once again we would be miserable when we were separated, and then come back together and discover a miraculous reunion without a flaw in it. I became once more she who is there because she wants to be. I had escaped the fate of she who is there because she wouldn't know where to go if she weren't there. With *Thérèse* I rediscovered Carné, and I told him all the things he didn't know about our life as extras in Vence. I liked Vallone. Vallone liked me: I loved Montand, and Vallone respects the wives of Italians who love their husbands.

I've just noticed that I've said "husband" twice running. We married in December 1951, but we've maintained the habit of backdating our married life as from August 19, 1949. We were married in the town hall of Saint-Paul by our pal Marius Issert. My witness was Jacques Prévert, poet; Montand's was Paul Roux, owner and hotelkeeper of La Colombe d'Or. It was a tiny wedding. The guests were the Prévert family; the Roux family; André Verdet; the Pagnol family, which means Marcel, Jacqueline ex-Bouvier, and Frédéric, their seven-year-old boy. (Frédéric was madly in love with me; he had broken all Montand's records—they were made of wax in those days—in his parents' collection. And one day when we were all having lunch, he crept up behind my fiancé and hit him on the head with a hammer. During the wedding dinner, which was held in the bar of La Colombe, he was drawing up plans for what he called the "escape scheme," designed for my kidnapping after what he called "that twerp's

137

wedding.") There was also a very distinguished and kind lady who was there with her husband: Her name was Jeanne David, better known as Deanna Durbin, who had been one of the biggest stars of the American cinema during her adolescence and mine. There was also the village weaver. There was Michelle la Cambraisienne. And there was Catherine.

That day the doves did something very unusual; they flew inside, and one of them landed on my head and spread its wings, looking exactly like the drawing Picasso had made for the peace congress. Everyone said it was an excellent omen. At just that moment Picasso's chauffeur pal arrived carrying a copy of *Verve* with a new drawing on its end papers and multicolored good wishes written with the first felt pens to come on the French market. The drawing and the greetings were signed "Pablo Picasso and Françoise Gillot." No doubt the drawing was by him and the greetings by Françoise. She was already writing. One day not so long ago we carefully detached the end paper and framed it. It's the only original Picasso in the house, and it's unstealable because it's unsalable. It carries both our names and the date, December 22, 1951.

We would see Picasso when he wanted to see us. He was then in his Vallauris period. Entire delegations of pains in the ass and bores made his life impossible, preventing him from working. He told us about it. He was funny and cruel; not wicked: cruel, and accurately observant. He did wonderful imitations of these gate-crashers: On the one hand were the fashionable ladies and on the other were the comrades, who had a tendency to dig him in the ribs and treat him as a none too serious propaganda illustrator for the party. He often came up to Saint-Paul with Françoise, Claude, and Paloma. He knew that in Saint-Paul he would find Prévert, Paul Roux, whom he liked immensely, and the two of us. Sometimes Braque would be there too, and it was a kind of miracle to be seated at the same table with those two men who were both so marvelous, but so different. The stocky Spanish bull would attack the big

Norman, and would get him to tell about the blue of the birds on the ceilings of the Louvre. I mean what I said: *tell*. They would tell color just as I can tell a film script. It was a game, a game they had been playing for over fifty years. Madame Braque didn't join in the game. She didn't like Picasso. She was fond of reminding people how it was she who had prepared Paulo's afternoon snack when he was little and practically a waif. She didn't like all the clamor and fuss that surrounded the Picasso lengend. She preferred Braque's quiet reserve. She preferred Braque's paintings. In fact, the only painting she liked was Braque's. The only other person of whom she spoke with affection was Modigliani. She had known him when she was a model. She would say, "How handsome Modigliani was...." Right into the fifties that seemed still to annoy Braque. She never talked about Modigliani's paintings; she talked about his face.

Picasso came often to La Colombe, which is why I said earlier that we'd see him only when he wanted to see us. Once in a while he would take us back to his studio. I always felt uncomfortable there. It's terrifying to say "That's beautiful" to someone who knows that everything he touches, be it color, papier-mâché, plaster, or iron, is immediately converted into sums of money in the minds of the people around him. And he did know that. He got enormous pleasure out of comparing the behavior of his guests. Once, we were all very gay. He was in the process of sculpting the famous goat. One could still recognize the bicycle handlebars that had become its horns, the two willow calabashes that made up its thorax, the central network of a palm branch that was its spine, the hollowed-out tin can that was its sex, and the two terra-cotta gourds that were its breasts. He had just begun covering it with plaster; four thin logs propped it on its feet. When I said we were gay I meant that nothing about the occasion was solemn; the goat wasn't finished, mounted, on exhibition. It was already a goat but it was still a toy made by a child whose parents can't afford expensive presents.

He always had charcoal crayons in his pockets, and it amused him to sketch frescoes and corridas on the whitewashed walls of the Préverts' house. A couple of storms and the mistral wind would erase it two days later. He always arrived without previous warning and it would be sparkling. It would never have crossed our minds to simply drop in on him, but he would have been outraged not to find *us* in when he decided to come up our way.

In 1957, after our tour of the Eastern countries, he called us and we went down to La Californie, his big house in Super-Cannes. The bronze goat stood in the middle of the lawn. Since she was an old pal whom we had seen born, she didn't particularly impress us. We stayed for hours; he wanted to hear all about it. David Douglas Duncan, the great American photographer, was preparing his book *The Private Life of Pablo Picasso*. In the grandiose Hollywood houses, which inevitably contain one or two Picassos, this book, too, is inevitably lying around. We are in it, and the owners of the paintings, who never knew Picasso, are a bit jealous. Which is morally quite right.

If Saint-Paul and La Colombe d'Or appear periodically in this tale, it's because they are our third home. Chronologically they are our first home, because that's where we met. Some people make pilgrimages to the place of their first meeting. That's sometimes loaded with surprises. In the place of the little café where they shared their first coffee there is now a laundromat.... That can't happen to us, because we've never stopped going to Saint-Paul. We've lived through the transformations. The main street we can remember deserted changed slowly into a commercial street; that's life.... But La Colombe hasn't become a Hilton. La Colombe has remained what it was, and even though Picasso, Braque, and Paul Roux will never again sit in the shade of the huge fig tree on the terrace, they are not far away. If La Colombe hadn't existed, perhaps the *grande rue* wouldn't have become a commercial success, and maybe Aimé and Marguerite Maeght wouldn't have created their foundation in Hauts-de-Saint-

Paul. I know that in the minds of people who have never been there, La Colombe d'Or sounds a bit like the Hotel Crillon. I don't think you'd see much of the Crillon family at that hotel, but at La Colombe there is the Roux family.

When we first met Francis, he as seventeen years old; François, his older son, is today twenty-two. We have accompanied the Rouxes along their lives. And they have lived a part of ours. Paul Roux was Montand's witness at our marriage, and Montand was Francis's witness when he married Yvonne. Pierrot, the barman, poured out Catherine's grenadines for her before her head reached the level of the bar. Today he's pouring them for Benjamin, her son. Titine Roux, "Madame Paul," still enchants little boys and girls trying out their first wobbly steps with "And this is how they go, go, go, the little marionettes." Her voice is low and crystalline, and her eternal black dress (actually, she has seven identical ones) seems to reassure them. It's the only four-star hotel I know where the bar is still the village café. Lots of people think La Colombe belongs to us. It doesn't belong to us. It is entirely owned by the Roux family. But we are really part of that family.

Our third real home is our own. Autheuil. Montand bought it in 1954. And I mean Montand. "There are loads of 'Battling Joe' and 'Feuilles Mortes' in it," he likes to say when he looks at it. And he looks at it often. I do too. And still today we are amazed by its proportions and its beauty; and above all, we are amazed that it belongs to us. The standing-room-only performances at the Théâtre de l'Étoile and the sales of records have made this miracle possible. The place symbolizes luxury for us, but not in the usual sense of the word as applied to a house. It symbolizes the luxury of being able to buy something with the fruit of one's labor, rather than to labor in order to buy something. That's what we mean by luxury; it's a very important notion to us. I meet quite a few people who say, "I'm making this film so I can have a house in the country." Autheuil was bought with the sous earned by an artisan who exploits himself by producing only the things he likes.

The best of all possible worlds is when this work is offered to an audience to which you like to give, and which likes what you have to give.

Autheuil is a big house. In 1954 the eighty-four kilometers that separate it from Paris made it seem like the end of the world. Because it was far away and big, it was reasonable; if it had been fifty kilometers from Paris, it would have cost three times as much. The house is furnished with "good stuff," which doesn't mean "really good stuff," but it is beautiful; everyone who enjoys wandering around a flea market will know what I mean. It's a house for summer and winter and autumn and spring. It's the opposite of the "caravan" because a lot of people can live and work there at the same time without being in one another's way, or even meeting except for meals—or not at all if they're not hungry, which never happens. It quickly became a kind of communal house in which people laugh a lot and work seriously. The house is as good at taking in big parties, at which charades or "the murder game" are played, as it is at giving house room to rehearsals for a recital or the writing of a scenario or a novel. It's a good house, a real house, and all who stop there seem to come back. When we thought it so big, the day we first visited it, little did we realize that often it would be too small for the number of guests who would come. There were always a great many children at Autheuil; now there are the children of those children.

For Catherine it was already "the country house," such as many of my Neuilly schoolmates used to have and, of course, none of Montand's little pals had. For Benjamin, Catherine's son, it's Autheuil-Georges-and-Marcelle. In 1954 Georges and Marcelle were very young. Marcelle was the cook in the "caravan." Georges worked in Les Halles market and pined for the country. Once again, we did everything backward; which probably means we did everything right. We didn't look for people to help with the house after we had bought it; we liked these people who liked the country, and so we took Georges and Marcelle

142

with us the second time we went to see Autheuil before we bought it. They liked it. We bought it. Which is why, for Benjamin and many others, Autheuil is also Georges and Marcelle. I think my pal José Artur, the broadcaster, describes Autheuil in *Micro de Nuit* much better than I do.

It is at Autheuil, where almost the whole cast had come to spend the weekend, that Raymond Rouleau conceived the first stage draft for *The Crucible*, well ahead of the initial rehearsals. *The Crucible* had been staged in New York without great success. The author, practically unknown in France, was himself a "Salem witch" banished by McCarthy. All we knew about him and his play was what we had been told by our friends Jules Dassin and John Berry, themselves refugees in France. They were always talking about having the text of the play sent to Paris, but they never did it. We knew that *The Crucible* was the story of the Rosenbergs cloaked but clearly evident in the characters of John and Elizabeth Proctor, victims of another repression, in 1692 in Salem, Massachusetts. From time to time we would remind John Berry that he had still forgotten to write to Arthur Miller, and he would say, "I'll do it tomorrow." But in Brooklyn, where Arthur Miller lived and which he couldn't leave because they had taken away his passport, he entrusted his play to his literary agent.

One day Elvire Popesco, the Rumanian-born actress and stage producer, phoned us. "There's this play, dearrr monsieur, dearrr madame, by an Englishman whose name I can't remember; it's full of devils and dolls. I haven't rrread it, but verrry prrretty translation be rrreaddddy next week, and I'd like you to rrread it and me to prrroduce it."

If I've tried to give you the flavor of Popesco talk it's because I'm full of affection and admiration for her. It took a lot of imagination to reconcile what she said about the play and what we knew about it. But, it appeared, we were dealing with one and the same object. We found this out a short time later when we read a very fine literal translation that came to us via A. M. Julien. He had "borrowed" it from Popesco's office, and, to speak frankly, he had tried to take over the rights. But this was just a little incident along the way. Elvire and Julien made their explanations and finally fell into each other's arms and decided to coproduce the play. Miller, in Brooklyn, made one stipulation: He wanted it to be adapted by Jean-Paul Sartre or Marcel Aymé—no one else. It had to be offered first to Sartre, and if he refused, to Aymé. Sartre refused. Or rather Jean Cau, who was his secretary at the time, refused for him, without Sartre having read the play. Marcel Aymé declined too. He detested America and didn't want to read the play. But thanks to an excellent actress who had also heard about *The Crucible*, and who had heard about the part of Abigail, he did read it. He accepted the job, and *The Crucible* became *Les Sorcières de Salem*, and Abigail was played by Nicole Courcel—who is not the actress mentioned above. Popesco and Julien hired Raymond Rouleau. Rehearsal was called for October; it was then July.

I limbered up to be ready for this great challenge. I hadn't set foot on a stage since I had been thrown out of the Mathurins in the Gabin–Pontius Pilate sandals, and I was very scared of what lay ahead. I made Rouleau promise that he wouldn't be easy on me. Should I prove not to be the "goods," he was not to be awed by the fact that I'd become a "film star"; he was to replace me. I was in the garden at Autheuil and thinking in this fashion when Marcelle announced: "Monsieur Clouzot wants you on the telephone."

Since *The Wages of Fear*, my relations with Clouzot had taken various turns. When he called me for *Les Diaboliques*, Clouzot's motivations were not those that had made him want Montand for *The Wages*. He had never been shattered by me or by my talent, if any. He considered *Casque d'Or* a "nonfilm" and once had scientifically proved to me how it could have become a film if he, Clouzot, had been the director instead of Jacques—and if Martine Carol had been the principal actress. I liked Martine Carol, who was a very sweet person, and I advised him to remake *Casque*. This will give you an idea of the tone of our conversations. We fought, we made up. Véra would arbitrate or pour oil on troubled waters, depending on the state she was in. They had discovered La Colombe and lived there permanently since the end of *Wages*. This allowed us to have an ambiguous and aggressive relationship which, when all was said and done, amused us greatly.

Clouzot is a great director. He's also a man who can learn anything; he's the most concentrated student I've ever known. I have seen him learn canasta from books and then play better than anyone, especially me. (I never dared admit to him that I understood nothing of his explanations.) I have watched him learn painting from manuals and start to paint. I have watched him read works on bullfighting, and though I didn't actually see him in action in the arenas, it was because this happened in Spain; but he really, truly, did have a go at it, at Luis Miguel Dominguin's place. He did not know how to swim, so at forty-five he learned, in the pool at Eden Roc with a swimming instructor, along with three-year-old kids. Ten days later he swooped off the high diving board into the Mediterranean. Then came the aqualung. Next was music. How could one listen to a Beethoven symphony without following the score, unless one was a completely uncultured nitwit? (The last apprenticeship I saw personally was with God. Since I lost track of him about nine years ago, I don't know what he's up to now.)* All this is to say that Clouzot is an honorable man in the most Shakespearean sense of the word.

When I said "yes" that splendid afternoon in July 1954 to his offer to play in *Les Diaboliques*, I knew that I was letting myself in for a hell of a time. I had no idea that it was going to be as wretched as it was for sixteen weeks. Clouzot asked me because he needed me for the part.

*H. G. Clouzot died after publication of this book in France.

Above all, he needed an actress whom Véra knew. She wasn't an actress at all, and he wanted her to work with a friend, in a kind of family atmosphere.

The truth of the matter is that it was she who wanted to make this film. I could write three volumes on Véra Clouzot. She was funny, unbearable, generous, crazy, unhappy, and capable of making others unhappy. I adored her and detested her, and strangely enough, I miss her. She wanted to make this film, and she wanted people to think that he was forcing her to do it. Actually, we knew each other too well. People should discover each other in the course of work. That's what happened with Jacques Becker. And it happened for me with all the directors with whom I've worked.

We all have flaws in our personal makeup, flaws that aren't always perceived by our workmates. One sets these flaws carefully aside for home use, for domestic consumption, when one is one's self and not a character. They're not for when one is she-me, the other; but for when one is me-me.

So there was Clouzot, suspicious of my nasty flaws, as I was suspicious of his. I'm sure I had all sorts of other faults on the set, but they were not the ones he was worried about. And this upset the equilibrium that must be established between a director and an actor. At table in the Toto Hotel, I sometimes told Clouzot to go to hell. But it would never have occurred to me to say *merde* to him on his own set. But he hadn't understood that, and his way of letting me know clearly that we were neither at La Colombe nor at the Toto Hotel proved that he hadn't understood. In short, everything was out of true!

The tension between us reached a high pitch the day he said very nastily: "I should never have allowed you to read the end of the script." He had said something fantastically intelligent, and this time it was I who didn't understand. I've already said that the filming was extremely difficult, so I can shoulder all the blame from that moment on. The woman I was playing was guilty; she was a murderess and the accomplice of her lover, played by Paul Meurisse. She was pretending to be allied with the character Véra was playing. Despite myself, I had a tendency to play her as guilty, whereas the suspense relied on the fact that the audience should believe her innocent until the last two minutes of the film. But when Clouzot said that, I took it badly. I was wrong, I repeat, not knowing then what I know today. After a period of unbearable tension came a period of pure hell, and then the apocalypse in the form of a registered letter from the Théâtre Sarah-Bernhardt demanding my presence for the second week of rehearsals for *The Crucible*. I had signed an eight-week contract with Clouzot, and we were beginning on the fifteenth week of filming. We did sixteen. He paid me only for eight. He had drawn up a very clever contract, which I had read too quickly. I started rehearsing *The Crucible* in the evenings in order to catch up with my workmates, who had a two-week head start on me. I went straight from murderess to New England Puritan, without any transition, and then next morning I would be a murderess again at the Saint-Maurice studios, where the director, his wife, and I were no longer on speaking terms. Thank God, Meurisse and Vanel were on that set, and Jean Renoir on the set next door. He was making *French Cancan*. And they were having fun. *Les Diaboliques* made a fortune and Véra got her picture on the front page of *Match*. Georges Sadoul, who wasn't so finicky on this gruesome subject as he was on attacks on the working class which he discovered in *Casque d'Or*, wrote a delirious review. Of course, he did rectify things in his end-of-year roundup, deploring "the presence of our dear Simone Signoret in such an immoral film." But all that was much later. By then we had already been playing *The Crucible* for months.

Putting on *The Crucible*, with Montand and me playing the parts of the Rosenbergs-Proctors, in the middle of the cold war in an immense theater was an aberrant idea that stemmed from the Rumanian madness of Elvire Popesco

147

and A. M. Julien's good business sense. The Rumanian madness consisted of thinking that a music-hall singer and a movie star were capable of playing a tragedy. The business sense consisted of thinking that Montand-Signoret sounded like good box office, and might bring them in. The really bright idea was getting Rouleau to direct. That one was our idea. We read that first fine literal translation one night after a performance at the Étoile, in bed, passing the pages to each other. At five in the morning we had read it all. It was a shattering experience. Of course, we wanted to say yes the next morning to Elvire and Julien. We said, "Yes, on condition that Rouleau is the director." It was made clear, naturally, that Rouleau must really want to direct us. We didn't want to be "stars" hiring a director. But the first time we met, it was evident that Rouleau liked the play and liked the risk of working with famous beginners. From the moment he accepted the job, he became the boss of this enterprise that would have us onstage with that admirable play for a year. We really—all of us who shared in the adventure of *The Crucible*—owe it to him and to Lila de Nobili.

I must say that I was helped and protected to an extreme. I don't "project" on stage. I had learned in films to reduce my effects to a minimum; to use a glance or a gesture to convey meaning. All of a sudden, there I was in the Théâtre Sarah-Bernhardt, which is enormous! My part, Mrs. Proctor, was much less difficult than that of Nicole Courcel, for example, who had to rant and scream. Mrs. Proctor was a dignified Puritan lady who never raised her voice. It was a part in which what I had learned in films could serve me well, if we could learn how to master it. They mastered it very well. For example, Lila put a ceiling on the Act II set. She built me a little resonance box. That may not seem important, but it is. All the other actors were completely at ease on a stage. I wasn't. Lila's costumes were simple and authentic, and they helped me move. They were attractive but did not flatter, in the sense that they were severe, everyday clothes such as a farmer's wife who worked in the fields and in the house would wear. Work and the countryside were the themes Rouleau sought to bring out during rehearsals. The play was a forceful appeal against intolerance. For four acts there would be the apposition of serious themes: social, metaphysical, and sexual. Rouleau knew that when our costumes were ready, they would make us seem like subjects in a Dutch painting. He fought against the imminent danger that we would move like figures in an elegant engraving. Every day during the two months of rehearsal, he emphasized that all these people were poor farmers, recently arrived from England, upon soil they had to clear in order to cultivate. Raymond's choice of Pierre Mondy to play the Puritan pastor, ascetic, firm in his beliefs, torn asunder in his moment of doubt, was absolutely perfect for exactly these reasons. Someone else would have chosen an actor with a mystical aura, a tall, thin inquisitor with unctuous gestures. But with Pierrot—strapping, healthy, open, and jovial— the appearance of the inquisition was all the more terrifying because it had this simple, healthy aspect. And when the inquisitor realized too late that he had been dealing with an innocent Proctor, there was the sight of a decent man breaking up, terrified by his mistake. Nicole Courcel, blond, fresh-faced, and chubby at the time, looked like a healthy peasant girl. Her role as Abigail demanded that she be a black-hearted liar filled with amorous passion—and that was Raymond's other stroke of genius.

Another strong theme during rehearsals was a constant reminder of the forces of intolerance that we French had known during the occupation. Raymond made great use of the yellow star that from one day to the next had obligatorily appeared over the hearts of French Jews. He talked to the actors who played the judges about the special occupation tribunals, instituted by the Vichy government. He reminded us of all those anonymous letters that had piled up in the offices of the Gestapo. Rouleau's direction contained extraordinary political imagery. And of course, there was constant reference to the Rosenbergs.

There were seventeen actors on that stage, and I think that, with the exception of Montand and me, very few of them had much political awareness. Raymond didn't go out and systematically select left-wing actors. He took what he thought were the best actors for the parts. And one can't really say that before May 1968 the tribe of French actors had discovered a decided taste for political causes. One day someone asked whether Miller would come for the first night, and when Rouleau explained that Miller couldn't leave America for reasons that were exactly those we would be interpreting for four acts, it provoked almost unanimous surprise. I quote this example to show you to what extent this homogeneous and convincing cast was made up of people who in everyday life were far removed from political events. Actually, all that doesn't really matter. I have known left-wing actors who were excellent militants but not always very good actors. And there are ghastly reactionaries who are prodigious actors. But for Montand and for me, our profound conviction that the Rosenbergs were innocent was an enormous help. I could be Elizabeth Proctor because I believed Ethel Rosenberg to be innocent. I also knew that the real Mrs. Proctor had been named Mary, and that Miller had given her the name Elizabeth so that the couple's initials would be J and E, for Julius and Ethel.

I always refused to read Ethel Rosenberg's letters in public when, just after the execution, people organized "galas"—yes, that's what they were called—for the benefit of their children and to perpetuate their memory. I refused, knowing full well that I would have had a triumph. I'm sure I would have been admirable, because I cannot read *Deathhouse Letters* without being overwhelmed, so overwhelmed that I would certainly have overwhelmed my audience. I would have been applauded for doing my job well. When taking part in a "gala" you go to the hairdresser, choose a very simple, well-cut dress, do microphone tests, and check the lighting. You're just doing your job. And if you do it outstandingly well, you reap an enormous personal triumph. In this case my little triumph would have been made of material that was still warm: the life of someone who had just been assassinated. Nobody ever understood what I was really talking about when I explained this. And as I was anxious to avoid the misconception that I was afraid of compromising myself by participating in these evenings, I would go and read a very beautiful letter by Émile Zola, which Roger Pigaud suggested to me. It was called *Lettre à la Jeunesse*, and it has been enormously useful to me every time I get involved in this sort of event. Not a comma of it has aged in any way, and it was written over eighty years ago, at the time of the Dreyfus affair. Unfortunately, this letter is still relevant in all the countries of the world. Well, almost all.

I never read Ethel's letters in public. I read them alone. And it was because I had read them that I could with dignity temporarily transfer to Elizabeth Proctor the emotions they had evoked in me. I needed them only in the fourth act, because until then Elizabeth Proctor is an exemplary Puritan woman; she forbids herself to exteriorize even the faintest glow of the passion and tenderness that burn inside her. Raymond had a marvelous image for her: "She's like one of those desserts where there's a hard white ice cream that contains a boiling core of chocolate." (I don't know where he had ever eaten that, but it worked for me.) Therefore, until Act IV I was an iceberg. But in the fourth act, in the farewell scene between Proctor and his wife—which was also their first love scene after all those years of a marriage spoiled by their Puritanism and her frustration—I needed all the emotion I had. It took some time to dredge it up, all that emotion. I think it arrived only a week before the opening. All I needed then was to be able to tap it again every night—healthy, honest, profound and sincere—for three hundred and sixty-five performances.

The opening night was a triumph. A triumph for the play and for Marcel Aymé's adaptation; for the work of Raymond and Lila, and for the cast. It was an exceptional personal triumph for Montand, who had crossed the frontier from the music hall to the theater, and for Nicole and Mondy. And it seemed that I had passed my exam—cinema to theater—with a good mark. Not with the prize for excellence, but still with a good mark. All the critics were full of praise, from Gauthier in *Figaro* to Claude Roy in *L'Humanité-Dimanche*. All our friends took a deep breath. All of them admitted afterwards—Jacques Becker, Gérard Philipe, François Périer, Bernard Blier, Pierre Brasseur, José Artur, Danièle Delorme, and Serge Reggiani—that they had worried incessantly from the moment we had decided to play together in this difficult, sober, and politically engaged play. They believed that had it failed, we wouldn't have come out of the wreckage alive. In the case of a semi-success we would have emerged like a pitiful couple trying to teach others a lesson; and a *succès d'estime*, a salute to "the courage of the two big names who attempted this experiment which is greatly to their honor, but . . ." would have been catastrophic, especially for the equilibrium of life in the "caravan" on the Place Dauphine. But it wasn't like that at all. It was a triumph, a real one. That Rumanian madness paid off; and so did the business sense. Nicole got her *Match* cover. She abundantly deserved it.

And the audience bridged the gap from the Proctors to the Rosenbergs. The Rosenberg affair had moved people all over the world. Even the Pope had tried to intervene with Eisenhower. Raymond made us play the fourth act with our hands in chains. The kiss that Montand-Proctor gave me, imprisoning my shoulders with his chains, before he went off to be hanged, was the exact copy of a photograph of Julius and Ethel which had appeared in the world press.

I've said enough about how the image of this couple helped us to play our parts in all good faith. At the risk of repeating myself, let me say again that we probably would not have acted as passionately if, at the time, our consciences had been troubled by other dramas, on the other side of the world. They had said to the Rosenbergs, "Confess, and your lives will be saved." They did not confess and they were electrocuted. But to others—in Prague, for example—they were saying, "Explain to us in what manner you are guilty, and then ask us to sentence you to death." And they were killed. During that abominable time in American history Julius and Ethel Rosenberg were the only people condemned to death and executed without proof. But on the other side of the world a great many were killed for having supplied proof of the guilt that those who judged them knew did not exist. What I've just said is extremely serious. So is the subject matter. These are my thoughts today; I didn't have them at the time. We were all delighted we'd got it across, as actors generally are when the theater is full to bursting every evening.

Marcel Aymé, who had thoroughly intimidated me in the beginning, dropped into the habit of stopping by the theater every other day or so just to see us. He was no longer uptight. He talked. He was funny and tender. He was a free man. He had been "purged" at the Liberation, and then, a few years later, when officially listed for the Legion of Honor, he sent back the paper on which he was asked to reply carefully to all questions concerning his merits, with this brief sentence he was rather proud of: "Monsieur le Président de la République, you can go shove your medal." He easily admitted that his work of adaptation had been greatly facilitated by the superb literal translation that had been given to him. Marcel Aymé didn't speak a word of English, was proud of this fact, and had not tried to corrupt the play with inventions of his own which might have watered down or changed Miller's thought. He had simply used his talent to formulate the thought of another. He had changed one thing, however. He had introduced Mrs. Proctor at the end of Act I, when in the original she didn't appear until the beginning of Act II. I think he did that to test me. When I met him the first time, I asked him why he had made this change, and, eyes shyly downcast, he replied, "I felt that lady actresses, when they're stars, prefer to herald their arrival by making an appearance at the end of Act I." I told him he was wrong! After that, a warm dialogue, always punctuated by long silences, was established between us.

At the third performance, Sartre came to see the play. He came to our dressing room—the famous Sarah Bernhardt dressing room—saying, "This play was for me. Why didn't you ask me to do the adaptation?" We told him he'd better keep an eye on his secretarial staff.

I said that we performed that play for a year. It's true, but in fact we played it three hundred and sixty-five times over two separate six-month periods. In those days, the Sarah-Bernhardt was reserved for the Théâtre des Nations season during the summer. And it was during that summer of 1955, before we resumed the play in the autumn, that I went on my first trip to an Eastern country. More precisely, to East Berlin. And even more precisely, to Babelsberg, the ex-Hollywood of the Hitler era.

Chapter 7

WOLFGANG Staudte, who had made the first German postwar film, *The Murderers Are Among Us*, shot entirely in the still-smoking ruins of Berlin, and in which Hildegard Knef was superb, had come to Paris to ask me and Bernard Blier to act in Bertolt Brecht's *Mother Courage*. The producer was to be DEFA—which is the German Democratic Republic itself. Bernard would play the cook, and I Yvette, the French whore. All the other parts would be played by actors of the Berliner Ensemble, with, of course, Helene Weigel (Madame Brecht) in the leading role. The Berliner Ensemble had performed *Mother Courage* in Paris and it had been a triumph. In fact, the Berliner Ensemble was one of the best companies in the world, and it had been the East Germans' good fortune that Brecht had chosen their side of the border and not the other when he returned to the country where he was born. Since there was not yet a wall, first nights at the Theater am Schiffbauerdamm were the most coveted theater seats in both Germanys. Brecht was performed on both sides of the border, but the East Berliners were the prestigious group, and my pal Bernard and I were more than slightly proud to be invited to act with these people.

DEFA had huge sums at its disposal, as state productions do in socialist countries. They had turned out one or two very good films, such as Staudte's *Rotation* and *Der Untertan* (based on a story by Heinrich Mann); as well as ghastly Zhdanovian frescoes. None of these products had ever been shown outside the domestic circuits. With *Mother Courage* they wanted to enlarge their market, and they had gone shopping to get some names that were known in the West. Bernard and I were known in West Germany, and known together. *Dédée* and *Manèges* had been great successes. DEFA must have had confidence in the taste of its Western compatriots, because actually, I was hired blind. In East Germany no one had seen me in anything. I was completely unknown. Not the films of Allégret nor those of Becker or Carné or Clouzot had been considered worthy of showing to a German democratic audience. Now at last they would get an opportunity to discover me in my German-language debut. For a month I'd been hammering away at my lines. I studied my text. I had taken German as a second language in my last four years of school, and it came back to me quickly enough to permit me to learn the part intelligently. As for Bernard, he relied on what he remembered from when he was a POW. I left first, by train.

The train rolled along in the West, then passed over into the Eastern zone, went back to the West, and ended up in the East. When it stopped in the West Berlin station, I went to the window. On the platform I saw a rather nice-looking gentleman who was running like a madman. In one hand he held a huge bunch of flowers, in the other a placard bearing my name and my photograph. He turned out to be the biggest film distributor in West Berlin. He had come to welcome me onto German soil. He insisted that the entirety of the German people were pleased that I had come to participate in a work written by the greatest contemporary German dramatist. He didn't really know the people at

DEFA, but he was sure they were very nice. I should not hesitate to phone him if something wasn't right. . . . He gave me his card and my flowers and the train moved off, and after a while it arrived in the huge East Berlin station.

On the platform, a delegation awaited me, composed of the head of the studio and representatives of the Ministry of Culture, red carnations in hand. French actors loathe carnations. It is a stupid and persistent superstition. Scores of stories are told backstage and on film sets about the fateful carnation sent by a rival, causing a nosedive into the prompter's box or first-night memory dry-ups. Let's get this straight: There are throughout the world people who save pennies in order to offer carnations—an enormous luxury in countries where there is little sun—to ungrateful French actors who, when they see the aforementioned flower, think only about the grippe that will render them speechless or the airplane that will crash. So there were these carnations, and all those smiling faces, happy to finally see at last, in the flesh, someone they had never seen on film. Among all these officials there was one woman, Rosaura Revueltas, the Mexican star of *Salt of the Earth*, a film I will talk about later. She was there, I think, to promote that film.

When the contract was being negotiated, they had very courteously inquired whether I wanted West marks. No, I'd take East marks. Did I want to live on the Kurfürstendamm in the West while filming? No, I wanted to live in the East. If I was going to work in the East, I wanted to live in the East. So I was put in a car and sent to Babelsberg. Babelsberg was the Beverly Hills of the German equivalent of Hollywood when it was run by UFA. Now it was run by DEFA, and the villas of the UFA stars and the big Nazi industrialists had been given over to the artists, writers, and directors of the German Democratic Republic. The biggest and handsomest of them, which had belonged to Siemens, had become a *Gasthaus* (inn). It was located in a narrow and most elegant street, overlooking the lake; it even had its own little harbor. There was a long dining table big enough for all the guests—mostly actors, some of whom had come from the West to work with DEFA. Fräulein Erika, who was great fun, was headwaitress, governess, and switchboard operator of this establishment.

The first night, when I arrived, I asked them to call Autheuil. I had left behind, for the coming four weeks, Montand, Catherine, Becker, José Artur, and the Périers. Despite our sad adieus, they were doubtless relieved at my departure. My efforts to revitalize my German (I wanted to arrive knowing my lines to a T) had rather spoiled their holiday. You are cute and conscientious and darned lucky to go and play Brecht in the original. So buzz off, play your part, and then come back to us after you've done it. No, we can't give you your cues in a language we don't know—we just can't! That was just about the tone in Autheuil before I left. So I wanted to reassure my little family, as one does after a long trip across frontiers, but then Fräulein Erika explained to me that one could call only East Berlin. Yet within fifteen minutes the whole thing was arranged. I don't know who Fräulein Erika contacted after my obvious surprise at finding myself cut off from my own little world. So I spoke to Autheuil. And during the entire time I spent in East Germany I could phone whomever I wanted wherever I wanted.

The elegant alley on which the *Gasthaus* was situated was closed off by a wooden stockade. It kept out people from the lakeshore, about a hundred meters away. It had been erected some ten meters from the *Gasthaus* entrance, so in order to get to the house you had to pass this little frontier. It had its own customs officer in the person of a young people's policeman. He had erected a very pretty little sentry box and had the companionship of a beautiful German shepherd dog. Had I been an avid reader of anti-Communist propaganda, I would have had my fill that evening when I arrived. But I was not that sort of person. I understood. I had crossed West Berlin and I had crossed East Berlin. In the West I had seen all the lights, the neon; I had seen the reconstruction. I knew it was all done with

American money. I'd had the time to see that things weren't cheerful in the East. That didn't bother me. After all, the Russians didn't have the same means or the same reasons to make the presents the Americans had made. The ex-Nazis, whom an accident of geography had suddenly transformed into militant socialists, had to pay through the nose. I had insisted on living in the East because, in a very childish fashion, I really believed that throughout the Eastern bloc (I had seen all those brochures, indifferently tinted but still luxurious), everything was exchangeable. I thought everything was traded. I thought I would find Chinese pineapples that had been swapped for Polish coal, splendid Zeiss eyeglasses exchanged for Ukrainian wheat, Russian caviar exchanged for Hungarian uranium. So even though it bothered me, I found excuses for this wooden stockade, which was, nonetheless, a little wall. After all, the West was two kilometers away; they were vigilant and rightly so. And then, here in Babelsberg there would be this marvelous script, a good director, and splendid actors; and it was in this frame of mind that I greet my old friend Bernard Blier, who had opted for life in the East for the duration of the film.

And then we began to work. Bernard and I both fell in love with the director. He loved his actors, and had good reason to do so. He was the son of an actor and had acted himself in his youth. He had even been one of Professor Rath's students in *The Blue Angel*, and he liked to tell how all the "schoolboys" noticed Jannings's growing anxiety as the part of Lola grew in importance during the film's progress, when he had fondly imagined that his character was the only important role in the film. Staudte lived in West Berlin and worked for the Bavaria studio in the West as well as DEFA in the East. He had hired us because he had seen us act. He had also recruited Max Douy, one of France's best set designers. And on the huge, perfectly equipped stages, Max had built superb weird and desolate sets, suggesting war—all wars!

The Berliner Ensemble told us about their lives. It was

nothing like anything we knew. The actors were completely looked after. Being broke and out of work simply didn't
exist for them. They sometimes would rehearse a play for
six months, or even nine, if that was what Brecht wanted.
They had music, dance, and mime courses at their
disposal. Naturally, they played what they were given, but
since it was generally Brecht, they were very pleased. They
would, of course, have liked to be better known
throughout the world. The films they occasionally made
were distributed only in the Eastern zone. In the West,
people like Peter Schalle or Geschoneck would have been
big movie stars.

The gentleman who was the distributor in the West very
rapidly resurfaced. The Western cinematographic press
wanted to interview us, Bernard and me, and hear our first
impressions of work in the East. We accepted on condition
that the Eastern press be admitted to the conference. They
accepted this condition, and it became a small moment of
significance in the history of the two Germanys: the first
time since the 1949 separation that journalists from the two
Berlins were in the same room asking questions—except
for the Cannes and Venice film festivals. There we were, in
the middle of West Berlin, in the salon of the Kempinski
Hotel. It was a very friendly, warm occasion. Of course,
the first questions dealt with the reasons for our stipulation:
Why had we brought them together? We explained that we
didn't have two sets of brains, one for the East and one for
the West; consequently our answers to their questions
would be the same for both sides. When more questions
came, they were neither perfidious nor dangerous. They
were the sort of questions journalists ask film actors
anywhere in the world.

Then we dined with the Staudtes, hung around awhile,
and then went back along the highway that crossed the
borders of both Germanys twice. When we arrived in
Babelsberg it was a little after midnight. The young
people's policeman, followed by his big bowwow, came
out of his sentry box and refused to open the locked gate of

the little wooden wall. It was at this moment that all the German Bernard had learned in Silesia rose to his memory. It didn't sound like Brecht. He roared in the middle of that elegant alley (I could even make out some French): "...fucking bastard...shits...for four years...." Here and there a window lighted up. Fräulein Erika came out and negotiated with the policeman behind the stockade. At last the young hero of the people allowed the new heroes of the East-West reconciliation to go home to bed.

Our little incident had caused some comment along the alley, and its echoes obviously traveled farther. The next day the Minister of Culture sent us a message apologizing for what had happened; it wouldn't happen again. Nonetheless, Bernard racked his bags and emigrated to the West, having glimpsed the charms of the Kempinski the day before. I stayed on. I had a nice room, I had made friends among the other guests, and I was near the studio. And I went on trying to understand.

What I never managed to understand was the interruption of the film. One bright day we were told that Helene Weigel didn't want to go on. Every actress who had ever played Courage anywhere in the world was contacted. But no one was willing to replace her. I had a few scenes left to do. Some of them included Courage, and we made them without a partner. The script girl read Weigel's lines, and the chief cameraman asked me to direct my eyes as if at someone around medium height, because they didn't know the size of the new Courage.

There was never a new Courage. This was 1955. Stalin was dead, all right, but a great many things still hadn't been settled. I was to learn later that Brecht's life had not always been easy in this country where his honest insolence and his courage sometimes led him to write things that displeased the powers that be.

I had finished playing Yvette. So I went home to take up *The Crucible* stage production. The day before my departure, the Minister of Culture gave me a long audience. He wished to excuse himself once again for the incidents. He was grateful that neither Bernard nor I had circulated the story about the locked stockade. I must say, at the time, a newspaper headline something like "Two French Actors Prohibited from Going Home after Midnight in the Eastern Zone" would have been quite a scoop. . . . He asked me please not to carry home a bad impression of my stay. They were beginning something new and they were making beginners' mistakes. Would I please come back one day, whenever I wanted to; would I please not hesitate to propose any film I might like to make—I would always be welcome, whenever I wanted. None of this fell on deaf ears. And it was because of these last words that a Borderie-DEFA coproduction deal for *The Crucible* was signed up a little while later. The film was to be made in July of the following year, the year 1956.

As soon as it was obvious to us that the play was a great success, we had considered the possibility of making it into a film. I don't think the film would ever have been made without the DEFA contribution. The negotiations were held in Paris. The Germans offered to take charge of the locations, the extras, the large sets, and the horses—all the things that were most expensive. In return, Borderie kindly offered us, but as Montand and I had agreed to take a percentage, his *beau geste* was rather symbolic. Raymond Rouleau was hired to direct. And Sartre was to be the screenwriter. Marcel Aymé had fully understood that for us to film these characters we had been playing onstage for such a long time, fresh dialogue was indispensable. The production dates were arranged to fit in with our schedule. We would finish doing the play in December. I had already signed an agreement with Buñuel to do a film with him in Mexico in spring, and Montand had agreed to do a film in Italy with De Santis as soon as he was finished with the play in Paris. Rarely have I see film negotiations conducted as quickly and as simply for a project that was to take shape several months later. The top and tail filming dates were of capital importance. A year and a half earlier Montand had signed an agreement, through l'Agence Littéraire et

Artistique, to do a huge month-long recital tour in the Soviet Union (Moscow-Leningrad-Kiev) and then one week in each of the socialist republics. He was to leave at the end of October 1956, and was to be accompanied by his wife, seven musicians, and a couple of lighting supervisors. L'Agence Littéraire et Artistique was, and perhaps still is, the only organization authorized to arrange tours in the Eastern countries, and its clients included the Comédie Française, the Théâtre National Populaire (TNP), and the Opéra. It had already spent two years working toward an East-West cultural rapprochement. One of the heads of this agency is Georges Soria. He is an agent and a writer (writers consider him an agent and agents consider him a writer). It was he who arranged this long tour, and there was no question of budging the dates. Period.

At the end of negotiations between DEFA, Rouleau, and Borderie, it had been agreed that the film absolutely had to be finished in mid-October at the latest. Once the terms had been agreed upon, the participants each went their separate ways. *"Prosit!"* *"À la votre!"* replied Borderie, who'd just concluded a very smart deal.

La Mort en Ce Jardin is surely not Buñuel's greatest film, but the three months that Michel Piccoli, Charles Vanel, and I spent on location in Mexico were an unforgettable vacation. Maybe this is true for Georges Marchal too, but as I have hardly seen him since, I haven't had a chance to reminisce with him, as I still do today with Vanel and Piccoli or Colette Crochot, the script girl. In the first place, there was Buñuel. Every actor who has ever worked with him has said the same thing; if you spend a day with Don Luis it's not like work, it's fun. It's like having fun with Becker or laughing with Picasso. And then there was Oscar—Oscar Danciger, the most Russian of Mexican producers, just as he had been the most Russian of French producers, after having been the most Russian of émigrés. The most Russian of charming Russians.... My thoughts stray also to Kessel and Tolo Litvak: All three know how to hum "Kalitka" ("the little gate at the bottom of the garden"). And then there were my two accomplices, Vanel and Piccoli, and some stupid and wonderful jokes, and those fights that began with throwing glassfuls of water at each other and ended with pailfuls. And finally, there was Mexico. I defy anyone not to fall in love with Mexico—and I don't mean the scenery, I mean the people. If that seems to you like romantic folklore, so much the better; folklore is sometimes all right, when it expresses something real, by which I mean when it's applied to the people. And long live the marvels of the Day of the Dead, even if there are firecrackers cracking off all over town while you suffer a terrible toothache—from a tooth which, incidentally, no longer belongs to you anymore because it's been yanked out by a charming political refugee, who is also a quack. Long live the little eleven-year-old shoeshine boy who refuses your glass of lemonade because he is a man, and a man doesn't allow a lady to pay for his drink. And long live the Mexicans, who hadn't an ambassador for the Spain of Generalissimo Franco. Long live the huge hats, trumpets, and guitars of the mariachis whom your friends bring along to serenade you on the day of your departure, and who play "La Gondoleria" and make you cry. Qué viva Mexico!

It was during the cracking of firecrackers, the clicking heels of bamba dancers, and the twanging of the guitars, all going on a few paces from where Trotsky's assassin lived in high style in prison, or so we were told, that the rumor of a report, not "attributed to Khrushchev" but "signed Khrushchev," reached us. It was lengthily commented upon by a bunch of old Spanish Republicans, Buñuel's friends, who met regularly to recount the battle of Teruel. They were all left-wing veterans of the POUM, the FAI, or the Communist party. For the past eighteen years they had met to talk about their lost war, and for eighteen years they had quarreled affectionately over glasses of tequila. That day, a great many things in their past were explained, and even justified. Stalin had not been what some people had thought; Stalin had been what others had said that he was. "Qué viva Khrushchev!"

On the other side of the world, in the Abruzzi and in the snow, Montand was listening to Italian commentary. For there, too, the report was not "attributed to" but well and truly *"firmato"* Khrushchev. The crew was mainly Communist, and as Gramsci had written, "Only the truth is revolutionary," the comrades decided that Comrade Khrushchev had shown the courage of a true revolutionary. I was not there; Montand told me about it.

I came back from Mexico, he returned from the Abruzzi. We were getting ourselves ready to shoot *The Crucible*. We were both in a really good mood. We were going to arrive in the Eastern countries with another point of view; there were mysteries and ambiguities which no longer existed. The bitterness of having been deceived for so many years was counterbalanced by the satisfaction of having been right sometimes, when we hadn't swallowed some of the grass snakes I've mentioned earlier. You may imagine our surprise when we came back to Paris and realized that the French Communists' reactions were not exactly the same as in other countries: In Paris the report was "attributed to," and its contents contested.

A whole army of French occupied the *Gasthaus* to make *The Crucible*. Fräulein Erika was still there, but the wooden stockade had disappeared. The Rouleaus had brought their children and we had brought Catherine. We took over the entire inn. There was Claude Renoir, the chief cameraman, and his crew; Mylène Demongeot, playing Courcel's role, and Alex, for all our hair and beards. There was no makeup artist; Rouleau, Lila de Nobili, and Renoir wanted us to be absolutely true-to-life seventeenth-century Puritans, without powder or false eyelashes. By the way, none of us had been made up onstage at the Sarah-Bernhardt, either; when there was an appropriate moment, we would be embellished by the lighting, nothing else. There were some frisky mornings on the Baltic shore when a little touch of the brush applied by Monique, Alex's wife—the makeup artist accompanying her husband on location but forbidden to work—would have given Mrs. Proctor, who'd been through so much, that comforting flush of beauty we all need when the camera comes in for the big close-ups. But there wasn't a brushful of mascara or a touch of crayon. We were the way we were every day at seven in the morning. As farmers were and probably always will be when they're over the age of twenty and are going out for a day's work.

Sartre's script was Sartrian but entirely faithful to Miller's play. It was, in fact, the result of a long correspondence between Miller and Sartre during its whole preparation. Miller still didn't have a passport (he was to get it back shortly, but that's another story—a love story). Sartre wasn't willing to go to America, and so they conferred by letter. Sartre's script delved more deeply into the real historical and social situation that was lived by those New England pioneers. They had all arrived equally poor, but already a few years later social barriers were starting to go up between those who had once been poor and those who were still poor. There were those who had chosen good land and those who had had bad luck. There were those who worked harder than others. There were those who were honest, and those who were less so. In short, within a very brief time there were the social superiors, and the others. All this had been said or was felt in Miller's play. The play fascinated people because the action told in four acts an abominable drama whose premises were externalized by words. Now we had to *show* people. We had to move out of the three walls of the proscenium. We had to go and show those huge estates, or those patches of land, depending on whether people were rich or poor. And we were going to enter that church they talked so much about in the play and see that there, too, the rich had their pews and the poor had theirs—and the

Negroes their designated places in the back, standing, with the dogs....

The black extras were recruited among the African students at the University of Leipzig. They were very pleased with the idea of being in a film—up to the moment when Raymond courteously asked them to take their places among a pack of big dogs. At which point they protested, left the church, and gathered in the main street of that town of Salem entirely constructed by Lila twenty kilometers away from the studio. It appeared that they had left their sunny native soil for the fogs of Leipzig in order to study chemistry, political science, German, and above all, Marxism, but certainly not to find themselves dressed in rags and standing among dogs behind a group of seated well-dressed whites. Then began a long explanation by Raymond of Miller's text and Sartre's philosophy, which ended with vibrant declarations of anti-apartheid. Then he went back to the beginning: The film we were making was in effect a brick in the edifice being created throughout the world, thanks to the good faith of men and women of all races and colors and complexions and philosophies, against intolerance wherever it raises its head, etc., etc., etc. It was the United Nations.... The African students were not idiots. They agreed to go back to their places, remarking as they went, not without irony, that contrary to what some might think, they did know how to read, and if someone had thought of sending a copy of the script to Leipzig, it would certainly have saved the producers time and money.

The white extras were recruited from among the citizens of the German Democratic Republic. There were a great many of them; DEFA really did its job very well, and Borderie had every reason to be pleased. The ladies and gentlemen of the little town of Salem arrived by bus in the morning. They were punctual, docile, and never asked embarrassing questions. They did everything they could to be cooperative. The days when we needed a big crowd,

Raymond would use a megaphone to direct his little army. Then you would hear his splendid voice wafted across the German plains, saying *"Ruhe, bitte—Konzentration"* (an abridged literal translation of his favorite expression: *"Allons, mes enfants, un peu de concentration, je vous en prie"*). In other words, "Come on, kids, let's have some concentration!"

There came the day when Proctor, Rebecca Nurse, and Martha Corey were to be hanged. The DEFA carpenters had constructed a huge scaffold; they had made it quite solid, as if made to last a long time. The prop people had made harnesses for Montand, Jeanne Fusier-Gir, and Marguerite Coutand-Lambert. Invisible strings attached the harness to the scaffold so that neither my husband, nor our lovely old Jeanne, nor our kind Marguerite would be stupidly hanged by mistake when the stools upon which they had climbed so the ropes could be put around their necks were removed. The whole population of Salem was gathered, and followed the rehearsals. The harnesses held, the cameras could roll, and Raymond had called for his beloved *"Konzentration."* At that moment there arose a kind of whisper from the crowd, and soon the whisper became a discussion.

Raymond repeated, *"Ruhe, bitte—Konzentration."* A spokesman came forward. He wished to alert Herr Rouleau to the fact that there was a slight difference between him and six of his *Genossen* (a *Genosse*, in East Germany, is a colleague; a *Kamerad* is a companion at arms). It was this: They could not agree on the manner in which Montand's feet, which were bare, should play their last scene after the stool had been removed. Montand's feet were not twitching correctly; there was a certain way, and no other, in which feet twitched after the hanged man was already deceased. He wished to present his excuses to Herr Montand, and he would be happy to show him, with his hands, how Proctor's feet should twitch. His six companions were also eager to help, so that this hanging would be immune to attack from the point of view of veracity. It appeared that all the hanged people that they had seen had not behaved in exactly the same fashion. From which arose the discussion.

Fourteen hands were lifted in the service of art, technique, and truth. They grew stiff. The fingers moved slowly apart. Some crossed and, for the space of a moment, fluttered like butterflies' wings. All this happened until each one, in its manner, achieved a graceful relaxation signifying that this time, finally, it was finished. Our technical advisers finally went back to their places. No one, among the French population of Salem, could fault them. Rouleau chose an amalgam of several methods. Then, he didn't repeat "*Konzentration*"; he simply said: "Roll." And that was the way Proctor was hanged: correctly, in the way any decent hanging should be undertaken everywhere in the world.

All this took time. DEFA's stagehands and electricians were remarkably serious and effective, but often what Claude Renoir wanted had to be translated. That took time. Sometimes Raymond had to tell a duck or a horse, both German, what he wanted them to do. Although this was done in German, it wasn't always understood as quickly as one might have liked. Catherine got the measles; Montand, Demongeot, and I spelled one another to take care of her, depending upon who was to be in front of the cameras. When all three of us were working, Fräulein Erika kindly powdered her for us. Not all of us lived in the *Gasthaus*, so a complicated transportation system between East Berlin and Babelsberg was organized. That took time. Borderie had thought that we would be able to film many of the more important things with means furnished on location than had been foreseen during the negotiations. Scenes that were to have been done in a Paris studio were done instead in the studios of DEFA. It was more economical, but it took more time. Actors we had thought we would need only in Paris suddenly had to be in Babelsberg; it had taken time to organize that. But we weren't really aware of the time passing because we laughed a lot. It's not indecent to laugh a lot when you're in the process of filming a tragedy. A company that laughs at the same things in real life while they are making a grave and serious film finds the right accent at the right moment for the story it is telling. If you can't laugh together off the set, you can't cry together, or make people cry.

So we didn't notice time passing, and that was a mistake. We laughed a lot, and that was not a mistake, because we weren't going to laugh much longer, Montand and I. October 1956 was with us. The film wasn't finished. As I've already told you, the day for our dovetailed departure to the Eastern world was a date that couldn't be budged.

We had exhausted all the DEFA resources: the horses, the crowds, the huge open spaces, and the white sands of the Baltic, where amber could still be found. One morning Fräulein Erika said good-bye to us all. We kissed; it was a little sad. The *Gasthaus* would go back to its habitual calm. We would go back to Paris and the studio on the Rue Francoeur. What remained to be done were the less costly scenes from the point of view of sets and extras, but the ones that were the most difficult to act. Quickly, very quickly, it became abundantly clear that we would never finish in time for Montand to meet his contractual obligations for the tour.

So one afternoon, still wearing our Puritan costumes, seated in Borderie's office at Pathé, we broke it to Soria that we would have to delay the tour for about a month. That meant turning everything upside down. It was a little like changing an entire railroad timetable. Two hours later the Russians called from Moscow. They were very upset, but they understood. It would be very complicated, but we must, of course, finish our film. The Soviet audiences were waiting for Montand as they had waited for the Comédie Française and the TNP. Not to worry; they would arrange everything. We heaved a sigh of relief. We would be able to go on working. We no longer had to badger Raymond with "Hurry up; we've got to finish."

These phone calls were made around the second week in October; thus we would be ready to leave the second week of November. It gave us the time to concentrate on the most moving scenes in the film. We concentrated.

At the same time as we were submerged deep into our characters, we were taken up by thoughts as superficial as worrying about where we would find heavy coats and lined boots that would see us through the intense cold of Moscow. These two different lines of thought meant that we weren't following international news with an attentive eye. Around mid-October came the Polish revolt. Newspapers were passed around the set. We had all just come back from East Germany, and thus everyone had his own opinion about what he had liked or detested in a socialist regime. The Germans we had met there never mentioned their own rebellion, in Potsdam, a few years earlier. It had been put down very quickly. It was true that the police had fired on the workers, but that was one of the errors of the past that Khrushchev had talked about so well. . . . Actually, in Babelsberg we talked very little politics; we talked cinema.

On *The Crucible* set on the Rue Francoeur we also talked cinema. Then, suddenly, the one subject was Poland. There were three days of intense worry. In the end the Poles won the round: The Russian tanks would not enter Warsaw; Gomulka reappeared and with him the hope of a new liberty that seemed to accord with the report "attributed to." Everyone let out a sigh of relief. The French loved the Poles, and the Poles to their great credit still loved the French, who'd dropped them so coolly in 1939.

So the set became the house of Proctor once more, and the "caravan" a rehearsal room in the evenings. Montand had not sung for two years. It was exhausting for him to be Proctor all day and a singing and dancing Montand a good part of the night. We began to curse the German horses and ducks that had not obeyed Raymond's orders quickly enough and so had caused our lateness. It was their fault that we were in this situation, or rather it was their fault we were still here rather than in Moscow.

Finally November came. You remember November 1956. I say this very seriously. November 1956 shook the world, sowed death in Budapest and in Suez. November 1956 made millions of good people despair and delighted a good many bastards. For Montand and me, November 1956 was the most absurd, the most cruel, the saddest and most destructive month of our twenty-seven years of life together.

Budapest exploded on the set, if I may express it this way, as the last hours of October expired. Right at the beginning of November, Budapest burst into flames throughout the world. Budapest burned because the Russians had sent in their tanks to quell what some called a revolution and others called a counterrevolution, and which may have been neither one nor the other at the start. Within a few days the French battalions had chosen sides. The defenders of the Hungarian "revolutionaries" paraded up the Champs Élysées led by Georges Bidault, Maître Tixier-Vignancour, and Maître Biaggi,° laying a wreath before the grave of the Unknown Soldier for the glory of the revolution. The ardent defenders of the Soviet army, whose tanks were in the process of shooting down Hungarians, paraded on the grand boulevards shouting: "Fascism won't get through." They were, of course, both persuaded that they were right. Some remembered that the Hungarians had been the allies of Hitler's Germany right to the end of the war. Others quoted verses of Petöfi, the great revolutionary poet, which they had read in *Match* for the first time in their lives the week before. If we'd liked the Poles two weeks earlier, now we adored the Hungarians. Paris had two shock battalions. Their objectives were clear, but their tears came from the crocodile. I think the only real tears were shed by those who were desperately trying to understand and who could

°Well-known right-wing activist lawyers.

not. They were members of the third battalion. The pains in the ass. The left-wing intellectuals. Not so much a battalion as a light squadron, they included Sartre, Vercors, Claude Roy, Gérard Philipe, and Roger Vailland, among others, and they signed a manifesto denying "the right to protest what was happening in Hungary to those who had not lifted their voices the year before when Guatemala had been crushed."

There were huge meetings of the peace movement, to which we belonged. And there was an explosion within the movement. I will never forget that Sunday afternoon. The meeting took place in a conference room which, strangely enough, was in the house where Philippe Henriot° had been gunned down during the occupation. There were a great many people. Vercors had begun his book *Pour Prendre Congé*. He delivered a superb speech in which he said he had been an exhibition piece for a long time, happy to be a splendid exhibition piece exhibited on special occasions; he had been an exhibition piece at the time of the Rosenbergs, but now he felt he could no longer continue being an exhibition piece. . . . We, too, had been exhibition pieces; sometimes we had been up on the shelf all by ourselves, where we looked just fine. Our thoughts were exactly the same as those of Vercors, only I think we were the only people in our particular situation in that Sunday afternoon audience.

I realize that there is something indecent about lingering on our small problems in the midst of a historic tragedy. We were sad and upset, and upset and sad, but above all, we were very deeply in a fucking mess. . . .

The film wasn't finished, and we were thus "findable." All one had to do was go to the Rue Francoeur and we could be found. The set on which we were trying to act became a waiting room for delegations of advice-givers, who buttonholed us between two takes. This tour of the East, signed up a year and a half earlier, benefited from

° A collaborationist.

widespread publicity of a somewhat flattering nature when it was announced. So everyone knew that we were due to leave, and everyone took it upon himself either to make us go or to make us stay. Both shock battalions came to lean on us. There was a cartoon by Sennep on the front page of the *Figaro* that showed Khrushchev on the telephone, saying: "Send the tanks to Paris if necessary, but Yves Montand must sing." The night before, the Olympia Theater had capitulated to the threats of a fascist group that promised to set fire to the hall if Montand sang a gala performance that was to have been his final rehearsal in front of an audience. Wearing long faces, the Olympia management came to the set on the Rue Francoeur, where Montand, wearing his Proctor costume, was requested not to change into his stage clothes for the performance, and to stay at home. Montand insisted that the radio station that was to broadcast this performance "live" announce every hour why it would not take place, so no one would think that he had backed out. Which it did!

And Montand's musicians often appeared on the set. They had been hired a long time before for a tour that was to last four months. It had already been pushed back a month, and they had refused work in order to be free for Montand. They were sorry about the mess Montand was in. What was going to happen? The musicians were hired and paid by Montand. They were to be paid in French francs while Montand was paid in Eastern currency. The whole tour was more for prestige than it was for money. At the time of the agreement, no one suspected how the tour would turn tragically sour. The musicians weren't very keen on the scheme, but they said, after all, a contract is a contract. And by the way, they had decided to double their fees if Montand did decide to go. That may have been their way of urging him not to go. On the other hand, if Montand decided not to go, he still owed them their pay for four months.

One morning I woke up with an idea that seemed to be luminously intelligent. It was November 7. I remember the precise date because November 7 is the day the October Revolution is celebrated at the Russian Embassy, and Louis Aragon, Elsa Triolet, and her sister Lily Brik had just left there when they rang the "caravan" doorbell in response to an invitation from me that morning. Here was my idea: Get hold of Aragon quickly and ask him to ask the Russians to ask us to put off our tour until a little later, when things had cooled down. The point was that the request should come from them. I had just learned that they had canceled the departure of their own artists who were to perform in foreign capitals where they might be exposed to their audiences' political anger. If they were aware of the danger for their own, they should be equally concerned for those who were coming. The Russian Embassy's walls on the Rue de Grenelle might be very thick, but still something must have filtered through of the attacks Montand was being exposed to in Paris. And since Aragon had just come from there, I asked him please to go back and see the ambassador; to be an ambassador himself. To be the ambassador of a man upon whom was being imposed militant party discipline when he didn't belong to the party.

During all the years I lived with Allégret, the Aragons never recognized me. Whenever I was introduced to them they always seemed to be searching their memories . . . but no, really, they just couldn't place me. Four or five times in three years they managed not to remember. It saddened me a bit because though Aragon had never seen me act, I nonetheless had read and reread all his works. But as soon as I began living with Montand, I was suddenly worthy of being recognized as the wife of the great popular singer, and in my own right as a dramatic artist. One day I asked him why, for so many years, he had seemed unable to recognize me. His bright blue eyes shining with malice, he explained it was just *because* he recognized me that he didn't want to know me. I was living with a man who had been Trotsky's secretary in 1935, and he couldn't allow himself to shake hands with a woman who was the companion of a Trotskyite. Since everyone was in a good humor that day, we counted up which hands one could and which hands one could not shake in the city of Paris.

We never saw much of Aragon, but when we did see him, it tended to be around the time of some cultural event, when he would come to ask one or the other or both of us whether we wouldn't like to take part.

So the three of them came in. It was late. Lily Brik, who had come from Moscow to spend a few autumn days with her sister Elsa and her brother-in-law Louis, was quite displeased by the atmosphere that reigned in the streets of Paris. The ambassador's cocktail party, it appeared, had not had the social brilliance of preceding years. Many of the people who had been invited had denied themselves the privilege of drinking vodka and eating the excellent caviar that they had appreciated in other circumstances. In short, Lily's trip to Paris had been disappointing. Elsa asked for tea; she had a cold. All these events upset her, and Aragon admitted that the situation was grave. It was at this moment that I launched into my speech about the mission I wished to entrust to him. Only he could go to Vinogradov, the ambassador, and ask him to send a cable to Moscow explaining Montand's situation, and asking them to take the decision that would relieve him of the responsibility of abiding by his contract at any cost. Montand, who was exhausted by the filming and the late-night rehearsals, had gond to bed. Aragon's beautiful blue eyes grew sad. He understood, of course, but he was only a French poet, and he really couldn't take it upon himself to get involved with Soviet affairs. . . . Yes, of course, he was a member of the Central Committee of the French Communist party, and he knew very well that neither of us belonged. Yes, of course, it was all very sad, but one had to remain strong in the face of the reactionaries. . . . In short, he couldn't be the bearer of the message. And even if he could, he wouldn't have done it. There was only one solution for Montand: He must go. He had to, that was all. There was a long silence. Elsa and Lily, who had surely seen plenty during their lives as Soviet citizens, said nothing. I felt like crying. At which point Aragon, following heaven knows what series of associations, started making a long speech about Claudel, the well-known poet-ambassador.

I can't remember what he said about Claudel. I wasn't listening. My scheme had gone askew. Montand was quite alone. No one was going to give him a helping hand. The Aragons finally left, saying, "Well, be brave and bon voyage."

On the television screen, pictures of Budapest in flames and interviews with people who had crossed the border were shown much more often than anything to do with Suez. The kidnapping of Ben Bella and his four pals was treated as a huge joke. The smile of the stewardess and the laughter of the pilot who had been assigned to reroute the plane were on all the screens and in all the newspapers. Pedrazzini, a *Match* reporter, was killed in Budapest; Jean Roy, a *Match* reporter, was killed in Suez. In Paris, the two shock battalions made more and more noise, and never in the history of show business had a variety singer-actor and a film actress–nonsinger been the object of such attention.

Sartre said, "If you go, you stand surety for the Russians; if you stay, you stand surety for the reactionaries." We knew that. But he, contrary to Aragon, didn't give us advice. We were flooded with threatening letters and encouraging letters. The first were disgusting and often scatological. The second were often irritating because of their hidebound sectarianism. After a while, our only normal relationships were on the set, among people we had been working with for months and who had been involved almost hourly in the evolution of this impossible situation.

One day in mid-November, the world's most famous newly-wed appeared at the Rue Francoeur. Arthur Miller had finally come to meet the Proctors. He found them not at all gay. He wasn't gay, either. The American left-wing intellectuals had no reason for being joyful then. We were meeting for the first time, and yet it was as though we

177

already knew each other. By then we had been living with characters of his invention for two years, so he, Montand, and I already knew each other well. He may not have been gay, but he was warm and handsome, and he spent the day with us and then went back to London to Marilyn, whom he promised to bring to see us if we didn't leave.

Finally we did leave. What made the decision was the famous drop of water that caused the pail to overflow. Montand had signed a contract to do *Modigliani* with Max Ophuls. The film was to be made after the tour was over. One morning Deutschmeister, the producer, phoned and said, "If you sing over there, the film's off. My backers and distributors have told me that if you go they want no part of any film you're in." I hadn't been listening on the extension, but from the other side of the room I looked at Montand. He was very serious and very calm, and then he said, "I haven't been sure whether I was going or not, but now it's very simple: I am going." That was it.

Two months later, when we were in Leningrad, we received a telegram from Gérard Philipe asking Montand whether he ought to accept the Modigliani role. Montand replied that he should do what he felt was best. We were in Belgium when we learned of Ophuls's death in March 1957. In the end Becker made what was later entitled *Montparnasse 19*. Jeanson wrote the script. As for the producer (now no longer with us) who had phoned Montand, he produced a film called *Normandie-Niémen*, the first Franco-Soviet coproduction. . . .

Thus, we were leaving. It had been decided. We finished *The Crucible*, and over a little farewell drink to celebrate the end of the film, we all said good-bye to one another.

It only remained for us to pack our bags, and to get hold of those boots and coats which had ceased to be our favorite subject of conversation since the beginning of that abominable month of November. What should have been a happy shopping trip became a terrible burden. In the stores everyone knew we weren't off to the Alps for a skiing trip. . . . There are really moments of life when the old popular saying "It isn't written on your face" loses all its charm and meaning. My old friend Monsieur Capobianco, to whom I wish to pay tribute, made me two pairs of fur-lined boots in record time. He came to the house to try them on and attempted to comfort me. I needed it. I cried all the time. Catherine was ten years old; she had laughed with us in Babelsberg, and she couldn't understand why suddenly everything was so sad around the house. I went to see the principal of her school, a wonderful principal such as you read about in the nineteenth-century novels, who promised me she would watch out to make sure that Catherine wasn't plagued by the other children because of us. She also promised to allow her to stay home if this occurred. She embraced me and wished us bon voyage. Once more there were tears. The more I cried, the more Montand remained calm and resolute. During the week before we left, the house was never less than full. It was like the house of someone gravely ill; people keep coming for news or because they think they've found just the miracle medicine. It was devastating. Everything was devastating: the solicitude of some and the hatred of others. One evening Montand sat down in front of a sheet of paper, and we wrote an open letter to Obraztsov, the director of the marionette theater in Moscow. I've found the text. Here it is:

Paris,
December 3, 1956

My dear Obraztsov,

You and your troupe and the Moiseyev Ballet of Moscow are among those who have contributed most to a cultural rapprochement between our two countries, and consequently to a détente; if for no other reason than the success you had in Paris.

As far as I personally am concerned, you have made it possible for the Soviet audience to know my work, and if today people hum my songs in the streets, it is thanks to your godfatherly help.

This is why I chose to send this letter to you.

I would like to tell you today about the profound distress felt by a great number of French people because of the Hungarian drama. I mean most particularly the members of the peace movement, which is the only organization within which I am active. A great many French people resisted the enormous and monstrous anti-Soviet propaganda machine, and they proved it by not associating themselves in any way with this propaganda in public. Nevertheless, they wondered about certain things, and they continue to do so.

I am among these people.

Today there was an extraordinary meeting of the National Council of the French peace movement. There is a wide divergence of opinion among the militants on a possible interpretation of the events that have taken place in Hungary, while there is absolute unanimity against the French pursuit of the Algerian war, and against the Suez adventure. But we were all in agreement, all militants for peace, whatever our political opinions, whatever our religious conviction, whatever our philosophy; whether we are intellectuals or manual workers: We all took a firm resolution to try to prevent by any means we can a return to the cold war, and consequently the possibility of a hot war. And this is why, as far as I personally am concerned, I am happy to ask you to tell Soviet audiences that I shall arrive in the near future, in hopes that I will thus be able to help a little in the maintenance and development of those cultural exchanges which are a contribution to the consolidation of peace.

So, *à bientôt*, my dear Obraztsov.

With kind regards,
YVES MONTAND

The next morning this letter was published in *L'Humanité*, *Le Monde*, and *France-Soir*. It was our only recourse in defining our position to our fellow citizens and to the Russians.

The evening before our departure I finished packing my bags. My big trunk was full of "natty little numbers," as they say in the *maisons de couture*. At that time I was quite frivolous and I really had enough to wear for any circumstances. Since the West was going to the East, I thought the West should appear in its most attractive form. The doorbell rang; it was Claude Roy. He often dropped in. He was not madly cheerful, either. However, he wore that sly look of someone who is about to surprise you. That is what it was: Seeing that we had a lot of baggage, surely I could stow a few goat cheeses and packets of Gauloises cigarettes into all that stuff. They were for Ilya Ehrenburg. "You know how much Ehrenburg adores goat cheese. No one ever goes from Paris to Moscow without bringing cheeses and cigarettes to Ehrenburg. And even under these strange circumstances the tradition must be maintained." And as he wanted to make me laugh, I think he added that this was well within the domain of those cultural exchanges we had all heard so much about. After all, it was thanks to Ehrenburg that the Soviets finally gained access to Picasso's paintings, and surely that was worth a couple of cheeses. . . .

But that wasn't the true surprise. The real surprise was a little sentence he dropped just as he was leaving: "A few days ago, in a Parisian salon where your coming trip was being discussed, Aragon, who was present, said: 'I find this trip very inopportune.'" Claude kissed me and left. I felt the house had fallen on my head. I phoned Aragon every hour till midnight. I just wanted to tell him to get stuffed before I left. His phone didn't answer.

The next morning we kissed Catherine before she went to school. We were to meet the musicians at the Invalides air terminal. There were a few friends who wanted to say good-bye. It called for great courage on their part. There was Périer, José Artur, Pigaud, Rouleau, Lila de Nobili, Danièle Delorme, Yves Robert, Francis Lemarque, and Hubert Rostaing. There was also a marvelous man whose name is Jean Roire, who is a Communist and the director of the Chant du Monde record company. Just a few members of our family.

There were also some *France-Dimanche*° people. Though not invited, they took our bus all the way to Orly. There was a young woman who was determined to get her scoop at any cost. I have not forgotten her name. The comedy of our situation made her laugh loudly and constantly, and she shared this laughter with her photographer. That was my last impression of Paris: a woman laughing and making fun of some sad people about whom she knows nothing. This image and Aragon's were to haunt me during the entire trip.

Air France took us as far as Prague. The stopover was to last an hour. It lasted the night. They took us to a hotel far outside town, where they furnished us with food, drink, bed, and explanations which, although they were meteorological, were nonetheless shady. For the Jazz Band, it was their first trip to the Eastern zone, and their questions to the head of the expedition began to be pressing. Georges Soria, who is never without an answer, quickly developed the theory of prudence in the air, which is one of the great qualities of the Eastern countries' airlines. One is never too careful. Quite true, agreed the company, and then they began to relax. The next morning a splendid plane from Aeroflot took us aboard and headed for Moscow. Another untoward event caused it to land in Vilna, the capital of Lithuania. The stopover was to last an hour. It lasted seven.

There were meteorological explanations for this delay too, of course. But was that due to the kindness of the crew? or the lack of snobbery of the stewardess, who wore no uniform and came around in an apron offering *chai* from a samovar? or our arrival in this airport that looked like a Tolstoyan castle? Whatever the cause, the relaxation that had begun the evening before came over us in full force. We had left, rightly or wrongly, but we had left. Beginning then, people would no longer look at us in a way that was judgmental. We ourselves might be judgmental, but about the things that lay ahead. Those seven hours in

°A scandal-mongering weekly.

Vilna were seven hours of recreation. We were greatly in need of it. In that airport there were big rooms arranged for stopover passengers to rest in. There was a nursery for children in transit. There were tables heaped with food and drink. And everywhere there was the portrait of Lenin seated in an armchair covered with a white slipcover. Soudieu, the bass player, asked who that man was. Before he had joined this orchestra, he had played with Django. The only things in the world he loves are music and mechanics. His question was the signal for complete relaxation. At last we could laugh again. Crolla interviewed me in Chinese for a leading Peking newspaper, Paraboschi drummed on the table with forks, and Azzola played Gypsy music on his accordion, music he had learned when he was a "little Italian" in Paris, decked out in buttercup satin smock with golden buttons with the white Russians in Montmartre. Castella contemplated his company, which had recovered its good humor. Soria telephoned.

While "in transit" we didn't see many other passengers. Maybe we were in a VIP lounge without knowing it. Maybe not. There was a very pleasant ginger-haired man who photographed us. He was from Vilna and worked for the local newspaper. Great was the joy of the Soviet people to know we had at long last arrived, he said. Since I didn't understand Russian, he tried Yiddish. I knew enough German to understand. He took photographs, brought us pastries, and appeared to have something to say which he never said.

A few hours later, in the middle of the night, one month and one day late, we finally landed in Moscow. Three hundred journalists were waiting on the airfield, Russians and all the correspondents of the foreign press, newsreel, TV, and radio. Obraztsov made a welcoming speech in which he mentioned Montand's letter. Montand replied, repeating the terms of his letter, and emphasizing the questions he was interested in having answered, which he would not hesitate to ask during his stay. Obraztsov replied that they would be replied to. . . . It was our introduction to official speeches in this language we didn't understand and which is the only one in the world that can transform flat clichés into little love songs. But that night, in the light of the projectors, we could see the tears in Obraztsov's white-blue eyes, and what he said was no cliché. Obraztsov was responsible for Montand's enormous popularity in the USSR. He had come to Paris with his marionette theater, the most famous in the world, and had seen Montand at the Étoile. He had taken home records and had his marionettes sing them. It was in this fashion, and no other, that Montand began having a following in Russia. There were no political reasons. Gérard Philipe was popular because of *Fanfan la Tulipe* long before his tour with the TNP, and good Soviet citizens whistled the tune "Grands Boulevards" long before they saw *The Wages of Fear*.

As for me, the only thing they had seen me in was *Ombres et Lumières*, racked by my traumas caused by Tchaikovsky concertos. Mostly I was known as Montand's wife.

Obraztsov knew well what it meant in our lives to have finally decided to come. He was one of those whose worldwide tour had just been postponed.

A fleet of Zim cars was there to take us all to our hotel. It was snowing as we crossed Moscow for the first time. It must have been about two in the morning. It was surprising to see so many windows lit up, almost all of them orange. Our hotel, the Sovetskaya, is a marble palace where heads of state are accommodated. We were given a princely apartment: living room, dining room, grand piano, and several refrigerators. The musicians, Nino, the stage manager, and his wife, Maryse, were calling to one another up and down long corridors, overwhelmed by rooms that had nothing in common with the normal tour hotel. The lady floor supervisor smiled at us all. Our four interpreters explained curtains, faucets, and telephones. They were named Nadia, Sasha, Slava, and André. They spoke perfect French. The three boys were at the University of

Moscow. They were twenty years old. Nadia had already interpreted for the TNP tour as well as for French Film Week, headed by René Clair. They would live with us for a month and a half. They were funny, intelligent, kind. They were the Oscar Dancingers, Tola Litvaks, Kessels.

I said a while back that we would no longer be faced with judging eyes. It was true, but it was wrong as well. For a month and a half we would meet the eyes of many Russians, and I will spare you my number on the warmth, kindness, and passion that one finds in those eyes. We were also aware of an enormous sadness which says more than all the things that are not said. And as there were still a great many things that weren't said, there were a lot of those sad eyes. And a few judging eyes. Those seemed to say: "By coming here, you have betrayed us." You had to be extremely watchful to detect those looks; they appeared rarely in the faces of the people around us. We'd bump into them in the street, or in a subway, a few at the University of Moscow, and two that I will never forget in the Litchatchev factory. You had to be extremely vigilant to detect those looks, and we only acquired that sort of vigilance after a certain time.

Chapter 8

THE night following our arrival, we went to bed after a day whose every hour had been tightly scheduled. But we already knew one thing: Moscow was one of the few cities in the world where no one talked about Budapest. We suddenly realized it in the middle of a luncheon with one of the ministers of culture. The few officials there sincerely believed that our problems had stemmed only from our position concerning the Franco-British bombing of Cairo. All they knew about Budapest was that "quiet has been restored," as Nadia translated it. The error was rectified a bit and the luncheon was slightly spoiled. We talked films. Things were spoiled even more when I asked where *Salt of the Earth* was being shown in Moscow. *Salt of the Earth* was written by Michael Wilson and produced by Paul Jarrico; both had been living in Paris for the past year because of their anti-McCarthyism. The picture had been directed by Herbert Biberman, one of the "Hollywood Ten" who had been jailed for refusing to answer the questions of the Un-American Activities Committee. *Salt of the Earth* had been shown in major cities all over the world, including New York. A little film made clandestinely in 1953 on the Mexican border, it was hailed as a masterpiece. I knew it had been bought by the Russians; I simply wanted to know where one could see it.

My question threw Mr. Culture into disarray. *Salt of the Earth*, translated Nadia. *Salt of the Earth*, repeated the minister. He went off to telephone, and came back a few minutes later announcing that he was hot on the track of the film. It wasn't being played at just that moment; it was probably in the process of being dubbed into Russian. It was patently clear they would rather not let Soviet citizens know that in America there were people who took risks. Dubbing or no dubbing, Moscow was one of the few cities in the world where *Salt of the Earth* wasn't being shown. That was our second discovery.

The third concerned us directly, or rather concerned Montand. Besides his recitals, where Montand sang for two hours every evening, a whole schedule of "singing visits" had been established. They wanted to show us everything: schools, factories, kolkhozes, and universities, and of course, at the end of all these visits, a few songs for those who wouldn't be able to get to the concerts would be looked upon favorably. Which meant in effect that Montand and the musicians would be working without respite. It would be tiring, that was sure, but it would probably be interesting. It wasn't interesting, it was fascinating; it wasn't tiring, it was exhausting—and instructive.

It was instructive, for example, to saunter around the Litchatchev foundry, wearing our well-cut Parisian clothes and guided by the clown responsible for the factory. The men and women who worked there looked at us and smiled. They looked hard at their comrade clown, who had verbal diarrhea, and their slightly mocking smiles said to us: "Don't swallow everything that clown is selling you." One face did not smile. It was the first of those special looks I mentioned a moment ago. This one was a woman.

Another that day was that of a master welder in the act of fusing metal. He gazed at us all, one after another, for a long time as we stood there, and then resolutely turned his back on us and went back to the metal, one hand shielding his face. We asked our clown what this meant. His answer was the sort of dialogue you wouldn't have dared put into the mouth of an evil employer in a bad 1936 film. "You know how they are—we give them masks and they won't wear them." It was "There's no point in giving them bathrooms, they'll just put coal in the bathtub," all over again. We didn't much care for that factory clown. But an hour later, in the biggest of the machine shops, on a stage improvised from several rows of trucks parked side by side, Montand gave his concert, at eleven in the morning. He sang for anyone who had been able to come, and there were thousands of them. It is hard to sing at eleven in the morning. But we had forgotten the factory clown. Where else in the world would you find a foundry where the workers are offered the kind of attraction normally available only to the upper crust, during the course of their working day at the factory?

The upper crust came too. The first night at the Tchaikovsky Theater (three thousand five hundred seats) was, we were told, the most acclaimed opening Moscow had seen since the Comédie Française. All the foreign embassies were represented. The only exception was the empty seats of the French ambassador, Monsieur Dejean, and his lady. They didn't even bother sending an excuse. Nothing. The two best seats in the hall simply remained steadfastly empty. They could be seen from all around. Especially from the balconies, which were crowded with standees who had somehow managed to get in.

There were a great many uniforms in the hall, and a slightly chilly wave could be felt when Montand began "Quand un Soldat." The songs had been translated into Russian in the program, and from where I sat I could see a few heads, their uniformed necks clad in raspberry-colored serge, beginning to realize what was being said in this song, whose martial rhythm in no way predicts the end, which is resolutely antimilitaristic.

As happens everywhere, the upper crust somehow got seats. The others stood in line. The line curled around huge blocks centered about the Tchaikovsky Theater. A bronze Mayakovski contemplated the stamp of icy feet as the fans queued up for their seats. The Ministry of Culture noticed what was going on and changed the venue for four nights to the Luzhnik Stadium, which can seat twenty thousand people.

Twenty thousand people! Of which a maximum of two thousand can catch the subtleties of what's being sung. Three thousand can just about cotton on. The other fifteen thousand trusted their pals' reactions and the public-address system. And the PA system was excellent. There were twenty thousand people for four days who loved, loved, and loved him. You have to be damn well balanced and have no talent at all for megalomania to come out of an experience like that intact.

We received telegrams to the effect that children born at the outer edge of Siberia had been named Yvesmontand. I'm sure they're embarrassed by it, now that they're of university age, after having been "different" to their schoolmates. There was even a set of twins, who had the good grace to be a boy and a girl, who were Simone and Yves. Nadia took me to GUM, the big department store, where I bought two silver beakers and had them engraved—in Cyrillic, of course—"For Yves, from Simone," and "For Simone, from Yves." This *beau geste*, which carries a whiff of the behavior of noble families in edifying novels, was celebrated by the press and filmed by television cameras. . . . Yves and Simone, wherever you may be, you're twenty now. Auntie Simone and Uncle Yves say, "*Zdravstvuite.*"

Once I was in GUM, I took a turn around the "special section." An old gentleman showed me the different qualities of sable. He was an old sable specialist. Blowing gently on the lovely fur—Siberian gold of another kind— he instructed me in his specialty. I learned, for example, that "in this quality, our government had a long evening coat made for the Queen of England"; and in that quality, "our government offered a big stole to the Maharani of Kapurthala." By the time he had gotten to "the cape our government sent to Princess Liliane de Rethey," I knew all about sable. I bought a few skins. They were not "offered by our government"; they were given to me by my husband, who was being paid in rubles.

He was being paid in rubles for singing in the evening. Actually, he was singing almost all day; the musicians were playing all day, and I was a "speaking extra." We were taken everywhere, and wherever we arrived someone would begin the popular song of the moment, "Ami Lointain." *L'ami lointain*—the faraway friend—was Montand, and the song is very pretty; it was written by the Russian Sinatra, called Bernès. He was very handsome and tremendously popular.

Everywhere we went we were also the audience. All the schoolchildren seemed to be able to sing and dance. They would do an opening scene, we would applaud, and they would applaud us for applauding. It is something I've seen done only in the USSR, and it's a very warming gesture.

In the kolkhozes, too, people sang and danced. Of course, perhaps our arrival was sometimes not as spontaneous and unexpected as people would have liked us to think. We would always get out at some model farm that just happened to be on the way that brought us back to town after an expedition to some distant factory. It would provoke great joy in the kolkhoz, buzzing with cultural activity—and it would just so happen that the folklore group was rehearsing that month's show. However, there are other countries where surprise visits are scheduled in exactly the same way....

Slava, Sasha, André, and Nadia had become completely integrated into the company. We may have cried a lot in November, but in December all thirteen of us laughed a lot, and often. We also talked a lot. They didn't have all the answers to our questions, but we had all the answers to theirs. Theirs had flashed out, fast, and been coped with from the first day on. Their naïveté proved that nothing was known in Moscow about what had happened in cities all over the world during the first week of November. Nothing. The three young university students and that cultivated, intelligent, and perfectly bilingual young woman who knew our literature from Villon to Vercors were as ignorant of the Hungarian invasion as their great-grandfathers would have been, with rags wrapped around their feet for lack of shoes. It was vertiginous; they listened to what we told them with tears in their eyes, realizing that they were members of a nation that at that moment was hated for good or bad reasons by a large part of humankind. It had all been hidden from them. When they learned about it, it caused them enormous pain.

We talked a great deal with Sasha, Slava, André, and Nadia. And with Ehrenburg. We had brought his cheeses and Gauloises cigarettes to his apartment. But not fresh news. The peace movement, of which he was a chairman, had exploded not far from the Solferino métro station in Paris; the *boom* had rippled as far as the Gorki Prospekt in Moscow.

And then there were the others. The others. The others formed a group of very affable and very fashionable people. Their eyes were neither sad nor judgmental. They're the kind one finds everywhere in the world in the wake of successful people, as long as they are successful—actors, directors, and writers. They were always hanging around when we were around; in the corridors and the great marble lobby of the Sovetskaya, or in the little sitting room next to the dressing room in the Tchaikovsky Theater, or in the Praga restaurant. They were the upper crust, the people who didn't have to stand in line to get tickets. With this lot we chatted, we didn't talk. And Obraztsov, with whom we might have talked, was on tour himself in Leningrad with his company.

Then something happened that probably couldn't have happened in any other country in the world. Montand and the musicians had just returned to the Tchaikovsky Theater after the four recitals in the huge stadium. One day at about noon at the Sovetskaya Hotel there was a surprise for us. Our friend Joris Ivens was there with his wife. For the purest and greatest revolutionary film-maker of his generation, the year 1956 had not been easy. Ivens, on his way to Peking, was in Moscow in transit. At the same table were seated Georges Sadoul and his wife. Sadoul had just been made doctor *honoris causa* at the University of Moscow and had come for the ceremony. Suddenly, in that immense dining room, it was like being back at the Lipp in Paris. I got around to asking Sadoul whether he was going to write a third review of *Casque d'Or*, now taking into account thoughts that might be inspired by the report "attributed to." He laughed and said he would think about it. We talked about all the lousy Soviet films of the Zhdanov period which had been imposed on us all. Especially on Sadoul, he admitted, when he had to write reviews of them. Joris talked about filming *Komsomols*, his first film made in the USSR, in 1932. We talked a lot, we were relaxed and happy, and during dessert Rutha Sadoul asked me to go with her that night to the Bolshoi, where she wanted to see her great friend Plisetskaya dance. I had accompanied Montand to the theater or the stadium every night so far; this once I would go to the Bolshoi and would join him afterward at the Tchaikovsky.

All thirteen of us had gone to the Bolshoi one evening. Afterward Paraboschi had decided that *Swan Lake* in its entirety didn't "swing so good." Ulanova hadn't danced that evening, but she had come to greet us in the enormous official loge that had been put at our disposal. She was a tiny woman, dressed like an English governess. She was at that time the greatest prima ballerina in the world, yet Paris had offended her, a few years before, by asking her to come and then refusing her the Opéra because besieged Dien Bien Phu had surrendered a few days before. Sartre had written a headline in *Libération* which had become famous: "Next year Ulanova will still be dancing, but Monsieur Laniel will probably no longer be prime minister." She remembered it well....

For my second evening at the Bolshoi I was wearing a splendid black velvet suit from Hermès, and I had hung unobtrusive but beautiful things on my ears and around my wrists. I crossed Moscow in the back of an enormous Zim with gray satin curtains, wrapped and hatted in pastel mink. I had always believed that those curtained cars had been the invention of American filmmakers who specialized in anti-Soviet pictures.

The ballet that evening was called *The Fountain of*...something-or-other. The story was taken from a Pushkin novella that neither Rutha Sadoul nor I knew, but as Pushkin more often than not took his sources from Polish folklore, and Madame Sadoul was Polish, I was sure she would understand and explain it to me as the story unfolded. The curtain went up on a disguised group that began dancing very beautifully. Given their squared-off berets, their boots, and the shape of their swords, no doubt existed that we were in Poland. Madame Sadoul would certainly know her way around. A quarter of an hour later she still didn't know what was going on, but as everyone danced so well, it didn't really matter much whether or not we understood the plot, which seemed passionate and nevertheless patriotic. At the end of the first act the prima ballerina made her entrance. She was superb. We were some distance from the stage, but we saw well enough for Madame Sadoul to point out that Plisetskaya was as distinguished and graceful on the stage as she was in everyday life. However, she did seem taller.... I whispered that that was quite normal, and told her how surprised I had been to discover that Ulanova was tiny offstage.

193

At intermission time, Rutha Sadoul asked one of the ushers to show her the way backstage to the dressing rooms. She wanted to congratulate her friend. I tried to discourage her, since dancers, like singers, need their intermissions to relax and recuperate. Rutha wouldn't hear of it. She wanted to see her friend. Immediately. At this point the usher started a long speech in which there were a great many *nyets* and which ended with the word "Kiev." Finally we got the message: It had been the understudy; Plisetskaya, that evening, was dancing in Kiev.

Highly amused, we went to one of the huge gilded galleries where pastries and drinks were served. We were among the families of workmen, peasants, intellectuals, and government civil servants. Intermissions are very long in Russia, and we had time to notice the sense of community among those different people sharing the same pleasures.

The second act was about to begin, without Plisetskaya and without subtitles, when the door to our little box opened, and as the crystal chandelier was dimming, I saw the face of our André. Behind him, standing still and pale, was "Mr. Culture." I must come back to the Tchaikovsky with them immediately. It was very serious. I excused myself to Madame Sadoul, thinking Montand must be sick, or perhaps there's a fire, or bad news from Paris. . . . Everything except what I was about to see. Everything except the thing they wanted me to discover for myself after having nonetheless done their best to reassure me.

A little while back I made a few ironic comments about surprise visits. Perhaps I shouldn't have. When we got to the theater I saw two policemen standing guard at the stage door. That was all. I went backstage. Montand was singing to a full house, but for the first time since our arrival in Moscow, the enormous first box on the right-hand side of the apron stage was occupied. It had curtains much like the huge Zim cars, but until then they had always been drawn. Now they were open, and sitting there, in exactly the same order as one always sees in official photographs, were

Khrushchev, Molotov, Mikoyan, Bulganin, and Malenkov, applauding the end of a song.

From where I stood backstage there were three simultaneous spectacles for me to see: Montand from the back, the five gentlemen in their box, and the audience. The audience, too, had a bonus, a couple of shows to watch: Montand on the stage and the five men. I'm sure that most of them were seeing these men in the flesh for the first time in their lives, or in any case from so close.

At the end of the recital, all five of them stood up to applaud. The whole audience stood up to applaud. They alternated: They applauded Montand, and then they applauded the Presidium. Montand bowed. Between two curtain calls he just had the time to say, "Did you see?" while he sponged himself off with the towel I handed him. After the last curtain call there was that "Oooh" of disappointment which is the same all over the world. Montand raced to his dressing room, just as he does at the Étoile or in Melun. Whether it's Moscow or Paris or Melun, it's in the chilly corridors after leaving the warm stage that you catch cold. His musicians and his groupie followed, as they always did. Mr. Culture then knocked on the door and said that the comrades from the Supreme Soviet of the Union of Soviet Socialist Republics were waiting for us. Before we even had time to speak to each other, Montand replied that he was waiting for them in his dressing room. He just needed the time to dry off. Mr. Culture then explained that a little supper had been prepared in the theater. He was simply coming to extend the invitation. The comrades from the Supreme Soviet knew that an artist needed to rest after his effort. If they hadn't come to him in his dressing room, it was only because they didn't wish to disturb him. They would wait; we were not to rush.

We had expected a protocol visit in the dressing room, handshakes for the cameras (which means without really looking at one another). At the most, perhaps a paternalistic slap on the back recorded for posterity by the cameras. In other words, all the little gestures made to capture a moment during which nothing real happens or is said.

Instead of that, we were invited to a little supper. The term "little supper" has a frivolous ring. As we followed the man in charge of the theater, Montand, Nadia, and I didn't realize that we were about to live the most interesting moments of our respective careers as actor-singer, translator, and actress, things being what they were in the world of December 1956.

They were waiting for us just across the threshold of the little dining room behind the official stage box. One after another they stepped forward to introduce themselves, as though we might not know who they were. Bulganin was tugging at his beard, living up to his image of a debonair granddad; Khrushchev cracked jokes; Molotov looked sinister; Mikoyan was laughing and Oriental; and Malenkov seemed very sad. They said their names, we said ours, and Nadia said hers. Mr. Culture said nothing.

A table had been set. There were nine places. There were the five of them, and Mr. Culture, Montand, Nadia, and I. There wasn't a single photographer, no television camera. If there were hidden microphones, I swear that all they recorded that night were scenes of truth and good faith: in the questions that were asked and in the answers that were given, on both sides.

The table was long and narrow. Nadia was seated at one end, between Mr. Culture and Malenkov. Mikoyan was at the other end, between me and Molotov. Montand and I were thus opposite Molotov, Khrushchev, Bulganin, and Malenkov.

I can't honestly say that the first five minutes were extraordinarily relaxed. Mikoyan spoke first; Nadia translated. Everyone around the table agreed that it had been a very fine recital. Montand thanked them; I smiled. Then there was a bit of chat about the severe climate, which must be a shock for us, coming as we did from the temperate zone. We were then at the borscht. Mikoyan proposed the first toast of the evening. I seem to remember that it was dedicated to the friendship and glory of our two nations. Or to the peace of the world. Whatever it was, the evening really got off to a start after the toast.

Once the ball began rolling, it lasted for three hours. Three hours during which one heard only the voices of Khrushchev, Montand, and myself—and especially Nadia, who was translating at an extraordinary speed both what was said by Khrushchev and what we said. The four other men remained silent. From time to time they nodded agreement to something said by Khrushchev or they laughed at one of his jokes, or one of ours. There weren't many.

Khrushchev triggered the discussion. "It wasn't easy for you to come here, was it?"

"It's not very easy to come to your country at this moment, Mr. Khrushchev."

"Because of fascist pressure?"

"No, because of what happened in Budapest, Mr. Khrushchev. The fascists are really more or less delighted by what happened in Budapest. . . . But let's forget about the fascists."

We talked to them about the others. All the others, whose existences they seemed not to know about. At first we spoke about ourselves. That was when my good clothes and my trinkets stood me in good stead. Quite honestly, we tried to define ourselves. We tried to explain that our public agreements with Communist positions, when they seemed right to us, came from the heart; our personal interests played no part. My expensive suit and fine jewels, I said, touching my diamond bracelet and my pastel mink hat, were bought with money I had earned in capitalistic countries. Montand continued, describing his lovely house in Autheuil, the results of work freely accomplished. He stressed that he. alone reigned over what he chose to choose. By which we meant to say that we personally had no reason to complain about a capitalist regime, but that was no reason to think that it was perfect for a lot of others. We were sentimentalists, not discerning politicians. And since we were sentimental, the thing that had shocked us most was pictures of the Red Army shooting in the streets of Budapest. We and many others who were not fascists had had great difficulty in understanding our departure, which, to speak frankly, we would much rather have delayed. Just as they had delayed the tours of their own artists. "No, it wasn't easy to come to your country at this moment, Mr. Khrushchev."

Nadia had translated our words almost as fast as we spoke them. She could have finished our sentences for us. We'd often had the same conversation with her.

So Khrushchev decided to explain things to us from his point of view. In essence, he went over the report "attributed to." In order to understand the situation in the socialist republics, one had to go back to Stalin, and this was particularly true in the case of Hungary. He explained Rákosi, the Stalinist leader, and his Stalinist errors. Then he talked about Poland, and told about how Stalin had completely liquidated the Polish Communist party, as well as some of the Spaniards in exile in Moscow. He mimed Beria. He talked about the camps—he beat rhythmically on the table each time he came to "sixteen million dead"— and about planned deportation of the Russian Jews to a state where they were to be concentrated. Nadia translated. She was reliving her childhood and adolescence. I looked at Khrushchev, and I looked at Molotov, who was looking at no one. In my eyes one might have read the question: "And you, what were you doing all that time?" Khrushchev replied to that question before I could ask it. "I see what you're thinking," he said, pointing his finger at me over the table. "You're thinking: You, what were you doing during all that time? . . . I could do nothing, because whatever one might have done against Stalin would have been against socialism."

At this point Mikoyan proposed the second toast of the evening, in honor of Comrade Khrushchev, who had the courage to tell the truth, for the greater glory of socialism. *Za vashe zdorovye!*

That was doubtless true, but was Mr. Khrushchev really sure that when he sent the Red Army into Budapest, he was doing something that was good for socialism?

"Yes; we saved socialism from a counterrevolution."

"But," said Montand, "in the past you thought Tito was a counterrevolutionary and a traitor."

"An error of the past," replied Khrushchev.

"And there's no possibility for present error?"

"Our army is in Budapest today because the Hungarians called us for help."

"The people?"

"Yes, the people. They want to be protected against Hungarian fascism and the agents of imperialism."

"Perhaps it was rather that the people believed they had a right to demand greater liberty, within the new socialism you had promised them, Mr. Khrushchev, and this gesture was misunderstood?"

"It's you who have misunderstood," he replied, smiling.

"Well, in that case, there are a great many of us who have misunderstood!"

And so we told them about Paris in November 1956. Not about our personal troubles, about the troublemakers at Olympia, or about *Modigliani*. We told them about the disarray of certain French Communist militants, who got themselves beaten up or insulted for defending *them*. We told them about the explosion within the peace movement, which had caused it to lose the support of thousands of faithful fellow travelers throughout the world. In the course of the activities of one week, they were no longer the heroes of 1917, and the victors of Stalingrad. They had become, in the eyes of some, tank commandos in a colony. In the eyes of some who found it very difficult to justify acts that resembled those they usually condemned when they were committed elsewhere. Precisely because they were good fellow travelers.

Nadia translated. In a monotone.

And I swear they were listening. Here we were, telling

the representatives of the biggest Communist party in the world to their faces just those things that we had tried to say to militant French Communists, who had replied, "I don't want to be in an anti-Soviet position." It gave us the most extraordinary feeling of relief. How much healthier to say these things directly to the Supreme Soviet!

Their way of listening made us think two contradictory things.

Possibly we were giving them information they didn't have, which their faces seemed to indicate. In that case, their official informants had somehow omitted some very important things. Mr. Vinogradov, for example, knew full well that there was a difference between a position taken by Jean-Paul Sartre and the action of the nasty little reactionaries who'd flung muck on the walls of his embassy on the Rue Grenelle in Paris. And if Mr. Vinogradov hadn't passed along to Moscow the truth about what was in the French newspapers and journals that were not part of the professional anti-Soviet press, or what was being said in the circles and salons where he was so very often seen, why then Mr. Vinogradov wasn't doing his job. That was hard to believe. Particularly when one remembered how many Mr. Vinogradovs there were. Was it possible that in all the capital cities of the world these gentlemen hadn't done their job?

Yet when certain well-known people were mentioned, whose talent, honesty, and notorious antifascism were equally well known, they seemed surprised. They put their heads together: Gérard Philipe, Vercors, Claude Roy, and Roger Vailland—all these had demonstrated against the intervention. We weren't denouncing these people by quoting their names; we were carrying messages that seemed to have gotten mislaid in the diplomatic pouches. Why had they been told that only the fascists had demonstrated and that the rest of humanity approved their action? They listened.

There remained the other hypothesis. That they knew all this, and they didn't give a damn. It was their business to run a nation of two hundred million Soviet citizens. That's a lot of work. The disenchantment of certain Western sympathizers and the despair of some of their Eastern friends really left them quite cold. Perhaps they just didn't want to speak the sentence we may have deserved: "You left-wing intellectuals are a pain in the ass." It's a sentence often heard in Paris. The one that always winds up our discussions with the Communist-party people. They generally add: "You've come part of the way with us, but we can carry on without you."

No, Khrushchev didn't pronounce that sentence, and Nadia didn't have to translate it. She did translate one of Montand's. He wanted to make it very clear that his coming to the Soviet Union represented no form of guarantee, although it might appear to give that impression. Khrushchev smiled, thanked him for his frankness. He called on his companions to witness his admiration for this virtue, which he called the only one suitable for the times, and got lots of *spasibos* and *pravdas* in return.

Mikoyan seized the moment to propose a third toast (the glasses were tiny and I believe they often contained water). This one was to Montand's father, mother, brother, and sister. He obviously knew the story of this family hounded out of its homeland by Italian fascism. They had emigrated to France for the greater joy of those music lovers who found in the French singer Yves Montand the perfect alliance of two Latin cultures, two countries that had always been great friends of the Soviet people. . . . Nadia translated, everyone applauded, everyone smiled. Except Molotov.

For two and a half hours there had been very hard things said around that table. After the last toast there was an uncomfortable silence.

That's when we heard the voice of Mr. Culture. We had completely forgotten about him. He must have been very bored up to now. Or, on the contrary, he may have felt that with us around, nobody was ever bored—that is, if he remembered hunting for the *Salt of the Earth* print, somewhat unceremoniously brought to his attention over our first lunch, two weeks earlier. Whatever the reason, one thing was certain: It was damned difficult to have a quiet meal in our company.

He was addressing me. He wanted to know whether I had cinematographic projects. A pertinent question, coming from a minister of culture.

That was when Khrushchev said that he had read somewhere that I had been offered a Franco-Russian coproduction deal to play *Madame Bovary*. I answered that a few months earlier I had been made an offer of this kind, which I had politely turned down. In my opinion, the only valid reason for coproductions is to tell stories dealing with characters of different nationalities. In this case, I couldn't be an Emma Bovary married to a Russian Dr. Bovary. Everything had to be French—even the cows, I added archly, which produced howls of laughter in my audience, with the exception of my husband, who smiled politely. He was well acquainted with my number on coproductions. Mr. Culture raised his head, took a deep breath, and sighed, "Ah, *Bovary* . . . Balzac!"

I looked at Nadia. She was crimson. But her eyes were begging: "Please say nothing, please, please say nothing." I think she was more frightened at that moment than she had been while she was translating the far more dangerous exchanges a few minutes before. Nadia, who knew pages and pages of Stendhal by heart, as well as Victor Hugo and, what's more to the point, Balzac and especially Flaubert; Nadia was a knowledgeable nuisance. The only person who seemed to react, strangely enough, was Molotov. He gazed for a long moment at his minister of culture, and then, for the first time, he really looked at me.

Now that we were talking literature, Montand and I inquired why *Les Thibaults* had never been published in Russia. Mr. Culture didn't know. He would find out. Nadia spelled Roger Martin Du Gard's name in Cyrillic, and Mr. Culture wrote it down.

It was late. Only the sweets were left on the table. I have no memory of what was served between the borscht and the sugared cherries and cinnamon marzipan at the end. Khrushchev rose to propose a toast. It was a toast to the divergencies between our points of view—which would certainly dwindle and vanish—and also to the pleasure it had given him to confront those divergencies of points of view elsewhere than in conference halls or through official emissaries. We were *cheloveks*, and he thanked us. He was as warm as Jean Renoir, as malicious as Popov the clown.

Then Montand rose. He presented his excuses; he was not expert in the proposal of toasts. He simply wanted to thank them for having allowed him and his wife to say here things which, had they been said elsewhere, might have served in a bad cause. He had come here on this visit to the Union of Soviet Socialist Republics although it had not been easy, as he had said at the beginning of the meal. But he was sure now that he had been right to come, if only for the privilege of opening his heart to them. He thanked them for having made this possible by inviting us to this gathering that was so unfettered by protocol. He had not been completely won over by Mr. Khrushchev's arguments. He hoped they had benefited from ours. He thanked them for having come to hear him sing, and he lifted his glass to the people and the audiences of the Soviet Union. *"Za vashe zdorovye!"*

Everybody applauded.

Mikoyan handed me a little glass of Armenian brandy and asked me to propose a toast.

I rose and said that my husband had spoken for me, and that I wished only to raise my glass to *pravda*—not the newspaper, but to *pravda*. Period. That got a big laugh. We drank to truth. Then we separated. It was almost four in the morning.

Before dropping off to sleep, I thought about all those in Paris who had criticized us. And all those who had urged us to go. And of Sennep's caricature, and of a photograph that had appeared all over the Soviet press: a beautiful photograph showing the two of us in a troika, wrapped to the ears in fur rugs. I was laughing and Montand was pointing to something in the distance. This picture had appeared in some French newspapers, but the heading had been: "Look at that smoke over there, Simone; that's Budapest burning." The picture had appeared two weeks after we left. I thought about the piece written by the Moscow correspondent for *L'Humanité*, a very nice piece about our arrival in Moscow, which André Stil, the chief editor, saw fit to caption with "Yves Montand says: 'Here I found pals.'"

I thought about the ugly, unkind laugh of the girl from *France-Dimanche*, and of course I thought of Aragon. I also thought about others. I thought about that whole gang of pains in the ass whose spokesmen we had been for those three hours. I think they would have been pleased. Montand, as he was turning off the light, summed it up: "From now on we're going to be on bad terms with everybody—but on what good terms we'll be with ourselves!"

(A few years ago I read in the *Figaro Littéraire* that a first edition of two hundred thousand copies of the Russian translation of Roger Martin Du Gard's *Les Thibaults* had been sold, and that the book had gone back to press. And since I am incurably sentimental, as I read the piece I heard Nadia's voice spelling the name. If I had had it handy at that moment, I would have put on Bernès's record, "Ami Lointain." So even if they retained nothing else of what was said that evening, the time wasn't completely wasted, neither theirs nor ours.)

I've just told you the high point of our Moscow trip. All that follows may seem dull by comparison with this confrontation, which by the next morning had become the talk of Moscow.

Everyone knew that we had spent three hours with

them. And everyone wanted to know what had been said. Everyone included the French ambassador, Ilya Ehrenburg, the Moscow correspondents of the foreign press, the cosmopolites of the city, and Soria (who had missed the whole thing because he hadn't been at the Tchaikovsky Theater that evening). Even the old bearded doorman at the Sovetskaya Hotel, who had taken to kissing both my hands each time I went back to the hotel, and the chief electrician of the theater, who had the sense of humor common to all chief electricians in all theaters and studios throughout the world—even they wanted to know all about it. So I will try to summarize.

We told the French ambassador, who appeared for the first time in the two weeks we had been there, that we would call him as soon as we came back from Kiev.

We told the American UP correspondent, who happened to have been a one-time neighbor in the Place Dauphine (and whom I called "gringo" out of loyalty to Mexico), that the conversation had been very interesting.

We reassured and undoubtedly disappointed the fashionable set by telling them they had never been so much as mentioned.

We told Soria that he probably wouldn't have liked what we said.

We told the old doorman nothing; we just smiled.

The chief electrician asked us whether we had been able to speak, and we told him yes.

We told Ehrenburg all about it. He had sent his secretary to our hotel. She bore a message inviting us to lunch in the country, at Ehrenburg's dacha eighty kilometers outside Moscow, the day after next. When I say us, I mean just the two of us. Alone.

Ehrenburg's secretary was a very beautiful woman. She had lived in Paris until she was seventeen, with her mother, who was a White Russian. In Paris she had fallen in love with socialism. So she left Paris and went to Moscow. Three weeks after her arrival she was arrested and deported to Central Asia. She spent seven years in a camp without ever knowing why she had been arrested. She had just been rehabilitated. She was the first victim of "the errors of the past" with whom we spoke. Her faith in the socialist state remained unwavering. She even wondered whether Khrushchev had been right to so brutally disillusion a people that had accomplished what it had accomplished only through its faith in Stalin. She had spent the best years of her life in a camp, but it never occurred to her not to spend those that remained to her in her own country.

We told Ehrenburg all about the dinner. But we didn't tell him much he didn't know. He knew our position and he knew that of the Presidium. We did surprise him a bit, I think, when it came to the form of the whole thing. When we described the courtesy and the easygoing tone of our debate, he stopped us with a roar of laughter and told us this story: A few days before our surprise supper, a serious, interesting woman, a militant in the peace movement, had come from Belgium at her own expense in order to try to meet Khrushchev and tell him the same things we had told him. She had finally managed to obtain an audience. But he hadn't allowed her to get a word in edgewise, had finally impolitely thrown her out and practically expelled her from the territory. But there were very few people in Moscow who knew this story....

Ehrenburg was very funny. He had lived in Paris a long time and spoke perfect French with that touch of old-fashioned Parisian slang which characterizes foreigners who lived in Paris before the war. He had turns of phrase that were all his own. "They gave a little haircut to my text in the last volume," he said, in order to explain the disgrace he was in once again. "But it's only momentary," he added. "I've always fallen on my feet, sometimes even on my hands. We Soviet writers are alive today only because we're the greatest acrobats in the world. All of us ... except Pasternak." It was the first time in our lives we heard that name.

So Ehrenburg told us about Pasternak, the greatest

Soviet poet, and the greatest translator of Shakespeare, the only man who had refused to give in to Stalin and the only man Stalin hadn't dared touch. He wasn't published, but he was alive. He lived retired, but not forgotten. "He's the only one among us who deserves respect." And Ehrenburg told us how Stalin had awakened him, Ehrenburg, one night by telephone to instruct him to replace, in a political serial he was writing, the word "Nazi" in all the places where they had previously told him to use "German" instead of "Nazi." Which is how Ehrenburg had known before anyone else that the Russian-German Pact had had its day.

And he told us about how Stalin had called them all to the Kremlin one day for an urgent meeting. "There are only two ways of writing. One can write like Shakespeare or like Chekhov. I'm not a writer, but if I were, I would write like Shakespeare. As for you, my counsel is to write like Chekhov. You may go."

Ehrenburg was funny, disenchanted, and lucid. His wife was lucid, disenchanted, and funny, and there were two little old Jewish ladies who said nothing but who contemplated their younger brother, knowing quite well that without his talent they would never be there in that pretty dacha.

There were splendid paintings on the walls: Picassos and Mirós and works by young Soviet painters which had never been shown in any exhibition. I glanced at the library and took off one of the shelves a little book called *Paris*. It was a collection of photographs taken in Paris and published in the Soviet Union around 1933, at the time when Ehrenburg had been a foreign correspondent for *Izvestia*. It showed little children in rags dragging a shopping basket out of which poked a bottle of red wine and a loaf of bread; bums asleep on warm air vents; prostitutes in Les Halles market in Paris; a dismal area in the industrial zone of Aubervilliers; and beggars, lots of beggars.

I asked him whether really, for him, at that time, Paris

had been nothing but this. "We all omitted a few things, *chérie*, us acrobats..." and as he was very funny, we all laughed.

The Writers Union in Moscow is in a beautiful ex-palace that used to belong to a grand duke. If, as is asserted, its salons were the scenes of abominable orgies up until October 1917, one evening in December 1956 they were the scene of an abominable scandal.

The previous week we had accepted an invitation to come after the theater to a reception at the Writers Union. Fate or the devil arranged to have this party the day after Ehrenburg's luncheon.... To the bearer of the invitation Montand had made it quite clear that he would not sing. He sang morning, afternoon, and two hours in the evening. He was perfectly willing, he said, to do overtime for those who couldn't come to the theater, but he wasn't willing to do overtime for those who seemed to spend practically every evening in the theater.

I must say in passing that the bearer of the invitation was part of the group we were continually running into. He had burst out laughing; what did we think they were? We were invited. We were invited to drink and nibble a little snack after work as well as, maybe, exchange a few ideas. ("Exchange against what?" Jacques Prévert would have asked.) No, no . . . Montand had misunderstood. There was no question of anything beyond a friendly cultural get-together. Another recital! Of course not. Unthinkable. The musicians would be perfectly welcome if they wanted to come along too. Well, that's fixed now. Thank you. See you next week.

When we arrived at what we were to call henceforth the "house of acrobats," imagine our surprise at finding ourselves installed on a platform on which were chairs, a piano, and a microphone. And in front of this stage were our hosts, the writers in grace and favor, installed in comfortable chairs. They were waiting for the show to begin. Someone in the audience made us a compliment.

Then, in our honor, the basso Petrov came on the stage to sing one or two grand arias. Then it was the turn of an old lady who had been a popular *diseuse*. She honored the assembly with some French nineteenth-century melodies. It was late; Montand was hungry. But we applauded, wondering what we were doing there.

The lady was really a very, very old *diseuse*. Probably she had captivated audiences for generation after generation, perhaps even in this very salon of the grand duke himself. She was about to offer us yet another encore when someone suggested she might be feeling tired. With some difficulty she was removed from the stage, but with respect and caution. Then a few voices, and finally the whole room, began to chant: "Yves Montand . . . a song." I rose, took the microphone, and attempted to live up to that reputation for grace and humor that seems to be part of our French reputation throughout the world. I asked them please not to insist, to do it for me. If he gave in, he'd take it out on me. He was tired, and when he was tired, I was the one who got it. . . . I was sure they would understand. "Bravo! Bravo! She's so funny. A song . . . a song. . . ."

Montand got up and signaled to Bob, who was beside us on the stage. Bob went to the piano. Montand then took my place at the microphone. He sang half a verse and then he stopped and said, "Okay, kids, let's get out of here." With one quick, supple movement he grabbed Bob from the stool and me from my chair and catapulted us off the stage. Only then did he begin to insult them. In record time he covered their present impoliteness, their past cowardices, and probably those to come. He told them that he hadn't read most of their books, but the simple fact that they were there, alive, at their age, was enough to tell him that he would never want to read their books. He asked them for news of Pasternak, he called them a pack of lousy old pen pushers, courtesans, opportunistic demagogues, and he rounded off the whole thing by calling them a bunch of dirty bastards.

Tired as he was, his voice projected, as it always does in

anger or indignation. That is, very well. There was lots of
noise. There was no longer any question of exchange of
ideas. They were all petrified. They were all very
cultivated people and understood French perfectly. What
they did not understand was why this nice, tall young man
was behaving with such unfathomable impoliteness.

Soria was there. He had missed the little supper. He
hadn't been invited to the Ehrenburg luncheon. But in his
capacity as a writer he had been the agent of this little
party. He did not follow us in our flight. He remained
among his literary brothers and probably explained to
them that great artists are sometimes also overgrown
capricious children. . . .

One evening in 1962, at the brasserie Lipp, we learned
how this episode had enchanted another Moscow—the
Moscow of the young poets and writers whom we never
ran into, who were never in the lobby of the Sovetskaya or
in the Praga restaurant. We knew nothing about their
existence, but they knew about ours. And for good reason.
Because they were writing pamphlets mocking us and the
people we kept company with. But after that evening in
the house of acrobats they started writing poems in which
the comic characters were no longer the two of us. When
translated, over a *choucroute*, six years later, these
pamphlets and poems . . . it was sad and it was funny.

The year 1956 ended in apotheosis. In the great Hall of
Saint George in the Kremlin, a little party was given for
three thousand people. Two thousand nine hundred and
ninety-one of them were Moscow's complement of
ambassadors, scientists, ministers, functionaries, military
officers, artists, and rehabilitated war heroes. And then
there was the French group: Montand, Crolla, Castella,
Paraboschi, Soudieu, Azzola, Nino, Maryse, and I. Nadia,
Slava, André, and Sasha were celebrating the New Year
with their families.

In the course of this banquet, the greatest artists in

Russia performed on a stage behind the table reserved for the Central Committee, but facing the three thousand invited guests. The Oistrakhs, father and son, played the violin accompanied by the scrape of thousands of forks, and the Moisseyev dancers performed their prodigious leaps while the chicken was served. I began to have the strange impression that I had already seen all this somewhere before.... Of course—when I was a *dame du château* in *Les Visiteurs du Soir*.

On the twelfth stroke of midnight the chandeliers went out, and I kissed my husband in the dark. Then a hand grasped my shoulder as the lights came on again. Nikita Khrushchev, owner of the hand, pulled me up from my chair, and he kissed me on the mouth in front of his 2,990 guests. Then he shook Montand by both hands and with the speed of a sprinter made his way to another table, where he dislodged the Chinese ambassador and brought him triumphantly to the table of the Supreme Soviet. And in keeping with rural manners, everyone squeezed closer together, and then the Chinese ambassador sat down between Khrushchev and Madame Furtseva. From the back of the hall appeared Marshal Zhukov, in disgrace until a short time previously; his face was all flushed and he was preceded by an emissary. He, too, took his place at the Supreme Soviet's family table—but at the bottom of the table.

Neither the Chinese dissident nor the turbulent general ever told us what they thought on that early morning of January 1, 1957. However heteroclite it might appear, a guest list including one marshal of the Soviet army, one companion of Mao Tse-tung, and one French singer and his lady who had either been publicly pardoned for having been wrong, or publicly thanked for having been right, could mean one thing or the other. Work it out for yourself—if you can! About 3 A.M., Khrushchev and Bulganin were dancing in one of the Hall of Saint George's small salons, tapping their feet, squatting on their haunches like young Ukrainian peasants. A ring of Western ambassadors, like spectators at Scheherazade's court, clapped hands, keeping the tempo to encourage them.

When we arrived in Leningrad, Peter the Great was waiting for us at the station. He had come with Alexander Nevsky, Ivan the Terrible, and a deputy from the Baltic. He was Nikolai Cherkasov, the greatest Soviet actor of his day, who wished to welcome us to his city. It was his city. He was its deputy to the Supreme Soviet. He was also the son of an old lady and the father of a young boy whom neither his titles nor his glory had been able to save from death during the siege of Leningrad, which had lasted nine hundred days. His son and his mother had died of hunger, like the others—that is, a million people.

Leningrad has been Saint Petersburg, Petrograd, and Leningrad, and it's superb. It has the most beautiful palaces, the finest museums, the handsomest river, and the best bridges. It also has the Hotel d'Angleterre, and this is where we lived, all thirteen of us. It was the first time that Nadia, Sasha, Slava, and André were really living with us. In Moscow they would go home after their day's work. But here they were discovering Leningrad along with us, and after the concert we would all go to *doma*—home— together. It was in the Hotel d'Angleterre that Esenin opened his veins and wrote his last poem. That was in 1925. Sitting on the floor of our princely apartment after a last glass and just before we went off to bed, one of the four Russians—I don't remember which one—remarked that it was perhaps on this very carpet that Esenin's blood had flowed. At which point all four of them recited in chorus, in Russian, the last verses of the young madman, which were:

> In this life, to die is nothing new.
> But living is surely no newer.

A few kilometers from the outskirts of the city, along the road that leads to the airport, there is a little wooden sign, black, bearing a white inscription. This is the boundary. This is the kilometer the Nazis were never able to pass. The verst they were never able to enter. To the left of the road, facing the sign, there stands a narrow forest of young trees planted at regular intervals. It extends as far as the eye can see. There is one tree for each of the dead. A forest of souls.

It was on our way to the plane for Kiev that we discovered the forest of souls. Our week in Leningrad had been quite different from those spent in Moscow. The local lounge lizards and acrobats had not shown up. Maybe there were fewer of them around the Hermitage than in the shadow of the Kremlin. There were the usual visits to factories, of course, each with a little concert, of course; but my clearest memory is of children's faces. They took us to visit the House of Pioneers, with its play park, with slides, and a great crowd of happy little kids who spoke French and were insolent to their instructors, who laughed along with them.

And then there was a dinner at the Cherkasovs'. Rolled in my napkin I found a pair of sixteenth-century earrings that Madame Cherkasov had put there for me. A friend of theirs sang "Kalitka" when dessert came. (Not "Kalinka.") It was the song that Michel Piccoli, Georges Marchal, and I had sung with Oscar Dancinger in Mexico: "the little gate at the bottom of the garden." And then Cherkasov, who was in the middle of making *Don Quixote* and thus had to get up very early in the morning, insisted on taking us home to the Hotel d'Angleterre. "Here, in our country, guests must be taken home right to their beds." Nikolai Cherkasov died some ten years ago. He was a prince among men.

Leningrad is an old city full of phantoms and survivors. Kiev is a new city. Its survivors rebuilt it. After ninety percent of it was razed, there remained a few vestiges of what had been the old capital of the Ukraine. We had flown over kilometer upon kilometer of this land, which, a few years earlier, was one huge fire, set by the Ukrainians themselves to repel the enemy. In the city you are faced with the anachronistic sight of people in traditional clothes silhouetted against the huge white Stalinist buildings. It brings your thoughts back incessantly to the war.

Montand sang at the opera house. And then in a kolkhoz and then at a dancing school. I would like to know what happened to that twelve-year-old little girl who danced so well and was so beautiful.... Kiev seemed very far from Paris and very far from Moscow. We laughed less often, less loudly. It was the last week of our trip. Sasha, André, Nadia, and Slava were pensive, not to say "not gay." Their working vacations were coming to an end.

When we got back "in town," the French ambassador asked us to the embassy. We went there at eleven in the morning the day before our departure, for an old-fashioned drop of port. Madame Dejean was waiting for us in the salon of this beautiful palace where "until October 1917 it is said that orgies took place which...." As we came in, she was leafing through an issue of *Théâtre de France*, and had just stopped at the page where Montand and Signoret, photographed by Thérèse le Prat, were John and Elizabeth Proctor. Diplomatic life is riddled with coincidences that would make an intellectual surrealist essay such as "Najda"° seem like a comic strip.

Had we had a good trip? She hoped that we had liked Leningrad, the Venice of the Eastern world.... Monsieur l'Ambassadeur made his entrance. He kissed my hand and dragged my husband off to a corner of the salon, announcing that he was sure the ladies preferred to be left alone for their chat. I could hear enough to know that Monsieur l'Ambassadeur was trying to winkle out information about what had been said during our little supper with the Supreme Soviet. Very interesting things, said Montand, who is not a spy for the French foreign office.

Monsieur l'Ambassadeur brought back my husband

°By André Breton.

214

and interrupted the ladies' chat. He wanted us to know how sad he and his wife were because they had been forced to ignore us. Ah, if only we had arrived now, in January, things would have been so much simpler. But this idea of coming in December... inopportune. Ah, yes, we'd already heard this somewhere before (thank you, Aragon). Now, of course, everything was back to normal. It had looked bad for a while there. But all's well that ends well, and he wanted Montand and me to know that these six weeks of recitals across the whole continent had done much for the prestige of France. It was the least he could do, to tell Montand that before his departure.

Monsieur Dejean is not a bad fellow, and he has a fine face. Madame Dejean is charming and very beautiful. As we left them, we said to each other—and I think we said it to them too—that we would rather be in our shoes than in theirs.

A few officials had risen very early to offer us one last toast in their airport VIP lounge before our departure. It was five o'clock in the morning. André, Sasha, Slava, and Nadia did their stuff. They translated *mir* (peace), *spasibo* (thank you), *rabota* (work), *dorogoy* and *dorogaya* ("dear," masculine and feminine), and *Za vashe zdorovye* (To your health). They translated speeches buried in which we recognized the key words of empty phrases. They were sad. We were too. We were like lovers whose last moments before a long separation have been officially and indiscreetly stolen.

It was very, very cold when we walked up the plane's gangway. We turned around one last time to say, or rather to signal, *à bientôt*. During the first hour of our flight I kept thinking of the tiny stalactites and stalagmites that might seal their eyelids, but as tears are hot, I told myself they would melt.

Warsaw was our destination. But our plane was most unusual. The inside was like a flying drawing room. As

Soria, busy with other tasks, had been lost from our sight since we went to Leningrad, he was not one of our party. We were greeted in Warsaw by his assistant, Roger Boussinot.

So the comments made by Crolla, Soudieu, Paraboschi, Azzola, Nino, Maryse, and Castella, along with Montand's and mine, about our unusual plane could be exchanged only among ourselves. The comrade stewardess who handed out glasses of tea couldn't understand a word of French. The seats were festooned with pompons, like the armchairs in the Hotel d'Angleterre. There was a corner designed for reading and a corner designed for card games. We had never seen a plane like that. We decided that it was a very nice "planelet" and that it was fun to arrive in Warsaw in a plane all to ourselves.

The planelet came down in Vilna. The same redheaded photographer was there, with his little boy and the photos he had taken on our way in. He still seemed to be on the point of saying things that never came out. The photographs were . . . photographs. But it was nice of him to have thought of bringing them, especially when one remembered that our planelet didn't figure on any official flight schedule (we didn't think about that until much later).

A few hours later our planelet landed in Warsaw. From the looks on the faces of our reception committee we immediately realized that something was wrong. Our planelet, it turned out, belonged to the Presidium.

It was the result of that New Year's kiss in the Hall of Saint George. We didn't just land in Warsaw. We came down upon Warsaw directly from the Kremlin.

So we were off to a bad start in Warsaw. The Poles—socialists, semi-socialists, and anti-socialists—have two things in common: They hate the Germans, and this goes back well before Hitler; and they hate the Russians, and that goes back to the Romanovs, passing through Stalin and ending with Khrushchev. Khrushchev's latest visit had not left a kindly memory. It had been in October, and it had been a surprise visit. It had also coincided with the encirclement of Warsaw by Soviet troops "called out in aid of socialism." Khrushchev had not greeted Gomulka, pretending he didn't know who he was. He had behaved like a czar among serfs. But the Poles were no longer serfs, they were socialists, and in no mood for another occupation, even in the name of socialism. They made this abundantly clear, courageously and intelligently. That's how Warsaw hadn't become Budapest, and why Khrushchev got back into his plane and left.

So making your smiling way down the steps of the same airborne apparatus that had brought Khrushchev in October was inopportune... once more. And especially on election day, the day when Gomulka took his well-deserved revenge after ten years of disgrace as a Titoist deviationist.

Our interpreter was very pleasant. And very discreet. It was only after a few hours that he decided to ask us—with many apologies for poking his nose into what was none of his business—why Montand had insisted on being paid in gold dollars!

Then we realized that the atmosphere of hostility we had felt from the moment of our arrival was not due entirely to the conveyance we arrived in. The plane was the final straw in a well-managed press campaign that had been circulated throughout the Polish newspapers. They had been told, and so they had written and the citizens had believed, that our entire tour of the East had been remunerated in gold dollars. Nobody had told them, and so nothing had been written, and so the citizens knew nothing about the various incidents in Moscow. Nothing about November in Paris. Nothing about our letter to Obraztsov. As far as they were concerned, we were people who had no problems. We were there to take their money after we had taken the Russians', and before going to scoop it up in other people's republics. And not any old money. Montand was there to sink the Polish economy, just as he was the best pal of Nikita, who'd lent him his personal plane.... That was our first day in Warsaw.

So we had to begin all over. First, foremost and very

quickly, we had to tidy up those rumors, contracts in hand. Then we would start on the ideological problems. Montand insisted that the press print the sums that he would be earning in zlotys. If they started off thinking us bastards, now they would consider us dangerously unhinged. They'd been through enough—maybe too much—not to be aware that their currency was almost impossible to convert anywhere in the world.

By the next day, the atmosphere was different. People arrived who wanted to explain. They had vaguely heard about the little supper and, quite normally, thought that nothing more had been said than the kind of banalities usually trotted out on such occasions. Since there were no witnesses and no tapes (that we knew of), they had to take our word for it. They were furious that Khrushchev hadn't thought fit to tell us about his surprise visit. It was quite true that although he had emphasized the liquidation of the Polish party by Stalin, he had been very discreet concerning the events of October. And we were too, because we had been conditioned by Budapest. For the Poles, Budapest was not all that interesting. Or rather it interested them only to the extent that it illustrated what they had managed to avoid in Warsaw. But as far as Hungary's future as a people's republic was concerned, they reminded us quite forcefully that there was no parallel in the pasts of the two countries. Leaving aside the fact that both Hungary and Poland had suffered under the czars, they could not forget that Hungary had been the first fascist country in the world, under the regent Horthy, and Hitler's undefecting ally up to the very last hours of the Second World War. Whereas they had been the absolute victims of Nazism. The two things could not be compared. They could understand that the whole world pitied Hungary, but they could not understand that the whole world wasn't celebrating their victory as Polish socialists. It was then January, but it was "springtime" in Warsaw. Their conversation would return again and again to those crucial days in October. (I remembered us on the set of

The Crucible, egocentrically reassured when we read that "everything has been arranged in Warsaw.") They needed to talk about those days in October, just as they needed to talk about the ten years that had preceded them. They talked and talked and talked, but they were no longer aggressive, as we were no longer the accused. They were passionate and fascinating.

These conversations took place in our hotel, in restaurants, in an apartment, and in Montand's dressing room. Anyone who didn't know where to find him in the city simply came to the theater, where there still remained the small matter of doing his job after a certain hour. But they didn't always come to hear the recital. They came to talk. And they talked until the moment the curtain went up. Then Montand would gently show them to the door, pointing to the hour. Of course they understood; and they said they would come back to take up the conversation after the show. In fact, during that week in Warsaw, singing ended up being a kind of intermission between conversations for Montand. I don't know how he survived. But he sang, and he sang well, and the halls were full. The last night, after the final curtain call, the audience sang "Stolat! Stolat!" to him, which must be a kind of equivalent of "For He's a Jolly Good Fellow."

Our zlotys paid the hotel bill, and they paid for a portrait of a charming adolescent Countess Potocka, a contemporary of Marie Walewska. Henry, our interpreter, had taken me to the state store, a kind of nationalized flea market. The young countess hangs in Autheuil, where she plays the role of a distant ancestor. The zlotys that remained . . . remained. They've been asleep in an envelope, waiting for us to go back, for the past twenty years.

When we left Warsaw for East Berlin we had the feeling of leaving happy Poles. They loved Gomulka, whom they had just brought to power with a 93 percent popular vote. Once in a while a conversation would still include a phrase like: "Unfortunately his wife is Jewish," but as they say, nobody's perfect.

I said a little while ago that Kiev is far from Paris and far from Moscow. In Warsaw, the week Gomulka was elected we were far from Kiev, but we felt close to Paris, Moscow, London, New York, and the Vatican. I've talked so much about the people of Warsaw that I haven't talked about the city.

Warsaw was razed and then reconstructed with fervor, stone upon stone, exactly as it had been, said Henry, when he showed me the polychrome square. For months teams of Polish architects had researched documents for the tiniest details of historic accuracy which, put into execution, gave back to this city one of the most charming central squares in the world. The little pink, ocher, and green houses have grown right back in their original places. A second team had offered the martyred city a skyscraper. It houses the Journalists League or the House of Culture; I've forgotten which. Its plans, too, were drawn up only after a great deal of historical research in the Polish architectural past, but it is a servile duplicate of the University of Moscow. We were to learn later that there are these copies everywhere. As there are Nîmes arenas and arches of triumph everywhere. There was also, at that time, a huge derelict area in the middle of Warsaw. It was, or rather it had been, the ghetto.

We did not see Poland during that week in January 1957. We saw the people of Warsaw. For the first time in six weeks we were meeting people who spoke loudly in the street and in their bistros. They were insolent, aggressive, charming, proud, and free.

Nothing seemed to have changed in East Germany since our last visit. Montand sang in an enormous theater whose name I have forgotten. One evening he gave a recital at the Theater am Schiffbauerdamm, home of the Berliner Ensemble. Helene Weigel and her company gave us a little party. Brecht had died six months earlier, and the two Germanys had, together, given him a national funeral. Our arms full of red carnations, we got on the train for Prague.

At the Czech border two gentlemen, their arms full of red carnations, climbed into our compartment. If in Leningrad one accompanied one's guests home right to their beds, it seemed that here, in Bohemia, one welcomed them at the door of the country.

They had come to welcome us, but also—combining business with pleasure—so they might use the few hours of travel together to outline to Montand his program for the week. He would sing in a very large hall, and they were happy to tell him that there wasn't a seat to be had. It was really very kind of these gentlemen to have taken the trouble to travel so many kilometers one way and now the same number back in order to present us with this bit of good news. Surely there was something else? Ah, yes! Two small requests. The Czech police and the Czech army would be so very appreciative if Montand would sing a little supplementary concert for them; would that be possible? They seemed painfully disappointed, not to say tragically up crap creek without a paddle, when Montand explained gently that he had never in his life devoted an evening to the police or the army of any country whatsoever, and surely they couldn't expect him to change these old habits in Prague. It then behooved me to ask if the Czech police intended to invite Madame Slanska* to their party. I didn't know at that time and in that train that in Prague there were still names you didn't mention. Even though they were the names of victims of "errors of the past," duly recognized as such.

Their terrified faces announced things that would be confirmed during the ensuing days. Prague was not Warsaw. They simply paid no attention to my little "joke" and began talking vaguely about the possibility of a

*The widow of Slansky, hanged in 1953.

concert in Bratislava. The Slovak population had complained of being exluded from this cultural manifestation. They gave us a little course in ethnic geography from which we learned that it was very difficult to please everybody. They talked about the Slovaks the way some Parisians talk about the Bretons. Since Montand had always sung for the Bretons, he had no reason to make declarations about the Slovaks as he had done about the police and the army. Well, nothing had been definitely decided, we were told; one would see....

The train rolled on, and from then on there were nothing but banalities. Yet something extraordinary and decisive had happened which neither of us had noticed. It took me until 1969 to reconstruct the puzzle and finally to slot in its two major missing pieces. And it wasn't until 1974 that I had confirmation of what I had discovered in 1969 and missed entirely in 1966.

The two missing pieces were two names pronounced within a few seconds of each other: the name of Slansky's wife and the town of Bratislava.

I had uttered the name of Madame Slanska. That was really a reflection of the black Warsaw humor we had been steeped in during the previous week. They had reacted with a terrified silence. Then they had talked about Bratislava. My reaction was nil. Bratislava meant nothing to me; prior to their geography lesson, I didn't even know where Bratislava was. They knew where it was. They also were very well aware that I had family there. They knew, but I didn't yet, not in this train.

I was to discover it the next day. I had a cousin in Bratislava. In Neuilly-sur-Seine we had never taken stock of those bits of our family that were in Central Europe. So it was quite normal for me to know nothing of the existence of my cousin in Bratislava. She phoned me the day after our arrival in Prague, at the Hotel Alkron.

She spoke English. She explained briefly how she came to be my cousin, through my paternal grandmother. She had read in the Bratislava press that Montand was going to give a recital there, and she very much looked forward to meeting us. I told her that nothing had been decided, and she seemed to be surprised. It had been officially announced. She hoped *very much* to see us. There was something so pressing in the way she said that she hoped *so much* that she would meet us, that when I hung up the phone, I mentally classified her among those pains in the ass who work hard at it when they discover some family link with celebrities, just to call attention to themselves among their neighbors. She told me her name. I forgot it. I also quickly forgot the whole telephone call.

The Hotel Alkron was a kind of crossroads between East and West. Its lobby and restaurant were always full of foreign correspondents and Czech journalists and people on their way to Peking or on their way back from Moscow: Western industrialists, writers, and people connected with embassies. The lobby of the Alkron was a combination of the Café Flore, Fouquet's, and New York's Algonquin. But I didn't know that yet. The lobby of the Alkron was also difficult territory to navigate without getting trapped by people who generally had nothing to say to you but wanted to see you close up.

Montand sang in a huge hall, not a theater but a kind of hall for meetings. We never saw the spokesmen for the police and army again. They must have made their reports, and surely we were not looked upon with favor. In any case, it was the third night, I think, that Montand didn't sing. There was a brusque, brief telephone call telling him at about six in the evening that the hall would not be available that night. The government needed it for an unusual meeting. If he wanted to, he could sing somewhere else. No, Montand didn't want to sing somewhere else; he would simply not sing that night. The next day the hall was available again, but nobody ever explained. Nobody ever said anything more about Bratislava, either. In East Berlin we had been joined by a new member of the Agence Littéraire et Artistique, Monsieur Lenoir; he hadn't been given an explanation, either.

During the day we met a lot of people. The film students at the university had invited us to come and see them. They were great fun and very lively. It was they who would, in a short time, give us what is now known as the Czech cinema—Forman, Passer, Kadar. They were later to remind me of this visit, though at the time they were little more than adolescents. Jiri Trnka, in his little studio, showed us some film cartoons; he was having problems in getting them released. He gave me one of the stars of his *Midsummer Night's Dream:* a little wooden goat, which still stands firm on its frail birchwood hoofs in a cabinet in Autheuil among Russian Easter eggs, Mexican angels, and Bulgarian flutes. He was hoping that with Shakespeare played by marionettes he would have fewer difficulties than with contemporary subjects.

The night Montand's recital was "canceled," we dined with Nâzim Hikmet. Montand may have forgotten this meal, which probably caused him to say in Chris Marker's film that he'd never met Hikmet, whose song "Comme un Scorpion, Mon Frère" he sings. (I'm going into this detail to clarify that I'm not making things up.) We dined together at the Alkron. Nâzim Hikmet was handsome and huge. He had been imprisoned in Turkey for years because he is what he is—the greatest revolutionary poet of his country and his generation. He spoke very, very loudly in that dining room. He talked about liberty, and lack of liberty. He was on his way to Moscow, where he was going to complain about something-or-other. He wanted to be sure everyone knew. The Czech writer who had come with him visibly wondered whether this meal was a good idea.

One day we lunched at the French Embassy, a superb baroque palace. I've forgotten to mention that since the drop of port with the Dejeans in Moscow, the foreign office had obviously flashed a green light, and in all the countries we visited, the ambassadors were always warm and friendly. The French ambassador in Czechoslovakia had very fine Lurçat tapestries on the wall, and he told us a story about the embarrassment of the visiting Czech dignitaries when they discovered that Lurçat, whose non-socialist realist art they detested, was a long-standing French Communist-party militant.

Our week was drawing to an end. One evening Montand inquired about the Bratislava recital, which had not been mentioned since the train, and someone said it couldn't be arranged. Too complicated ... and too tiring, all these comings and goings. The Slovaks would understand. Fine.

The next morning my Bratislava cousin phoned. She had just read in the Slovak press that Montand had decided not to come and sing in Bratislava. That was a great pity, she said. I explained that it had not been his decision; we had been told that it was too complicated and too tiring to come. I explained to her what they had told us. She repeated that it was really a pity. "It's too bad, it's too bad," she kept murmuring. Her voice was very sad. So I said that really it was only something we were putting off; I said something like, "We'll surely meet someday." She said, "Maybe."

As I hung up, the thought crossed my mind that it was certainly a pity that we would miss a very beautiful city, but on the other hand, missing the family dinner that my Bratislava cousin had undoubtedly organized had its advantages too. So I left Prague with a perfectly clear conscience, after a week in which some pleasant things, some inexplicable things, and, above all, some unexplained things had happened to us.

One day in London in 1966, as I was in my Savoy Hotel room getting ready to suffer in my role of Lady Macbeth—and cause suffering to the ears of a number of Shake-spearean purists—my bedside telephone tinkled, as it is wont to do at the Savoy, and I was told that Mrs. Sophie Langer would like to speak to me. "Mrs. Sophie Langer says she is your cousin from Bratislava." Nine years after having missed me in her own country, here she is in London, I thought. I took the phone and announced that I was working very hard. She was aware of that, but she was in London with her daughter and they would like very much to meet me at long last. We arranged to meet the next day at three in the afternoon.

I was then going through a period of monstrous egocentricity. I was trying to achieve something dictated by my vanity—or my lack of wisdom. Moreover, I wasn't doing it terribly well. (We'll come back to the *Macbeth* adventure later on.) I was available only to myself. I had about as much use for my cousin from Bratislava as I would have had for the Pope if he'd requested an audience with me. I was concentrating only on Lady M., and I went over and over the lines all day long. It was the first time in my life I was behaving like that—and believe you me, I've forgotten nothing of those weeks when I was disconnected from the rest of the world, exactly like all those people whom I often consider contemptuously when handing out accusations of indifference.

My cousin was very beautiful. Her daughter was graceful and charming. They were in London because the girl had gotten an *au pair* job with an English family. Well done, well done, I said, mentally going over the lines I would be saying on the stage of the Royal Court in the near future. I really was wrapped up. Nonetheless, my cousin wanted to tell me the story of her life. After the Nazi invasion, she and her husband, young Czech socialists, had left their country and gone to live in exile in America during the war. In 1945 they had rushed back home to help construct a socialist state. Her husband, Oskar Langer, a lawyer, had been arrested, with many others, for deviationism in 1952. She was about to go on when I said, not really to interrupt but to show off my knowledge, I suppose, "But he surely would have had trouble in New York too."

She stopped speaking. I asked her to continue her story. She said there wasn't much point now. She finished her tea, signaled her daughter, excused herself for having disturbed me, and left my luxurious little apartment—not, however, without remarking that people like me really knew very little. My cousin from Bratislava was not the pain in the ass I had imagined in Prague; but she didn't strike me as being particularly likable. As far as I was concerned, well, I had to act. Besides, if she was in London, and with her daughter, those things she mentioned must already be ancient history. Things must be all right now in Czechoslovakia, since people travel as they wish. And that was that.

Those were my thoughts as I closed the door. I turned to my blackboard, on which I had chalked in capital letters: "*Wouldst* thou have *that which* thou *esteem'st* the *orn*ament of *life....*" A difficult little line enclosed in the middle of a long speech that was no less difficult. And I gave no more thought to my cousin or her daughter or her husband, whose story I had never let her finish. "*Wouldst* thou have *that...wouldst* thou have *that....*" She had mentioned, at the beginning of the conversation, another daughter, who sang; who knows.... "*Wouldst* thou have *that....*"

In autumn 1968, on returning from Stockholm, where I had been filming *The Seagull*, I discovered in my pile of mail an envelope postmarked Germany. It contained two pink pages of flimsy paper; it was dated August 30 and had been waiting for me for a month. It was written in English, and happily I have kept it.

I had decided never to get in touch with you again, since it was so obvious that you did not like us. When I wanted to tell you my story, all you could think of to say was that, as Communists, we would have been treated in the same way had we stayed in the United States. I hope that *today* you can understand the difference. I crossed the border forty-eight hours ago between Russian tanks and guns. It was a nightmare. But from now on life in Czechoslovakia will be a nightmare. We got out with two suitcases, thanks to the little car bought with *the price of my husband's blood*, the money paid at the time of his rehabilitation....

I felt ill at ease as I read that letter. And I deserved to. I could have written to an address in London where she said she would be for the next week. But I didn't. A month had already gone by. I made no attempt to find my cousin Sophie Langer. Yet I didn't chuck the letter away. I put it aside and started packing to go off to Los Angeles with Montand.

When I came back to Paris in March 1969, I read *L'Aveu (The Confession)*, by Artur London, *Les Nôtres (Our Own People)*, by Elizabeth Poretsky, and Josefa Slanska's autobiography, one after another. In Josefa Slanska's book I read the story of my cousin Oskar Langer, the story I had not wanted to hear in London. I was dreadfully ashamed. I found the two pink pages and, as one throws a bottle out to sea, I wrote to the improbable address in London, now seven months old. My letter begged her pardon for my egotism and my sins of ignorance. A week later I got an answer from Västerås in Sweden, four single-spaced typed pages. It is an overwhelming document that rightfully ought to be reproduced in its entirety. She pardoned me. She thanked me. She was sorry that we were now discovering, twelve years later, things that we could have learned from her if we had met in Bratislava. In 1957 her husband was still in prison. "You two might have been able to shorten his detention time, and thus prolong his life, simply because 'they' knew that I had written proof of his innocence, and consequently the innocence of many others. Often 'they' wanted to give a good impression to sympathetic foreigners." I found out that she had come to Prague and had sat in the lobby of the Alkron. She had seen us go by but hadn't dared accost us, as she knew she was being followed and she didn't want to be the "badgering cousin." At that moment she still thought we were coming to Bratislava. Her daughter was singing under a name other than that of her father, the "traitor." She was singing in the bar of the hotel where we would surely have been accommodated. She was no longer allowed to appear with

228

the orchestra with which she had been a soloist. Both she and her daughter had worked out an elaborate plan for informing us. But we hadn't gone to Bratislava...and so from afar she had seen disappear her only hope of convincing honest people who had been duped, as she herself had been duped in her youth at the time of the Moscow trials. She kept reverting to the notion of twelve lost years. And to the silence that enveloped the detention of people, some of whom were rehabilitated only in 1964. She also said, "Despite all I had endured during those years, in January 1968 I found I was capable once more of enthusiasm." Now she was learning Swedish, her seventh language. Her letter ended thus: "Excuse me for having written at such length. Perhaps it is because there are many people here with whom I can make conversation, but no one with whom I can talk. Thank you for having written; it has done a little to restore the faith I used to have when I believed in human dignity. Oh, how I believed—what tremendous faith I had in those days! Love, Sophie."

My cousin Sophie came to Paris last year. We spent a day together. Now she speaks Swedish. We spoke a mixture of English, French, and German in order not to lose time searching for words. We had so much to say to each other. We often had tears in our eyes—sometimes of laughter, sometimes of sadness. She is eight years older than she was in my Savoy suite. I am too. She is seventeen years older than she was in the lobby of the Alkron. Of course, I never saw her in the lobby of the Alkron. Since that letter from Västerås, in my mind's eye I've screened and rescreened that scene in close-up. The tight close-up is the face of a woman who sees passing the only people in the world she wants to speak to. Who are sneakily being prevented from going to Bratislava, without their knowing why. She is looking at someone whom they tried to pressure to perform a gala evening for the police and the army; which would probably have been presented as his personal initiative. She is seated there, she sees us go by, she can do nothing, nothing, nothing. No doubt we were smiling, in a hurry, shaking hands, and we didn't see her. We pass by. I think back on those Russian faces whose messages had not escaped me. Hers had escaped me. Now she's here beside me, and she's telling her story. She could still feel the anguish of that day, and it was wonderful to be able to do, even seventeen years too late, what I might never have been able to do. Listen to her and kiss her.

With the help of her memory and mine, we were able to reconstruct that puzzle whose twisted design was now illuminated by a dark clarity. Today I can truly maintain that during that week in February 1957 in Prague, everything was put into place, or sometimes displaced, so that a meeting between the wife of the political prisoner Oskar Langer and her cousin, the wife of the singer Yves Montand, would be impossible. That mission was accomplished. It started when we were taken in hand right at the frontier. It ended at the moment when we fastened our seat belts in the plane that took us to Bucharest. Only then did those in charge of this delicate mission heave a great sigh of relief.

For a week, without knowing it, we were actors in a story written by Kafka. From high in the sky we looked down one last time on Prague the majestic.

Bucharest, too, has a skyscraper. It, too, is deeply inspired by Rumanian history. In Bucharest the copy of the University of Moscow is called the House of Culture. We were invited there by the minister, a charming, intelligent lady. She announced that the government wished to give us a dinner. They had heard about the little supper in Moscow and didn't want to do less than their big brother. She asked us to please prepare any questions we wished to ask, that they would be welcomed.

A young couple had come to see us at the hotel. He was French, she was Rumanian; he had come to this country as a reporter for French television; he wanted to marry her and take her back to France. It was officially forbidden. If the little supper in Moscow did nothing more than introduce Martin Du Gard to Russian readers, the big dinner in Bucharest at least served to bring about this marriage.

On the eve of our departure we were given a lovely engraved Chinese scroll rolled around a bamboo stick, on the back of which was written a letter. I will reproduce here just the end, respecting the charming turns of phrase. "May a little Simone and a little Yves soon be the fond fruits of our happiness, which you have helped to bring about. Our words are pale thanks. But please remember that our kindest thoughts and wishes will always be with you."

It was signed: "Plinie Cretu and Henri Chapuis, February 22, 1957." The engraving is also in Autheuil, not far from Trnka's little wooden goat. In Bucharest we were the agents of a marriage; in Prague we let someone rot in jail.

Anna Pauker had less luck than our fiancés. "She's very well" was the answer to our question. "She's grown old, she's resting." Quite true, the old revolutionary was "resting."

Anna Pauker speaking at a political rally, Madame Lupescu at the Chantilly racecourse, and poor King Carol in exile; those were the prewar newsreels that I remember from the Chézy cinema in Neuilly. Anna Pauker with her short hair and her men's shirts, Madame Lupescu with her huge hats and silver foxes, and the poor, sad king, also at Chantilly.

During our week in Rumania I was, visibly, not the only one playing games with nostalgia.

We didn't see Rumania. We saw Rumanians. Not the impoverished peasants described by Panait Istrati; Rumanians of Bucharest, who didn't require too much egging on to start yarning about how gay their city used to be: like a little Paris. Yes, indeed! Along with the Iron Guard, the alliance with Hitler. The Russians weren't loved in Bucharest. Exactly the same thing was applicable in Warsaw. In Bucharest the desire to be socialist wasn't seen. In Prague it was.

Sofia, too, has its skyscraper, descended in a straight line from Bulgarian history. In Sofia the University of Moscow is...I can't remember whether it's the Press House or the Medical Union.

In Sofia they love the Russians. That goes back long before Khrushchev, Stalin, or Lenin; it goes back to the Romanovs. The Russians saved the Bulgarians from the Turks.

The mausoleum in Dimitrov is dedicated to a revolutionary who refused to plead guilty at the Reichstag fire trial. He was a Bulgarian. That was in 1933.

Kostov was the only defendant in those rigged trials who tried to demystify the machinations. He was a Bulgarian. That was in 1949. They hanged him anyway. But he tried.

In Sofia, it's all a matter of frontiers. They don't like the Greeks or the Yugoslavs, and they detest the Turks, who in turn can't stand the Greeks, who don't much like the Yugoslavs, who hate the Bulgarians, who don't like the Hungarians and loathe the Germans.

We came to these weighty conclusions one evening at dinner, after the recital in Sofia—our fifth stop in the socialist camp after we left Moscow. By that time I could only dimly remember my concept of that grand comradeship, that fraternal exchange of regional products, I had imagined on my way to Babelsberg: "Let's have a spot of your coal and we'll pop off a pile of our uranium; and let's share our apples, our caviar, our bread, and our salt...."

In Sofia we saw a people that was strong, calm, and gay.

(Today is September 28, 1975. Yesterday morning Franco sent five young men to the firing squad. I'm going to write down their names so that they will remain in print longer than in this week's or maybe even in next week's newspapers: Angel Otaegui Echeverria, José Francisco Baena Alonso, Ramón García Sanz, José Luis Sanchez Bravo, and Juan Paredes Manotas. And I also want to list the names of those who went to Madrid on September 22 to deliver a collective text written by Sartre, Malraux, Aragon, Mendès-France, and François Jacob—since neither the *Express* nor *Match* saw fit to mention it in their pages. Their names were Costa-Gavras, Régis Debray, Michel Foucault, Jean Lacouture, the Reverend Father Laudouze, Claude Mauriac, and Yves Montand. They didn't sit quietly in their cozy chairs, and they were carted off to the airport for the return flight to Paris in a Spanish paddy wagon.)

Belgrade does not have its skyscraper inspired by Serbo-Croatian history. There is no University of Moscow in Belgrade. In the hotel restaurant there were Gypsies singing "Kalitka" ("the little gate at the bottom of the garden").

Speaking of songs, it's been a while since I mentioned my husband's show. It would be a prime example of conjugal immodesty to repeat that here, as elsewhere, every seat was filled and he was a huge success. Never mind; I'll repeat it.

In Belgrade the movie houses show films from all over the world in their original versions. And in Belgrade I saw *The Crucible* played by an all-Croatian cast, and I understood it all.

And it was in Belgrade that we met Mr. and Mrs. Broz.

One morning, a voice on the telephone said: "Marshal and Mrs. Broz would be very happy to receive you tomorrow afternoon for a cup of tea. A car will be sent to your hotel around three in the afternoon." There was no more protocol than that to the invitation, and the car that was waiting for us at three o'clock the next afternoon was an ancient Ford with no distinguishing features except that it was old. There was a man at the wheel and another who opened the door for us. Neither of them spoke French.

They smiled; so did we. We left Belgrade and then crossed a suburb, and soon we were in a very dense forest. This is when Montand and I started playing our version of *Le Mort en Fuite*. In this film, Jules Berry and Michel Simon are two second-rate actors, and at one point Berry is mistakenly captured by a group of Croatian revolutionaries and is taken to the Carpathian mountains.... Was it the fatigue accumulated over the past few months, or certain mysteries of the East that had been swirling around us almost constantly for some time now? I panicked. But I bottled it up inside.

The car seemed like nothing that might belong to a head of state any more than our two companions seemed like official emissaries. The voice on the telephone that had invited us seemed entirely anonymous. The forest became increasingly dense.... At just that moment Montand said, "Where are we going? And who are these two guys?" Obviously our thoughts had met. Suddenly it was all very simple: We had talked too much wherever we went and we knew too much, so they were going to do away with us. And what place had they chosen? Of course; the territory of the ex-traitor Tito, recently rehabilitated! Suddenly it all made sense; we were childish not to have thought of it before! Montand said in a low voice, "Don't get scared. Watch the driver and I'll take care of the other one; if the car slows down, I'll jump him."

But the car never slowed down. Gradually the forest grew less dense, and then we weren't in the forest any longer. We were rolling along a road bordered by spacious gardens, in the middle of which stood splendid villas, occasionally with a visible guard. Then we came to the finest of the houses, and there were two guards. On the steps leading to the house were three figures: Marshal Tito, his wife, and a very tall and distinguished gentleman.

Tito was dressed in gray flannels cut in good English style, and there was a large diamond stickpin in his tie. Madame Broz wore black, and her jewelry was as unostentatious as that of a girl taking her first communion.

They were beautiful people. The tall gentleman translated words of welcome. Madame Broz held both our hands while the tall gentleman translated: "It's marvelous; I feel as though I were at the movies." I asked him to reply: "We do too—a newsreel."

Tea had been laid, but Tito proposed champagne. Cool bottles arrived, and on their labels was written "Reserved for Marshal Tito." And then, for two hours, Tito talked.

We exchanged toasts, and then we began to wonder whom he had really invited to drink champagne with him in his country house, receiving us with family-style informality. Was it the actor-singer and the actress he and his wife had seen in films? Or was it the fellow travelers of the French Communist party? Or was it the voyagers who had just sojourned in six countries where people had once been hanged for Titoist allegiances? Or was it the people who had supped with the Presidium of the Supreme Soviet three months earlier? Or was it a couple who were to land in Budapest a few days later? We were a combination of all those people, and he addressed himself to them all.

He obviously thought we were party members; so it was with definite sarcasm that he asked us whether, now, we were convinced that he was no longer the traitor who had sold out to imperialism, as they had said he was from 1948 to 1956.

We replied that we had never been convinced of anything as far as he was concerned, which was, in fact, one of the reasons why we had never become card-carrying French Communist-party members. It was not the only reason; but the others were of a cultural nature. This clarification undoubtedly contributed to changing the course of the conversation. Once again we were in the fortunate position of being able to define our point of view to the person concerned.

Tito, his wife, and the tall gentleman were surprised and very pleased. They had been misinformed. That's quite understandable, we said. Without holding the card, we had participated in a number of things together with the

French Communists, including, probably, a number that concerned him. But, well, that's the way it is. . . . He hadn't invited members of the French Communist party. We had never been to a cell meeting where Titoists were excluded, nor had we been Titoists. We were free; we were even free to be wrong sometimes.

The tall gentleman translated. From his ear a thin cord was plugged into a small black box on the table. Occasionally he would adjust the sound after someone spoke. I thought: At least this is frank and honest. They're taping but they're doing it openly. At that point, Montand, having kicked my shins several times with some obscure signal, asked me to please speak a little louder. The tall gentleman was deaf; the microphone was a hearing aid. We were not in the forest, and we were no longer playing *Le Mort en Fuite*. We were with Marshal Tito, who wanted to talk about Paris.

He appeared to attach enormous importance to the attitude of the French Communist party during the preceding eight years. Those who had condemned him knew him very well; they were the people he had met when he was a clandestine militant in France, during the time of the Spanish Civil War and before the Second World War. His irritation against Jacques Duclos and his book *Traitor Tito and His Gang* was particularly strong, and for once he had two French people to talk to; he wanted to speak out. His rehabilitation was still quite recent and his memory was excellent.

He talked of the Paris he had known during those years of clandestinity, just the familiar suburbs and the little "safe" hotel run by comrades. Nowadays, when he went, he saw only the insides of a palace and a palatial hotel. He still didn't know Paris.

He talked about the Parisian railroad stations. It's often in railroad stations that revolutionaries are picked up by the police. He had evolved a system that he still recommended to his juniors in revolution. You dress inconspicuously to look like everybody else, and above all you have a dog. The plainclothesmen watching the arrival of certain trains coming from certain countries aren't looking out for a traveler in an ordinary ready-made suit who loiters to pee his pooch on the platform. What they're looking for is the man in a hurry in a black leather jacket and cap. You walk slowly, with your dog, showing your ticket to the man at the gate. If you have a fine pedigreed dog, he attracts attention. Which is also excellent, since everyone knows that the clandestine traveler has no interest in being noticed. All you have to do the next time you cross the border is to change dogs.

Tito laughed a good deal as he told this story, and the tall gentleman smiled as he translated it, and we laughed a lot as we listened. Madame Broz watched us listen and watched him as he spoke. It was surely not the first time that she had heard his number on the perfect method of clandestine travel, but she still seemed to be listening with pleasure, as women who love their husbands tend to do. And since I'm an incurable romantic, I wondered whether the first time she had heard his course on the perfect incognito traveler was in the mountains when she was a young partisan.

Later he talked about films. They saw all the films at home, at private screenings.

Then he spoke ill of Molotov.

Finally, he talked about his country's enormous economic difficulties. His "treachery to the socialist ideal" (he was still harping on it) had not solved all his problems. The people, or rather the peoples, of Yugoslavia had lived through difficult times, and they were not yet finished. "At least," he said, "I warned them. I never lied to them. That's why they love me and believe in me, and that's why they didn't abandon me when I was alone in 1948."

Then he talked about the Bulgarian partisans who had held the mountains during the war and refused passage to the Yugoslav partisans. We already knew that story: The Bulgarians told exactly the same story but with the roles reversed. Then he talked about Stalin's liquidation of the

Polish Communist party, and we knew that story too. Mr. Khrushchev had told it to us during the little supper in Moscow. "Oh, did he? Did he also tell you he didn't recognize Gomulka when he went to Warsaw in October?" "No, but the Poles told us, in Poland." "Did he talk about the Spaniards?" "Yes, he did." "About the ones who were liquidated?" "Yes, he did."

Then he began a list of names that meant nothing to us. He would say a name, and after each Spanish name came the same word, which the tall gentleman translated: "liquidated...liquidated...liquidated...." For us they were names; for him they were faces. It was a bit as it had been in Mexico a few months earlier, with the veterans of the Spanish war. And for this man of sixty-five or sixty-six, it was as it had been for them: a way of remembering the time twenty years earlier, in front of people who knew nothing, who were too young to have lived through all that. He was talking about a family, his own family. He talked about his family, the Communist International, somewhat in the manner of an uncle who'd been vilely slandered before his credulous nephews, and who'd suddenly reappeared to set family stories in their true perspective. He had been "Cousin Josip, who had gone to sow his wild oats in foreign parts," and now he was Uncle Josip, who knew where all the skeletons were in the various closets and who was ready to tell all to the listening nephews.

We had come full circle. We drank another glass of champagne. There were no toasts spoken aloud. We clinked glasses and smiled at each other. Madame Broz, who had said very little, asked me about Catherine. I suspect she reads about the private lives of the "stars." A photographer took some pictures of the group. We said good-bye. Madame Broz kissed me.

The next day a courier came and brought three photographs to the hotel. One had been signed by Marshal Tito and Madame Broz. In a second envelope there was the same set of three pictures with a note asking us to sign them and return them. Signing photographs is not an unusual experience for us, but I must say we were a bit stumped to find the right words to match our memory of that extraordinary afternoon. Finally, we found the right thing to say. We said, Thank you.

A year later, Montand went off to do some filming on the Dalmatian coast. Cleverly, I slipped the signed photograph into our bag. It was better than any passport. And that's how Catherine and I were able to swim quietly on a little beach after the local policeman tried to turn us away in a language we didn't understand. I had the "speaking" photo in my bag. It's the only time I used it.

Arriving in Budapest in the second week of March 1957 was a little like arriving at the house of the widow four months after the death of her husband. It's no longer mourning; it's a kind of half mourning. And the widow, however great may have been her sorrow at the time it happened, no longer wants to talk about it. Go ask Jacqueline Onassis whether four months after Dallas she still had the face of Antigone.

Budapest had been the world's most famous and most suffered-over widow since the month of November. Also the most betrayed and the most manipulated. From both sides. Her tragedy had served everyone. Now the Hungarians were visibly tired of their stardom.

Four months later they summed things up with a kind of black humor. "Now it's our turn to be Papa's little darlings. The food's a lot better than it was before November. And the ladies can buy the hats and dresses they couldn't get before. Hungarian ladies have always been very particular about their appearance. Now Budapest is the show window of the Eastern bloc. Visitors can see how we're being spoiled, now that we're such good children. In fact, we've been so good that for the first time since 1945 we're being allowed to celebrate our national holiday in a few days. That wasn't allowed under Comrade Rákosi, or under Gerö. We can celebrate by going to the factory or the office or by sweeping the streets, because we don't have a day off, but in the evening we're being given a lovely present. For our national holiday the Red Army chorus is coming specially, to sing us their repertoire. . . ." That was more or less the tone.

True, the stores were much fuller than in Warsaw, Prague, Bucharest, and especially Belgrade. And it was also true that the fine vocal group was coming to give them a military band concert in their splendid uniforms. (Montand was all for jumping into a plane to warn his friend Nikita that he was on the point of blundering again.)

The people who talked like that didn't ask us to define ourselves. They'd given up asking anyone to define himself. Especially not people from the West, which had encouraged them, with radio broadcasts, to fight during the "events" (they strictly avoided the words "revolution" and "counterrevolution"), and then had dropped them. They detested the Americans, the English, the French, and the Swiss as much as they detested their own who had fled to the West. They stayed put. They loved themselves. This, however, seemed not to indicate that they loved one another. They never came in a group to talk to us. We would meet them backstage; they were journalists, or they worked for the radio, and their humor always ended with something like this: "But of course, now everything's fine here"; especially if one of their colleagues appeared at just that moment. They had their jobs and they didn't mean to lose them. If they'd had their ration of dead, now they'd buried them. They had no desire to talk about their October-November experiences. And when they did talk, their accounts were often contradictory. Frequently it was not dissimilar to the way a Parisian—on a much smaller scale—might have talked about the riots in February 1934; all would have depended upon whether he had happened to be on the Place de la Concorde with Colonel de la Rocque* on February 6, or at the counterdemonstration on the Place de la République a few days after, with what

*Leader of the Croix de Feu (Cross of Fire) neofascist movement.

later would become the leadership of the Popular Front. The Gardes Mobiles of my childhood, on their horses, played the same role that the Soviet army had just done in its tanks. That is, firing into the crowd. A crowd of Hungarians. It appeared, however—here the tales differ— that the tank soldiers, recruited in Central Asia, thought they were in Suez. But this may already be one of those legends that appear during, or after, wars. When all's said and done, I myself have told the story about the three horsemen from Hanover who were scared when they saw the sea disappear in Saint-Gildas in 1940.

We saw some gutted houses in one part of town. The chauffeur who took us around claimed they were the result of an accidental fire the week before. However, the lady who was with us said they were still the result of the tanks of November. But not in front of the chauffeur. The chauffeur had been assigned by the Ministry of Culture, which in turn must have gotten him from the Ministry of the Interior. The Hungarian lady who accompanied us spoke very little in our apartment.

She preferred to do her talking in the park that surrounded the hotel.

The hotel was a huge palace situated on an island that separates Buda from Pest. It went back to the splendors of the Austro-Hungarian empire. It was against this background, like a set for a Max Ophuls film, that she told us a number of things. Not about the past, but about the present.

Ever since November, it was the Communists who were being arrested. Of course, there were still fascists in this city, which had been the first fascist city of Europe, with its spear-headed crosses, so akin to the Rumanian Iron Guards, though they no longer represented a danger. They were no longer young and their little aborted plots really bothered no one. In fact, they were often helpful.

Those who made the trouble were the dissident militants. The people who were in prison in Budapest in March 1957 were the same as those who were singing in the streets of Warsaw, free. Since mid-January, Kadar had increased police surveillance, and at the very moment our companion spoke, besides the arrested leaders of workers' councils, there were some fifteen writers in prison. She wanted us to know this because it was most unlikely that the Minister of Culture would tell us, if ever we met him.

We did meet him. He had a handsome, sad face. He had just been jailed for years under Rákosi; he was crippled and received us in a wheelchair. He asked me if I had found Gyula Illyés in good health.

Gyula Illyés is a great Hungarian poet and writer; he is a Peasant Socialist, not a Communist; at the time he was on the line, but untouchable. I had, indeed, seen him, but nobody else had, and nobody except the person who had brought me his message to come and see him knew about my visit. In fact, I had just come back from seeing him. He lived in the country, and Madame Illyés had given me a present for someone in her family living abroad. That's all. It was Illyés who had confirmed the fact that there were about fifteen Communist writers in prison since the end of January.

As I appeared surprised that the minister knew where I had spent part of my day, he added, "Illyés telephoned to tell us that he had seen you." I couldn't bring myself to tell this crippled minister that he was a liar, but I suddenly remembered Illyés's face when he saw my chauffeur. My chauffeur was a very well known chauffeur in Hungarian cultural circles. . . . I told the minister that I had found Mr. and Mrs. Illyés in good health. "Very glad to hear it; he is our greatest poet, you know. And now, what brings you here to see me?" So Montand asked about the Communist writers in prison.

His face grew even sadder. We had been duped. There was not one single Communist intellectual in the Budapest prisons. There were perhaps a few bogus fascist intellectuals, the ones who had hatched this counterrevolution, which had been brought to heel only by the providential arrival of the Red Army. We must believe him. In the name of everything he himself had suffered when he was a prison companion of Comrade Kadar's, and above all Comrade Rajk, who had died so unjustly. That was past history! The political prisoners, if indeed there were any, were all fascists. And now that he came to think about it, there were no writers among those who might possibly be in prison.

He was quite convincing in his wheelchair. As for us . . . we didn't know what to think anymore.

The audience was young and gay. It may shock you that I speak this way about a city over which so many tears were still being spilled. The audience was exactly as our first interlocutors had said it would be. Especially the girls. They were pleased to be well dressed, they were often very beautiful, and they seemed to take pleasure in their freedom. The Hungarian lady who would talk only in the park had explained that very well. The young were the survivors, and they intended to make full use of it. The girls who had carried Molotov cocktails in November, and who had learned how to construct homemade bombs by watching lots of Soviet films celebrating the revolution of 1917, had discovered that all this had come to nothing, and now their only thought was to enjoy life. They had exchanged their overalls for sunburst pleats, because at last pleated skirts were in the shopwindows. They had no great respect for their parents, or for their grandparents. Their grandparents had been fascists under Horthy, and their parents had been Stalinists under Rákosi. They had been revolutionaries in November. Now they had decided to take things as they came. The girls . . . the girls . . . I'm talking about the groupies that week in Budapest. Visibly, nobody prevented them from getting what they wanted, or from going where they wanted. They were in the theater every night. They loved the music and adored the musicians. They also adored the singer, but unfortunately for them, and perhaps for him, the ancestral groupie was always there, planted in his dressing room, just as she was at the Étoile.

The girls had absolutely no desire to talk about the "events." They hardly remembered them.

The only account of the day of October 23, 1956, the beginning of events in Budapest, we heard at the French legation during a formal dinner. We heard it from a young cultural attaché who had lived through the entire thing, roving about the city. According to him, there was a great wave of happiness, the joy of being able to express oneself freely after so many years, and it was in this spirit that an enormous delegation of true socialists—and not counterrevolutionaries—had gone onto the streets. Everything had begun very joyously, with songs. People came with their kids. The procession had stopped for a moment before the statue of Kossuth, and then had continued its march, swelling all the time. Almost everyone joined this human tide without any kind of counterrevolutionary intent. The afternoon papers appeared in the kiosks at around four, and many of the marchers left the column to buy the papers; they wanted to see if they were being written about. They were astounded to discover that there wasn't even the smallest squib. It was then that they got angry, and the mood changed. Dusk faded into night. They decided to go to the radio station, to demand that they be received by the news department, insisting they should be heard. In this spirit the crowd arrived in front of Broadcasting House. Inside, hysteria struck. Apparently somebody gave orders for the lights to be switched off in the square. Suddenly the crowd was plunged into complete darkness, and they began to light torches; torches made of the newspapers they had just bought. Inside Broadcasting House the atmosphere became increasingly feverish. Fear of fire. Then a shot rang out; nobody ever knew where it came from. From then on the catastrophe grew.

Nobody in the legation seemed to know much about the

current situation in Budapest or about the political imprisonments.

I had promised Lila de Nobili that I would go see her uncle and aunt. They were very old, and they had seen so much in their years of Hungarian life that they no longer had anything to say. Their part of town was intact. They hadn't gone out during the "events." It all happened very far away from them. In a lovely little salon full of froufrous, which hadn't been renovated since the turn of the century, they wanted me to tell them all about Lila's Parisian stage sets.

We packed our bags. For the last time. We were going home. The groupies were all over the lobby of the hotel. The Hungarian lady accompanied us to the airport.

Five minutes before we were due to board, a woman approached us. Perhaps I had already seen her among the journalists and radio people? She had something to tell us. She said it very fast and very low. Did we know Aragon? Would we be seeing him? And how! Well, we must give him a message. A friend of his, a young Hungarian poet, was in prison along with a number of other writers, since January. Neither she, who was his ex-wife, nor his present wife had been able to obtain the slightest information concerning his fate. A letter had already been sent to Aragon a month and a half ago. Aragon knew Tibor very well. Elsa did too. Tibor had joined the banned French Communist party during the war, in 1942, in France, where he had been a political refugee since 1938. Aragon must do something to help; he knew that Tibor had never been a fascist. I promised her I would deliver the message. I did not promise her that Aragon would do anything. She gave me a long look, in silence, and then she took both my hands and said, "Well, then, ask him not to sleep for one night." I wrote down the name, Tibor Tardos.

Full circle. It had all begun four months earlier; now I had one more reason to make the telephone in the Rue de la

Sourdière ring and ring and ring until there was an answer.

Now I had all the time in the world!

Two days later, Louis Aragon, striding—as he likes so often to describe himself—around the big room of the "caravan," checked on his appearance coming and going in the mirror above my chimney. He was handsome; he was courteous. I was dead beat, but I attempted to emulate his courtesy. For once the roles were reversed.

Question No. 1: Had he or had he not declared in somebody's well-frequented salon, the day before our departure, that this departure was "inopportune"?

Reply: He had, he thought he had, a vague recollection of a dinner during which, questioned by the other guests, he had admitted that the moment was, perhaps, not extremely well chosen... "inopportune... let me see." Yes, no doubt, it may have been the word he used because it was the right word, wasn't it?

Question No. 2: Did he remember that evening of November 7, during which he had instantly discarded the possibility of changing the date of our trip by having a word with the Russians? And did he remember that, faced with my absurd insistence, he had clearly indicated that the only possible attitude was to change nothing and above all, to go? Did he remember that afterward he had talked about Claudel for hours, and when he said good-bye, he had wished us *"Bon courage et bon voyage"?*

Reply: Yes, yes, of course, well, it was a little vague in his mind; it was a while ago.... He remembered mostly that Elsa had the beginnings of the grippe that evening and he was worried about her.

Question No. 3: How could he, knowing what he knew, have instigated libel suits against people like Kravchenko or Koestler, or question their integrity when they dared declare there were camps in which, as Khrushchev himself said, sixteen million people had died? And deny, deny constantly!

Reply: "What do you mean, sixteen! You must be joking, my dear friend. Not sixteen—eighteen million dead! And as for the denials, of course I had to deny everything: I had family there."

I looked into his splendid blue eyes, his smile, and I remembered those Russian eyes, the ones you had to watch so carefully to see. I suddenly felt like crying. But I didn't want to cry in front of Aragon. I didn't want to run the risk of being comforted by Louis Aragon.

So I delivered the message given to me by the ex-Madame Tardos. "Tardos? . . . Tardos?" He searched his memory. "Yes; Tardos. Tibor Tardos, Aragon; a poet." "Oh, yes, now I remember! The little poet! I didn't know he was in prison. But what can I do? I'm a Frenchman. And really, what happens in Hungary is none of my business. . . ."

Naturally! Well, it was perfect, because we had already answered for him; I would have been much surprised by any other reaction from him. "Since I promised that woman I would do it, I must deliver the rest of the message. She asked me to ask you, simply, not to sleep for at least one night." Aragon's fine hand traveled to the gray mane of his splendid head, and he said, "But, my dear friend, I haven't slept for twenty years!"

I took Aragon to the door of my house, and there I told him that I never wanted to see him again in my life. I put him out, and I have never spoken to him since.

However, I did scribble him a note after Elsa's death. But that was due to an old Belgian gentleman who used to come to La Colombe with his wife for years and years. One day he came alone, sat down at their usual table, and saw me at mine. He tried to smile and suddenly burst into tears. Because of that widower I wrote a note to Elsa's widower.

(A few months ago, I met Tibor Tardos. He now lives in Paris. At the time of my Aragon conversation he was in solitary confinement in a Budapest prison. At his trial—or theirs, I should say: the Dery-Hay-Zelk-Tardos trial—which took place in November 1957, a witness did bring a message from Aragon and Elsa. He had met them in Moscow, and they were worried about Tardos. They wanted the tribunal to know that the Tardos they had known in his youth had been very respectable. The message bearer made it quite clear that this judgment did not concern the present. . . . Nevertheless, Tibor Tardos asked me to point out that this so very prudent intervention had undoubtedly helped in reducing his sentence. He got out of prison in April 1958. In 1965 Aragon offered him a column in *Lettres Françaises* with a caption written by himself: "Tardos lives and works in France as a Hungarian writer: It would be good if there were more like him—it's loyal, it's just." Well, there you are, Tibor; I delivered the message!)

In the end, Aragon was the only person to hear and listen to the balance-sheet summary of those four months.

In the same week both *L'Humanité* and *Match* were dismissed from the Place Dauphine, for opposite reasons. André Stil wanted a "vivid account of Montand's vibrant experiences," and *Match* wanted a "vibrant account of the experiences Montand had lived through"; plus a few words against the French Communist party.

We had nothing to say to them; not to one or the other. We had a lot to say to our family, to Catherine, and her friends, but that was our own private business. Our enemies of November would not have the satisfaction of gloating over our bitterness, and our November friends would not have the pleasure of putting out the bunting with a pretense of alleged enthusiasm.

Both enthusiasm and bitterness are unclassifiable. And above all, they must never be utilized by others. That's all we knew, but we knew it very thoroughly.

It was a joy to be back in the Place Dauphine with Madame Paul, Monsieur Lavaux the bookbinder, the steps of the Palais law courts, and Mademoiselle Danloux, the bookseller. It was a joy to unwrap all those little objects brought back in the drawers of the steamer trunk, things I had piously swathed in wads of Kleenex which my Occidental prudence had made me pack before leaving, in vast quantities. There were the "babas," little ceramic bears, traditional dolls, Yugoslav belts, Polish wooden painted birds, Ukrainian ribbons, biscuits shaped like squirrels or sleeping babies from Prague, a miniature Bulgarian zither, not bigger than half the palm of my hand, made of colored balsa wood—exactly the same size as its little sister, the Mexican guitar—eggs, or simply their shells, painted in mad colors. Russian eggs, Polish eggs, Bulgarian eggs, Rumanian eggs with frescoes on them.

Unpacking one's bags means first of all making sure that everything one has brought home is intact. When you're bringing back nothing more than trinkets, toys, and eggshells, you're all the more anxious as you open the drawers of the steamer trunk. When the steamer trunk proves to have been a good steamer trunk and the Kleenex good protecting Kleenex, you're enchanted. You keep unwrapping little objects that are really priceless: They cost nothing, and they were offered by hands and faces you'll never forget.

That's what the ritual of unpacking one's bags is all about—that, and having packed only what the traveler didn't consider worthy of leaving behind, half hidden, in the hotel bedroom cupboard, before departure, to give the impression that it had indeed been forgotten: The forgotten objects are usually in the heavy-goods category: huge lacquered boxes whose illustrations show only grandiose scenes; official gifts, undoubtedly very costly. They bear no personal touch; the tender look, the extended hand are not discernible. Whereas the trinkets are all connected at one end to an invisible thread. It runs for thousands and thousands of kilometers, and at the other end there's always a hand holding the thread. But the people who ask you serious questions when you come back from the East in 1957 are never interested in that particular network. They want facts, conclusions, declarations.

249

They had to do without them.

It was François Chalais and Frédéric Rossif* who first gave Montand the opportunity to talk publicly about the trip, with complete freedom. On their television show, he talked about the circumstances surrounding our departure, and about the artistic results of it all. At the time, it was the only neutral offer he received. He accepted, and it was good that he did. The show was honest and he spoke freely; no one asked him to serve one side or the other. It was a refreshing experience.

Refreshing too, but in quite another way, was our financial balance sheet at the end of the year 1957. The accounts of the box-office receipts and sales of the film of *The Crucible* (which I remind you, at the risk of displaying sordid cupidity, we did on a percentage basis) had been kept with a discretion that made them as inaccessible as Kafka's castle—which, incidentally, they have remained until today. Our trip, which provoked the flow of so much ink and tears, was evaluated by the Ministry of Finance at the official rate of exchange of the zlotys, rubles, lei, leva, crowns, and East marks involved; Montand was asked to pay French taxes on them. The whole thing became such a joke that one day we sat down with pencil and paper. We tried to remember how to do long division—that took us quite a while—and we sat around arguing about things like "Nine, that's two fours with one left over," etc. After a couple of hours of these exercises, there we were, impregnated with the smell of chalk and brownish ink, sitting at the splendid table in the handsome salon of our beautiful house in Autheuil (Eure), with a result that seemed to indicate that Montand had received a fee of 2,650 old francs (about four dollars) per performance, in theatrical-agency parlance.

We were vastly amused by the idea that all this Moscow gold, all expenses paid, musicians' salaries and hotel rooms

---

*Chalais was a TV journalist and critic, Rossif a television producer. The two worked together frequently.

accounted for, finally provided the singer with an unskilled workman's salary. The only tangible objects we brought back with our Moscow gold were the skins of those poor little sables captured by a nasty Siberian trapper. They were presented for the appreciation of some gentlemen who were probably the cousins of the old gentleman at GUM. They blew on the fur pelts with deference. They were superb. A fluffy beige at the roots, brown in the middle, and whitish at their tips. Lovely, valiant little sables. The gentlemen were sorry there weren't more of them. But they declared there were enough to make a lovely stole. That's what they became. But then, since a stole isn't exactly my favorite "prop," they were transformed into a big shawl collar. However, that wasn't really what I wanted, though a big shawl collar is magnificent for having your picture taken for a glossy magazine, two fingers negligently holding the fur in place. . . .

There was one more stage to come in the life of my little sables. One day they were fitted with a system of snaps, and now they can be found one day on beige, one day on black, one day on silk, one day on velvet, one day on jersey. Idle observers are left with the impression that every one of my neatly tailored suits has its personal sable adornment. My little sables have been very useful to me; a simple, straightforward relationship between us is established when I snap them onto a new outfit. They came from GUM, and since then they have seen many lands— many more than their little sisters who spent a boring life on the shoulders of Liliane de Rethy, or the Maharani of Kapurthala. Most women have a sharp eye and when they notice that here are real sables! Even on cotton. Especially on cotton.

So much for our Moscow gold.

Finally, as at the end of *Uncle Vanya*, we decided the time had come to rest. For despite the Ministry of Finance's arithmetic, we were able to rest. And that we did.

Chapter 9

AMONG actors, the word "rest" has several different meanings. You rest on your days off. You rest after a long tour. You rest after a difficult film. Rest is sacred.

But rest stops being rest when it goes on and on. Then it isn't called rest, it's called being out of work.

Being out of work, for an actor, means not being in a position to turn down parts. It consists in not reading plays or scripts, because nobody's offering you anything. In other words, your telephone doesn't ring.

And since we actors like imagery, we discreetly call these periods "the trough of the wave." But sometimes there are waves that become ground swells.

The trough of my wave lasted nine months. Nobody asked for me. I was neither frustrated nor embittered. I made myself a list of the ladies whom I'd played. It was a very nice collection, running from the little serving girl in *Démons de l'Aube* to Mrs. Proctor. I had Montand, I had Catherine, I had a lot of friends, my life was rich, and we were not poor. I was about to be thirty-seven years old, and the future belonged to the pretty young things and the attractive young women. I fully realized that there wasn't much call for a ripening lady, especially when she had just come back from a tour of the East. I was at the bottom of the "new wave."

Then, one day, the phone rang. A call from London. Without knowing it, I was about to find myself on the crest of the "new wave."

One morning in the spring of 1958, Montand and Catherine took me to the Gare du Nord, and I got into the Golden Arrow, a train that becomes a boat and then becomes a train again from Dover to London. I had no notion that this train I was boarding would lead to my saying thank you in April 1960 in front of millions of television viewers, to three thousand people seated in red velvet seats in a Hollywood cinema. In the French film industry there's always a smart guy who says before the umpteenth take of the same shot: "Come on, let's do it again and we'll get the Oscar."

I had chosen this means of transportation because I was a little fed up with airports, but above all because I was trying to recapture my first visit to England, when I was sixteen and stayed with Audrey, who loved only her pony, Pixie. I was off to act in an English film called *Room at the Top*. I had read the script and liked it very much. It's thanks to the stubbornness of Peter Glenville that I made this film, which relaunched a career that had seemed finished. Glenville, whom I didn't know, came one day to ask me to do a film in Hollywood. Since this was very shortly after our return from the East, I explained politely, even before I read the script, that he was wasting his time. I had no visa for America, I had never asked for one, and each time there had been a vague offer of my participating in an American production made in France, negotiations had rapidly broken off. . . . Peter Glenville replied, "But McCarthy's dead!"

Bill Goetz, his American producer, was in Paris and wanted to see me. So Mr. Goetz came. In the meantime, I had read the script. It was a comedy. I decided that I was neither young enough nor frivolous enough to play this charming, archetypically French, lady. I told them so. That's no snag, they said. They would change the character. Fifi, or Lulu, or Madeleine—I can't remember the name—would be kind of a cross between Madame Curie and Simone de Beauvoir; tailor-made for me. I repeated to Mr. Goetz what I had already told Glenville. He, too, assured me that McCarthy was dead and all that stuff was gone forever. He himself had signed a kind of Stockholm petition; he slipped into the conversation that he was a friend of Picasso's and he visited the artist each time he came to France. He owned several Picassos, Mr. Goetz was a liberal American, and nobody had ever stopped him from offering a part to anyone he wanted. Really, he was a charming and sincere man who was trying to please his English director, who wanted me for the film.

Montand took us all to dinner chez Allard, and as I was stashing away my pickled pork with lentils, I reflected that it was more than slightly amusing to be implored to come to Hollywood when in my own country the people in my profession wouldn't have me around, in order not to get in bad with the Americans!

The conversation concluded with the decision to send me a new script very soon. All the rest was small potatoes. The visa, the work permit, the Equity permission—all that would follow with no snags. The only thing that mattered was that I like the new Fifi or Lulu they would remanufacture over there. They left for Hollywood the next day.

A few days later I received from Hollywood a long telegram of several pages. Bill Goetz explained to me that for reasons he couldn't explain, the dream he and Peter Glenville had had of seeing me in the film they were about to begin unfortunately had to be abandoned. But he wanted to be sure that I realized this was only a rain check, that our relationship would continue, and that he was not ready to forget those pleasant hours he had spent with me and my husband in that picturesque little bistro in old Paris. So see you soon, here, there, or somewhere else! I should know that I had a new friend in the world. A film is only a film, while a friend is something infinitely precious. Warmest regards.

I wasn't a bit sad. Fifi or Lulu hadn't the slightest chance of becoming a character I would be mad to play. Not even if she were fiddled with and fussed over by the most reputable plastic surgeons in the realm of scripts. The episode had taken only a few days. It had come to its natural conclusion. McCarthy was not dead, even if the citizens of his country thought they had buried him.

Thus I rapidly forgot the only offer of work that was made to me during the rest period. I was convinced that I would never see Bill Goetz or Peter Glenville again. I was even faintly pleased that I had predicted to them what would happen. They had tried a kind of smuggling operation, and it hadn't worked. I had told them it wouldn't. My self-esteem was saved.

But Peter Glenville's self-esteem had gotten some kind of a knock. He was a British subject and one of the best-known English directors. Nobody had ever tried to tell him whom to hire or whom he couldn't hire. He was very irritated that someone had enough power to keep him from working with an actress he had chosen. Which is why, a little later, my phone rang with a call from London.

To tell the truth, the call really came from Orly airport, which makes the story even prettier. Glenville was spending a few hours in Paris, and he wanted to see me right away. Half an hour later, he was in the "caravan." He had found another actress for the comedy. He would begin working next week; he had just arrived from London and was leaving that very evening for Hollywood. He was making this detour via Paris especially to ask me whether I would be in his next film. That film would not be American, it would be English; with an English producer. The script was not yet finished, but he had brought me the book. He was much too involved in his monologue to leave me the time to say that I thought it was very nice of him to have reappeared, and still nicer of him to offer me a part despite the complications that an involvement with me was likely to raise. Like a good director, he timed the scene carefully. He opened his suitcase and took out a book, covering the title with his hand for a second. He said, "This is the book," and put it down on the table. It was a fairly fat hardcover book, and "*Room at the Top*, by John Braine" was printed on the jacket.

If you had put this object down on the living-room table of any English actress of my generation, there would have been a bombshell effect. *Room at the Top* was that year's best seller in England. All the English film producers had fought fiercely for the rights. I had before me the object most coveted by people of my profession on the other side of the Channel. But Peter Glenville had muffed his entrance. I had never heard of *Room at the Top* or of John Braine.

Glenville rectified the lacuna in my knowledge. He urged me to read the book as soon as possible, announced that his producer, James Woolf, would soon pay me a visit, and then he left, again in a whirlwind.

I didn't do *Room at the Top* with Peter Glenville directing; the film was directed by Jack Clayton. But it's impossible for me not to associate Peter with the watershed in my professional career this film proved to be.

James Woolf came. (I have trouble calling him James, since he was to become our friend Jimmy, but that day he was Mr. Woolf.) I liked the book. It wasn't a masterpiece of contemporary literature, but it had a wonderful "story." John Braine, the happy author, had been a librarian in Leeds, and he had obviously studied the tenants on his bookshelves. He must have burrowed into Balzac, Stendhal, and Colette. He may also have glanced at Theodore Dreiser's *An American Tragedy*. Be that as it may, his story about a young working-class opportunist from the North of England who decided to make his way in the world by any means whatever was fascinating.

One of the most fascinating aspects of the story was his love affair with a lady who was no longer quite young (she was then in her forties), whose name was Alice. Alice Aisgill. Alice was intelligent, generous, understanding, maternal, sexually liberated, and socially without prejudice. Alice was a character who had everything going for her, including her death before the end of the novel. Alice was a piece of cake to play. (I almost forgot: On top of it all, Alice was married to a complete cad.) Did I say a piece of cake? A wedding cake is more like it: a part whose like one seldom encounters in the course of a career.

I had absolutely no desire to repeat with Mr. Woolf the kind of brief encounter that had occurred between me and Mr. Goetz. "Fifi-Lulu" had been taken away from me for Washingtonian reasons, but if I was going to lose Alice, I wanted to know immediately. So that was my first question. Or more precisely, it was my entry into negotiations. I wanted very, very much to play Alice, so I wanted to know whether there were Americans involved in the film's production. If there were, I knew there was no point in beginning to negotiate. I wouldn't be allowed to play Alice.

Jimmy looked at me a long moment. Then he explained that he and his brother John were independent producers, and that he had never been preoccupied with the life or death of the aforementioned Mr. McCarthy. He was very pleased that I wanted to play Alice. I would have to sign my contract based on the book because the script wasn't finished yet. Did I prefer a salary or a percentage? A salary, I said, thanks to my experience with *The Crucible*. (In passing, let me say that in this way I missed what was probably the most lucrative financial operation of my career; I was very well paid, but if I had accepted a percentage, I'd be very, very, very rich today.) Before he left, however, he did say this: "I am not dependent on the Americans; but my right to hire does depend on two authorizations: that of the Ministry of Labor and that of British Actors Equity. I must tell you that our verbal

257

contract is subject to the approval of these two organizations, and doesn't become effective until we have them." And then Mr. Woolf left for London.

The Ministry of Labor authorized the immigrant actress to come and work on British soil, and Equity agreed to let one of the best parts in the contemporary English cinema be played by a Frenchwoman.

In the novel, Alice was English. To justify my temporary immigration, she became a Frenchwoman married to an Englishman.

In 1953, the British film industry had given me its highest award for my part in *Casque d'Or*. It gave it to me again in 1958 for *The Crucible*, and it gave permission to play Alice in *Room at the Top*, for which performance, in 1959, for the third time, I got the British "Academy Award." It will hardly surprise anyone when I say that I'm not an Anglophobe!

The Golden Arrow rolled through the English countryside. Once again I sniffed at that familiar mixture of lemon-flavored cleaner and Players cigarettes, and I reread with delight the script signed by Neil Paterson. John Braine had better luck than his fellow writers Dostoyevsky, Balzac, and Durrell: The script was better than the novel.

I changed trains in London, and after a while I arrived in Bradford, Yorkshire, the wool capital. There I met the people who were to become my mates for three and a half months and my friends for life: Jack Clayton, Laurence Harvey, Heather Sears, Jimmy Woolf, Freddy Francis, the cameraman, and all the others who breathed life into a story that caused so many English and American tears to flow—between fits of giggles. As I've said earlier, it's only with complete complicity, and consequently shared humor, that one can tell a serious, if not a tragic, story. Once again the location miracle took place. If you want to start a family, you move in together under one roof. A film unit, if it's to work well, must be a family. If you begin a film by going out on location, it's the best way of cementing your foundations. The roof can be the Grand Hotel in Monaco in full sunshine. Or it can be a commercial hotel for traveling salesmen in wool-combing machines, opposite the station in Bradford. (Which caused Harvey to ask every morning what time the hotel would pull into the London station.)

Bradford (along with its neighbor Leeds, John Braine's hometown) is a busy industrial city. Factory smoke mingles with local fog, and great wealth nudges great poverty. This is part of what Clayton wanted to show in his film. So to tell the story well, it was better to be right there. And once there, all might just as well live under the same roof. It might be a temporary roof, but you soon develop habits much as you do under your own roof. There are common meals, and bedtimes and rising times calculated for the work you all do together. There is always that bit of guilt that haunts you at the end of the day because you're absent from your own roof. You take care of that with the daily telephone call. There hasn't been a fire, nobody's sick, great, talk to you tomorrow....

Without that reassuring daily telephone call that keeps you in touch with your real life, locations could become crucibles for divorce. But if you know how it all works, they really consolidate unions. If you have the good fortune of being able to have a real dialogue with your real family, who know—because they've been in the same situation—that you are happy, pleased to be doing the thing you love with people you like a lot who at the moment are a kind of family for you, locations are marvelous.

Montand was filming in Italy. We understood each other perfectly. And we loved each other immensely for both loving what we were doing.

In Bradford, too, the people liked us. It was the first time the town had served as background for something other than boring documentaries about wool combing. The people of the "upper top" paid no attention to us, and their fortresses never did open for us. No doubt they had read the book. By contrast, the houses in the working-class quarters were wide open for us. I remember two nights of filming during which the kettles never seemed to cease boiling in beautifully clean little kitchens. The people of Bradford—these, in any case—were gay and full of humor. I was discovering the North of England. The rest of the world wasn't far behind me: Most of the people who revolutionized the cultural and artistic life of Britain during those years, the "angry young men" and their contemporaries who waged war on the Establishment, came from the North. When we went down to London to do the studio shooting, I became aware of this fact, but my three weeks in Yorkshire had prepared me well.

In 1947 I had lived in London for three months during the filming of *Against the Wind*. Then London was still full of great bomb craters, and there were still ration tickets for certain things. In the sedately elegant Burlington Arcade the jewelers' shops displayed an extraordinary quantity of court tiaras and antique jewelry. Their sale had allowed the gentry to survive the war, it was explained to me. Eleven years later there were no longer any bomb craters or ration tickets, but there seemed to be just as many court tiaras and antique jewels in the Burlington Arcade. For me, that's one of the mysteries of London. But it has nothing to do with *Room at the Top*.

And yet there is some connection. It wasn't unusual for me to come back from the Shepperton studios at around seven-thirty in the evening, dirty, with half my makeup still on and in my working outfit, and in the lobby of the Savoy Hotel run into groups of ladies in evening dress complete with tiaras, accompanied by dinner-jacketed gentlemen walking solemnly toward the grill. A change had begun to overtake England, though it was still invisible to these people. It was happening backstage.

At home in France, everything had already changed and was visible for everybody—except for me. I experienced the events of May 1958, when de Gaulle came back to power, mostly via the radio. At the risk of getting a bad mark for indifference toward the destiny of my country, I must confess that I was then living essentially the life of Alice Aisgill.

The friendship and reciprocity between Jack Clayton and his cast grew and grew. Our working days in the studio ended as they had in Bradford. We separated with regret. We generally ended the day in a little pub, where we had a snack before going to bed early. I left my apartment in the Savoy at about five-thirty in the morning, just as the maids began vacuuming the corridors. We'd have a little chat while I waited for the elevator. After a few days I no longer had to wait: My friend the night elevator man, knowing my hours, would be there, waiting for me. He had six flights during which to continue (exactly where he had left off) the story he had interrupted the day before. What he talked about were his memories of France, at Armentières, where he had been a soldier in 1914–18. As his memories were copious and the Savoy elevator quite fast, the three months of morning trips hardly began to deplete his stock. Sometimes he did remember to ask me whether I was pleased with my work. Everyone at the Savoy kept asking me whether I was pleased with my work. It must have showed on my face that I was.

I was happy because I had a marvelous director. Without throwing his weight about, and without pretentious explanations, he made us do exactly what he wanted. And as the rushes showed us that what he wanted was true and right, I was happy.

Besides, I had a producer who wasn't a horse trader but a man who loved the cinema and respected the people who worked with him.

Furthermore, my leading man, about whom I had been told every possible variety of tale, was someone I got along with very well.

And I would spend Sundays with my old pals from the Ealing studios, Michael Truman and Gordon Jackson, which was very nice.

When Montand had a short break in the film he was making, he came to spend a weekend. Catherine was in Autheuil, and every night I phoned to reassure myself that there hadn't been a fire.

Then came the final days of shooting. The last day was very sad. As it most always is. Maybe even a little more than usual, because the same town and the same language would no longer bring us together.

So I went back home.

When people asked me where I had been all that time, I said, "I was making a film in London." That impressed no one. Everyone in Paris knew that the English cinema was dead. Still, I would say timidly that it seemed to me that I had made a very good little film. Nobody wanted to be unpleasant about it; after all, I was still in the trough of the wave. It would have been uncharitable to hold my head under water.

After I came home, Alice Aisgill left me day by day, in dribs and drabs. For a little while I went on wearing my hair as she did and putting on my ready-made blazer that I had bought at Simpson's. Then I had my hair cut and took out my Hermès suits. One day I realized that she had left me for good.

Montand had decided on a new recital at the Étoile, so of course I became a groupie again. It was the end of summer 1958. All the musicians came to live in Autheuil. At the beginning of autumn there was the first night at the Étoile. It was a little less than two years after our "inopportune" departure.

A lot of water had flowed under the bridges of the Seine. Those high angers, sincere or not, had diluted. People welcomed back Montand. The feeling was reciprocated. He chose to sing his old songs and new ones. The old ones, which had always been successful, were still so. He decided not to sing one of the old ones, though.

That was "C'est à l'Aube," which he could no longer sing with sincerity. In it there was talk of "the worlds of hope." But Montand no longer knew where those worlds stood in the world.

Instead he sang "Le Chat de la Voisine" ("The Neighbor's Cat"), which said a great deal more.

Again, Montand stayed for six consecutive months at the Étoile.

One day in November, Jimmy Woolf and Jack Clayton phoned me from London. *Room at the Top* was about to come out. Alice Aisgill reappeared in my life.

I packed one lovely dress and my wandering sables and left the concrete walls of the Étoile basement for two days for the carpeted corridors of the Savoy Hotel.

The hotel staff, who had seen me come and go in my blue jeans, carrying my script, for three months, complimented me on my evening outfit when I came down to the lobby at exactly seven-thirty. I was off to the gala premiere of the film I had so visibly enjoyed making during those summer months. They felt more than a little involved. Everyone said, "Good luck," to me as I stepped into the rented Rolls Jimmy had sent. My new splendor may have fooled the hotel guests, but it didn't fool the bell captain, who tipped his hat and murmured, "Well, miss, they're doing well by you this evening! Good luck!"

And they *were* doing well. But mainly, they *had* done very well. They had made—we had made—a very good film. As midnight chimed that evening we, the people of *Room at the Top*, were the kings and queens of London Town. This cliché-like talk is used intentionally here. Let those who have never savored such a magic crowning, when the lights come on in the auditorium, cast the first stone. When all doubts that assail you—the same doubts that will inevitably worm their way back once you're fully lucid—are swept away by the total allegiance of the first-night audience, it's difficult to spurn the laurels symbolizing your coronation!

At midnight that evening, for good reasons or bad, we were kings and queens. We had made this movie hoping that a few of our friends would like it. And now here were hundreds, perhaps thousands, of strangers who adored what we had enjoyed doing. For certain disgruntled people that might have been disquieting. But we weren't disgruntled. We were damned happy.

The next morning the English press unanimously celebrated the virtues of what it called the rebirth of the English cinema. The staff of the Savoy was like a clipping service and slipped the reviews under my door. Anything having to do with Alice Aisgill was underlined in red. Jimmy Woolf read me on the telephone passages I already knew. I thought it was very sweet of him, so I didn't want to interrupt him by telling him that I'd already read them. Somehow those he read always contained a reference I had missed. "There hasn't been the like since Greta Garbo." It was either at the beginning of the review or at the end. Namely, in the best possible place. At the end of the third review, I got the message...so I replied with my own inventions, boosting him. He was the world's greatest producer since Irving Thalberg, my fake news-clipping service would announce.

Clayton phoned every fifteen minutes using different voices and names, asking me for interviews for papers specializing in chicken farming or the hothouse propagation of tropical plants. It's the kind of humor kids have the morning after their final exam. We had every right not to take ourselves seriously. That morning we were being taken so seriously by the entire British press that a bit of levity was not only a right, it was a duty.

That same evening, still in a state of stupefied euphoria, I appeared backstage at the Étoile just in time to see my husband take his last bows after his last song. The audience was still shouting, "Another, another!" He had no idea that it was Greta Garbo handing him his Turkish towel.

He didn't know, nor did anyone in France. The success of *Room at the Top* remained an insular phenomenon— until the film emigrated and was solidly installed in the "New World." Jimmy sent me press clippings from America, but I couldn't decipher their meaning. *Variety*, for example. You live quietly on the Place Dauphine for years, and then along comes a tiny scrap of paper which the accompanying letter assures you is a priceless document. You read: "*Room*, boffo!" followed by figures in dollars. Since the exchange rate, too, is unfamiliar and the figures are preceded by a kind of Mercury's wand, it really means nothing. So you get in touch with some of your blacklisted friends from America and they translate the whole thing for you. They turn out to be very happy for you, and very happy to take their nostalgia out for a little canter with this vocabulary they haven't used since their exile, so you get initiated into this language with fever, joy, humor, and pride. After that first lesson, you can translate.

"*Room*, boffo!" means a triumph.

Montand had had his "boffo" for two months at the Étoile when Norman Granz appeared one day to propose a recital in one of the Broadway theaters at the beginning of 1959.

Norman Granz was one of the rare American impresarios known in France. He was the happy representative of Ella Fitzgerald and Oscar Peterson; he owned Verve Records and was the inventor of *Jazz at the Philharmonic*. We had never met him, but in Autheuil we had a wonderful album he had produced in 1952. Long before today's vogue for the thirties, he had the splendid idea of asking Fred Astaire to rerecord all the songs and steps of all his films. He had offered him Oscar Peterson and the musicians of *Jazz at the Philharmonic* as accompaniment, and we had spent hours and hours not only listening to the music of our adolescence but also looking at the photos and drawings and reading the texts. The album is a splendid example of good taste, intelligence, and affection. We had a numbered copy, signed by Fred Astaire. Georges Beaume had brought it back from America in 1953.

That evening, in the dressing room, Norman Granz was, for us, the gentleman who had had the idea for that "Astaire Story" we were so proud of owning. Norman Granz isn't always affable; often he is rather abrupt. But that evening he was smiling, smooth, and direct. He knew that various Americans had, on a number of occasions, tried to get Montand to come to New York, and he knew that some of the big nightclubs had tried to get him to participate in galas like *April in Paris*. He knew that Gene Kelly had tried to get him for a film of his a long time ago, and he even knew the old story about Jack Warner. He knew about our trip to the East; he knew about the Stockholm resolution, the Rosenbergs. He knew all about us.

His suggestion for Montand wasn't an elegant high-priced nightclub, or a gala for the American Legion; it was the equivalent of what Montand had at the Étoile—a theater, a real one, and on Broadway. He would see to it that a visa was obtained. Things have changed, he said, and he would prove it to us.

Norman Granz is not always affable; he's often abrupt—but he's stubborn.

So, a few days later, we found ourselves seated before a batch of official forms containing twenty-two or twenty-three questions to which we were requested to provide answers we solemnly believed were true.

A hell of a good memory was required to remember all the places we had been to over the past twenty years and all the illnesses we hadn't had. It required a good sense of humor to swear we'd no intention of assassinating anyone during our stay. And very little self-respect to answer the question: "Have you ever prostituted yourself?"

And then there was Question No. 20. "Are you or have you ever been a member of the Communist party or an organization affiliated with or having common activities with the Communist party?" The first half of that question didn't concern us; the second, however, was perfectly applicable to our situation.

We dutifully wrote "Peace Movement" and "Confédération Générale du Travail"—the trade union's full title—not simply the abbreviated CGT, so as not to appear to be shysters pulling a fast one as travelers of the Compagnie Générale Transatlantique. Those were our answers to Question No. 20.

There followed Question No. 21. "Have you fully understood the meaning of Question No. 20?" We had fully understood.

This interesting *curriculum vitae* was duly delivered to the Visa Section of the United States Embassy. I made a copy of the answers we'd filled in, so that if our first application met with disapproval and we had to redo our homework, our replies would be identical.

Indeed, a young cultural attaché from the embassy phoned us a few days later. She was very sad; she had been asked to tell us about the great sorrow of the consul, who asked to see us to explain why our visas had been refused. Could we stop by his office?

I consoled her. I asked her to console the consul. But as for going to see him in his office . . . well, it was a very kind invitation, but we didn't really think we wanted to cross town to have explained to us why we weren't admissible candidates. However, if the consul wished to speak with us, he would be welcome any afternoon. Not too late, since my husband left very early for the theater.

The next afternoon both of them arrived at the "caravan." I don't know whether by coming to see us they'd infringed diplomatic corps regulations, but what I do know is they were in perfect agreement with their consciences.

It just so happened that at that same time, when we'd flunked our exam, a lady who had happened to be the mistress of Lafont, the head of the French Gestapo during the Nazi occupation (a mistress so faithful that she even lived on the Rue Lauriston, the scene of inquisition and torture), had just flown off to the United States, armed with a visa for life. We knew about this; everyone knew about it. It was the current joke of the town. It didn't make the young consul laugh at all. His wife was a French

Jewess. Undoubtedly she'd commented on the value of good-conduct points he was authorized to distribute or withhold.

He had been ordered to refuse our good-conduct points because of our past. I said that perhaps I ought to have laid greater emphasis in the application about the time I worked for the pro-Nazi newspaper *Nouveaux Temps*. His face uncreased. He laughed with us. Once more we weren't sad. After all, the trip to Broadway hadn't been our idea; it was an American idea—generous and seductive, but if our answers to the questions had caused displeasure, just too bad!

There followed a small exposé, delivered by Montand and me, to the effect that had we been able to swear, without perjuring ourselves, that never in the course of the past twenty years had we taken any position whatever concerning the crises offered by the history of the world, and particularly that of Europe (twenty years meant from 1938 to the present), then Monsieur le Consul would have had the joy of giving his good-conduct points to vegetables, chairs, ectoplasms, or jellyfish, but certainly not to human beings.

Which was exactly what he had come to tell us.

Norman Granz is not always affable; he's often abrupt—but he is both stubborn and proud.

Norman Granz had decided that he would be the first to import Montand to New York, to open his 1959 autumn season. But at the moment we weren't *grata*, as they say when they allude to certain *personae*. We were soon to learn that the American citizen Norman Granz was made of sterner stuff.

Granz took this refusal as a personal insult. On top of all the other things I've said he is, Norman Granz is also touchy.

Monsieur Benassy, who had taught us English at the Neuilly-sur-Seine secondary school, had made copies of a little pamphlet called "Beware of Deceitful Friends." It was made up of a short list of words which, because they were the same, or almost, in the two languages, made you run the risk of saying precisely what you didn't want to say, unless you were very careful. Or worse, they said exactly the opposite of what you wanted to say. "Deceitful Friends"—oh, those false friends!

"Actually" was the uncontested star among these traitors. "Actually" means "positively," not "at this moment." "Susceptible" in English means "sensitive, open, accessible," whereas the French equivalent is "touchy."

Norman Granz is one of the few people in the world who would justify both interprètations of that word.

He is sensitive and he is touchy. So we'd see what we'd see! He'd coped with stiffer problems before. He was quite right to start getting things going so far in advance—it was only December 1958.

A few days later it was already after December 10, 1958.

On the tenth of December, 1958, at around five in the afternoon, in the waters near the island of Sein, my brother Alain died. He died the same death as those whose lives he was then filming: the fishermen of the island of Sein.

Now the half-Jew, made Protestant by Pastor Ebershold "so his papers would be in order," lies in the very Catholic sailors' cemetery of the Île des Veuves (the Widows' Isle).

Since then, without fail, I know whether a tale I'm about to tell, whether gravely sad or hilariously funny, took place before December 10, 1958—or after. It's a border.

I think it was toward the end of January. Norman Granz had had his breakfast in Stockholm, his lunch in Rome, tea on a British Airways plane, and a champagne cocktail on the Air France plane bringing him from London just in time to have dinner in Paris in a restaurant where he had reserved a good table for eleven forty-five two days before from Lausanne. There he announced to us that it was time we started on our homework again.

Three days later we had what we thought was a visa.

269

Our passports had been very officially stamped. Our passports announced that we were authorized to set foot on the American continent between July 15 and December 15, 1959. A very large, red, handwritten sentence announced: "One entry." Then—also in handwriting, but very small and blue—there followed a long line of numbers stuffed between parentheses; it looked like an equation, or a pharmaceutical formula, or a fragment of the obelisk in the Place de la Concorde, read horizontally.

As we were not Einstein or Louis Pasteur or Champollion, Norman explained that it was a "waver." At least that's what it sounded like to me. To wave means to agitate a small flag or your hand, preferably with a handkerchief clutched in it. It had overtones of "Come, come, you're most welcome.... Finally you're here.... We've been waving to you for so long.... Welcome, welcome."

Since this image pleased me, I didn't ask for more explanation or translation, and I forgot the word.

A short time ago—to be quite honest, an hour ago—I was curious enough to consult Harrap's dictionary, which is to translation what the Michelin Guide is to gastronomy. "Waive (verb): vaccilate, quiver, hesitate, float, be undecided...."

Thus, a waiver: "Pay attention. Signed, Washington, D.C."

In other words, I had understood the exact opposite of the word. I had made a spelling mistake in 1959, but oddly enough, I had still known in advance what would happen a few months later.

In the meantime, Norman, who was scheduled to be in Montreal at noon the next day and in Los Angeles at about six in the evening, made a contract with Jacques Canetti for a partnership that would make them the coproducers of a one-man show called *An Evening with Yves Montand*, due to open during the second half of September 1959. This one-man show would be produced in New York (New York), in a theater on Broadway with a seating capacity, acoustics, and reputation of the first order.

Norman was smiling. He takes care of the outer edges of his eyebrows the way some men take care of their mustaches; it made half his face resemble Taras Bulba. It had just occurred to him that if he changed planes in Geneva, he could catch a plane from there to Montreal on Air France. Norman likes Air France. It's his way of living a French life—with French food. Norman Granz is not always affable, he's often abrupt, he's stubborn and proud, he's sensitive-generous-susceptible, and is a gastronome.

Before leaving that evening, he gave me the latest news of Alice Aisgill. In *Variety* we were no longer "boffo"; we had become "whaaam." I had to consult my blacklisted linguists once again in order to understand that things were becoming serious. "*Room*, whaaam." How about that!

In February, Nina and Maryse took down the gray tulle fly curtain at the Étoile, and in March the cuadrilla, the groupie, and Jacques Canetti landed in Tel Aviv.

Waiting below the steps to the plane were a lot of photographers. Among them was one so busy smiling and waving his arms that he forgot to use his camera, which hung uselessly around his neck while his colleagues were busy immortalizing our descent from angles that showed off the El Al plane's markings to best advantage. He was red-haired, and he hadn't changed a bit. The sun had given him a coppery color, that was all. He hadn't brought his little son, but he had brought the pictures he had taken the last time he saw us. In Vilna.

The next day he appeared in our apartment at the Dan Hotel. In his newly acquired English, and his not yet discarded Yiddish, he explained to us what he had twice tried to tell us at the Tolstoyan airport. At that time he had hoped that our arrival, and then later our departure, would somehow help him to get out. He had finally managed to leave his native Lithuania via Warsaw. He and his family had crossed France, and in Marseilles they had found a ship that took them to the Promised Land, of which they were now citizens.

He hadn't cared for Stalin, although he acknowledged

that during the war in the unoccupied areas where the Jewish community had been evacuated, the officially recognized anti-Semitism was theoretically punishable by a prison sentence.

He hadn't cared for what came after Stalinism because of its anti-Semitism—still punishable with a prison sentence—but nevertheless plainly visible in the streets of Vilna.

Now he was wondering whether he was going to like his new country.

He wasn't sad; he was funny. It's not impossible that we may meet him again one day somewhere or other, beside another airplane.

We have never returned to Israel since 1959. In 1959, one day in Tel Aviv, we were visited by an extraordinary group of five people. All five were socialists and citizens of socialist countries, like our Vilna friend. But they were gloomier. They had come to alert us to the Palestine situation. They talked about camps....

It was in Tel Aviv, in the residence of the French ambassador, Monsieur Gilbert—an ambassador who had taken the trouble to learn Hebrew—that we lunched with Ben-Gurion and Madame Ben-Gurion. Madame Ben-Gurion was the most perfect example I've ever encountered of what is affectionately known as the Yiddishe mama. She had seen and heard Montand the evening before, and even though he isn't a bit Jewish, she had liked him enormously. As for me . . . she hesitated.

She sized me up, pondered, and summed me up. My half-Jewish condition was distinctly not in my favor. After all, if my mother wasn't Jewish . . . who's to say if my father was really my father? But she didn't say that. Actually, she said nothing to me. However . . . after the cheese she was suddenly seized with a desire to communicate. With a superb Russian-Polish accent, she said in English, "And you, what kind of an actrrress arrre you—a good one orrr a bad one?"

I was working out an answer that would be both

earthy French and Talmudic, when Ben-Gurion, running both hands through the hair at the sides of his head, said, "Mama, Mama, please...I'm surrre she is a verrry good actrrress."

"And how do *you* know?" she answered.

I've tried to avoid telling anecdotes, but here I couldn't resist. But remember that it's about two very young pioneers, still unfamiliar with protocol. After all, they were only in their seventies and still had time to catch up with the jet set.

Eighty kilometers from Tel Aviv, we discovered the kibbutz life. It was a poor kibbutz. There are rich ones and poor ones. Two guys came to fetch us in a jeep that was far from new. They had telephoned. They knew when it was Montand's night off. No one had put them in touch with us. They had invited us to dinner. There would be no press, radio, or television people present. They had simply invited us to dine. It was a French-speaking kibbutz; a kibbutz of Moroccan Jews.

We arrived at the same time as the kids, who'd come to spend an hour or so with their freshly washed, shaved, rested, and available parents, before returning to their own quarters, the little kibbutz within the kibbutz—the children's house. The children laughed a great deal. I can't bring myself to believe that they had been rehearsed for their illustrious visitors. A young man of seven made me a present: It was a penguin. It was made of a big pebble on which he had painted all that the pebble lacked, although it was exactly the right shape to be a penguin. They were free, cheeky, and happy.

The parents laughed a lot less. They were grave, intelligent, not religious or racist. They'd immigrated to Israel because they'd decided it was preferable to live beneath its sky than beneath that of the mother country they'd never known—under whose far-flung jurisdiction they'd been mobilized, repudiated, then solicited once again. They'd been fed up to the back teeth with being a species of French—not quite French because they were Jewish—and fed up with being Jews who were too French for the Arabs. They'd fully understood the situation. They were wise.

Their dining hall was a kind of canteen. They were happy to have us there. After dinner they danced. The music and the rhythms were entirely Slavic. They had faces like Italians, Arabs, and Spaniards. They clapped to the music like Cossacks. And Montand danced the hora with them as though he had been doing it all his life.

The same two guys in overalls drove us back to Tel Aviv. They had come eighty kilometers to collect us, eighty kilometers to bring us to the kibbutz, and they were going to do eighty kilometers to take us to town—which left them eighty kilometers to go home themselves.

When we got to the Dan Hotel, we asked them to come in and have a drink with us before they went back. They said they would gladly take a coffee. The uniformed doorman in front of the nightclub basement of the Dan Hotel pulled a face heralding the sort of snide remark one might expect to hear at the Hotel Crillon. The overalls displeased him. Montand pointed out to him that without people in overalls there probably would be no state of Israel. Our friends had come for a cup of coffee with us and they were going to get it. He smiled, and the kibbutzniks drank their coffee in this place where, fleetingly, they hobnobbed, for the first time in a very long while, in a world the continued existence of which they'd taken great care to ignore.

In Tel Aviv, Jerusalem, and Haifa we met young sabras who spoke of the latest arrivals, the immigrants of the fifties, as "soap Jews." By that they meant those who had passively accepted the possibility of a raid, deportation, and, finally, the transformation of the bit of fat still left on their bones into one of those cakes of soap on exhibition in the Museum of Nazi Crimes.

It was in the Bet She-arim, the Orthodox ghetto of

274

Jerusalem, that I heard an old grocery woman, her store full of shoelaces and little bags of holy soil especially packaged for American tourists, mutter in Yiddish that Hitler had been right. The Jewish people had committed the sin of heterodoxy, and had paid the price of their crime!

On the road to Jerusalem we picked up a hitchhiker, a handsome boy who said not a word for the first quarter hour, and then, during the remaining hour and a half, told us the story of his life. He was American. In 1945 he was one of the first who had walked into the Bergen-Belsen concentration camp. When his military service was over, he went back to New York to kiss his father and mother. A week later, after this short return to a homeland he had thought was his, he landed on this soil, which he had since reclaimed, irrigated, and defended.

With the exception of the sabras, in 1959 everyone in Israel came from somewhere else, and everyone had a story to tell. The accents changed with the age of the teller. The eldest told their tales in a singing Slavic accent. The less old told their story with a heavy Teutonic rhythm. The young might have a Polish or *Piednoir* or Hungarian or English or Rumanian or Bulgarian or Belgian or Parisian accent. Of course, they all used Hebrew. Some of them had learned it long ago—they were the pioneers. The others had set themselves to learning it. The new ones were learning it now. But for all of them, their first words, the words of their childhood, had not been Hebrew.

And the music, the lullabies, the nursery rhymes, the old tales, silly refrains, or verses of sublime poetry—all these had found homes in the ears of tiny tots, never to be cast away.

For some, then, it was "Kalitka" ("little gate at the bottom of the garden"); for others it was the Siegfried Idyll or Brahms's Lullaby. There was the duet from the tango in *The Threepenny Opera*, or "Somber Sunday" in its original Hungarian version, or "Tea for Two" or "Bei Mir Bist Du Schön" or "J'ai Ta Main dans Ma Main" or the "Lambeth

Walk" or the shrill voices of little girls singing Prokofiev or bits of Bartók. "Paris Reine du Monde"..."Ploum Ploum Tra-la-la"..."Une Petite Phrase de Vinteuil"...the "Internationale" or "Deutschland über Alles"....

For Montand, singing to an audience of these people was like singing in ten European cities in a single evening....

In Tel Aviv I stupidly caught up with my thirty-eighth year. By way of compensation, the next morning I received a phone call from London announcing that Alice Aisgill had won. I was the year's best English-language actress. In Cannes, a few weeks later, André Malraux, Minister of Culture, gave me the Golden Palm for my performance in the role of Alice Aisgill in a film called *Les Chemins de la Haute Ville*. I said thank you—in English.

Les Chemins de la Haute Ville did not have the same commercial success in France that *Room at the Top* had in the Anglo-Saxon countries. It was easy to understand why. The North of England, with its old prejudices and new signs of coming change, with its memories of the German bombings and its reminders of paying respect to superiors even in civilian life, with its mediocre and pretentious petite bourgeoisie still in the feudal grip of a wool lord—all this meant very little to a French audience. And then there was the Yorkshire accent, which very few could make out in the original version and whose savor had been completely lost in the dubbed version, which meant absolutely nothing to most of the French. It was hard for them to smile at the ridiculousness of this amateur dramatic group taking themselves so very seriously as they rehearsed and then played appallingly badly the repertoire of a typical "elegant" London theater.

Of course, there was the love story. In London and New York, *Room at the Top* broke through certain taboos. But *Les Chemins de la Haute Ville* really surprised no one in Paris when it showed lovers in the same bed; and the theme of the aging woman cousin of Léa (of *Chéri*) and Madame de Rénal (of *The Red and the Black*), living the last unhappy affair of her life with an ambitious young man, didn't seem surprising or daring.

I have just given you a summary of the film's reception by the critics after Cannes. No one argued with my prize, but I was a little saddened by the lukewarm enthusiasm for the film.

A few days ago, in Autheuil, I acted like Gloria Swanson in *Sunset Boulevard* when I asked Montand and Chris Marker to run the 16-millimeter print of *Room at the Top*. (I'm unmechanical.) Since I was going to talk about it here, I wanted to see what a film I had liked enormously looked like eighteen years later.

Neither my husband nor my friend of Sabot Bleu days is a model of diplomacy or courtly politeness. You're taking a great risk if you ask them to look at an old film with you. Sometimes, after the first reel, they stop with a comment such as: "You *really* want to see the rest?" Sometimes I'm just hypocritical enough to insist that if they're bored with what I want to see, I wouldn't mind a bit if they left me alone—I'll call when it's time to change the reel. And sometimes they do exactly that . . . and they're clever enough to calculate the time of the reel exactly, and to reappear at just the right moment without my even calling them. One or the other of them comes to switch the reels, and they do it exactly like a good projectionist: silently, with precise, economical gestures and a total indifference to what the machine will throw onto that little white square.

Sometimes, however, they don't follow my suggestion, and they stay. Then one of two things happens: If they don't like it at all, they make snide comments in a kind of stage whisper; or else they like it and shut up, or they laugh at the right moment, or they say, "Hey, that isn't dated at all!"

So I have two witnesses who, last week, confirmed what I've always believed: Long ago, I helped make something that was, and is, and will remain, a very good film.

The evening that the prizes were awarded in Cannes (it was six months after the death of my brother), the photographers spent a great deal of time on me and André Malraux as he gave me the prize—and when the ceremony was almost over, suddenly, to my surprise, all those photographers came back toward me. At that moment, someone at the officials' table rose and announced that a posthumous prize was being awarded to the young French film-maker Alain Kaminker, who had died while he was filming. I was taken completely unaware, and just as my heart was jolting with emotions at what had been said, the flashbulbs went off. And of course it was these photos that appeared the next morning in most of the press, with captions saying: "Ecstatically happy, she couldn't contain her feelings when her prize was announced."

I say "most" of the press because *Match* had sent me a very nice young man who took pictures in the garden at La Colombe for five hours; but the magazine accomplished the typographical miracle of never mentioning the prize for an actress's performance in their issue devoted to the Cannes festival. I never saw those pictures, but in case that young man should read these lines, and if he still has those negatives, I'd like to say that it would give me pleasure to see them and show them to my grandson, Benjamin. Granny, bleached blond; in the garden of La Colombe. They might amuse him.

All that remained now was to get ready to leave for New York. The job was divided between us in a very egalitarian fashion.

Montand rehearsed his musicians, working feverishly on his little English texts that had been concocted by our blacklisted friends. They were to serve as introductions for the songs he would sing in French to the American audience. They were little masterpieces of humor or *amour* which summarized the story or the atmosphere of the song. They were most important for the song sketches—the songs that tell a story in three little acts. I know that all the blacklisted authors weren't necessarily talented, nor were all the talented people necessarily blacklisted, but these particular ones fitted into both categories. So Montand's little English texts were written by good authors, and he studied them, rehearsed them, worked on them, recorded them, and wrote them on bits of paper and blackboards. He would use different colors of ink for words with a tonic accent, and then he would suddenly change to some phonetic method, which made the bits of paper and blackboards seem full of poems from Thailand and Breton prayers. All this took a great deal of his time, and with good reason: At the time he neither spoke nor understood a single word of English.

As for me, I was snowed under, what with fittings for lovely dresses at Lanvin, super suits at Hermès, and wonderful shoes at the workshop of Monsieur Capobianco, who told me I was a lot gayer than during the fur-lined-boots period. The shoes were a half size larger than usual, as he'd learned from the horse's mouth, as it were—from New York socialites—that in their city the foot tends to swell unpleasantly due to the humidity. So you see, I too had my problems.

Our departure was set for the month of September. Montand had decided to do a series of shows in the French seaside resorts so as to be in tiptop form. It was a real Tour de France, which began in Nice and ended in Deauville. I remember that in Biarritz, Lauren Bacall, who was to become "Betty" to us later on, made a date with us for opening night in New York. In the town of La Baule, Poiret and Serrault, in shorts, wrote new sketches. And it was in La Baule that I got a phone call from the New York office of a man I knew by name, Ed Murrow. It was about a program called *Small World*—they would explain it to us when we arrived. In Saint-Malo the piano hadn't been tuned because the local priest didn't like Montand and so he had forbidden the piano tuner—who was also, I think, the parish organist—to repair the damage caused by humidity, which is as bad for pianos as it is for New Yorkers' feet. And I think it was in Saint-Malo that the phone rang in the middle of the night and someone asked me whether I would like to play in Colette's *Chéri* on Broadway.

It was odd and gay to be simultaneously plotted step by step over *there* and yet remain firmly anchored to our own world *here*.

It was July 1959, and the beaches of the Atlantic and the Channel were as marvelous as they had been when I was a child. A great many sand castles were being built, and the young people were still on bicycles, just as they had been at the time of Saint-Gildas. But the "pacification" in Algeria was beginning to take a strange turn. I'm ashamed to say that we, champions of just causes—well, we thought about it, of course, but maybe not as much as our reputation would like to have it. During that month of July 1959, we were mostly thinking about ourselves. About what was happening to us and what awaited us.

Then a minute incident occurred that called us to heel. Our Tour de France—not bicycling, but singing—being over, we crossed the border and arrived in Ostend, Belgium. While Montand was supervising the lighting at the theater, I went for a stroll. Suddenly I saw *La Question, La Question, La Question*, an entire bookshop window crammed with *La Question*, by Henri Alleg. We might be on vacation from just causes, but we were not at a point where we were beyond indignation when the French government ordered the pulping of this book, which told about torture in Algeria as practiced by the French army. And more precisely, torture which had caused the death of Maurice Audin.

For a moment I thought that the pulping had miraculously stopped, and then I remembered that I was no longer in my country.

The bookshop was huge and well appointed, as are the buildings and shops in this Biarritz of the North Sea. The man behind the desk wasn't young, and his face was that of a shop owner, not of a bookseller. I asked him for three copies of *La Question*. He gave me a penetrating look and then said, "You're right to take three, since you come from a country where you're no longer allowed to read books."

This was said without the hint of a wink; it was said in cold anger and complete contempt. When he gave me my change, he added, "And besides buying books, what are you doing about what's being done in your name?" I murmured, "Not very much." When I left, he didn't say, "Good-bye, madame." He took absolutely no notice of my departure; he just went back to reading the book he had put aside when I came in.

I found myself on the sidewalk of a foreign city where, for the first time in my life, someone had spoken to me as I had often spoken to others. It was a new experience. It was unpleasant. But it was healthy.

We read *La Question*. We circulated our three copies, and I know that some people mimeographed certain passages. It was a tiny contribution, but it was better than nothing.

Our time of departure was drawing near. Again we were concentrated exclusively on ourselves. I suppose that's quite normal. (Although the Ostend bookseller was to reappear in our lives, and I'll tell you why a little later.) It was normal because we knew we were going to a city where the success or failure of the whole game is played off in one evening.

Catherine knew all about it too. She knew that if Montand's first night was a success, she would come over to join us. Just as she knew that if it was a flop, she would see the family back home forty-eight hours later.

There were plenty of examples of catastrophic homecomings of talented people, or people who thought they were talented, or people whose talent shone across the footlights everywhere except Broadway. There was a whole heap of anecdotes.... All of them had been photographed at the gangway of their plane—always at an angle favorable to the airline, which, by the way, never carries anyone free. Very few of them had a welcoming committee when they returned. All this crossed our minds as we were waving at the airport. "Good-bye, Paris—hello, New York," the captions would say, just as they had when Sarah Bernhardt left from Le Havre.

It's strange how departures for America, or rather New York, keep an anachronistic symbolism out of time and out of reason.

For show-biz people, in any case.

Maybe because of the risk. The risk of a flop.

In this spirit we made those ancient gestures, and I'm not sure that one newspaper didn't actually say: "À *nous deux*, New York!"*

___

*"Now it's between the two of us, New York!"—a parody of Rastignac's challenge in Balzac.

Chapter 10

THE gentlemen of the immigration service, in their glass cages, huddled for ages over the coded messages in our passports. They never lifted their heads to look at the two travelers, still completely dazzled from having seen with their own eyes that Manhattan *really* was an island. They ran their fingers down the pages of the two fat black books, looking for something, which they either found or didn't find. Then they went back to studying the hieroglyphics. In the end, they stamped our precious documents several times, as though regretfully. They extended them to us, and finally, for the first time, they lifted their very blue eyes to our faces and muttered, "Welcome to the United States."

Our "waver" was not the happy "Come, come, come" I had once thought it meant, as I've already said. Nor did our "waver" mean "These people are to be watched." Our "waver" wasn't a "waver." It was a *waiver*.

(It wasn't until yesterday's lunch with James Baldwin that I finally, after seventeen years, got a correct definition for this word, whose wandering etymology does, somewhere way back, have something to do with the waves of the sea and hand gestures.)

"Waiver" (see Harrap's): "abandoning of a right ... end of revendication."

Waiver: "We have every right to say no to these people, but we're giving them a dispensation. Love and kisses. Signed, Washington, D.C."

I now understand the sad faces of those officials. As they stamped our passports they were abandoning their rights. It was written black on blue sky. One of the numbers, the "28" in parentheses in the middle of the equation that summed up our lives, gave them this order. They obeyed the order, but without conviction.

Those two fat black books reminded me of the train that had stopped in the middle of nowhere on my way back from Dax in 1943. I remembered the disfigured Maréchal. I wondered whether the lady from the Rue Lauriston with her visa that was good for life had been greeted with a happier "Welcome to the United States" than the one we had been subjected to.

But glass cages last only a fleeting instant, and immediately after these formalities we and our baggage faced a bunch of wisecracking guys who asked us to open our bags for them. It wasn't a real search. It was all very good-humored, at that time anyway. One said, "You don't have to open that one, baby," and then, "I know you. You in show biz or something?" Another: "Did I see you in *Room at the Top*? I didn't understand those English accents." The first: "You're Italians?"

There was a certain familiarity about it all, or more accurately, a lack of obsequiousness. It made for a good transition. At the other side of the customs barrier Norman awaited us. He smiled like an uncle from the big city waiting for his small-town nephews, waiting to show them the sights.

The astonishing thing about crossing New York from the airport to the heart of Broadway is that one isn't astonished. Or rather that one is astonished by the absence of one's astonishment. For the French who love the cinema, arriving in New York for the first time is like an editing job at the Cinémathèque in which Langlois has pasted together pieces of *Scarface, Mr. Deeds, You Can't Take It with You, King Kong, Angels with Dirty Faces, The Naked City, Breakfast at Tiffany's, Easter Parade*, and *Twelve Angry Men*. All the sets are just the way they should be: the fire escapes; the elegant awnings to protect the lady about to enter her big limousine while the liveried doorman holds open the car door and salutes. Three strange, empty streets where there seems to be nothing alive and then you turn a corner and are in an enormous avenue full of old men and old women dressed as youngsters. One had the time to notice all this during that short trip, or rather to recognize it. At the terminus, there was the Algonquin.

A few snobbish Americans had laughed at us when we had announced before leaving Paris that we were going to stay at the Algonquin in New York. The Algonquin! That was the place to go twenty or thirty years ago, when Mr. So-and-so and Mrs. So-and-so and Miss So-and-so lived there, wrote their music, their plays, or their terrible reviews that demolished everyone else's plays, there in their rooms, or in the bar. Since we'd never heard of any of those So-and-sos, we let them talk, and instead of going to one of those big palaces they suggested, we followed the advice of Uncle Norman: Out-of-date provincials that we were, we were going to stay at the Algonquin.

The Algonquin is like La Colombe. It belongs to a family, the Bodnes. If we had lived at the Waldorf-Astoria, I doubt very much whether we would ever have met Mr. Waldorf or Miss Astoria. At the Algonquin, the Bodne family awaited us in the lobby.

The lobby reminded me of the smoking room of the Savoy, with its mahogany and overstuffed armchairs; it reminded me of the lobby of the Alkron, with all its traffic; and it reminded me of a Viennese teahouse, with the quiet good manners of all that bustle.

Mrs. Bodne said she was sure that Catherine would join us very soon. That one sentence said it all. Welcome. I don't know you but I do. Your show is going to be a success, you'll see; I know you're only going to bring over your daughter if it works. This is my way of saying good luck.

Norman, the Californian who likes New York only for its jazz musicians and his stays at the Algonquin, where the switchboard girls serve as his secretaries and the Bodnes as his true family—Norman had told them all about us.

Fifteen minutes later we were in Apartment 8005-8006. Uncle Norman showed us the secrets of doors that can be securely locked by pushing a little button on the knob; how to regulate the shower, depending upon whether one wants it tepid, hot, ice cold, rainy, or sharply piercing; how to draw the curtains, operate the TV set; how to use those long strips of impregnated cloth to shine your own shoes; how to cope with those ready-made lists offering every kind of imaginable breakfast (it simply requires not putting an X in the inappropriate place); how to get your laundry done—again a wide choice is offered: silk, nylon, cotton (it simply requires...). In other words, everything the average contemporary Frenchman would have no trouble in discovering were he to spend a night in one of those "contemporary" hotels that have recently sprung up.

That evening in September 1959, Norman was like Nadia, André, Sasha, and Slava; he was showing us the things about his country that we didn't know.

Before we went to bed, Montand asked where the theater was. "Let's walk there," said Norman. The Algonquin is on West Forty-fourth Street; we hadn't realized that we were in the heart of Broadway. Three minutes later, Norman showed us something about his country that we knew well, so very well—something every actor in the world knows: Times Square. It was Luna Park, the Fête de Neuilly, fireworks, blinking lights. A square like a golden door opening on nine streets that were short but magical. The streets with the theaters. The streets of triumphs or flops, depending on whether their marquees are lighted or dark.

The Henry Miller Theater, on Forty-third Street, had a dark marquee. By the light of the next-door theater we could press our noses to the glass of the closed doors and look at the lobby with its box office in the middle. In a bad film, at this point there would be a sound effect of a shivery bell: one minute till curtain time. I wonder if bad films aren't just maladroit blueprints for authentic natural reactions.

Monsieur Capobianco was certainly right to make my shoes a half size larger. But he had forgotten that the very special September heat wave in New York means that a stiletto heel has a terrible tendency to sink into the asphalt, which slows down the tourist's progress, dirties the delicate white of the shoe forever, and leaves a kind of stippled track marking her first walk in the city.

A sharp detective following this stippled track the morning after we arrived would have tracked us to a large building and then, investigating further, would have found himself in a boxlike room in which the principal feature was a dentist's chair. It was there Montand learned his first words of useful English—"Am I hurting you?"—not to mention "gums," "jaws," "tooth," and for obvious reasons, "teeth." This English lesson was given by a Dr. Weinstein, who was the first New Yorker to have the privilege of hearing sounds emanate from the famous French singer whose show had been announced two weeks previously. The toothache had erupted out of the blue, at the crack of dawn; the previous evening there'd been nothing wrong.

Montand was in tremendous pain. I could do nothing for him except translate his pains into English, and then the dentist's questions and instructions into French. From where I sat, I could read "Time-Life" on the roof of a big building and see the second hand on an illuminated electric clock leaping forward like something out of a McLaren animated film. If my memory is so accurate, it's because, unfortunately, we were condemned to watch that clock every morning for ten days. Dr. Weinstein took very good care of Montand, whose pain decreased as his progress increased in a somewhat specialized vocabulary not easily dropped into casual conversation. Though by learning "wisdom teeth" you also learn what the word "wisdom" means, which can come in handy.

The daily visits to Dr. Weinstein hadn't been included in the schedule that had been so carefully worked out before we arrived. But by putting the alarm clock half an hour forward and delaying the day's first appointment by forty-five minutes, we could manage not to demolish the construction that had been so lovingly built by Norman and Richard Maney.

Richard Maney was not young. When he smiled, he had the clear blue gaze of an Irishman—that is, of any Irishman not employed as an immigration official in a glass cage. He was to the Broadway theater what Paul Poiret must have been to French couture. He was a legend; a legend he avoided telling himself. He was the best publicity agent on Broadway. His methods were old but they were in no way outdated. They weren't showy; they were effective. And they were serious.

He had sliced up Montand's mornings, which were destined for the press. The ladies and gentlemen of the press were accorded fifteen minutes, twenty minutes, a half hour, or an hour, according to their merits. A stream of journalists came and went in the little living room of Apartment 8005–8006.

Thanks to "Time-Life" and McLaren, we were never late for the first arrival at about ten-thirty. At that early hour it was often a young man or a young woman who had been granted only twenty minutes; the beginner who carefully writes down all the answers to his prepared questions, leaving his black coffee to grow cold in order not to lose a second. Those interviews rarely rose above the level of: "How long have you been married? And how come you were born in Monsummano? And you in Wiesbaden?" They had studiously done their homework, and they addressed their questions to Mr. Monntaind. Mrs. Monntaind would translate them to Mr. Monntaind, and then Mr. Monntaind communicated his replies to Mrs. Monntaind, who worked hard not to make mistakes as she translated the little lesson in European history explaining how two apparently typical French people were born in Tuscany or the occupied Rhineland. All that took quite a while. So just at the moment when the young man or the young woman was finally getting around to asking questions about the recital, Maney's assistant, who had been silently tending the black coffee or the tea with lemon, would get up and, looking at his watch, would murmur with a gentle smile, "Sorry, Joe [or Susie], but time's up, I'm afraid." So our beginner would pick up his papers, leave his cold coffee, say thank you, and go. Sometimes he would turn around on the threshold and, usually blushing deeply, say breathlessly that he had seen *The Wages of Fear* at college, or knew the words of "Autumn's Leaves" by heart, and in French.

At that point it would be ten fifty-five and we would have a five-minute breather. At exactly eleven, the questions would begin again. The ceremonial would be the same; it was still the proper time to offer coffee or tea.

During the slice of time that ran from eleven to noon, the age of the callers would be higher than during the preceding slice. They, too, had done their homework, but they would get to the heart of the matter with greater speed. They wanted to know how many songs Montand was going to sing, what French or American singer had a roughly comparable style; they were asking him to define himself. I translated. Their questions were never indiscreet, but they were caught in an impossible situation. They had been asked to do articles on someone whose work they had never experienced, and if some of them had heard a few records, they still couldn't understand why in Montand's replies there were suddenly allusions to dance steps. They were trying to be nice; they would mention the great success of *Room at the Top*, which was still playing the first-run movie theater.

In Paris Montand is Montand, and I'm myself, and we

are man and wife. In Moscow, I was Montand's wife. In New York, for the few days that preceded his opening, my greatest worry was that they would see Montand as an actress's husband.

In the time slice that went from noon to one, we were generally dealing with specialists. Depending on their age, they had generally seen Montand at Carrère's after the Liberation, or at the Étoile, or even at the ABC when he replaced a sick Piaf. They asked their questions; they had generally requested an interview with this man who reminded them of their weeks or years in Paris. These same people also knew that *Room at the Top* hadn't been my first film. During this time slice Maney's assistant would serve Bloody Marys or Scotches on the rocks, and visibly would get a bit bored listening to some journalist hum bits of a song that for him carried no waves of nostalgia.

The next time slice was the deluxe slice. Now came the lunches in the Algonquin dining room with the press VIPs. They were people who were as much at home there as those Parisians who regularly frequent Lipp. The maître d' would greet them, calling them by their first names. We knew these people as little as we knew the others. We knew no one. However, judging by the respectful looks that came from the tables about us, we caught on: This was important promotion.

And in fact, it was. These people had earned their jobs. They were great journalists. There were courteous, funny, polyglot, liberal, curious, and impossible to fool. In the course of one of those lunches, a tall young man from *Time* magazine began asking real questions. He had a smile that bared at least forty-eight teeth, the shoulders of a baseball player, he wore a signet ring that said something about his European ancestry, and he had pale eyes in which one could read both candor and malice. He attacked his clams, and after a few remarks about the unusual heat, to which we were surely unaccustomed, he asked, "Why has it taken you so long to come to America?"

I translated to Montand. Montand asked me to translate

his reply sentence by sentence. It was something like this: I might answer that we were so busy with recitals, films, and couture collections that we never had the time to get around to crossing the Atlantic. (I translated.) But as you are an editor at *Time*, you know your files certainly contain more than those of the Paris Préfecture de Police, the FBI, and the KGB combined. (I translated.) Consequently you know perfectly well why we haven't come here before now. And I would be very grateful if you would explain those reasons to your readers. (I translated.)

So we made a list of all that had kept us away from America for so long. Sometimes he would add a detail that we had forgotten. Our frankness amazed him.

So we were very frank. We didn't box clever. We were intelligent. It was far better for us not to seem to be something that we were not in America's most widely read weekly. We were what we had always been; it was America that had revised its stand. And that's what appeared in the article written by the young baseball player (who may have been a philosophy Ph.D.) and published a few days before the opening.

From those sliced-up mornings Richard Maney had pulled together a kind of bouquet. It was composed of superficial observations, amusing or unamusing interviews, thumbnail sketches, caricatures, more searching articles, reflections about Europe, descriptions of what Montand and I were wearing during the interview, etc. All the things that make up a press kit. Old man Maney had done his job very well; New York now knew that there was a variety performer named Yves Montand in town.

Now it was up to Montand.

Norman looked after Montand's afternoons. They were not divided into slices, unless it was that of "the musicians' quarter hour," that break practiced in all languages and all latitudes.

Montand was rehearsing with a new orchestra. Bob Castella, as piano accompanist, was the only French musician allowed by the New York union. Hubert

Rostaing, the orchestrator, had received permission to come for a few days to put the new musicians in the picture. The new musicians had been recruited by Norman. They were marvelous jazz musicians.* As far as swing was concerned, they swung. But they were being asked to learn something new, which was the exact opposite of what they had learned to do better and better all their lives. They were used to telling a story with their instruments, depending on the inspiration and mood of the day. Montand was asking them to help him tell *his* stories; consequently to follow him as his inspiration and mood dictated; and, moreover, to follow closely some things that had to be very firmly established and precise, especially in the funny songs, or the effects might not come off. In order to understand all this, they had to know what the stories were about. Montand told them as well as he could, and those little texts by our blacklisted friends did a great job. His new musicians became his first audience, a very good audience.

At the end of a few days all the various traditions had merged: blues with bal musette with ragtime with commedia dell'arte.

I didn't go to rehearsals. My presence there would have been completely useless. They all understood each other perfectly well without an interpreter.

The evenings were sliced up by no one. The days were very tough. The sessions with Dr. Weinstein meant getting up early, and Montand was aggravated from trying to understand and make himself understood. So we dined at the Algonquin.

Most of the staff were Italian, and thus it was in Italian that they took our orders and inquired after our physical and psychological health. Sometimes other old-fashioned provincials like us—Laurence Olivier, Luis Buñuel, Peter

*The orchestra consisted of Nick Perito, accordion; Jim Hall, guitar; Jimmy Giuffre, clarinet; Al Hall, double bass; Charles Persip, drums; Billy Byers, trombone.

Brook—passing through New York, would come and share our pastrami with us.

Ella Fitzgerald and Oscar Peterson were also guests at the Algonquin; which proved that Mr. and Mrs. Bodne's conception of their vocation as hotel owners and American citizens was no minor merit—nor their least attractive. Ella and Oscar had a drink while we dined. Their show began at around 10 P.M.

Norman sat contemplating his little family. Ella and Oscar were "sure things"; they had been recognized geniuses for a long time, though it was surely partly his doing that they were respected as they were: In 1959 not every hotel would have welcomed them on its guest list.

Montand wasn't a "sure thing." The countdown was just beginning. I'm sure that at that moment Norman was counting too. But he didn't cast a shadow of doubt. He seemed pleased to see us all together. In different ways, he had broken two taboos.

Finally, opening night came.

Again, if I were directing this film, I would pan in, the morning after the premiere at the Henry Miller, to a shot in the office of the principal of the Lycée Français of New York. I would be there, enrolling "Catherine Allégret" into her fourth class (their eighth grade). I would do a quick sequence of the maid making up Room 8007, which could be made to open into Apartment 8005–8006, and you would have understood in a flash that the evening was a triumph.

I would include photographs of Marlene Dietrich, Ingrid Bergman, Lauren Bacall, Marilyn Monroe, Adolph Green, Goddard Lieberson, Sidney Lumet, and Monty Clift, as well as a lot of people whose faces, however famous, I couldn't connect with names, plus highlights of the article written by the most famous columnist in New York.

I would do a flashback on the only evening we had spent at Sardi's, a few days earlier, where we had felt so provincial and out of it that we had decided not to have our little party, after opening night, in this inner sanctum of a world that was not yet ours.

And I would end this flashback sequence (which would come just before the one in the lycée principal's office) in the lobby and the two dining rooms of the Algonquin, cracking at the seams with people who were kissing Montand, who were kissing me, and who were kissing one another.

At two in the morning, the fresh galley proofs brought in by a *France-Soir* correspondent, Maney's assistant, and a pal of the Bodnes', circulated from hand to hand. There are seven critics* who write at night in New York, and it is they who decide, at around dawn, whether the theater will remain lighted up or whether it will go dark. These people may or may not have seen the press kit so carefully prepared by Richard Maney, and couldn't care less whether you'd rather wear a sweater or a dinner jacket. They're not a bit curious to know what you think of the cold war or about the joys and difficulties of ten years of married life. They are specialists and no one can pull the wool over their eyes.

They come to see and hear, and to describe what they've seen and heard.

They don't ask for much. They want to be taken out of their surroundings, amused, moved; they want to laugh and to understand—especially when what they hear isn't in their language. They want to be astonished; they want to be surprised into clapping their hands and asking for more when it's done.

All seven of the reviews were superb. It was fiesta time at the Algonquin. At about two-fifteen that morning, Montand became a member of the Broadway family.

If Montand had had the same success in a well-known New York nightclub, he wouldn't have become a member of the family. Not the big family, in any case. Then the

*There were seven critics in 1959.

elegant people from the elegant parts of town where the elegant nightclubs are located would have come. A few well-known stars would have reserved their tables in advance, and a few of the broke would have scratched together what it takes to pay for the Scotch which grows warm so quickly, and which they keep watering down because it has to last all evening, given the price of a drink in those places. It would have taken just the same amount of energy to conquer the stage fright that goes with singing fourteen songs as it does for singing twenty-four, and he would have gone back to a dressing room full of salmon- or cream-colored satin to be gracious about the compliments of people come to end their evening in a fashionable place.

But the Henry Miller Theater isn't a fashionable place. It's just a theater, which has had, and will continue to have, its lighted moments and its dark ones. It was now quite clear that with *An Evening with Yves Montand* it would stay lighted quite a while. The dressing room was a cement box in the basement, as are most of the Broadway dressing rooms. Those nine streets are filled with catacombs where at the same time of day, different sects prepare themselves to sing or dance, play Shakespeare or Tennessee Williams.

On the way from the Algonquin to the theater there was a tiny store. The dust that covered its window from the inside was so thick that it was impossible to distinguish what had once been sold there. On the outside, the dirt was a kind of mud. Still, if you rubbed with a Kleenex, a small rectangular sign appeared on the far left-hand side, on which was handwritten: "Aquí se habla Yiddish."

There was much graffiti on the walls and doors of this part of town. It was not yet psychedelic. It often had to do with lovers' dates, and some of it was smutty, of course; Forty-second Street is not far away. What I consider the most wonderful graffiti of all wasn't found by me, but by Pierre Olaf: "Nostalgia isn't what it used to be." Pierre Olaf read it because he was there; he was there because *La Plume de Ma Tante* was a hit on Broadway. The Dhérys and their company had become members of the Broadway family a few months earlier. And Catherine Dhéry was already a veteran at the Lycée Français.

Our Catherine arrived three days after the marvelous reviews. Colette came with her. Colette was the young fiancée, now widowed, of my brother. Apartment 8005–8006–8007 was beginning to look a bit like the "caravan."

Forty-eight hours after she arrived, Catherine had learned how to cope with Manhattan. All you had to do was read the numbers and make sure you knew whether the address you wanted was west or east of the island's spinal column, Fifth Avenue. This simple step had taken me a week. Once I found myself on an Eighty-third Street that resembled the Puteaux slums before the big mini-skyscrapers were built, when I was expected somewhere like the Faubourg Saint-Honoré. . . . That taught me to pay more attention to the Easts and Wests in the addresses I wrote down.

Catherine took her bus, lunched with her pals in a drugstore, and knew that one shouldn't go into the park after four in the afternoon. She learned English with Mrs. Bodne, the doormen, the elevator men, and the waiters—although in the latter case it was slightly Italianate English. She wouldn't have learned as much in three years of Berlitz courses.

On her free afternoons, Thursdays, the eighth floor of the Algonquin, as well as the halls of the eighth and ninth floors and the connecting staircases, became marvelous playgrounds for hide-and-seek. Sometimes she would go to play and sleep at the house of her best pal, the Laporte kid, whose father was the French consul. During the time of Raymond Laporte and his wife, the French consulate in New York was really a home, not an administration.

When the owner of the Henry Miller Theater had made his arrangements with Norman for *An Evening with Yves Montand*, he had done something very audacious. It took courage to sign up a two-and-a-half-hour one-man show done entirely in French. But his courage had turned to panic when someone said to him, "I hear you're expecting Yves Montand. That's great. She's fabulous!" So the owner had been careful to take out his insurance—another booking. Which is perfectly comprehensible, and that's how at the end of three weeks, the Miller's box-office people, who had spent their time telling people they were sold out, looked on unhappily as we moved out. The manager, the ushers, and the fire marshal had to get ready for the next booking, which the cautious management had contracted "in case of disaster."

So *An Evening with Yves Montand* moved over to the Longacre, which had just had a disaster. . . . *An Evening with Yves Montand* stayed at the Longacre long enough to see the lights go on and then go off very quickly at the Henry Miller four streets away: There had been a disaster. . . .

The story I've just told might seem mean to you. But what I've just told is really very kind. Nowhere else in the world have I met theater people who take their triumphs or flops with so much good humor, grace, and absence of vanity as in New York.

Since the time of our provincialism and timidity was now behind us, we did go to Sardi's once in a while. It's here that theater people come to celebrate after their opening night, and it's here that the first copies of reviews are eagerly scanned.

We would see people who had rehearsed and acted in plays they had believed in, rightly or wrongly, and whose hopes were guillotined as they read those reviews. But they would read them aloud, announcing that as of now, two in the morning, they would be out of work the next day. They laughed and joked, or seemed to, which isn't as easy as all that. Tables would be joined together and toasts proposed: "To the biggest flop of the year—cheers."

They knew when to put an X across the thing and go on to the next. Maybe they cried when they got home. But in public and among their peers, they laughed.

But they really were moving on to the next job. There

were so many outlets that there always seemed to be work for everyone. What with the theater, films, and the several television channels, as well as tours, repertory companies, and off-Broadway productions, which were beginning to grow in importance, you had to be very bad or very lazy to stay out of work after a flop. Or, in those days, you had to be very black not to find work right away.

After the show, the dressing-room door at the Henry Miller and then at the Longacre would often open on people who were among the greatest stars of the New York scene. We could measure our ignorance by the facial expressions of Pat Saunders, Montand's dresser. At the time we behaved as provincial as the owner's pal who declared, "Yves Montand . . . she's fabulous!" But then, how would most of the French react to names like Jack Benny, Buddy Hackett, Zero Mostel, or Tallulah Bankhead?

One evening the door opened on a very tall, very handsome man, who said, "My name is Henry Fonda." And we said, "We know." We hugged. He said that he had some spaghetti at home, just in case, and if we had nothing better to do, he'd be delighted to take us both with him.

We met Arthur Miller again; we hadn't seen him since that sad afternoon in November 1956 on the Rue Francoeur in Paris. He hadn't come to the first night, but he came on the second, with Marilyn, who had come to the first. They, too, had prepared a little supper in their huge, all-white apartment, just in case. They were with Norman Rosten and his wife.

But what was best of all was the arrival of those taxi drivers, millionaire sugar daddies, crazy aunts, stationmasters endangered by Indians, rich lovers, proprietors of shoddy bars, last-minute witnesses, confiding pals, unscrupulous reporters, and flunky headwaiters. . . . They all came. They would say: "You don't know me, my name is . . ." at which Montand would stop them. And then he would tell them everything he had seen in films from his earliest childhood on, and would mime their most glorious moments for them. He knew them all. They had their triumphs in his dressing room. Which made everyone concerned feel very good.

It's a while since I've talked about old Alice Aisgill. When we arrived in New York, and up to Montand's opening night, I had found her a bit of a menace to my daily routine. Of course, it was delicious to hear "Hello, Simonn," or "Are you Miss Signorett?" or "Hi, Alice," from taxi drivers, or in stores, or in the streets of a city you're seeing for the first time. But we weren't here to shore up the incredible success of *Room at the Top*, which, as I said, had been playing in the same first-run movie house for a year now. We were here for *An Evening with Yves Montand*, and our only preoccupation was to see that the expedition didn't end with "*One* Evening with Yves Montand."

Montand went through his routine pangs of worry before an opening night, as well as his language problems, his problems with the new orchestra, and his terrible toothache. I had only one pang to worry about, but it was a sharp one.

If somehow Montand's first night had been a flop, I would have started to hate Alice Aisgill and accuse her of unfair competition. You see, every day at the same time this dame would deliver the same performance, and this she would repeat unaltered six consecutive times. She was able to do this only because all the best takes of a film made a year and a half earlier had been intelligently stuck together. Because of this she had become a pal of taxi drivers, a spiritual sister to aging ladies who had had a late adventure with a young man, or the symbol of the expert older mistress so many young men dream of meeting. It might be too hot, it might rain, there might be a draft in the movie house, but Alice was invulnerable.

My husband, on the other hand, wasn't invulnerable. Each evening he was a man who just couldn't be miserable because of the heat, nor could he have a rain-induced cold, or be stabbed by a draft, or be the victim of a line fluff or a memory dry-up, or be let down by the lighting—nor could he be, quite simply, just a little bit off. . . .

Moreover, the spectators before whom he was to appear had to be in a good mood; they couldn't be too hot, or be bothered by a cold they had caught in the rain, nor could they have a crick brought on by the draft. . . .

Also, I had just gotten to the bottom of the famous system of "You win or lose in one evening." It was true, albeit a slightly Jesuitical truth. It was true that on Broadway the game was won or lost during that single evening before the Broadway reviewers; but under normal circumstances a first night took place after a long tour in key cities to get the kinks out of the show. A Broadway opening was never a real opening. It was very often the fiftieth time the curtain went up. In fact, frequently there was no opening night at all: The theater would stay dark because the play had died on its way there, in Boston or in Pittsburgh.

This discovery increased my own private worry. So I was careful not to share it with my husband.

I had a recurring nightmare that we would be forced to leave in disgrace from this city where Alice continued to work for me while my husband had missed his entrance. You may imagine my relief the morning after the opening, when Alice and I went back to being friends.

Being "discovered" at age thirty-eight gives you an odd feeling. Sadly, I discovered that apart from a few film buffs who lived in the Village, nobody had seen *Casque d'Or*. But it was pleasant when the three of us arrived at parties: Eaves, Simonn, and Alice. She was no longer a nuisance. My husband put up with her very nicely.

The parties . . . sometimes they were dinners for six or seven and sometimes they were parties for a hundred people. But they were always real parties, a little like they still are in the country in France, when at the end of the meal everyone takes a turn with his song or dance or story.

In Paris, people in show business reserve their talent for the show. They don't show off. It's a combination of modesty (sometimes false), timidity (sometimes a bluff), and pride—which can also be called vanity. Whatever the reasons, that's the way we are.

Perhaps in New York it's really the remains of a tradition of nostalgic immigrants. There is a kind of simplicity of encounter, a sense of fun, and the sharing of what one loves to do. There's nothing of the showoff about it; it just somehow happens, and it's marvelous.

It's like a campfire with stars, an Actors Equity gala in a corner of a living room, or a hora in a kibbutz that isn't necessarily entirely Jewish.

Before leaving New York, about which I've spoken with great egotism, possessiveness, and the superficiality characteristic of people who have survived an adventure no more important than a drop of water under the aspect of eternity, I would like to thank the following people for the precious moments they have evoked in my memory: Mrs. Betty Bacall, Mr. Adolph Green and his fiancée, Mr. Goddard Lieberson and his wife, Brigitta (who greatly resembles Vera Zorina, because she is Vera Zorina), the mounted policeman who said to his horse, "Say good evening to Alice," Mr. and Mrs. Leonard Bernstein, Miss Ruth Gordon and her husband, Mr. Garson Kanin, the gentleman at the French library, Miss Jane Fonda, Mr. Mike Nichols, the Armenian tailor gentleman, Miss Lillian Hellman, Mr. Duke Ellington, Mr. Sidney Lumet, Mrs. Lotte Lenya, Columbia University, Mr. and Mrs. Richard Seaver, and, of course, the immigration officers at the airport.

We left New York. A lightning survey might add up as follows: a handful of privileged streets and residential suburbs, fashionable restaurants. The outer fringe of Harlem, to wind up an evening in a club that specializes in welcoming O.K. white jazz fans. Contagious laughter with newly acquired friends. Loads of wicker baskets containing wondrous fruit protected by layers of cellophane like bridal veils. The Hermès department of Saks Fifth Avenue.

We had stopped going to Dr. Weinstein a long while since. I sometimes wonder what it would be like for an immigrant who didn't speak the language and woke up in Brooklyn or the Bronx his first morning in the new country with a terrible toothache.

We left Catherine in New York to finish her semester at the Lycée Français. Colette, Mrs. Bodne, and the Laporte family would look after her, and she would meet us in Paris at Christmas time. Montand still had three items on his agenda: a week in Canada and, in California, a week in Hollywood and a week in San Francisco.

Canada, give or take few skyscrapers, was apparently still the country we used to learn about in our geo and history books long, long ago. But the Maria Chapdelaines* were beginning to be emancipated, and there was Félix Leclerc and the Bozos; although Charlebois and Gilles Vignaud were still in short pants, they were already born. There were others, too, who would soon prove themselves. Quebec had begun to move, and, as in Moscow, you had to be very vigilant to ferret out the dissidents. On the side of the enemy, "L'Anglois," nonetheless, there was the National Film Board, laboratory of the genius McLaren and many others, such as those who made *City of Gold*. The Film Board sold us a 16-millimeter print for fifty dollars, and it is one of the gems of our film library in Autheuil.

We thought we had only a couple of weeks to spend in America before going home. I spent twenty and Montand thirty-two before we both got back home.

"Hollywood" . . . I use quotation marks because "Hollywood" is rarely Hollywood. It's Beverly Hills, Burbank, Westwood, Malibu, Culver City, Downtown, Venice,

Maria Chapdelaine was a well-known old-fashioned novel by Louis Hémon, whose French-Canadian heroine was very pure.

Watts, Santa Barbara—as well as Hollywood. It's also Los Angeles, known as L.A. when you're from that neck of the woods.

I'm not a local lady, so I'll go on calling L.A. "Hollywood" in memory of when I was sixteen: the Harcourt Studio; love at first sight between Annabella and Tyrone Power; Mireille Balin pining away with love for Tino Rossi, who'd remained in Paris; Danielle Darrieux dolled up with sausage ringlets across her head for *Coqueluche de Paris*, a hairdo I'd tried to imitate one lunchtime before Vantieghem's Latin class; those "chipolatas"° which had caused so many articles to be written in movie fan magazines (all one had to do was heat the curling irons on the pilot light of the bathroom gas heater: "Chipolatas" were obtained; they also left behind a pungent smell of frizzling, equally revolting in the bathroom and on a schoolgirl's head). "Hollywood" for me is the memory of Jean Harlow's death; Deanna Durbin's first film kiss; Lupe Velez's suicide; Carole Lombard's "bangs," which hid an ugly scar; the golden key to Simone Simon's garden gate; the immense shadows highlighting Marlene's cheekbones; ditto Greta's, Katharine's, Kay's, Irene's, and Barbara's (Dietrich, Garbo, Hepburn, Francis, Dunne, Stanwyck), made by eyelashes that grew longer than anywhere else in the world.

As you can see, I was hardly up to date. I was just up to my own date as the plane flew over that section of Los Angeles, and I could look down and read HOLLYWOOD, traced out in capital letters as though written by a child.

I'm always sorry for the people who reject gifts their adolescent memories may offer. As that plane circled down, I was eating one of Proust's memory madeleines, as big as a donut. I knew perfectly well that what we would find below wouldn't be that "Hollywood," but it was fun remembering Neuilly-sur-Seine.

Consequently, I'm sorry for those French people I

°Small sausages, generally served with cocktails.

know who have never set foot elsewhere than in Le Lavandou, Boulevard Saint-Germain, or Zurich, but who tell me that flying over Hollywood—excuse me, L.A.— would mean nothing to them. Especially if they're my age and assert they love the cinema. One of two things: Either they're bluffing, or they're lying when they say they love the cinema. Probably they were the little kids who knew that Santa Claus didn't exist long before their pals put them wise; the sort who set out to prove to you that a bean can't grow into a stalk stout enough to be climbed, and who sniggered when told that a poor and beautiful girl had been identified simply by the size of her foot when she lost one of her slippers on the stroke of midnight.

I feel sorry for them because they have censored mythology. Up there, in our airplane, we were mythologizing with the wisdom and smiles of people who have done what they had to do elsewhere, and for whom it's a wonderful pleasure to finally arrive at the Mecca of their adolescence. Even though that Mecca had never been responsible for, or productive of, or godmother to, what either of us had done.

On landing in L.A., Jack Warner's and Howard Hughes's former contractees didn't have to account to anyone. They were what they were; they hadn't come ten years earlier. They'd come to spend a week.

I have five Hollywoods in my life: 1959-60, 1964, 1965, 1967, 1968-69. Not one is like another.

Everything happened right away. Before we left New York, one of the three French ladies of Hollywood, Anne Douglas (the two others are Quique Jourdan and Véronique Peck), had phoned to tell us that she was preparing a little party for the day after our arrival. That little party, so lovingly prepared, simply prolonged the mythology of our adolescence. Anne and Kirk had invited *le tout* Hollywood. It was grandiose, and at the same time it was intimate. That same evening, the unfortunate Richard Nixon, campaigning for the presidency, also gave a party, in one of the big hotels in town. Judging by the number of guests thronging the living room, the garden, and the pool at the Douglases', one might be given to wonder who had gone to the party given by the future ex-President of the United States. But perhaps a few of them dropped by at Nixon's party on the way home? Only one guest had the courage of his convictions: Jack Warner announced that he had come from Nixon's party and that he would be going back there, but he did want to stop by to see that "sonofabitch" he had tried so hard to import in 1949. He was vulgar and funny, and proud of his role during the time of McCarthy. He bore no grudge against those he had wronged. Before returning to serve in the cause of his candidate, he nevertheless declared that it was much more amusing there at the Douglases' than at the hotel. . . .

And it *was* amusing. Montand asked Walt Disney why he had never answered the letter he had written to him when he was thirteen years old. Judy Garland sang in a corner of the living room. Romain Gary explained that one should never trust the bored look that his role as consul forced on him. He was never bored at all. In one evening, the Douglases had introduced us to the whole town, and had allowed us to meet again the few people we already knew.

There were a lot of big names among the guests: the Coopers, the Kellys, the Pecks, the Wilders, the Hathaways, George Cukor, Dean Martin—a whole long list I can't enumerate because it's too long—and a little lady who wasn't the most famous of the guests but who greedily relished our "debut." She was Minna—Minna Wallis. She kept seeing herself under the orange tree at La Colombe, in a tizzy—ready to leave empty-handed, ready to face her boss's fury for having come back without me, ready to agree with me on all counts after a rough two-day siege. She was radiant at the sight of us there—at last! She kept telling people the story of her own encounter with that evening's king and queen when they were still just French yokels, madly in love.

There was also Mr. Goetz and his wife, Edie. It didn't take me long to discover that Edie Goetz was the Duchesse de Guermantes of what was left of mythological "Hollywood." And Mr. Goetz justified his multi-page telegram. He reminded me that he had said it was just a rain check.

There was Charlie Feldman, with whom I'd broken faith by not following Minna Wallis. There was Capucine, who told me that a private screening of *Room at the Top* had been stopped at the end of the second reel because the hosts wanted to play gin rummy—and they were the same people who had just thrown themselves into my arms, telling me how "fantastic" I was, and how I had done a "great job," and would surely be nominated for an Oscar.

And there was Dalio. Marcel contemplated his old pal from *Dédée d'Anvers;* he saw the adolescent who had sung "Moi j'm'en Fous" at the Club des Cinq when the Liberation had brought him back to Paris. During the war Marcel had spent five years playing waiters and bit parts in this town that had forgotten, or had never known, that he was Rosenthal in *La Grande Illusion* and La Chesnaye in *The Rules of the Game*.

As you can see, the Douglases gave a marvelous party. A party put together with love ....

Montand sang at the Huntington Hartford in old Hollywood. The theater was enormous. Once again he had a new band of musicians, since California union rules forbade the use of the New York musicians. Once again Norman had chosen the best. Profiting by the New York experience, rehearsals were easy. Montand sang for a week to standing room only. We were already in San Francisco when the phone rang with a call from Hollywood; they were asking Montand to come back. I'll tell you why in a minute.

In San Francisco the theater had velvet and gold trappings, the dressing room was furnished in scarlet damask, and the armchairs were decorated with pompons. The mirrors were beveled, and if one had searched long enough, undoubtedly graffiti would have been discovered, etched long ago by diamonds Wild West adventurers had offered to some long-forgotten diva.

The Golden Gate was just as everyone knows it is. The Top of the Mark looked out on the whole bay, and made one feel like Jeanette MacDonald or Clark Gable.

On opening night there was a second star; Harry Bridges, the most famous longshoreman in America, was in the audience. This man could paralyze all the ports in the West with a phone call. It had happened once, when the Un-American Activities Committee had had him arrested. An hour later they let him go. Or so the legend goes.

In San Francisco we irritated a taxi driver who wanted us to look at the prisoners of Alcatraz through a telescope placed opposite that awful island for the greater joy of passing tourists. He muttered unpleasant remarks about foreigners who had no taste for American prisons.

In San Francisco, in a small movie house, they were playing Leni Riefenstahl's *Triumph of the Will*. In the lobby there were display cases containing arm bands with swastikas on them, SS insignia, Iron Crosses, and belts with daggers. The two male ushers were very tall and very blond, and the audience was entirely Aryan.

In San Francisco I recorded the program Ed Murrow had phoned me about in La Baule, *Small World*. But I'll return later to this incident, which ended up being of exceptional importance for me.

So we went back to Hollywood. Twentieth Century–Fox, alerted by the impact of the one-man show at the Huntington Hartford and the fan mail that poured in after Montand's appearance on the Dinah Shore show, had offered him a film. It was called *Let's Make Love*, and the director was George Cukor. The leading lady, already signed up, was Marilyn Monroe.

It occurs to me that if I were to try selling a script based on the story I've embarked on telling here, whether beginning in Cabucelle and Neuilly, or starting only in

1956, or after the glass-cage episode at the New York airport, I would be courteously thanked by the specialists in the matter, who'd point out that soap opera is definitely old hat.

Soap opera or not, the contract was signed, and Catherine was informed that her parents wouldn't be home as early as anticipated.

Bungalow No. 20, in the garden of the Beverly Hills Hotel, became the younger brother of the "caravan," the cousin of Apartment 8005–8006 at the Algonquin, the nephew of the Babelsberg *Gasthaus*, and a replica of the small sixth-floor apartment in the Savoy Hotel.

(Here I am with my mania again: hotels. I talk about them more often than I do about the dreads of actors, the joys of creation, the motivation of characters, and diverse paradoxes—none of which I talk about very well, because they are things I prefer not to talk about, in order to maintain their mystery. I think that if I were to try to clarify these mysteries, I would be in danger of losing them altogether, by dint of knowing them too well. For I would be in great danger of no longer being surprised when they explode in or around me. So I'll just go back to where I was: Bungalow No. 20 in the garden of the Beverly Hills Hotel.)

The word "bungalow" applied to the Beverly Hills Hotel is not what most people expect, especially when they think of safaris or if they've read Kipling. The Beverly Hills variety are rarely little individual cabins. When they are separate, they're five-room apartments with two bathrooms.

Bungalow No. 20 was situated on the second floor of what looked like a little suburban house. It was composed of a living room, a small kitchen, a bedroom, and a bathroom. On the same floor was Bungalow No. 21. That was where Arthur and Marilyn lived.

On the ground floor of this house was Bungalow No. 19. Now comes the moment in my unsalable script when the producer throws it out the window. For Bungalow No. 19, which was much bigger than the two apartments above it, had its curtains permanently drawn—and was inhabited by Howard Hughes and his family.

Nobody was supposed to know, and yet it was notorious. His guards would wander around trying to look like people just taking a walk down the little paths that crisscrossed the gardens. They would circle the block of bungalows that ran from No. 16 to No. 21.

I could hear babies crying, and the sound came from No. 19. One day I saw Jean Peters taking a sunbath on the small lawn in front of her window. I recognized her because I had seen *Niagara*. She said hello, and disappeared behind the curtains.

I saw Howard Hughes only once in my life. Arthur Miller pointed him out to me. But I'm anticipating; that happened after weeks together in the little suburban house. However, let's get it over with now. Arthur and I had agreed that he would wake me if he could prove that what he had told me was true. So at midnight one night, he knocked on my door. I was to go out on my kitchen balcony and look. From the wooden balcony at the back of the bungalow one could see a lane where there was an old Dodge or Ford that had obviously been abandoned there by its owner. It was grayish or beige.

That night there were snakelike tubes leading to the old abandoned car and bringing heat, ventilation, and the telephone from Bungalow No. 19. In the rear of the car was a man, his feet propped up on the back of the front seat. There was a small pulpit that served as an office desk. Howard Hughes was running his empire . . . or perhaps it amused him to offer us this show.

But let me go back to where we were. Spyros Skouras gave an enormous cocktail party in the dining rooms of the Fox studios. In 1959 he was the big boss. A few months earlier, when Nikita Khrushchev was in America, he had appeared on the set where they were making *Can-Can*. Skouras gave a speech, which finished with these remarks, if I can recall correctly what I've been told: "Look at me, Mr. Khrushchev. I was a poor Greek shepherd, and now I'm the boss of thirty-five thousand employees. That's America! Top that one." "I can top that," Khrushchev replied. "I was a poor Ukrainian shepherd, and today I'm the boss of two hundred million citizens. That's the USSR!"

Well, Spyros Skouras gave this huge cocktail party to celebrate signing the contract with Montand. He hadn't been stingy on the champagne, or the Scotch, or the vodka, or the canapés, or the zakouskis. There were at least fifty photographers present, and they weren't stinting on film. It was the afternoon that most of those well-known photographs were taken showing four smiling faces: Marilyn, Montand, Miller, and myself. Those pictures were to be the delight of the cheap newspaper folk a few months later.

On the stroke of midnight on December 31, 1959, the lights went out in the well-known restaurant we were in. I kissed my husband, the lights came on again, and there was a hand on my shoulder and another on Montand's: It was Gary Cooper. He said, "Happy New Year," and then he added, "I limp a little, but may I dance with your wife?" Montand said, "Of course," and so I spent the first minutes of the year 1960 chastely in the arms of the handsomest man in the world. It was true that he limped a little, but I don't dance very well, and the music was a slow fox trot from the forties.

At exactly the same hour three years earlier, we had been in the Hall of Saint George in the Kremlin, where the ex-Ukrainian shepherd had popped up to surprise us in the dark. Now it was Gary Cooper, and the restaurant was Romanoff's. (This is where my script becomes totally indigestible.)

To reply, "Of course," to Gary Cooper, to muddle through everyday life with words scooped up at random, to be clearly understood when clearly enunciating little texts announcing one's songs in which the basic message is communicated anyway—that's one thing.

Learning lines, dialogue—that is, asking questions and replying to questions as the character you're personifying, when all the questions and answers are riddles as you try to decipher them in the script you're reading, because you've been hired to act in a movie story you've only been told—that's quite a different thing.

It would have been crazy to say no to Cukor. It was also crazy to have said yes. Montand was crazy. But he was right. So the walls of Bungalow No. 20 were covered with placards and little colored bits of paper and signs. Those poems from Thailand and the Breton prayers came back into my life.

At the time of day when Hollywood stars relaxed after their day's work at the studio, sipping bullshots and bourbons, Montand began to work. After a full day of work. (I must be very careful when I use the word "work" in reference to Montand. It has always irritated him intensely to be commended for his "hard work," or the "clockwork perfection" of his song recitals. Such praise is generally misconceived. The "work" of rehearsal always comes after the inspiration. If that's good, one cultivates it so that it can bloom fully. Then one has to "catch it," in a way, so that it can be revived every evening in its most effective form. That can't be done untidily, or in madness. Primordial madness at the moment of creation must be respected; it also must be revived every evening. There's no "clockwork" that can regulate it so that you can find it every evening. It's a token of what happened to you one day at a precise, graced moment. It's a ceremony that takes place in time, and if it has been well timed, it will touch the last spectators as much as it did the first. Above all, freshness must be preserved. This is what's often called "work." But it's really love.)

But this time it was really a question of work; and work with tools—words. But they were words he had never heard in his childhood; they were sounds to be used with the apparent nonchalance of somebody who's always used them. It's saying "by heart" things that must give the impression that they're coming from the heart, when they're simply a faithful reproduction of sounds you've been taught. You become a prisoner of those sounds if you want to be understood. And with all this going on, you're supposed to appear natural, relaxed, authoritative, tender, capricious, and naïve, like Gary Cooper or James Stewart. These are surely the stars Norman Krasna had in mind when he wrote his script, which was basically a charming reissue of the fairy tale in which once again the prince marries the shepherdesss.

Thus, my husband was *working*. And I became a housewife. That is to say, I was there when he came home from the studio, and I put a match under the log the Beverly Hills Hotel staff had laid in the hearth of the fireplace connected to a gas jet, guaranteeing the kind of Old World blaze one reads of in Dickens's novels. I would order dinner by telephone from room service, and I would check the clean laundry the service brought to us to make sure it was really ours. You can see I was a real housewife.

My days were very pleasant. They were much more pleasant than the days of many actors' wives in Hollywood. Many actors' wives got up very early to take their kids to school. The old black or Irish nurse is a myth that disappeared a long time ago. Many actors' wives did their own marketing. The cook-housekeeper is something that exists on television screens when they replay old films from the thirties, but they are in evidence in very few real houses. Generally, they had people who came in and worked by the hour in those pseudo haciendas, pseudo eighteenth-century follies, and pseudo trappers' cabins. But the lady who came in to do the cooking would under no circumstances also agree to take care of the floors. And the lady who would agree to put the plates in the dishwasher would under no circumstances be willing to do the ironing. It's a variety of economy, but it does complicate the lives of those exemplary housewives, who would accommodate a procession of different people with different specialties, with jobs to be distributed according to their talents and their personal schedules. I've known Hollywood actors' wives who finally decided that it was easier to do all these things themselves rather than become foreman of a work crew. So contrary to all legend, these women worked very hard. If the caricatures show them behind the wheel of a car with curlers on their heads, it's because they somehow found the time to put them there before going to market. When the time came to welcome you for lunch, their hair was done.

On the evenings when there were big parties they called in the extras. The extras were quite willing to play the parts of old family retainers. I knew one whom I met everywhere. And everywhere he went, he fitted the tone of that particular house. He was a little like Rémy, who worked for Aunt Irène and Uncle Marcel on the Square Lamartine. Three times I pretended not to remember that I had seen him in three different houses. But after a while we stopped playing the game. We would greet each other quite overtly and compare the merits and freshness of the different buffets we had known together. . . .

These women I've been describing often even found time to go back to school. They went to UCLA and took up studies they had abandoned when they got married. They were often New Yorkers whose husbands had been called to Hollywood after a Broadway triumph. At first they would be in California for just one film; they kept their New York apartments and rented a house for four months. Often they yearned for noise and lights and smells and the snow and the New York lights. They didn't hide it. After a while, the silence, the hummingbirds, the coyotes crossing the valley, the sun that greeted them every morning, the friendliness of the salesgirls, the splendid Pacific beaches, the poolside brunches, the pleasure of seeing their children climb the fence to play on the grass with the children next door, the pleasure of seeing their husbands come back from the studio in blue jeans and imported Italian sweaters, so much more relaxed than after a last glass at Sardi's—all would end up seducing them to this way of life.

When the first film was finished, they would go back to New York. But at the first call from Hollywood they gave up their East Coast apartments, and if it had gone at all well for their husbands, they decided that they would no longer rent a house, but buy one. And that was how they had come to own those haciendas and eighteenth-century follies and trappers' cabins. All those houses have their stories. They were built for some big star during the heyday of the movies. They were thus enormous, and often crazy. In the beginning it was fun to show your visiting friends the mirrors on the bedroom ceiling which X had put there, or the closet where Y hid his bottles.

But after a while, the constant sunshine, the luxurious routine, and the iridescent bubbles in which they lived (to say nothing of the discrimination that then still existed between new Californians and those who'd arrived in the thirties) began to weigh on them. So they went back to school.

Now I was in the period that corresponded to silence, hummingbirds, coyotes, sun, and relaxed saleswomen. I had absolutely no housekeeping worries. Room service functioned twenty-four hours a day. The iridescent bubble seemed absolutely delicious to me. Since I had all the time in the world, I wasted it with the feeling of having the right to waste it. I was totally lazy, and not the slightest bit bored. I lunched in the hotel's Polo Lounge, which at the time was like Fouquet's or the Lipp. Jimmy Woolf and Laurence Harvey and Jack Clayton had come to Hollywood to keep an eye on *Room at the Top*. So the garden of the restaurant was like London again. And then sometimes it was like New York, since show-business people often do the round trip from the East Coast to the West as we do Paris–Nice.

And it was also Hollywood. And even HOLLY-WOOD. . . . I felt fine in my bubble, because it was a temporary bubble. I often thought that I was very lucky that I hadn't come to this big village when I had been summoned ten years earlier.

Ten years earlier I hadn't done enough. I would have had to conform to what a contract would have legitimately asked me to do. Ten years earlier I would have taken the risk of believing life was this: the bubble. Though the period known as the cold war in Europe had been difficult, contradictory, exciting, disappointing, I regaled myself with memories that made my head spin during those California lunches in the sun. I was two thousand years old—and fourteen.

Walter Wanger was a producer. He was very fond of us both, Montand and me. He was special, as they say. He had once been jailed for having shot his wife's lover. The lover hadn't died, but Wanger had had a taste of prison. Since then, alongside his activities as a producer, he was extremely active in the cause of imprisoned people.

The most famous prisoner of the time was Caryl Chessman. Without real proof, he had been condemned to death for rape and murder, and he had written a book in jail. The date for his execution had been delayed several times.

One morning Walter Wanger asked me if I would like to have lunch with an archbishop. So at around one o'clock, after a hello to Howard Hughes's various bodyguards—they were still pretending to be innocuous strollers on the path the inhabitants of Bungalows Nos. 19, 20, and 21 took to reach the Polo Lounge—I found myself seated at a table with Walter Wanger and the archbishop. He was a very affable archbishop. Wanger had invited him in order to ask him to sign a petition demanding a pardon for the condemned man. I'd been called in as an extra. First of all, because I didn't know anything about Chessman's case, and second, because Wanger had asked me there only so he would not be alone with the archbishop.

Wanger's arguments were identical to all those we had trotted out so often and completely sincerely in the Old World in an attempt to "sell" them to people who weren't "buying." This was applicable from Henri Martin to the Rosenbergs.

The archbishop was undoubtedly a good archbishop. He listened carefully, with an air of someone learning for the first time about the life and fate of this interesting prisoner. He punctuated Wanger's sentences with nods of his head. Most depressing; humanity was at a low ebb.... He drank his coffee. And, politely, refused to sign the petition. And he left to comfort those members of his flock who were not in prison.

Wanger was livid with anger. He believed in "Chessman's case." I knew nothing about it at all. One never really knows anything about the true guilt or innocence of the people whose part one takes. Most of the time, one takes a stand against people who think they have a right to take a stand against the accused. And they have none.

Walter Wanger was sad. Sad as one is when one has lost an operation for the Committee for the Defense of ... or the Committee in Favor of ... and one is face to face with failure.

The archbishop was definitely out. His signature's absence on the petition would be a cruel loss. Walter stirred his sugar substitute (memories of the Café Flore saccharine, circa 1942) into his decaffeinated coffee and called on me to witness the indifference of churchmen concerning the life and death of their brothers.

At which point I activated all the charm and femininity my elegant clothes and fine shoes of that time would underline, and I asked, "Walter [pause] ... what did you do for the Rosenbergs?" "Nothing," was the reply.

Walter Wanger was very handsome. He was not all that young. He was warm and cultivated. His "Nothing," with the quiet blue smile that accompanied it, said more than any excuse he might have offered but had no desire to.

This little story only illustrates why I didn't have time to be bored....

And then there were the great houses I mentioned a little while ago. In these, even if the son was forty years old and lived in New York, one still met the old black nurse who had given him his first bottle. And there was no risk of bumping into the neighbor's butler.

This was Hollywood's elite. There really were real Renoirs and Van Goghs and Picassos on the walls. They had 35-millimeter projection rooms where a union operator would come to run the machinery after dinner. These parties were always on Friday or Saturday nights, the only nights of the week when the town didn't go to bed at ten-thirty.

Women always seemed to reign over these houses. They were the wives of producers, and often also the daughters of legendary producers. They had known everyone and everything in Hollywood. They would tell about the great changeover from the silent movies to the "talkies." They went to Paris for every collection. They never went to movies, movies came to them, and they would show a first-run film that was generally the latest product of a rival of their husband's film company. They would show these films to a few faithful old friends and the latest fashionable arrivals. They had the manners of a ruling sovereign, and sometimes the caprices of an empress. One heard about their infatuations—platonic, of course—that had ended with banishment.

Some of these houses would close their doors to you forever because the house of an enemy had been the first to welcome you as a new arrival. The reasons for these classic enmities generally dated back to the time of Rudolph Valentino and Rin-Tin-Tin. These reasons were obscure for the new arrivals, but they were well known to all the pioneers, and consequently never explained. It just was that way. Right from way, way back, Mrs. X didn't speak to Mrs. Y, and it was judicious to know that one didn't mention the name of Mrs. Y in Mrs. X's house, and vice versa. It was an acquired knack.

There was the house of George Cukor. No projection room there, but everywhere a collection of photographic treasures that made the succession of little Victorian drawing rooms like a still cinémathèque. And there was

Cukor himself. Cukor knows everything about the film world of the day before yesterday, yesterday, and tomorrow. He's a hundred years old—and eighteen. He's also the only man I know who phones you at seven twenty-six and is furious to find you at home when the dinner to which he has invited you is at seven-thirty. "You're late," he says. You live five minutes away, but he wants you to consider the hazards of the journey. He's also the only man I know who says at ten-thirty, whoever the company may be, "Time to go to bed." He's also the only man I know who, for the four hours he has set aside to distract himself from his work life, will show himself so funny, generous, and attentive; cruel to the mean, and mean to fools; derisive with the pretentious, ironical with the gossip-mongers, rude with the snobs, and infinitely delicate with the nobodys. And a great lover of talent.

There were also the little houses in the valley, far from the fashionable section. In these lived the directors, scriptwriters, and independent producers who had not regained the right to sign their names. . . .

As you can see, I got around a lot for a housewife! When I wasn't circulating, I read. I was reading a lot of scripts. They arrived with somewhat battered imitation-leather covers. They were almost always stupid stories with an admirable role for a no-longer-young actress. Given the condition of the covers, they were not altogether recent. I could imagine them passing from Bette Davis to Joan Crawford, ending up in the house of Ingrid Bergman. Some of them may have made a small detour via Magnani; Ingrid Thulin probably read them too, and Ava Gardner surely thumbed the pages between two *corridas*. They fluttered into Bungalow No. 20, and I swear I saw some of them again in a pile that accumulated around my pal Anouk Aimée beside the pool at La Colombe when she came back from Hollywood after the success of *A Man and a Woman* in 1967. They never were made into films.

Certain scripts had some merit. There was one, I remember, which never got made into a film, either. This one wasn't specifically a vehicle for a "star," but a fine story full of characters. Often these scripts didn't have a title page. It had been visibly torn out. When I say visibly, I mean ostentatiously. No title, no author's name, no director's name. One was supposed to smell treasure, but one smelled sulfur too. These scripts were usually as uninteresting as the others. Some smart guy somewhere had decided to label them with a "I can't openly say I wrote this but it's me" guarantee. These were rarely written by my pals in the modest little houses in the valley. Or if they were, my pals didn't really have the talent that their condition as victims of McCarthyism should have conferred upon them by divine right.

There was the Château Marmont. At the time, it was the hotel where New Yorkers stayed who had come for a two- or three-day role in a Hollywood film. That year Paul Newman and Joanne Woodward, their two little daughters, and their black nurse, who had already brought up Joanne, lived on the top floor. They hadn't come for a two- or three-day part, but they hadn't yet decided to become Californians. They were funny, warm, and passionate. They still are.

As for me, I circulated between the rich houses and the poor houses, my English lunches and my brunches, my archbishops and my French pals. I discovered the Farmers Market, the chic boutiques of Beverly Hills. From one week to the next, a small record store would be transformed into a shoe shop, and it would be fun finding the ex-record seller in a shop specializing in Indian weaving two streets down.

I would hear Miller's typewriter chattering away in Bungalow 21. Marilyn went to the studio at five-thirty in the morning; Montand would leave at seven-thirty. At about eleven-thirty the neighboring door would open, and there would be a knock on my door. It was a ritual. "I've made some coffee," Arthur would say. He would make me tell him my projects for the day. I would talk, we would drink our coffee, and I would leave on my voyage of discovery, promising him that I would report at the end of the afternoon. Arthur would go back to his machine. He never set foot in the big village.

Outside, Alice Aisgill worked for me. She worked very well. She worked so well that one bright day in February or March I found myself nominated for an Oscar.

Now let me go back to *Small World*, Ed Murrow's television program, which I had recorded two months earlier, at a time when I thought I would be home in France when it would be broadcast. The crew even promised to send me a print of the show when it was ready.

In due course *Small World* appeared on television. It was just before the nomination. Ed Murrow, whom I never met but with whom I talked a great deal during the show, was one of those truly good Americans, such as there are, as there have been, and as there always will be. He had been an American radio correspondent in London throughout the war. When he returned he talked to the citizens of his country, and he had told them about another world, in which he had lived. He was one of the Americans to whom one doesn't say in the middle of a conversation, "By the way, from which ghetto or which Sicilian village did your grandparents come?" He was a direct descendant of what is written on the cracked flank of the great bell in Philadelphia: "Proclaim Liberty throughout all the Land unto all the Inhabitants thereof." He was an American from way back. He also had the privilege of being white.

One day, after television had replaced radio, he decided to kill off McCarthy. It was all very simple, like most good ideas. All Ed Murrow did was to request the interesting senator who had been playing Torquemada for quite a while to consent to a long interview. McCarthy was delighted to express himself, and he expressed himself. All America saw on the screens in its living rooms a madman who no longer knew what he was saying. Three weeks later, McCarthy physically passed away. He wasn't dead; he had just passed away.

I had been told about all this in France. In La Baule, while on tour the previous summer, I already knew that I wouldn't be facing a TV "clown" if I said yes to Ed Murrow.

Small World was organized on this formula: Four people in four different places would converse on a subject set by Ed Murrow. Each of these four people would be filmed in his or her city during the entire conversation. Thus four cameras would be rolling at the same time—at different hours, due to the time lag.

I knew who my partners on the program would be: Hedda Hopper in Los Angeles (or rather Hollywood), Agnes De Mille in New York, and Ed Murrow in London; I spoke from San Francisco.

Hedda Hopper was a dud actress who'd swapped the stage for journalism. In her daily column, she doled out good or bad marks depending on whether she liked you or not. She had terrorized Hollywood for ages. She had broken marriages and contracts. She wrote her pieces based on gossip gathered by spies; she never went out to do her interviews, but she would order people to appear at her place, and then nonchalantly drop the information that the sinner, or the trollop, or the genius had taken the trouble to come to see her. She had denounced a great many people during the McCarthy period.

Agnes De Mille is the niece of Cecil B. De Mille, and a choreographer. She had been blacklisted and hadn't been able to work for eight years. And I was a late discovery of the seventh art; a stranger to Hollywood and a stranger in the land.

Murrow's first question was: "Do you consider *that* particular press important to a career?" De Mille and Hopper, who had an old feud with each other, took up their cudgels immediately, and I kept my nose out of their business, which was strictly American. I simply said that I was still unfamiliar with the kind of press they were talking about, and couldn't compare it with anything I knew in my own country.

Murrow's second question—and he knew very well what he was doing—was this: "Do you think it's right for artists to get involved with politics?" Without a second's hesitation, Hopper replied, "Yes, absolutely—if they're the right politics." Again the discussion between her and De Mille grew venomous. It was at this point that Murrow asked me for my opinion as a European. I said that I couldn't judge the differences that opposed Miss Hopper and Miss De Mille; it was none of my business. On the other hand, I could talk about my own country, and so far as I was concerned, it was impossible to have been twenty years old at the time of the Nazi occupation without being—whether one wanted to or not—involved in what some people called politics. I talked about the war, Communists and non-Communists, the executions, the raids, the fear, and the famine. A host of images crowded in on me. They were anachronisms in this splendid room overlooking the bay of San Francisco, a few yards down the street from which I had seen, the night before, *Triumph of the Will* and swastikas in the showcases. I was passionately sincere and was very good, as one is who really believes in what one is saying. Murrow, De Mille, and Hopper listened.

The program was recorded in December and broadcast in February or March. The whole town saw it. When the program was edited, Murrow kept on the screen the three listening heads while the fourth talked. So this story of the occupation years was received in very large close-ups. And Murrow had kept in—unfortunately for her—Miss Hopper's mute or spoken reactions. She was wearing one of her famous hats—she was said to have two hundred of them—and under the hat her face was not tender. She certainly had the courage of her convictions. The film editor had not betrayed her. While quarreling with Agnes De Mille she had said, "It's no secret that I was all for McCarthy." But her conclusion, which was also the end of the program, was probably spoken when she thought the camera was no longer rolling. She said something like: "I should have known better; I fell into a liberal's nest." The adjective "liberal" has a different meaning depending on whether you're involved in "good" or "bad" politics—and liberal was bad according to Miss Hopper's conceptions. That little sentence at the end was abundantly commented upon throughout Hollywood. All those people she had caused to tremble for years and who hadn't always had the opportunity or the courage to tell her to go to hell felt they had been avenged.

I was very much the beneficiary of that program. Hedda Hopper never forgave me for *Small World*. She had two weapons: words that wound or the silence that kills. As she was no longer young and she thought she was still living in the good old days, she chose the weapon that had worked so well for all those years—the second.

That was a mistake.

The day after the nominations, all the newspapers—the solemn ones, the serious ones, the frivolous ones—announced the score. There were five actresses nominated: Katharine Hepburn, Doris Day, Elizabeth Taylor, Audrey Hepburn, and Simone Signoret.

Miss Hopper wrote her column on the nominations somewhat as *Match* would have done it. She discussed my four rivals and forgot me.

That, it soon appeared, lowered her and elevated me. I owe her a great deal. She was to avenge herself on Montand a few months later. Then I was no longer there; I had returned to Europe.

I owe her a great deal, for whatever the merits of Alice Aisgill in *Room at the Top*, they were surely not overwhelming by comparison with my four rivals. We were unlike in age and in the kind of parts we played, but we had all valiantly defended the characters we had been lucky enough to be offered. Katharine Hepburn and Liz Taylor in *Suddenly, Last Summer*, Doris Day in *Pillow Talk*, and Audrey Hepburn in *The Nun's Story*.

Of these, *Room at the Top* was the only film not made in America. I was the only actress who didn't owe her career to Hollywood. I must say that I think both factors played in my favor, and that Miss Hopper's silences also worked in my favor. As did *Small World*.

I was happy, I was amazed. I never thought this would end up with an Oscar. Everything was super as it was; a nomination! In the weeks following the nomination all those nice people who had until then kept telling me, "You'll see, you're going to be nominated," started saying, "I told you you'd be nominated."

For the two weeks that preceded the presentations, the phrase changed. It became: "You're going to get it, you're going to get it...." People said it out of cars when they stopped for red lights, they said it at the switchboard of the Beverly Hills Hotel when I ordered breakfast, and I heard it from my friend the waiter at the Polo Lounge. So I discovered that this big village was heading toward its annual big party—with its bets, its favorite candidates, and its declared enemies.

I was the Beverly Hills Hotel candidate. The hotel people had no votes, neither on the first nor on the second round. But when we returned to Bungalow No. 20 in the wee hours of the morning of that April evening, and put the Oscar on the mantel beside the big photograph of our house in Autheuil, we gathered off the floor innumerable little notes that had been slipped under the door after the television broadcast of the ceremony. Written in English, Italian, and Spanish, they ran: "Congratulations, and thanks—you've made me win ten [twenty, fifty] dollars."

I couldn't personally thank all those who had voted for me. It's a secret ballot. I never knew to whom, among the two thousand five hundred people in my profession, I owed my nomination on the first ballot. Nor do I know to whom, among the twenty-five thousand people in my profession, I owe my victory on the second ballot.

In any case, I'll never forget the screams of joy that resounded in the big movie house when Rock Hudson, who was opening the envelope that contained the one name from that list of five names, literally yelled:

"Simauauaune Signoray." Nor am I likely to forget haring up that little staircase to the stage, where I was presented with that legendary statuette which, rightly or wrongly, for reasons good or bad, sanctifies you for a year, in the film capital of the world, as the "best actress in the world."

But I would be an abominable hypocrite if I said that all this was simply another turn of Fortune's wheel. It was fabulous! It was my victory. It was the victory of those who had voted for me. It was their response to the silences of Miss Hopper, and to two articles written the day after my nomination. One of them said that the voters had dishonored themselves by proposing my name, which was as shocking as would have been that of Mrs. Goebbels in 1938! In the other, I was summoned to supply the number of my card as a member of the Communist party, and I was asked to explain why I had performed in a film by Bertolt Brecht for DEFA.

So among the Oscars of 1960, there was one Oscar that a large North American village, HOLLYWOOD, awarded to itself; its members wished to proclaim that they had become free again, free to do what they wanted. That was the meaning of those screams of joy in the audience, that was the meaning of the telegrams that piled up the next morning in Bungalow No. 20, and the bouquets of flowers, the first of which came from Katharine Hepburn.

The ceremony itself followed a well-established and practiced ritual. That year Vincente Minnelli was the organizer of the exercises that provide both the town's main holiday and the prizes given to the best students of the year in the profession's various branches. It's also the most opulent variety show to take place on a stage.

Sunset; dusk in Los Angeles. The town's festive holiday was heralded by the crisscrossing beams of two enormous searchlights sweeping the sky, reminding the citizens that an all-important event would take place that very evening, and that they could throng before the place where it would be celebrated. They would have the chance to gaze briefly at their idols of the moment, and even at those of their youth, maybe of their early childhood, alighting from their shiny limousines before disappearing into the huge lobby of the theater. They came. They shouted. They whistled. It was a festive holiday.

It's a prize ceremony for the best students in the class because there is an Oscar for the best among the five best prop men, musicians, cameramen, costume designers, lyricists for musicals, sound engineers, editors, supporting players, authors of foreign films, directors of "shorts," cartoonists ... I may be forgetting some of the categories, but the organizers of this prize-distribution ceremony haven't forgotten a single one of the various branches, from the most obscure to the most visible. The three most visible are the last three to be crowned: "best actor," "best actress," "best film."

It's the most opulent variety show ever seen on a stage and televised throughout the country because before the opening of each envelope—which will make four people unhappy and one very happy (each envelope is opened by a different star, presented, that year, by Bob Hope, who was the master of ceremonies)—a famous performer sings, dances, or tells stories.

Montand and I, seated in the back of the big limousine that had come to fetch us at the Beverly Hills Hotel at eight in the evening, looked at the crossed searchlight beams in the sky and checked to make sure that we hadn't forgotten any of the cards. There was a bunch of them, each engraved with a small gold emblem of the magic statuette.

One card showed the number of our seats. Another said what one should do in the case of triumph—that is, how to get up on the stage. Each of the nominees would be placed in a seat directly on the central aisle, so that in the case of triumph there would be no time lost after the envelope had been opened. Another card invited everyone, winners and losers alike, to an enormous supper at the Beverly Wilshire Hotel.

Besides all these cards, Montand had one marked

"Performer," which explained the exact route he must follow and exactly what time he must leave the seat next to mine and head backstage in order to arrive onstage and sing two songs, as Vincente Minnelli had asked him to do.

So the two of us, in the back of that limousine, had four cases of stage fright. As well as a fit of giggles. La Cabucelle and Neuilly-sur-Seine were winking at us. Our rented limousine left us in front of the cinema at the same time as a certain young man's. He was much more famous than we are—I can't remember who he was—but he helped us make our way discreetly through the crowd.

At about ten-thirty, my stage fright for Montand and his stage fright for himself were forgotten. After the Oscar for the best film music, Bob Hope fetched Fred Astaire from the wings and asked him to introduce Eaves Monntaind. Eaves sang "Un Garçon Dansait," which is the story of a poor failure who thinks he can dance like Fred Astaire. He sang and danced this lovely fable in front of Fred Astaire. Then he sang "À Paris." That left us with two cases of stage fright to go.

Minnelli offered to have him escorted back to the audience and to me, but he said, "I'd rather wait for her here." Minnelli replied, "Let's hope she comes," but he only told me that later.

Now there was just my stage fright for me and his for me. From the start of the evening, *Ben-Hur* had won all the Oscars. At the beginning of the ceremony, for the special-effects prize, a team of three prop men had insisted on not being separated, so all three of them had seized the statuette at the same time, which was a very pretty sight. For the cartoon prize, a huge ovation had greeted the names of Faith and John Hubley. Later I found out that this ovation, whose real reasons I hadn't grasped at the time, was actually a salute to this couple, who were the most gifted and inventive people in the history of American film animation, upon their ascent out of the McCarthyist purgatory. With the exception of these two, and *Le Poisson Rouge* by Lamorisse for short subjects, all the prizes went to the superb superproduction *Ben-Hur:* costumes, music, scenery—all those envelopes opened by famous hands were for *Ben-Hur, Ben-Hur, Ben-Hur.*

Ben-Hur was at its ninth Oscar when the envelope sanctifying the best actor of the year was opened. It was Ben-Hur himself—Charlton Heston.

My husband had remained backstage. There was an empty seat beside me. Behind me there was a nominee who had just lost. In front of me there was a nominee who might still win. We had come to the moment for the best actress. I hunched down in my pretty black dress. There was absolutely no reason for the same voters who had chosen the huge superproduction again and again to choose old Alice in a small film with a small budget made at Shepperton Studios (U.K.). And yet, as soon as the voice said, "Simauau..." there was an enormous thud on my shoulders from the nominee seated behind me—but I was already up and running.... (For the rest, see above.)

End of unsalable scenario.

Chapter 11

ONE evening in August 1962, Montand phoned me in Toulouse, from Paris. I was having dinner with Costa-Gavras and Claude Pinoteau. They were then René Clément's assistants for *Le Jour et l'Heure*. I came back to the table and told them, "Marilyn is dead."

I was very sad. But I wasn't surprised.

A half hour later, the hotel manager told me that he had just refused to rent rooms to journalists from Paris who had asked him where I could be found.

Still, today, I am grateful to this gentleman. He helped me to avoid shining the limelight (posthumously now) on an incident that the press had unmercifully hammered away at two years earlier.

That same press had latched on to the four of us—Marilyn, Montand, Miller, and myself—in order to make us play parts we had never learned in a play we hadn't read. It's a pity that it was all in retrospect and that they never saw us live as we did for four months. They knew nothing about the quiet lives of the four people in Bungalows Nos. 20 and 21. If they had, they would have seen nothing resembling the blond heartbreaker, or the moody dark man, or the bookworm, or the admirable wife standing on her dignity, which were the labels they pasted on us afterward.

And it's a pity, too, that Arthur Miller, of whom I was very fond, wrote *After the Fall*. After her death.

I am not Norman Mailer: I'm going to talk about somebody I knew. Not about a myth; not about a "poster." I'm going to talk about my neighbor across the hall, who was fond of her neighbor across the hall; about two women who lived together as neighbors, as one does in any apartment house anywhere.

Montand would come back from the studio first; he would have a shower and then furiously attack the text he had to learn for the next day. He would close himself in his room and work there for at least an hour before dinner, often in the company of his coach, come to watch over his accent and tonic emphases.

When Marilyn arrived, she would generally find Arthur and me either at their place or at ours; it was the time of day when I would tell him about what I had done. We would drink our Scotches and I would make my daily report, or else Arthur would tell tales about the recent and not so recent past of his country, which he knew so well and I knew so little.

She was still made up, and would say, "I'll just take a bath and I'll be with you."

She would reappear wearing a blue polka-dotted rayon dressing gown. Without makeup or false eyelashes, her feet bare, which made her quite short, she looked like the most beautiful peasant girl imaginable from the Île-de-France, as the type has been celebrated for centuries.

The famous lock of hair that flopped onto her forehead had disappeared; that puffed-up, sophisticated phenomenon was the result of a hairdresser's vigorous teasing between takes. But now her hair had been brushed back. And her widow's peak appeared.

It was a very pretty widow's peak, which divided her

330

forehead neatly in half. But she detested it, despised it; it was her personal enemy. She hated it because, curiously, the roots of that hair, fluffy as the hair of a small child, didn't take the platinum dye as well as the rest of the hair on her blond head. The lock that fell over her eye so casually and so accidentally was produced by all that teasing, and it was a shield protecting those darker roots, which might be seen when the camera came in for close-ups. She explained it all to me at the very beginning of our neighborly relations. She had also said, "Look, they all think I've got beautiful long legs; I have knobby knees and my legs are too short." That was hardly true in her dressing gown bought at a local Woolworth's, and it was completely untrue as soon as she was in her "Marilyn" getup. I saw her in her "Marilyn" getup only three times in four months. Once was at Spyros Skouras's monster cocktail party, once was the only time the four of us went out for dinner, and the last time was when she went out to receive the Golden Globe—the only artistic recognition this town ever gave her.

In order to have platinum hair, and to kill her enemy the widow's peak, she sent for, and paid for, a very old lady who came all the way from San Diego. This old lady had once worked for Metro-Goldwyn-Mayer, and she now lived in retirement. San Diego is all the way down near the Mexican border, which is where this artist in peroxide had chosen to retire. She had been responsible for the platinum head of Jean Harlow throughout her short career—or so she said.

Which is why every Friday evening, as she left us, Marilyn would say, "See you in the kitchen tomorrow at eleven."

For every Saturday morning the hair colorist of the late Jean Harlow would board her plane in San Diego and arrive in Los Angeles, where Marilyn's car would be waiting for her at the airport and would bring her to our kitchen, or rather the kitchenette of Bungalow No. 21.

Before allowing her to remove the bottles from her old

331

carrying bag (products long since made obsolete by more modern techniques), Marilyn would ply her with food from a buffet—a combination of brunch and cocktail-party ingredients—she had carefully prepared. The old lady would indulge with gusto. Marilyn would knock on my door, telling me to bring my towels, and then the hair-dyeing party would begin.

Now the old lady began to relive her life. While the two of us blonded, she would tell about the color she had concocted for Jean Harlow's head thirty years earlier, which had been the secret of her success. Her tales were full of silk dresses, white foxes, lamé shoes, and parties. They were also full of silences—for she preferred not to tell everything she might have told. Her stories always ended with the funeral of the "platinum-blond bombshell." While she talked, the two of us wallowed in nostalgia, winking at each other when the old lady would stop in her tale because she was too full of emotion to go on. Then her stick with the cotton swab at the end, coated with the precious liquid that was supposed to be applied to the equally precious roots of our hair, would fly through the air instead of coming down, lending an incalculable factor to the incubation time of this delicate operation. As Marilyn worried only about her widow's peak, there, things became serious; when it was a question of the enemy, the stick must not fly through the air. But the rest of the time she would sink back and let herself be rocked in the cradle of the old lady's anecdotes.

As soon as the widow's peak had been treated in seriousness and silence, the old lady, punctuating her story with "dearies," "sweeties," and "sugars," would take up her tale where she had left off. Listening to her, you might come to the conclusion that Jean Harlow had her hair dyed twenty-four hours out of the day, since it would appear that this lady had never been absent for a minute from the daily, conjugal, and amorous life of her star, nor of course from her deathbed.

After another meal, she would take her plane back to

San Diego. When she left, the two of us would be impeccably blond—Marilyn platinum and I on the auburn side. Then Marilyn and I would clean up the kitchen, since the artist had always left a lot of cotton swabs lying around on the floor.

It amused me enormously to have my hair tinted by the lady who pretended to have created the myth who was splashed across the newspaper pages of my adolescence. But it didn't amuse my neighbor. It was no accident that she had tracked down the address of this retired lady. She believed in her. She liked her and respected her. She was perfectly willing to pay for her round trips from the Mexican border, her limousine rides, and her caviar. It was a kind of association through a third person between the Blonde Mark I and the Blonde she turned into. And in retrospect I think it was also a hand stretched out to someone who had been forgotten. This is so often the fate of those reputedly indispensable technicians who serve the camera of the moment, or who are responsible for the sound or the makeup or the hair style of the moment: those who—invisible to the audience but indispensable to the production company—contribute to making the star of the moment happy.

The twin kitchenettes were not only hairdressing salons. Once in a while they were actually used as kitchens. That was rare, I must admit, but it did happen once or twice. Then Marilyn and I would play at cooking. In particular, I remember a spaghetti party, artistically cooked up by Marilyn and myself thanks to sciences we had learned from in-laws: she from the DiMaggios and I from the Livis. That evening earned us compliments from Miller and Montand, who were both very proud of their wives. After dinner we did the dishes, and then we separated out what belonged to each kitchen, since we had pooled our utensils for this great event. We had been like kids with a toy dinner set.

She had another dressing gown, something in long crimson velvet. Miller had given it to her for New Year's day in 1960. Whenever she wore it instead of the little blue synthetic-silk peignoir, she would talk about it the way others talked about the wild minks they had found in their Christmas stockings. Whenever she wore it she would also wear a little amber necklace, either around her neck or in her hair like a tiara. It was the only jewel I ever saw her wear, outside of a pair of enormous paste earrings.

This is what Marilyn wore in Bungalow No. 21, and she hardly ever left Bungalow 21 except to go to work very early in the morning, coming back as soon as her work was over. On Saturdays and Sundays she never budged.

She would leave to go to a job she apparently didn't like very much. She didn't like it very much because there had been a whole succession of people in her life who had taken pains to explain to her that she was anything but an actress. They had made her believe that without them she was incapable of saying "It's going to rain" and have it ring true in any way. She had ended up believing them. They cost her a fortune, which she paid willingly.

She also paid for having been a starlet in a town that had forked out an enormous chunk of capital to turn her into a star. They had thought that the starlet Marilyn was cute. They detested her for becoming Monroe. They were unkind to her, which is why she preferred to stay at home.

But there was something else too. For that I must go back to my fireside chats in front of the artificial fire (guaranteed to function due to the gas jet in the hearth of Bungalow No. 20 or 21) with my neighbor, our author, her husband, my friend Arthur Miller.

He told the story superbly: How, in 1955, she'd extricated him from the anti-McCarthyite catacombs where he'd been driven. How, incognito, she'd accompanied him to Washington, where he had been summoned by the Un-American Activities Committee. How she'd taken refuge at his lawyer's place; how the press had got wind of the Blonde in town and had besieged the lawyer's office building. How she'd taken her time (she needed three full hours; I know; I lived through these sessions) to transform herself into "Marilyn," and appear as such before the three hundred hungry sharks, living up to her legend. Simpering and sighing.

And maintained the simpering and sighing attitude on the sidewalk in this Washington street. She asked them by what right had they taken the law into their own hands to force her to account for the love of the man she loved? If she loved him, it was because he was a respectable, good, and honest man, and therefore why was he at that very moment summoned to play the part of an accused man and face a tribunal of fascist clowns?

At that moment the scales could be tipped. She'd thrown into them everything she had. One of two things could happen: her total destruction, or the rehabilitation in the eyes of the public of a man who, among others, was deprived of his passport; a man whose works were neither played nor published. This, indeed, was the beginning of McCarthy's first death spasms.

I've told this story as told to me by Miller. Following the Washington caper, Spyros Skouras took in hand the career of "the blond bombshell" who had made her way out of her role of a prefabricated object by dint of expensive publicity. It was explained to her that if she continued to love Miller publicly, this same expensive publicity machinery would be set in motion to destroy all it had constructed.

Marilyn's answer to the ex–Greek shepherd was: "Go ahead and destroy me; we'll go to Denmark."

Denmark must have represented Elsinore and a place where a king walked the streets wearing a yellow star.° The ex-shepherd considered the reply of the blond bombshell. Then he probably checked her popularity ratings. Finally, he decided to continue betting on her. Which is how Arthur Miller got his passport back, and his

---

°King Christian walked through the streets of the Danish capital wearing a yellow star of David in protest on the first day of the German law imposing discrimination against Jews.

rights as a citizen. He retrieved them the honorable way. Nobody asked him to denounce anyone anymore—which he wouldn't have done anyway!

That was well worth an act, or a scene, or a few lines in the play called *After the Fall*.

After the Fall was directed by Elia Kazan in New York in 1964. Marilyn had been dead for two years.

One evening, in front of the same fire, I asked Miller to translate for me the word "Gadge," which I had found in a telegram inviting us to a party at Romanoff's. The telegram ran: "Hope you can join us at a party celebrating return to town of Gadge. Cordially, The Strasbergs." As everyone in that town knows (everyone except us peasants), Gadge is Kazan. Miller said to me, "You and Yves have absolutely no reason to go to a party given in honor of—" I stopped him right there; I didn't need his warning. I knew all about it. I have never met Elia Kazan in my life.

But I do think it's sad that the Kazan-Miller reassociation was celebrated across a box called a coffin. A coffin for the blonde. It seems to me that they disfigured her, at least in part; in any case, they betrayed what was best in her.

She irritated me too, Marilyn. It was a bit tedious to listen to her tell about how happy and inspired she had been during the months when she made that series of photographs with Richard Avedon. The series was, indeed, remarkable; they were pictures of her made up to impersonate all the big stars of the thirties. But listening to her, you'd believe the only satisfaction as an actress she had ever felt was during those disguises, when she suddenly turned into Marlene, Garbo, and Harlow. She talked about these photography sessions the way other actors talk about their films.

She seemed to have no other happy professional memories. None of those moments of uproarious giggles among pals, none of those practical jokes, none of the noisy hugs and kisses after a scene when everyone knows all have acted well together. All these things were unknown to her. I couldn't get over it.

She made me tell her my stories, which were neither more nor less original, comic, or emotional than any actress's stories in any country in the world. Basically, they're stories of marvelous complicity, the kind children have in their early school years.

Possibly she encountered that complicity for the first time in her life when she filmed with Montand, and that would explain a great many of the things that happened after.

She also made me tell her just stories. So I told her *La Sauvage, L'Hermine*—all those girls from the Anouilh repertoire, parts I thought were made for her, as I came to know her better and better, living beside her. She seemed to me to have all their fears and regrets.

One evening I told her the story of *They Shoot Horses, Don't They?*, a book I knew backward because I had done it on the radio in 1946 when I was pregnant with Catherine, and I advised her to buy the rights as fast as possible.

That same evening, while Montand was in his room going over his lines for the next day, she cooked up one of her tricks for us—it was the only time.

Miller was in Ireland with John Huston for a discussion of *The Misfits*. He had asked us to take care of Marilyn. We talked late that evening. Late for Hollywood. Too late for her, since she had to get up at five. At around eleven Yves stuck his head into the living room and announced that he was going to bed. I had finished my tale, so I advised her to go to bed too. But she wanted one more story. I really had the impression of a kid who's delaying the moment for lights out. Finally she followed my advice, kissed me, and went back to her own apartment.

At about ten the next morning Montand phoned me from the studio. She wasn't there. The car had been waiting for her since five-thirty, as it did every morning, in the little lane by the back door, next to Howard Hughes's office-car. Finally, the chauffeur had gone upstairs and knocked at the kitchen door. Then he went around and knocked at the front door. Then he went out into the garden, where he could look up into the windows. Eventually he had gone back to the studio empty-handed.

At around eight the Fox studio had started telephoning the Beverly Hills Hotel. The switchboard hadn't been able to get an answer out of Bungalow 21. The studio had tried at least twenty times; no reply. Now it was ten o'clock and they were scared; everyone at the studio was scared.

I went over and knocked on the door across the hall. First I knocked, then I banged, like policemen or firemen. Then I began shouting, at the front door and then at the back door. Since there was no sound whatsoever in reply, now I was scared.

My pal the switchboard girl reassured me. She told me that indeed Bungalow 21 did not reply, but Bungalow 21 had made a phone call that morning.

I called Montand at Fox.

Forty-five minutes later he was back at the house. A day's work would be lost if Marilyn continued to lie low. They would phone him from the studio if there was any news, but in any case, since he was on the spot, he would be the first to know.

So, with a little help from me with the English, Montand wrote a note that ran more or less as follows: "You can do whatever you like to Spyros Skouras and the Fox studio and all the producers in town, if that's what you want. But next time you decide to hang around too late listening to my wife tell you stories instead of going to bed, because you've already decided not to get up the next morning and go to the studio, please tell me! Don't leave me to work for hours on end on a scene you've already decided not to do the next day. I'm not the enemy, I'm your pal. And capricious little girls have never amused me. Best, Yves."

We opened our door silently, stole across the hall in bare feet, and slid this letter under the door opposite, making quite sure to leave half of it outside where we could see it.

Then we went back, but we didn't close our door. We watched in silence. It was just like a Western or a mystery. In a short time the message slid under the door and disappeared, in slow motion, millimeter by millimeter, as though the person behind the door were taking precautions like the carriers of nitroglycerin in *The Wages of Fear*.

Then we closed our door as silently as we had opened it and waited for the reply.

There was none. Then Montand decided he had had enough. The time for silent suspense was over. Very loudly, so that it would certainly be heard on the other side of the corridor, he said in French—or rather in Franglais— that since the day's work was loused up anyhow, the best we could do was go out for a very good lunch. There'd be no filming that day because of absentees. He shouted the operative words in English at the top of his voice.

We lunched out. Then I think we went to the movies. We went out for dinner, too. We were sure that when we came home, there'd be a message under our door.

There was none.

At around eleven that evening, the phone rang. We were already in bed. "It's Mr. Miller, from Dublin," the switchboard girl said.

"I'm sorry if you were asleep, but now that you're awake, please do me a favor and go knock on Marilyn's door. She's there, she's told me all about it, she doesn't know what to do. She's ashamed."

So I got up, went across the hall, and knocked. Suddenly I had in my arms a weeping girl, who kept saying, "I'm bad, I'm bad, I'm bad. I won't do it again, I promise!" All this happened in the middle of the hall. Montand, in his dressing gown, patted her head, saying, "Okay, okay; try to be on time tomorrow morning."

This story has never made me laugh. I told it a few times while Marilyn was alive. The catch phrase of the story always triggered peals of laughter: "She phoned Dublin so that Dublin would phone her next-door neighbors."

After her death, I would tell that story only to people I

knew wouldn't laugh. (After our reconciliation in the hall, we never mentioned that "lost" day again.) I never dared ask her at what time she had decided not to go down and take the car that was waiting for her, or when she had started to be angry with herself in that silence, that absence, that false death. I'll never know how long she remained sitting on the floor behind that closed door before deciding that she would read the message which was a line to the outside. It was a line she must have thought was broken during that whole day, since she was unable to knot the two ends together without help.

All this happened long before my nomination for the Oscar. But it was already in the air, and that delighted her. Despite all the movies she had appeared in (she must have relived all those parts, tucked away in her little corner), she had never been honored with even a nomination, yet she felt a part of the thing. She was always the first to bring me the little clippings she had read in the "bibles" (*Daily Variety* and the *Hollywood Reporter*) that automatically arrived with her breakfast tray.

As they always came with my breakfast tray too, I noticed that every time I was celebrated as a foreign "diva" (the publicity machine for *Room at the Top* was supplying the material), strangely the story always included some barb at her. They would quote her gaffes in public, or an inappropriate remark she had theoretically made in some fashionable restaurant. They were all invented. She couldn't have made a gaffe in public; she almost never went out. And as for fashionable restaurants, it had been a long time since she had set foot in one—with the exception of the one time the four of us went out together, rather pompously, as people from provinces go out for an evening to Maxim's, and for that occasion she had put on all her "Marilyn" war paint.

I mention that she was the first to bring me those clippings from the local "bibles," because an actors' strike was declared which concerned "residual" rights, claimed by actors when films made years earlier for cinema distribution were shown on television. It was like a corporation strike rather than the strike of a union in the sense that the French know it. In America, unions are like corporations.

So all of Hollywood was on strike. It was not like Paris in 1936 or Odessa in 1905, but as the strike of an entire profession it was exemplary. There were no big demonstrations or parades. There was simply a refusal to work. That included Gary Cooper and Gregory Peck, the newly arrived Paul Newman, Elizabeth Taylor, Debbie Reynolds, Marilyn, and all the others.

That's why, after a certain time, we were constantly together, and that's why she was the first to bring me the gossip in those "bibles." We were "confined to barracks" in our bungalows; the others were at home in their eighteenth-century follies and their Victorian houses.

They were all quite right. It was their thing, and we were foreigners, but still, my husband was on strike. So I was the wife of a striker. The enormous expense account, which was just enough to pay the enormous bills at Bungalow No. 20, allowed us to hold out.

It's funny to be on strike in Hollywood, but I'm wrong to joke about it, because that strike completely changed working conditions in the whole American film industry, whether for big stars, medium stars, or no stars at all. It's just that the fleeting image of me as the wife of the striker Yves Montand in Hollywood caused me a quick, quiet laugh. . . . The strike went on and on. Arthur had already been back from Dublin for quite some time when he decided that they would go off to New York and wait for the negotiations between the television companies and the union to be concluded. I had just been nominated, and they were pleased for me, they were pleased against Hedda Hopper, and they were pleased for the Proctors. Marilyn was pleased, but also probably a little hurt. "It's all quite fair," she said, but she probably thought that it wasn't totally so.

The morning they left, the four of us kissed in the hall

and then Montand and I went out on the living-room balcony to wave *ciao* and *à bientôt*. She turned around and called to me, "Good luck! I know! I know you're going to get it!" Then she ran to catch up with Arthur on the garden path. She had put on high heels and her ready-made white mink coat; it had a big unattractive collar that she always meant to have altered.

That's my last image of her. I never saw her alive again.

I've described here the woman I knew, and that's surely the same woman who went back to work after the strike was over.

By then I was no longer there. I was honoring an old contract that had been delayed several times. I was in Italy making *Adua et Ses Compagnes*. It wasn't a masterpiece, but I'd be a dirty hypocrite if I said that I was the lady gnawing her nails because she was away from her husband, whom she had left in Bungalow No. 20, next to Bungalow No. 21.

I was thoroughly enjoying the Roman spring and my return to Europe and my dinners with the film crew in the old trattorias. The crew was funny and gentle and as old as the Old World and as young as the young girls astride the pillion seats of Lambrettas, clasping their young boyfriends around the waist as they whizzed past. There were the splendid sunsets I watched from the balcony of my apartment on the seventh floor of the Excelsior. All the terraces of Rome seemed gilded. I always knew with whom I would have dinner. I could enjoy all that dignity conferred on me by the statuette. I had a marvelous time with people I loved very much. And I was acting for the first time in two years. I was acting in my own language; I'd be dubbed in Italian later: There was no language problem. I spent three delicious months in Rome, and that keeps me, even today, from judging what may have happened during my weeks in Rome and Miller's weeks in New York between a man, my husband, and a woman, my pal, who were working together, living under the same roof, and consequently sharing their solitudes, their fears, their moods, and their recollections of childhood poverty.

Therefore, allow me to reroute any fans of "slices of life" to the newspapers of that period. The press undertook to transform into an "event" one of those stories that can occur in any enterprise, big or small, any apartment house, big or small—and also during the making of many films.

The stories are often tender and disarming; sometimes passionate. According to their degree of intensity and the particular circumstances, they wind up neatly, smoothly, or else there's a brutal break with the previous life patterns of the people concerned.

And sometimes, as time goes by, they transmute into a friendship that's more solid than any fleeting passion.

It's rare that one's workmates or neighbors don't gossip. It's not mean gossip; it's indulgent, in the manner of those who have traveled the same road and secretly regret that those times are over.

But, as it isn't "in the papers," and it's never been "in the papers," it's in the faces of the people they meet in the cafeteria, or on the stairs of their building, that the heroes of the drama read judgment or complicity or disapproval. And most of the time they're free to decide themselves what they're going to do with this story which was their personal business at first, but which now seems to preoccupy the studio or the building at one remove. (My readers may turn back to Chapter 9 of this book if they're still with me.)

But when it is "in the paper" and the "scoop" begins to do the rounds of the rotary presses—and there are quite a few of them in the world—and Miss Hopper writes her little column, then your nice little story, or your beautiful story, or even your great story, is doomed!

Then it's no longer yours, that of your partner and you, or even that of your husband or your wife. It's now in the hands of the buyers of newspapers. And consequently it has become the "business" of the paper merchants.°

° It would be unfair if I forgot to mention the superb photos and lengthy articles on us featured in *Match* for two consecutive weeks.

And since these stories sell very well, they're translated into a great many languages. And depending on the temperaments of the different countries that replay the drama to which you have been assigned, the lines you haven't said begin to take on a character of melodrama or tragedy or vaudeville.

It's sad. And abysmally stupid.

It's abysmally stupid to receive in the mail letters encouraging you to "hold out," and explaining to you across four pages that "I too have suffered, but I got my husband back and this is how I did it . . ." or "My rival was blond as she is. . . ." It's abysmally stupid to have the shopkeeper tap you on the shoulder, when you've gone into her store to buy a yard of elastic (which happened to me in Auxerre, where I was filming *Les Mauvais Coups* [*Naked Autumn*] and having a wonderful time with my pals), and say to you with an encouraging wink, "He'll come back, you'll see." This happens at a time when your husband, who's now making a film in Paris (because all this is happening in October), phones you every evening. . . .

That little drama went on for months. It was not sad, but it was a bore.

Later we were privileged to receive mail that included both these qualities: It was sad and abysmally stupid—and third, it was anonymous.

This mail was about both my "misfortune" and my signature on the Manifesto of 121.

I came back to the old country loaded with honors. I had a bagful of stories to tell about those months spent in the iridescent bubble. My pals filed in and out to see what a real Oscar looked like. I was tanned like a Californian. I wore relaxed pants suits from Jax, moccasins embroidered with beads that were, I was told, fabricated on the reservations, where the Indians are so happy. I was frivolous and a bit elsewhere. It was obvious that I had to be put back into my natural environment.

It was Claude Lanzmann who did it. He had to see me

right away; he was on a mission from Sartre. Could he stop by? From his tone it was evident that he wasn't coming to admire the statuette or to hear my colorful description of Sunset Boulevard. When he took the paper out of his pocket, I knew that action was on the point of being renewed. My vacation was over.

I read. The text was concise, courageous, and too provocative—in the good sense—to pass unnoticed. Here are the last lines:

> We the undersigned, convinced that every person must declare himself concerning acts which henceforward cannot be construed as simple news items in our individual lives—we declare that all of us, according to our place and means, consider it our duty to intervene. Not in order to give advice, for people must make their own decisions concerning such grave problems, but to ask those who judge them not to allow themselves to be duped by equivocal words and values.
>
> We respect and find justified the refusal to take up arms against the Algerian people.
>
> We respect and find justified the conduct of those Frenchmen who believe it their duty to give aid and protection to the oppressed Algerians in the name of the French people.
>
> The cause of the Algerian people, which has contributed in decisive fashion to the overthrow of the colonial system, is the cause of all free men.[*]

[*]Signed: Arthur Adamov, Robert Anthelme, Georges Auclair, Jean Baby, Hélène Balfet, Marc Barbut, Robert Barrat, Simone de Beauvoir, Jean-Louis Bédouin, Marc Begbeider, Robert Benayoun, Maurice Blanchot, Roger Blin, Arsène Bonnafous-Murat, Geneviève Bonnefoi, Raymond Borde, Jean-Louis Bory, Jacques-Laurent Bost, Pierre Boulez, Vincent Bounoure, André Breton, Guy Cabanel, Georges Condominas, Alain Cuny, Jean Czarnecki, Jean Dalsace, Hubert Damisch, Bernard Dort, Jean Douassot, Simone Dreyfus, Marguerite Duras, Yves Elleouet, Dominique Eluard, Charles Estienne, Louis-René des Forêts, Thèodore Fraenkel, André Frénaud, Jacques Gernet, Louis Gernet, Édouard Glissant, Anne Guérin, Daniel Guérin, Jacques Howlett, Edouard Jaguer, Pierre Jaouen, Gérard Charlot, Robert Jaulin, Alain Joubert, Henri Krea, Robert Lagarde, Monique Lange, Claude Lanzmann, Robert Lapoujade, Henri Lefebvre, Gérard Legrand, Michel Leiris, Paul Lévy, Jérôme Lindon, Éric Losfeld,

For just a brief moment the thought flashed through my mind: How nice it was there, those peaceful days in the gardens of Beverly Hills...but the next moment I was insulting myself. You don't want to stick your neck out, do you? You're trying to wriggle out, find something wrong, some word that doesn't work....I read and reread the paper. Claude said nothing; he just looked at me. Then, suddenly, I saw Ostend. *Ostend!* The old bookseller, cruel but right, impolite and contemptuous. "And besides buying books, what are you doing about what's being done in your name?"—and no good-bye or thank you when he gave me my change....

Here was my revenge! And it's in that spirit that I signed the paper which became famous as the Manifesto of 121.

I couldn't take it upon myself to sign for Montand; it was something neither of us had ever done without the other's having read or listened to what was to be signed. He was on the other side of the world, and given the difference in time and our different schedules, I couldn't possibly reach him before the Manifesto's publication time, which was very close. It was a verbal bomb that disturbed everyone and created enormous problems for those who had signed it.

When Montand came home, he was angry that I hadn't associated him with me, but the time of his return was also the moment we were playing our parts in the drama I've

---

Robert Louzon, Marcel Péju, Olivier de Magny, André Mandouze, Maud Mannoni, Jean Martin, Renée-Marcel Martinet, Jean-Daniel Martinet, André Marty-Capgras, Dionys Mascolo, François Maspero, André Masson, Pierre de Massot, Jean-Jacques Mayoux, Jehan Mayoux, Théodore Monod, Marie Moscovici, Georges Mounin, Maurice Nadeau, Georges Navel, Claude Ollier, Hélène Parmelin, Jean-Paul Sartre, Florence Malraux, André Pieyre de Mandiargues, Ernest Pignon, Bernard Pinguad, Maurice Pons, J.-B. Pontalis, Jean Pouillon, Denise René, Alain Resnais, Jean-François Revel, Paul Revel, Alain Robbe-Grillet, Christiane Rochefort, Jacques-Francis Rolland, Alfred Rosmer, Gilbert Rouget, Claude Roy, Marc Saint-Saens, Nathalie Sarraute, Renée Saurel, José Pierre, Claude Sautet, Jean Schuster, Robert Scipion, Louis Seguin, Geneviève Serreau, Simone Signoret, Jean-Claude Silbermann, Claude Simon, René de Solier, D. de la Souchère, Jean Thiercelin, René Tzanck, Vercors, Jean-Pierre Vernant, Pierre Vidal-Naquet, J.-P. Vielfaure, Claude Viseux, Ylipe René Zazzo.

just described. So everything got mixed up: In the minds of some—and they were not our most distinguished spirits— the absence of his name next to mine for the first time, after so many years of the two signatures, was seen as a kind of moral divorce.

The enormous problems became official problems. Then they became reprisals. They were even posted in the radio and television stations, the theaters, and film-production offices. Anyone who had signed the text, whatever his profession (and there followed the list of names), was banned on radio, on the stage, or in any kind of televised news broadcast. Government subsidies would be withdrawn from employers who didn't heed the warning.

Which is how, in the Barrault-Renaud company, a Claudel that was about to be staged was paralyzed.

Roger Blin, Laurent Terzieff, Alain Cuny, and Pierre Boulez were on the list.

That's also how my nice producer, R. Thuillier, who had hired me for *Les Mauvais Coups*, found himself without a state subsidy.

That's why Frédéric Rossif and François Chalais interrupted their program, *Pour le Cinema*, with a grave announcement that they would continue as soon as everyone could again be interviewed. They went on the air again seven months later, with me on their first program.

That's why Jacques Prévert, who hadn't signed, and who was offered two hours of radio time, naïvely made it his condition that he would be able to work with all the people who had signed, from Danièle Delorme to François Truffaut.

And that's also why, naturally, Montand refused to participate in any of those end-of-year programs to which he was invited.

All this was going on while those letters, those sad, abysmally stupid, and anonymous letters, still poured in. They were at once pornographic, scatological, and

347

patriotic. They generally said that my husband had been quite right to prefer a gorgeous blonde to me. They suggested I go back to the Arabs, whose amorous aptitude is so well known. They often added that it served that Jew Miller right.

The year ended with this mess, when it had started off so well.

Nothing, nothing seemed left of the real work: our confrontation with New York, the dignity of having remained ourselves in that country where the door had been closed to us for such a long time, the long hours of battle with the poems from Thailand, the Breton prayers—nothing. Swept away! It seemed almost as though, in the minds of some, we had gone to America only to stir up this publicity.

I would probably not have gone back over this seventeen-year-old mess if very recently, and more and more frequently, certain historiographers who believe themselves at least in part sociologists—and who aren't completely disinterested—hadn't been publishing fat books devoted to the premature death of that young woman whom nobody took seriously while she was alive. Inevitably there comes the chapter that deals with us, and then those old quotes surface again, like the one about Marilyn's "schoolgirl crush on me" attributed to Montand. It can't be true, if for no other reason than by its grammatical form and its difficulties of pronunciation it would have cost Montand a week's hard work—if indeed he had ever pronounced those words to Hedda Hopper, as she claimed he did the day she decided to take her revenge.

And then, there are also those psychological studies, with names I know. People talking about Marilyn. Among those names are a few belonging to people she loved and who loved her. Unfortunately, there are also others belonging to people who hated her. They told me all about it, during that happy time in Bungalows Nos. 20 and 21. But she never knew about it.

Nor did she ever know my sadness on that August day in 1962.

She never knew to what degree I never detested her, and how thoroughly I had understood the story that was no one's business but ours, the four of us. Too many people were concerned with it during troubled times when many more important things were happening.

She's gone without ever knowing that I never stopped wearing the champagne-colored silk scarf she'd lent me one day when I was being photographed. It went well with what I was wearing; so well that she made me a present of it.

It's a bit frayed now, but if I fold it carefully, the fray doesn't show.

Chapter 12

I began walking hand in hand with myself at the age my mother took me for my Joan of Arc cut to hairdressers who didn't singe their instruments, and I've followed myself across all those borders that came later. Last night I left in my typewriter a forty-year-old bleached blonde.

I was so deep inside myself, inside that bleached blonde (what a bore, one's memory!), that I was astonished when I glanced in the mirror this morning and met there a person a bit too plump, graying, not to say white-haired, who looked back and said, "Hello there, it's me!" when I was about to brush my teeth.

Sixteen years separate those two people. A lot of things happened, and there were other borders to cross, or perhaps I should say tolls to pay.

I've already told about the real borders. The real discoveries—the way up the professional ladder, the taking stock of myself, the loves and the friendships, the important books, the irreversible choices—all those were played off during the first forty years.

In fact, they were so well played that the rest, these past sixteen years, is a kind of surplus, a present, an extension of the miracle. In a sense, I'm surprised that it's still going on, and grateful for the good and even the bad moments. It's a continuation of the voyage in a first-class carriage on smooth rails; but when I got onto that train aged twenty, it was a third-class carriage rolling on rickety rails, interrupted by all sorts of tollgates and unknown stations where one gets out for the first time.

My stations from now on will be ones I already know; rediscoveries and verifications, rarely discoveries.

Except for one. I became a grandmother for the first time on March 28, 1970. Bonjour, Benjamin!

Surplus, presents, the extended miracle....To be Roberte in *Les Mauvais Coups*; after having said no to all those scripts in their battered covers, not one of them with a really good part in a really good story, to find myself blissfully happy in the middle of Burgundy during that very cold winter of 1960. To be the wife of Laurence Olivier in Ireland, and to be directed—at last—by Peter Glenville. Traveling in trucks, subways, trains, and bicycles from Rethel to the Spanish border for three months under the direction of René Clément.

Sometimes thinking back to California, to the humming-birds and coyotes and the tinkling sound of ice in glasses, thinking it a place I would probably never return to; and then suddenly to be back there in 1964 to play the contessa in *Ship of Fools*, directed by Stanley Kramer.

My Hollywood of 1964 is also full of things.

There's the beach in Trancas, where Katharine Hepburn took me very early in the morning when I wasn't working. She rises with the sun, like the pioneers. If she hadn't told the story herself, I would never mention her life with Spencer Tracy; she watched over him with a kind of adolescent love. She no longer worked so that she could be with him, and he no longer worked since a heart attack had made him uninsurable. So Stanley Kramer had had a splendid armchair installed on the set, with Spencer Tracy's name on it, and every morning at around nine the handsomest of Irishmen with all that white hair took his place as the so-called supervisor, and made us die laughing. . . . When I wasn't working I was with her; when I was working I was with him.

There were the weekends with Lee and Betty Marvin and their four children in a little house they had rented on the beach. There was the sound of the sea as I hadn't heard it, so close to my bed, since living at Saint-Gildas. On Sunday mornings George Segal arrived with his wife, his baby, and his banjo. We picnicked or cooked. It was even more like Saint-Gildas. For Lee Marvin, *Ship of Fools* was the end of his time as a supporting player; he had been waiting for twenty years. For George Segal, it was his first important film.

To reach the beach entailed driving through a short pass between two red rocky cliffs. One morning Hepburn pointed out to me that there were hearts and initials painted in white at a vertiginous height; they were the equivalent of the hearts and initials you see in France, chiseled out with a pocket knife on chestnut or plane trees at a height a man or a woman can easily reach. At the peril of their lives, these rock-climbing fools had scrambled up there with a pot of paint to daub words like "Jane + Bill = Love," and the date.

All this would be no more than folklore and anecdote if, upon each trip back to California, I hadn't noticed that those perilous lovers' graffiti remained just as loving, but were often followed by "=Love and Peace" from 1966 on.

From 1968 to 1969 the rocks came to resemble gigantic totems. The Jane and Bill inscriptions were no longer in the center of hearts, or rather they were hearts, but they had the shape of a circle in which a schematic semaphore man lowered his arms. It was the peace sign, and the names and dates were as significant as a postage stamp.

I realize I'm doing a "flashforward," but if I'm going to

talk about those rocky cliffs I might as well tell their story now.

In 1964, while *Ship of Fools* was being made, there was an electoral campaign going on. Barry Goldwater would appear on television, to be greeted by his supporters with "Hello, Barry, nice to see you, Barry." They were the same people who put a sign in the rear windows of their cars showing the chemical symbols for gold and water. The people I was working with didn't have an excessive love for Johnson, but there was so little choice. Anything rather than Goldwater! So when a car passed them on the road that had the "Au H_2O" sign of the enemy, they would speed up to overtake it or to catch up with it at the next red light, and then "Up yours" signs, more European than Californian, would be exchanged between the drivers. Things had changed a great deal in the land of the hummingbirds. . . .

Kennedy had been assassinated, and his portrait hung everywhere people were encouraged to vote for Johnson. Or rather to vote against Goldwater.

The people I worked with never ate in a restaurant where there wasn't a portrait of Kennedy. However, one day I strayed into a pseudo cheap dive; there on the table stood a minute porcelain bust of Kennedy. It was a salt cellar, with holes in the precise spots where the bullets— fired by whom?—had penetrated his head.

(In Autheuil there are two framed letters side by side on the piano. One, signed "John F. Kennedy, President of the United States," thanks Montand for having accepted an invitation to sing for the tenth anniversary of the Democratic party conventions; it is dated January 20, 1963. The other, signed by Martin Luther King, Jr., thanks Montand for having organized and MC'd a huge meeting at the Porte de Versailles when Martin Luther King came to explain to the French the battle he and his brothers were engaged in; it is dated April 5, 1966).

In Hollywood, in 1964, Stanley Kramer had bought

twenty-odd advantageously situated seat tickets well in advance, and when the day came, he rented a minibus and took all the actors from *Ship of Fools* to the other end of town, to the big Los Angeles stadium. It was the day of the track meet.

But this was a very special track meet. It was the first Soviet-American encounter on U.S. territory.

All Saturday and Sunday afternoon a group of strong young men high-jumped, broad-jumped, ran long distances and short distances, flew over bars that rose higher and higher, and passed relay batons before seventy-five thousand people. The Americans were white and black. The Soviet athletes were Russians, Ukrainians, Georgians. ... Their names, accompanied by the place and date of their birth, were in the program. They were between twenty and twenty-three years old. There arrived a black giant, born in Montgomery, Alabama, and during a three-minute uninterrupted ovation he became the hero of the entire country, represented by the seventy-five thousand Californians, very few of whom, at the time, would have offered him a cup of coffee in their houses. There was a Soviet athlete who jumped higher than anyone, and after consulting the program one wondered how that young man could be so strong, since he had been a newborn in Stalingrad in 1943.

Certainly Stanley had hired his minibus and bought those expensive seats so that we would ask ourselves these questions.

At the stadium exit, militants of the Birch Society and the American Legion distributed expensively printed tracts explaining that these Soviet athletes had come to do spy work between two broad jumps and three javelin throws....

In Hollywood, in 1964, Vivien Leigh gave elegant dinners in the big house she had rented from London. She wanted them sumptuous, and they were. She was no longer Laurence Olivier's wife, but she wanted to remain

Lady Olivier. She asked us to dress, and my little wandering sables worked hard at her house. The dinners were served by the light of candelabra. They were cooked by a real Cordon Bleu chef and served by a waiter who also was no extra; both of them had been hired for the duration of the filming. She was as beautiful as she had been at the time of Scarlett O'Hara; she had fabulous memories of this town, and she clung to them. At the end of these evenings the phonograph played the theme from *Gone with the Wind*; it made her sad, but she did it deliberately. From one moment to another she was scintillating or desperate. She was very sick. *Ship of Fools* was her last film and she's prodigious in it.

In 1964, in Hollywood, there was already an establishment called Synanon, which is the drug-taker's equivalent of Alcoholics Anonymous; I went to visit it with Oskar Werner and Stanley Kramer. The average age of those voluntary candidates for detoxification was between sixteen and eighteen; this was their last chance after the clinics, hospitals, and prisons; they had begun taking drugs at around fourteen.

Upon my return to France, when I spoke about Synanon to people who were amused to see their kids smoking their first joints, they laughed at me. . . .

During that time in 1964 I sometimes had a truly luxurious Saturday. I would have myself driven to Leona Drive, up on the hill. There I would ring a bell and soon realize that I was much more excited than if I were going to see Greta Garbo: Jean Renoir would open the door.

I'd walk into a living room that was as it would have been in the country in France; sometimes there were Renoirs on the wall, sometimes there weren't, depending on whether they'd been lent to exhibitions or put in the vault when Dido and Jean Renoir were traveling. In one closet there was a somewhat rickety 16-millimeter projector that sometimes caused trouble, but with the help of a screwdriver always ended up running, and in another closet was a small screen, and finally there were reels of films.

So, on a hill overlooking the film capital of the world, with Jean and Dido Renoir as my projectionists, I saw *Le Crime de Monsieur Lange* once again. On the screen flickered all my little world, my world of the Café Flore when all those people were thirty years younger and I hadn't met them yet. They were already speaking words written by Jacques Prévert. There was even Sylvain Itkine, who a few years later would die under torture, which was perhaps inflicted by that superb blond boy wearing a swastika arm band in the last shot of *Ship of Fools*.

Hollywood, 1965. Stanley Kramer had asked Oskar Werner and me to come back for the opening night of the film. There was a week of parties: big banquets, small dinners, and the joys of meeting again. The reviews were superb and once again nominations were in the air. (A few months later, Oskar and I were indeed nominated, but that time we missed the statuette. It didn't matter; we had won Kramer.) I was just about to go home—in fact, my luggage was almost packed—when a young man named Bob Littmann brought me the script of a one-hour television show.

It was a two-character play, for a young actor and a well-known actress, who discuss and argue about a character in a play. It was very beautiful, very intelligent, and very Pirandellian. It all took place on the empty stage of an empty theater, and it was called *A Small Rebellion*. The director was the best television director of the time, Stuart Rosenberg. It was his last televison show; he was moving on to films.

I telephoned my husband, unpacked my bags, and went to work. Because of Rosenberg's schedule and mine, we had to begin right away. I don't know how I managed to learn all those long speeches—or rather I do know: by asking every pal I had to come and give me my cues, especially George Maharis, who was to give them to me when the cameras rolled. We made a sixty-minute film in six days, without rehearsals. I've rarely worked as hard. But I was well rewarded; *A Small Rebellion* brought me an Emmy, which is the Oscar of television, and that year I shared it with Frank Sinatra.

Surplus, present, extending miracle.

But that year in Hollywood, during the summer of 1965, something happened that was much more important than *A Small Rebellion*. There was what might be called an enormous rebellion: the Watts uprising.

Like all worldly people with artistic and folkloric pretensions, all I knew of Watts was a peaceful little street where Leslie Blanch, who was at the time Romain Gary's wife, had taken me and Montand one Sunday afternoon in 1960.

At the end of this peaceful street were two towers and a kind of crypt in the middle of a rather neglected garden surrounded by a fence. The two towers and the crypt were made of mosaic. But as you came closer and touched it, you realized that the mosaic was made of millions of pieces of broken plates, coffeepots, bits of bottles, and Coca-Cola tops. From a distance the whole thing glistened in the sun like Byzantine towers. It was the lifework of a local Facteur Cheval.° Since his death, two young film editors from some studio or other were fighting the municipality to preserve the edifice from demolition.

I had seen nothing else in Watts, and I knew nothing else about Watts except that the town administration wanted to do away with this legacy from a light-headed dreamer, a peaceful and persevering man who had left this treasure. Perhaps the town fathers spent too much time on the

°A now famous French country postman who'd spent all his spare time building, in a field near his village, Hautes Rives, an extraordinary collection of surrealist houses and palaces, with odds and ends gathered on his rounds.

towers and not enough on the people. Be that as it may, in the month of August 1964, the people in question rose up. And that was how I finally discovered that Watts was the ghetto of Los Angeles.

If my memory serves me right, it all began during the night from a Wednesday to a Thursday. On Thursday evening the television stations showed fires burning. Friday morning on the set, the stagehands and electricians had their ears glued to transistor radios and relayed the news. They were scared, and they wanted me to be scared with them. Watts was very near, they said; it was fifteen minutes from the Beverly Hills Hotel by freeway. "The radio's announcing roaming bands of niggers. Be sure to lock yourself in tonight in your bungalow," they said. A gigantic "grip," wearing John Wayne–style boots, his hammer in his belt like a Colt pistol, explained to Stuart Rosenberg and me that the best solution would be a small atomic bomb especially designed to be dropped exclusively on Watts. . . . Friday evening: Channel 7 had managed a phenomenon; it had canceled all its regular programs. All the sponsors of variety shows, plays, literary discussions, and political confrontations donated the time they had paid for. A helicopter with a marvelous cameraman on board flew over the Watts area continually. It came down so low that you could see people lighting bonfires and then running away; you could see them go into stores and begin pillaging. Another camera crew was permanently installed in police headquarters. Every fifteen minutes or so a voice would announce that what you were seeing was being brought to you by beer X or car Y, which had voluntarily relinquished its air time so that we, in our comfortable armchairs, could be in Watts; and the voice fervently exhorted us not to leave those chairs—nor were we to leave our houses, if we were within forty miles of the city.

Disdaining and insulting myself profusely, I nevertheless double-locked the door that evening.

I didn't work on Saturdays. Channel 7, which had the highest audience rating in the country that day, continued its nonstop report. Liberal sociologists and churchmen filed across the screen between scenes from the helicopter and said very sensible things on the deeper reasons that had unleashed this unreason. They were not gentle with the city administrators, and were even less so with the mayor of Los Angeles.

At this point the mayor allowed himself to be interviewed. I've forgotten his name; he was tall and stout and wore a white Texan hat. The sight of him suddenly reminded me of something. Five years earlier I had returned to France on an inaugural Air France flight. On board there had been a number of French officials who had been invited for the round trip. Among them was the Senate president, Gaston Monnerville, a black man born in Antilles. During the flight he had asked me questions about my months in California. My account had been idyllic; I truly had nothing to complain about. The president listened to me, smiling, and before going back to take his seat beside Madame Monnerville, he asked me whether I had met the mayor of Los Angeles. "No," I said. "Well, I didn't either. We had an appointment, but I was only received by his assistant," said the president of the French Senate, tapping my hand and smiling more broadly than ever.

Now, on the screen, the man in the white hat reassured his people, affirming that he had issued orders to restore order.

And order was restored. On Sunday it was all over. The area had been taken over by the police, and now Channel 7 showed nothing but endless lines of blacks being put into paddy wagons. Contrary to what is generally people's behavior when they're arrested, these people arranged to stop right in front of the cameras long enough to enjoy a close-up; they had to be pushed by the cops to go on. They would wave in a way that clearly indicated: "This isn't the end!"

In 1966 I was making *Games* with Curtis Harrington.

On paper it was a good story of theft and murder. The film was made at "Universal speed"—that is, very, very fast, and I was absolutely *not* nominated. There were two beginners in this film: James Caan and Katharine Ross. With Curtis's permission, I organized a screening of the rushes for Mike Nichols, and that's how Katharine got her part in *The Graduate*.

I mention this only because she herself has never stopped telling this tale, be it in London or Rome or Paris. I don't talk about people who never remember how things started for them—but talking about her is a way of thanking her for her good memory.

In 1966 there were fewer big parties. The Hollywood bubble was becoming less and less iridescent; its weight and colors were changing. People still gathered together, but it was rare when after a certain point in the dinner the conversation didn't switch to Vietnam and civil rights. One evening at the Gregory Pecks', things nearly turned very sour when one well-known guest used the word "enemy" in speaking about the Vietnamese. "Whose enemy?" asked Peck, dignified, calm, and firm.

In those same superb houses, and around those same pools where, six years earlier, the vile gossip of Hedda Hopper or X's bad review or the overpraised merits of a certain actor were subjects of passionate and partisan conversation, now no one talked about anything except Vietnam and the black problem.

In fact, in the Hollywood of 1966—with its wonderful sun, and the songs of hummingbirds, and fewer and fewer coyotes bounding across the hills because of ever-growing construction—it was patently obvious to me that the film people, the only people I saw, were much more concerned and courageous and active than their equivalents in my country at the time when we were engaged in our own colonial wars, or so-called pacifications.

They were not the only people in America to be concerned, of course. The campuses were in an uproar; but

I was not on the campuses, I was in HOLLYWOOD. And in the Polo Lounge of the Beverly Hills Hotel I heard things that I would probably never have heard at Fouquet's or the Lipp six years earlier.

I'll never forget those three young actors—two boys and a girl—who wept in Bungalow No. 17 the evening they heard on the radio that the bombing of Hanoi had begun again (following a sort of cease-fire in tribute to the Almighty—this was before Christmas) with far greater intensity.

Nor will I ever forget the pompous, imbecilic chauffeur who, the next day, took me to Malibu Beach in a limousine to visit Vadim and Jane Fonda and spend with them that Christmas that had been violated a little prematurely by squadrons of American bombers. The chauffeur was obsequious, as Americans rarely are, but he obviously thought this was the way to do his job as the chauffeur of a rented limousine. He told me all about the countryside, which I knew by heart, and advised me against the road that led between the two red rocky cliffs after I had asked him to take it. I was his prisoner, and this would teach me to learn to drive. All along the twenty-five miles that separated me from my friends, he shared his worries with me.

"It's a shame, what a pity . . . shameful . . . scandalous," he said. Judging from the back of his head and the tone of his voice, it was all three rolled into one. The Tournament of Roses wasn't going to take place this year in Pasadena. He checked in his rear-view driving mirror to make sure I had understood his news. I had received it, but the lack of concern that must have been visible on my face encouraged him to continue his part as an indulgent teacher who, although paid by the mile, would gladly include a free supplement as cultural guide in his price.

Every year a squadron of planes, or let's say several, let fly tons and tons of rose petals over Pasadena. But this year the shower of petals had been canceled, and can you imagine why? Why, the times were all topsy-turvy! Perhaps there were bad political influences trying to keep the good people of Pasadena from living their lives as free citizens, as they had until today. He himself wasn't from Pasadena; in fact, he had never set foot in Pasadena. But he and his wife had always sworn that someday they would go to Pasadena, for the Tournament of Roses. Well, maybe next year. If things were back in good order by then, which was not at all certain these days. Fortunately, Ronald Reagan was now governor of the state. Did I know Ronald Reagan? the rear-view driving mirror asked. As an actor, of course, he wasn't a patch on John Wayne or you, Miss Signorett . . . my wife cried so hard when she saw *Room at the Top*. No, you and John Wayne are real artists. But as governor, Ronald Reagan is exactly what we need. . . . He really didn't want to brag, but in a way he had done something to contribute to the governor's success; modestly, of course, in his own way. This very limousine in which he now had the pleasure of driving me had participated in the campaign. It was while he was driving some of Governor Reagan's supporters that he had become convinced, by the things he heard them talk about—which naturally he couldn't permit himself to butt into—that Ronnie was the right guy. But perhaps all this political stuff bored me? After all, I was French. He begged my pardon. Did we have roses in France? He had never been in France. He might have gone, but the war ended just as he was about to be drafted. He hadn't been in the Pacific, either. He was very sorry about it. He had no son, but if he had had one, he and his wife would be proud to send him to serve his country and finish off some of those Vietnamese bastards. . . . Was I too hot? He could put on more air-conditioning. The radio had announced fog for that evening. Maybe, after all, that was what had kept the planes from going up; that would explain about Pasadena. But even so, it was a shame that all those tons of rose petals would wilt rather than be scattered over the population of Pasadena. . . .

I have in my day gotten out of taxis during rush hour in the middle of Paris. Halfway through the trip I've said to the driver, "Stop. I don't want to listen to you anymore. What do I owe you?"... and then found myself on the sidewalk, miserably trying to attract a hypothetical vehicle, having firmly decided that this time the driver's conversation—whatever it might be—would leave me made of stone, in view of the hour.

But there, on the highway to Malibu, I lacked courage. I could see myself, or rather I could imagine myself, my arms full of little Christmas presents in big packages, plus my suitcase containing my nightgown and my toothbrush and my splendid dressing gown–Christmas party dress, hitchhiking on the road like a superannuated hippie. So I gave up that idea, but I felt it was disgusting cowardice. I listened. I never said anything; I just nodded. He had me framed in his rear-view mirror. My silence must have been the proof of his powers of fascination, and I could imagine him telling his wife that evening how Miss Signorett had been captivated by his commentary, and how sorry she, too, was that the Tournament of Roses had been called off.

Each time he mentioned rose petals I conjured up a flashback to Titine Roux on the second floor of La Colombe, letting fall a snowfall of red, pink, white, and yellow rose petals on me and Montand when we came back from the town hall on the day of our marriage. Not a ton; a few handfuls. And when he went on about the airplane, I superimposed Hanoi in my mind's eye—but that didn't show in the rear-view mirror.

He delivered me in front of the beach house, and when I say delivered, I mean in all senses of the word. I paid my fare, and with slightly belated courage I mumbled a few short phrases, in which I tried to convey the message that planes sometimes dropped roses and sometimes bombs. He nodded. It's a shame, he said, sighing. He gave me his card, in case I needed him for the return trip, and with a big smile wished me a merry Christmas.

I think I bored my friends a bit with my story about the chauffeur. But I had a very merry Christmas. There was Papa, and Papa was Hank, as they say here, but since I'm not from here, I say Henry. Henry Fonda.

There was also Peter, the little brother, and his pal Dennis. They talked endlessly about their pal Jack and the story they were writing, and about the film it would be. With slightly condescending indulgence, I listened to these young dilettantes. Their thoughts and projects seemed to me as unreal and improbable as all those others I had heard since forever between the Café Flore and the Montana bar. So it was with much humility and great surprise and joy that two years later I kissed Peter Fonda, Dennis Hopper, and their pal Jack Nicholson when the lights came on again in the Columbia studios' small screening theater after they had shown me the first rough cut of *Easy Rider*.

We were now in 1968. Or rather it was "after May '68" for us French.

It was "after August '68" for the Czechs.

And it was the end of 1968 for the Americans.

America had priests in prison; the Berrigan brothers had been jailed for having burned draft records. In HOLLY-WOOD, the sharpest sharks in the film industry had grown long hair and beards to keep in character and not miss catching the connection for the youngsters' bandwagon. The youngsters flung *Easy Rider* into their jaws. The most apparently apolitical fathers would tell stories about how they went down in the morning to make sure that a draft notice for their boy hadn't been popped into the mailbox. If it had, their check was ready for a trip to Canada or Sweden. The most popular show on television, *Laugh-In*, had once included the line: "I hope this war ends soon so our boys can come home...from Montreal." On television, thirteen channels gave air time to the opponents of their government's policy, and black actresses, who, until then, hadn't been exactly overemployed and who had overspent themselves for hair-straightening sessions, were now overspending themselves buying Afro wigs.

Just like the first time, I was a housewife again. Montand was working with Minnelli, and I would always be home in time to put a match to the gas in the fake fireplace of Bungalow No. 8. Bungalow No. 8 wasn't upstairs; it was a little villa—a real bungalow! But there was a fake fire under the chimney, just as in the others.

Like the first time, I wandered around a lot, as one can in a village where one has old friends. Nine years had passed since the first time, and by now I had often gotten off the train at this station, and so the changes struck me less than they struck Montand.

One thing hadn't changed, and hasn't changed yet, and that's the number 28 stuck among the hieroglyphics in our passports. Now, when I return, the gentlemen of the immigration service no longer say, "Welcome to the United States"; they say, "Welcome home." And then, after leafing through the pages, they reach the infamous page and the horrible truth. A great sadness and a kind of incredulity comes over their faces. I always have my formula waiting: "I'm special," I say. "You sure are," they reply, stamping and sometimes smiling.

That year, in 1968, it wasn't a gentleman but a "gentlewoman" who checked us in the glass cage at Los Angeles airport. Apparently she liked neither men nor women nor couples nor special cases nor foreigners nor, probably, herself. She didn't welcome you one little bit; in fact, she made you want to buy a return ticket immediately on the first plane that had two available seats. The gentlewoman was not at all gentle. But once again there was a smiling face beyond the glass cage.

If she didn't like foreigners, this lady must have suffered greatly that year. HOLLYWOOD had become Hollywood-on-the-Seine. On Alpine Drive there was a little house, and in the window to the right of the door there was a sign saying "Place de la Sorbonne." Inside, if you had invited yourself for lunch, which happened to me about five times a week, you found Agnès Varda, Jacques Demy, Rosalie and Monique la Nantaise.

Jacques Demy had made a film that may be the best film on Hollywood 1967, seen through a foreigner's eyes. It is called *Model Shop*, and it was unsuccessful, but it ought to be shown again. Agnès Varda had been taken for a ride by a stranger to the town, a vanishing artist and producer of rubber checks, so she had temporarily abandoned her project of filming a superb script she had been working on for months, but she went back to work, and in three weeks, operating practically clandestinely, she made *Lion's Love*, which she had written in two weeks. Monique la Nantaise had learned to drive a car, and she brought back from the supermarkets provisions that ended up as typically French regional specialties. And Rosalie, who was then about nine years old, quietly became bilingual at the Beverly Hills public school.

Philippe Noiret, Monique Chomette, their daughter, and a lady whose name I've forgotten occupied another house on the hill, whose owner often came around to check on the furniture. The preceding rental on the house had been a pop group and the final inventory had been a rude shock. Philippe was making one film with Cukor and another one with Hitchcock; he broke no furniture, and he cooked for relaxation on his days off.

Anna Karina was making a film with Cukor, and she had rented the house Agnès was later to use to make *Lion's Love*. The house belonged to the same fussy proprietor as that of the Noirets. Nothing was broken while the film was made, but everything in it was changed around in one night of artisan's work, including the color of the pool, which became psychedelic.

Anouk Aimée was working with Cukor.

Piccoli was working with Hitchcock.

Dirk Bogarde was working with Cukor.

And Montand was working with Minnelli.

Michel Legrand returned to his winter quarters in this town he now lived in for six months every year.

Ingrid Bergman had come back for the first time in a long time, and she was making *Forty Carats* at Columbia.

Polanski was giving parties at the bogus Norman farm house that was to become the scene of the crime.

Vadim, Gegauff, Serge, and Christian Marquand brought back fish they had caught in the Pacific, which became Mediterranean bouillabaisses after lengthy conferences held in the little kitchen of the beach house.

Jane was taking care of Vanessa, her daughter, and also working on her next film. She prepared herself with a seriousness, gentleness, and energy that are most extraordinary. The film was *They Shoot Horses, Don't They?* She was also preparing, without yet knowing it, a new direction in her life.

It was Jane Fonda, superb, gay, thoughtful, and gracious, who welcomed us—Montand, Piccoli, and myself—on December 25, 1968. We were invited to a family meal. Of course there was Papa, and of course there was Peter. And Papa looked at Peter, who had managed to change something in this town, together with his pals Dennis and Jack. Papa was proud, worried, and baffled.

There was also, at that time, living in a little house in the valley, James Baldwin, who was writing a script about the life and death of Malcolm X. I had once seen him often, solitary in the back of the Montana bar, at the time when the Rue Saint-Benoît was drawing its first breath just after the war. At the time we wondered whether the young black man was a trumpeter or a deserter, or perhaps both. We didn't speak to him, he didn't speak to us; we exchanged smiles. That may not have been enough. It can't have been, and to my great surprise—once more—I discovered one day that the small black man who'd sat at the back of the Montana had become one of America's greatest contemporary writers.

James Baldwin did write a script about the life and

death of Malcolm X, which was already quite an achievement three years after Watts. But for a number of reasons the life and death of Malcolm X never became a film. At least not so far.

There were three days of rain. Then the rain became a deluge and Beverly Hills became a disaster area. There was talk of evàcuating the bungalows, and Agnès prepared a little refugee bundle in case Alpine Drive was flooded. Splendid houses that seemed made of marble melted away in a night when they stood in the path of the torrent that gushed down from the hills.

The television screen was full of people of different sects announcing the Apocalypse. Some said it was their punishment for not having sufficiently loved the Lord; others said it was their chastisement for not allowing the free sale of marijuana; others, the majority, said that's the price we pay for the war in Vietnam.

And then the sun came back.

This brings to a close the tales of my different Hollywoods. I liked them all. They seem to have returned my affection. No little number 28 in my passport will make me say anything else.

Yesterday, March 7, 1976, Rome, France, Hollywood, and the world wept at the death of Luchino Visconti. And I remembered the last time we had all laughed together— he, Montand, and I. It was in America, and he had just shown us his passport. We had compared our number 28's. . . .

I cherish the idea that it was the legendary Gary Cooper who asked me to dance on New Year's Eve 1960, in a legendary restaurant that no longer exists. I cherish the vanishing memories of Spencer Tracy's laugh. I loved seeing Paul Newman begin to be Paul Newman, and not another Marlon Brando. I loved my meeting with a beginner named Jack Nicholson. And I loved enormously a Hollywood that gave Jane Fonda an Oscar in 1972. I particularly loved it when my Paris newspaper showed her film photo next to a news picture in which she was standing with Angela Davis, and another showing her on Alcatraz with the Indians. They had occupied that rock which was no longer a jail: that jail we refused to examine through the telescope, much to our San Francisco taxi driver's contempt, way back in 1959.

Chapter 13

A few years ago, in a street in Courbevoie, I was carefully returning to my start marks for a final technical runthrough. We were filming the location sequence of *Le Chat*, directed by Granier-Deferre, with Jean Gabin. *Les Diaboliques* had been shown on television the evening before. Two gentlemen who were hanging around watching sidled up to me wearing big smiles: "Hello, Simone. How are you, Simone? We saw you last night on television.... You aren't getting any younger."

I said, "Ah, no!" and I smiled. I refrained from asking, "And you, are you getting any younger?" Nor did I ask them whether they would have said the same thing to their cousin who had been abroad, and returned now twenty years later. It seems to me that the standard phrase in this case is: "It's incredible. You haven't changed a bit."

After forty—come on, let's say forty-five—you can take one of two routes: Either you can cling to parts that keep you looking thirty-five or thirty-six as long as possible, or you can be like everybody else, and quietly accept the idea that forty-five puts you on the road to forty-six rather than forty-four.

If you want to hang on to the characters that moved,

fascinated, enchanted, or enthralled those ex-adolescents who are now already balding a bit, and who besiege you with phrases like: "Oh, you just can't imagine how much in love I was with you when I was a schoolboy," then it's your turn to play . . . but play what?

If you've decided to be like everyone else—like their cousins, their mothers, their concierges, their family doctors, their schoolmates, their legitimate wives—then again it's your turn to play. Play with everything you've got. Be prepared to disappoint them when there are no carefully filtered close-ups to hide the lines and the bags under your eyes, which are so like their own.

Generally they can't afford to go off to the plastic surgeons. We can. I think it's the moment when we choose to go or not to go that determines those wonderful gifts from life and miracles and continuing chances I was talking about earlier.

I chose not to go. I didn't go because I've never been a star. Hordes of young girls never copied my hairdos or the way I talk or the way I dress. I have, therefore, never had to go through the stress of perpetuating an image that's often the equivalent of one particular song that forever freezes a precise moment of one's youth. I've mythologized too much myself not to know what I'm talking about.

It's very hard to be a star. It's very hard to be a star in whom people see diminishing talent only because she has become a star. They seem to forget that without initial talent she would never have become a star. It's very hard to remain a star. And it must be horrible to stop being one.

It's very easy to go on functioning at the same rhythm as your contemporaries; to mature together with them, and to age with them.

And it's miraculous when life brings you parts that seem to grow better each year; stronger, laden with the memories and personal experiences that have put those lines on your face. They are the scars of the laughter, the tears, the questions, the astonishments, and the certainties that are also those of your contemporaries.

For most women, those scars are the enemy. They try to track them down, turn them away, erase them. How well I understand them! One doesn't fraternize with the enemy when the enemy brings you nothing you can use.

For the stars, those scars are killers; they creep stealthily in prior to the expulsion from the garden: the garden of dreams. They have to go, for fear they will erase those dreams that they inspired for a few years. It's sometimes caused by self-love, but often it's out of respect and gratitude to the art of cinema for giving them the millions of anonymous lovers the cinema laid at their feet, and whom they don't want to disenchant.

(At the end of *Chéri*, Léa is sad when Chéri intrudes. She is in her fifties. He has returned without warning after years of separation. Léa has changed. Chéri wouldn't have noticed the change had he been there. But he hadn't. So he finds her changed.)

For people like me, who never had the push or the taste or the courage to do a star's job, those scars have been allies, or possibly even alibis.

The two gentlemen in Courbevoie were a kind of Chéri, if they had lost track of me since *Les Diaboliques*. These jokers had followed me to deliver their carefully thought out punch line rather than to really say something to me.

And yet they did say something to me, something I found reassuring. Okay; I hadn't gotten any younger—but I was still there! I was a continuation of that young, skinny citizen of Thebes who had chanted "Jocasta, the Queen Jocasta, is dead..." before she got fired and marched up the Rue des Mathurins wearing her pair of rented theatrical Spartan sandals, formerly allocated—so it was said—to Jean Gabin–Pontius Pilate, who was now my husband in *Le Chat*....

I was, I am, I will be, I hope, somebody who continues to wear disguises. I am like an actress in a repertory company playing different parts on different days, pleased and amazed that they are still offered.

When I talk about the lines on my face as allies or alibis, I mean that the aging process has helped me pass through a number of tollgates and that my lack of corporal discipline has furnished me with alibis.

That's a question Maurice Pons probably wouldn't have dared ask me during the course of our lengthy conversation. He probably wouldn't have dared ask me the following question either, to which I can reply because I'm asking the question myself: Does one act better after one has aged?

Well, one doesn't act better: One doesn't act anymore. One is. The compliments you get from people who speak about "the courage to show oneself in an unflattering aspect" are just pious remarks. It isn't courage; it's a form of pride, possibly vanity, to show yourself as you really are in order to better serve the character that has been offered you as a gift.

Thank you, François Leterrier, for *Les Mauvais Coups*. Thank you, René Clément, for *Le Jour et l'Heure*. Thank you, Stanley Kramer, for *Ship of Fools*. Thank you, Costa-Gavras, for *Compartiment Tueurs*. Thank you, Sidney Lumet, for *Call from the Dead* and *The Seagull*. Thank you, Jean-Pierre Melville, for *L'Armée des Ombres*. Thank you, Granier-Deferre, for *Le Chat* and *La Veuve Couderc*. Thank you, René Allio, for *Rude Journée pour la Reine*. Thank you, Patrice Chereau, for *La Chair de l'Orchidée*. Thank you, Alain Corneau, for *Police Python*. Thank you for the gift of all those women with whom I was able to pass chronologically and quietly from the "still loving beloved" to one "still capable of being in love" . . . in order now to end up among the grandmothers. Thank you for offering the part of an "offbeat" character, a bourgeoise, a revolutionary, a dud actress, a spy from the Eastern bloc, a Gaullist resistance fighter, an alcoholic cripple, a peasant from Dijon, an Aubervilliers cleaning woman, a pitiful Lady Vamos, and an omnipotent paralytic.

You'd think it was a list in a folder left at a theatrical

agency in the hope of landing you a job. But it's really only a sampler—the parts I've played that I'm proud of. There are others. . . .

In 1962 I took great pleasure in translating Lillian Hellman's *The Little Foxes. The Little Foxes* was written in 1939, but the action takes place soon after the war of secession, before the turn of the century.

The plays actually written around 1900—Ibsen, Chekhov, Strindberg, Becque—are not dated today. Some people find them a bit dusty, but they forget that these were avant-garde plays when they were written. They deal with the preoccupations of their time, preoccupations that doubtlessly belong to the past, but perhaps that's due to those authors, who lived with their time and caused things to change. These plays show things as they were; they witness their epoch.

The action of *The Little Foxes*, which takes place before 1900, was written in 1939 by an author who introduces the preoccupations of a liberal American of the thirties into her flashbacks. She tells about Southerners and Northerners at the beginning of their lives together. It's a kind of *Gone with the Wind* in reverse. It's *Gone with the Wind* seen by someone who remembers that her grandparents owned, bought, and sold slaves, and that fraternization with the Yankees could be profitable. Her heroine isn't a touching Scarlett; she's the abominable Regina. *The Little Foxes* is the demythologizing of the Gallant South (cf. *Strange Fruit*).

I still think today that everything in *The Little Foxes* speaks to Americans in a language which concerns them. There is still a South and a North, Alabama and Little Rock, Watergate and Lockheed, ITT and Dallas.

In France in 1962 *The Little Foxes* was greeted as a good but dated melodrama. It was considered a play by Mirbeau, written after the time of Mirbeau.°

°Octave Mirbeau, nineteenth-century playwright and novelist, who wrote *Diary of a Chambermaid* and *Business Is Business*.

I was wrong to play the part of Regina myself. I had a way of listening to the lines that had nothing to do with the way one should look at another actor when he speaks to a character you're playing. I was listening to and watching over the text. I didn't want them to spoil my translation.

But we were right to put on *The Little Foxes*. Every evening for six months, Flon, Bozzufi, Sabatier, Pellegrin, Josée Steiner, Claude Berri, Jean Michaud, Gordon Heath, and Darling were happy to be together. And sad to separate at the end of six months.

Not long ago I read a book by Lillian Hellman; a superb book: *Pentimento*. In it she tells stories that are true and overwhelming in their daily banality, and consequently they are crammed with the things that, when all is said and done, make up life. Reading that book, I had decided to forget her arrival the day before the opening of *The Little Foxes*. In *Pentimento* I met again the woman I respect and love. The woman who told McCarthy to go to hell. The woman who asked us not to make too much noise, the evening we dined with her in New York, because there was a sick man upstairs: Dashiell Hammett, who was dying.

Reading *Pentimento*, which is an autobiography, I saw myself in my mind's eye seated in those crimson velvet armchairs among her splendid mahogany pieces of furniture. I heard her laughter—a bit hoarse, marvelously warm, or formidably wicked when she was dealing with the wicked. I erased the image left in my mind of that opening night in Paris, which was also the day after her arrival from New York.

I was reading happily along, when suddenly I came upon a few pages that were meant for me. Unfortunately, I don't have a copy of the book at hand, which is a pity, because I would have liked to quote directly. In essence, she said that I am a charming film actress, but that I was a lame Regina in the Paris production of *The Little Foxes*. All right, I can take that. She goes on to say that the aforementioned production was the worst she had ever suffered, and God knows she had seen some awful performances of her masterpiece. Well, I could accept that too, since that's exactly what she told the whole cast, with a few added personal comments for several among us, comments I had to translate to my dear workmates, as Miss Hellman doesn't speak a word of French. Flon, Sabatier, and Berri got good marks, whereas Bozzufi suffered from one great defect—he didn't look like "Uncle Benjamin," who was the author's uncle and who had been the model for the character of horrible Ben, brother of the abominable Regina. Bozzu asked me to please translate that he was very sorry, he'd never met Uncle Benjamin.... Pierre Mondy's stage direction and Jean-Marie Simon's sets and, generally speaking, the entire enterprise were qualified as "bad, bad, bad...." She says all this in *Pentimento*. It doesn't make pleasant reading, but after all, that's exactly what she said that evening. She is perfectly entitled to dig around in her memory and tell the world about the atrocious pain she endured on that evening in December 1962 in Paris (France). They had killed her child. If I remember rightly, she also talked about the translation. Was it good or bad? Whatever she thought of my translation, it had been carefully examined by three specialists, all personally chosen by Miss Hellman. One of them was Professor Guicharnaud, holder of the chair of drama at Yale University. He had liked it. He and I became great friends after that, but that's another story.

Let me remind you again that all this happened the day before opening night. We had run through the play for her; for her alone. From the moment when we first went into rehearsal I had written asking her to come to Paris, even if she left for New York again immediately thereafter. She couldn't, she said. She had complete confidence in us. Good.

About two weeks before the opening we again asked her to come. She couldn't, but she had wholehearted confidence in us. Very good.

The afternoon we ran through the play with her, at the end of which everything was "bad, bad, bad," was the day after her arrival from New York. The cast met the author only twenty-four hours before they were to face the critics and the audience. That's a bit late to make changes. Caught between despair at having taken the wrong road, and nervous giggles that our recent cold verbal shower provoked in all of us, we took Miss Hellman out to eat the first sea urchins of her life at Dreher, opposite the Théâtre Sarah-Bernhardt. My friends, to whom I had exalted the great human qualities of this woman whom I admire, let fly a bunch of remarks which went from "I must say she's cute, your pal Lilly," to "Mischievous, don't you think?" Miss Hellman discovered that she liked the iodine taste of sea urchins. I translated to my friends that she liked them. "Good. That means she didn't come to Paris for nothing," was the reply. I decided it might not be the moment for a faithful translation. Miss Hellman coughed. "Oh, my God, if she gets sick on us.". . . That, too, provoked mad, mad laughter, such as only schoolchildren or actors exhausted by overwork, stage fright, and real anguish can indulge in—because tomorrow it's win or lose. Then Miss Hellman asked us where she could buy some pretty clothes; she hadn't been to Paris for such a long time. That did it! Sea urchins taste of iodine, but they became saltier and saltier as tears of laughter fell into those split porcupines. Answers ran from "I know a good mail-order house, but you have to write" to "I have a cousin who's in the garment business, but he's just gone to jail." I admit that's not high humor, but it was good to be able to laugh. Although we were very sad. . . . After the sea urchins, we went back to the theater and re-re-re-rehearsed. Miss Hellman, suffering from jet lag, went home to the Crillon to lie down.

I don't suppose I would ever have told this story if I hadn't read *Pentimento*. In *Pentimento*, Miss Hellman remembers herself in Paris a good two or three weeks before the opening (I really should find the book to check on her exact words). Disgusted by what she had seen at the Théâtre Sarah-Bernhardt and discouraged by our various incapacities to understand her legitimate grievances, she preferred purely and simply to retire and enjoy the comforting presence of an old friend, who took her out for walks and consoled her, since none of us could understand her.

Pentimento fell from my hands. I did finish it, but from then on every line, however beautiful, seemed suspect to me. Does one really forget? Or does one arrange? Or does one contrive? It's a question I'll soon be having to ask myself. And perhaps others will ask me. It's a question I'm asking Lillian Hellman today. Not Miss Hellman, as I've taken to calling her in my wicked but true story. Lillian, you know perfectly well that you arrived only the day before the opening. I don't know whether you'll read this book; it hasn't been written to settle old scores. Perhaps I should have written you a letter after I read *Pentimento*. I didn't do it. At the time it didn't seem that important. Today, since all this is a matter of my memory, I don't see why I shouldn't confront mine with yours. . . .

Then there's the work I didn't accomplish, and I've got nothing to boast about.

There's one part especially that I didn't accomplish, in both senses of the word, and that's Bouboulina in *Zorba the Greek*, Michael Cacoyannis's film.

I've just talked serenely about aging, and its advantages after a certain point. Twelve years ago I was just precisely at that point, the moment of decision. I was already forty-three years old. But I was only forty-three years old. And for this part I had agreed to add fifteen years to mine. I honestly tried. I had all sorts of props: a false derrière and false sagging breasts and cotton inside my cheeks and a fake gold tooth, as well as a plastic wart and ridiculously frizzy hair that Alex curled painstakingly. Even my eyebrows were replaced with some moth-eaten little lines by Monique (it was very tough for my two old makeup friends, who'd always done their best to improve me). I swear I tried. I worked for a few days, and I would have been all right if a small incident hadn't come along that changed everything.

378

The young designer suggested that there be a photograph of the young Bouboulina to be placed artfully on the set. Preparations for that photograph took all morning. Alex and Monique hummed as they went about their jobs, reconstituting the coiffure of *Casque d'Or*. The photographer was a genius, and there appeared one of the best series of portraits of me ever to come out of the developing bath. I was no longer forty-three years old; I had lost ten years....

I didn't have the guts to go on. The next morning I no longer had the heart for my work. I didn't want to be poor Bouboulina anymore; I left her on the beach in Crete. She was adopted by Lila Kedrova, who was more courageous than I was, and who was rewarded with an Oscar for the best supporting actress the following year. I wasn't even punished for my cowardice; Michael wasn't angry at me. The day before I left, he, Irene Papas, Anthony Quinn, Alan Bates, and the whole company broke glasses together as you see it done in films glorifying Greek folklore.

But I have something else to tell apropos of Greek folklore, or should I say Greek mythology?

A few days before I left for Crete, I was visited in Paris by a very young correspondent from an Athens newspaper, who wanted to know what had led me to go play Bouboulina. With a vanity of which I'm still ashamed today, I answered no to what I think was the first question he asked: "Doesn't it bother you to make yourself look older than you are?" Then I answered his other questions, most of which were of the kind: Do you prefer the theater or films? How does it work when both people in a couple are actors? There were about two dozen of the usual questions. The young man was very timid, and he seemed surprised by the absence of gold shoes on my feet, and by the general sparseness of the "caravan." It was obvious that he hadn't expected show-biz people to be like this. Nevertheless, he noticed everything, and I had the proof of it when I arrived in Athens a little while later. In any case, he had especially noticed and carefully examined the mirror over my mantel, that same mirror Aragon liked to parade in front of when he still came to our house. Wedged between the mirror and the mahogany frame there are a certain number of souvenirs and photographs, without which the fireplace would probably gain in neatness but lose in warmth.

Among those photographs stuck in the mirror there's one, about the size of a passport photograph, that has been there since 1953. It's of a very handsome young man, smiling and holding a carnation. Under the face is a caption: "Glory to the heroes of Athens."

Millions of copies of this photograph were made at the time Beloyannis and his comrades were killed. They were all heroes of Greek wartime resistance, and they were picked up by the monarchist police at the beginning of the cold war. Millions of people throughout the world had worn this little photograph on their lapels during the rigged trial, after which Beloyannis and his friends were secretly executed, standing against a wall starkly outlined in the beams of Dodge truck headlights. Picasso made a sketch of this photograph. It is called for eternity *L'Homme à l'Oeillet* (The Man with the Carnation).

Yael Dayan, Cacoyannis's assistant and the daughter of the Israeli general, was waiting for me at the airport in Athens. There was also the French cultural attaché, a representative of Twentieth Century-Fox, and about twenty journalists. Things were being done in style for the future ex-Bouboulina. A press conference had been prepared in the VIP lounge. A young man whose face seemed strangely familiar joined the group; it was Costa's brother, come to greet me on the soil my pal had decided to leave to his ancestors.

There were all the expected questions: "Have you read all the works of Kazantzakis?" "Is this your first trip to Greece?" Then a silence. Finally a tall man dressed in a battered Burberry slowly asked: "We have read in a Greek newspaper that you have on your mantel the portrait of a Greek hero. Can you tell us who that is?"

If you arrive in Greece in 1964 for the first time in your life, having firmly decided not to get mixed up in things that are none of your business, and you're made to pronounce the name Beloyannis just as soon as you step off the plane, it's about as diplomatic as arriving in New York for the first time ten years earlier, and when they ask you, "Do you know any famous Americans?" you reply, "Yes, the Rosenbergs." Or, if the same question were asked in Moscow, earlier still, you reply, "I only know one Russian, and that's Leon Davidovich Trotsky."

Some of the same temptations crossed my mind as on the day I was asked to sign the Manifesto of 121. A Greek hero? No, I really couldn't remember. . . . Oh, yes. I have a beautiful reproduction of a bust of Achilles. . . . There was a long patch of silence. They looked at me. I looked at them. About half the eyes there pleaded for my reply, and the other half dared me to give it. Perhaps if Costa's brother hadn't been there, I would simply have said, "No, I don't know what you mean." But in front of a witness who could squeal, I couldn't. So I said, "Yes, there is a photograph of a Greek hero over our fireplace. I could tell you that he's a mythological hero, but I won't. It's the photograph of a man named Beloyannis."

No one wrote a word on his pad. They all looked at me. They didn't look at each other. The lady from the embassy looked at her shoes, and the man from Fox, to whom the name meant nothing but who realized something serious was going on, looked questioningly at Yael Dayan.

Then the man in the Burberry plucked up his courage and asked me a second question: "Can you tell us why you keep this photograph?"

I had never asked myself the question. I told him so. But now that he was asking me, it appeared evident to me that a photograph showing a very handsome young man, smiling, holding a carnation to his lips at the moment they're about to tell him that he's been condemned to death, and who later is assassinated, is not an object one wants to throw in the wastepaper basket. One keeps it.

Maybe he had hoped for something better, something stronger, a declaration commemorating "Comrade Beloyannis, wept over by Communists throughout the world." But he had to make do with my reply; it was the only truth I could give him. The press conference ended rapidly.

The little local plane that flies from Athens to Crete left only the next morning. Yael, a bit worried, made her way through all the newspapers. No one had dared to print the name of Beloyannis, but all the newspapers mentioned the incident. The right-wing papers spoke about justice having been done a few years earlier, and the left-wing papers talked about heroes, and especially they talked about carnations.

The two of us, Yael and I, were waiting to board the plane. Two very young girls came toward me. Each had a carnation in her hand. They gave them to me, silently.

Despite the carnations, the little plane didn't crash.

In the Crete airport a tall black silhouette was waiting to take the same plane in the opposite direction. It was Mikis Theodorakis. He said, "Thank you, thank you, thank you." Word had spread quickly from Athens to Crete.

I was terrified that Cacoyannis would be angry. He wanted to make his film in peace and quiet. He would have preferred the press conference to deal with Zorba, and not controversial past history. Yael was my witness; I hadn't brought up the subject. Cacoyannis believed us, but advised me in the future to take inventory of the souvenirs exposed on my mantelpiece before allowing into my house correspondents of a country where I was about to make a film. I didn't promise him that I would.

I never saw that shy young man again. If he ever returned to his homeland, I hope nothing happened to him after the colonels took over in 1967.

I never read the message that he obviously wanted to circulate in what appeared to be a perfectly benign interview. Nor do I know when he had the time to examine my mirror so closely. Perhaps it was when I was called to the telephone, or when I went to the kitchen to get us something to drink. The photograph is so small that he must have recognized it rather than discovered it.

In Z, when Lambrakis-Montand takes over the little office of the committee, or perhaps when he is brought in after having been hit on the back of the head—I can't remember which—there is an enormous portrait on the wall. It is an enlargement of the little photograph I lent to Costa, blown up ten thousand times. He returned it to me unharmed, and while it was out of the house, he lent me a reproduction of L'Homme à l'Oeillet by Pablo Picasso.

If young Greeks come to lay carnations in the square where Lambrakis is killed in Z (filmed in 1968), it's because a young writer, Vassili Vassilikos, read the newspapers in 1964. So, naturally, he took up the theme of Beloyannis's carnation when he decided to tell the story of Lambrakis in his book Z. And of course there are carnations in the film. Vassili himself told me about it. Perhaps one day someone will tell about the death of Panaghoulis. . . .

If Vassili hadn't by chance been in Rome during the colonels' *putsch*, the manuscript of Z, not yet translated from the Greek, wouldn't have landed in the hands of Costa. . . .

If Costa and Semprun hadn't gone to work immediately to make a superb scenario from that superb book, which all the French producers had refused, so as not to get in bad with the Americans. . . .

If the actor Jacques Perrin hadn't decided to become a producer, on a share basis of the box-office takings of all the people who worked on the film. . . .

If all these people hadn't been full of mutual confidence, as opposed to and against the advice of all the officials of the film industry, Z would never have become a film.

And although it's surely not Z that overthrew the colonels' regime, it still didn't do much to improve their image around the world.

Certainly not in America, where its allusion to the role the CIA played in the death of Lambrakis obviously didn't

383

shock people as much as it had the French producers. In 1969, Z received two Oscars: one for the editing and one for the best foreign film of the year....

Sorry, William Shakespeare, I won't do it again.

I don't want to brag, but I think I've probably sweated more blood working on the part of Lady Macbeth than anyone else in the world—which still didn't prevent my stunt from misfiring completely.

In the first place, it wasn't my stunt. The whole thing was amicably cooked up in London in 1966 by friends who wanted to do me a good turn. Alec Guinness wanted to play Macbeth again, which was an event quite sufficient in itself. Sir Alec, the great film star, wanted to return to the classics in a dusted-off, unclassical production. My lords, ladies and gentlemen, Shakespeare lovers the world over: You see this announced in the press, and immediately you book seats at the Royal Court Theatre two months in advance. When, a few days later, my lords, ladies, gents, Shakespeare lovers, etc., read that Lady Macbeth is to be played by Casque d'Or Alice Aisgill, you may scratch your heads and wonder why. Nonetheless, you book those precious Royal Court Theatre seats, possibly in the same frame of mind as you'd get tickets for a royal charity ball in which a trapeze act, to be performed in the flies without a net by a blues singer, is billed.

It still happens to me today that I wake up of a morning and say to myself: "Great! This evening I don't have to play Lady Macbeth!"

An unaccomplished trapeze artist may fall. Some have fallen, and have required years of physical therapy to recover from having tried to prove for one evening that they could spread out from their own branch and, with the speed of light, learn something which someone else had been studying from the cradle on. Many of them don't fall, fortunately. They heave a great sigh of relief as they return to the sawdust of that unfamiliar circus ring.

I've never had the courage to learn tightrope walking or a wild-animal act, a magician's routine, how to leap through a flaming hoop, roller skate, or ride a bicycle you can take apart. They are definitely not up my alley! So what on earth—or in heaven—possessed me to even begin to suspect that I would be able to play (for a charity ball that was to drag on for a full month of an "exceptional run") Lady Macbeth when I was incapable of reproducing the Shakespearean accents they had every right to expect to hear?

"Nou pahtim cink sans may pah un prron ramphor
      Nou nou vim troa milan arrivan topor"*
wouldn't sound right to a Frenchman's ear, even if Laurence Olivier made a special trip to Paris to offer us his personal version of Rodrique. But this phenomenon will never happen, I know, because he told me so with much gentleness and humor the day after our opening.

I've probably exaggerated in the example I've just given. It's actually quite tolerable, my little French accent in English; some even find it charming. Only, unfortunately, speaking English quite fluently doesn't mean that you can speak Shakespeare, sing Shakespeare, scan Shakespeare's rhythms—in short, act Shakespeare. Even if someone has invited you to participate in a nonconformist and dusted-off production like that at the Royal Court.

Nevertheless, I took the thing very seriously indeed. I bought six different editions of *Macbeth* and retired to Autheuil to study my text for two months before rehearsals began. Then there would be two months of rehearsal in London before the opening night of that much heralded series of thirty-one special performances.

Six different editions...that was a foreigner's idea to begin with. No Anglo-Saxon actress would ever have taken it into her mind to read and compare all those texts. The

*Nous partîmes cinq cents mais par prompt renfort.
Nous nous rîmes trois mille en arrivant au port.*

385

only result of doing it was to still further deepen the mysteries that all good Shakespeareans have decided to put aside or ignore or treasure, and for good reason.

In one edition a speech of Lady Macbeth would end with a question mark, in another it would be between quotation marks, and a third would simply end with a period. In all of them, however, it was quite clear that the Macbeths had never had a child, and yet at a certain moment (Act I, Scene 7, if you want real pinpoint precision), Lady M. goes on about this babe from whose boneless gums she would have plucked her nipple! Mystery, mystery! So, having retired to the heart of Normandy, I was trying to solve these riddles. I was having a great time. My friends who innocently dropped in to say hello were lured into a terrible trap from which there was no escape. They were handed one of the six editions and made to listen to me "recite." As there were quite a few difficult lines, it was a little like playing "the game." Every evening during that month of terrifying "exceptional" performances, when it came time to say "Nor place, nor time," the beautiful face of my friend François Arnoul would appear before me, her finger on her wrist watch to remind me of the word "time," which I had such trouble memorizing.

With my lines learned by heart, I appeared at the first reading. I was very proud of my "by heart." Unfortunately, all my bad habits were already locked in place. I thought I had the rhythm right, but it was all wrong. I had done almost everything upside down. It's only today that I fully realize to what extent your pride in trying to take a flying leap into the unknown can make you forget everything that your natural instinct has taught you ever since you began acting.

For two months, day after day, I had slid imperceptibly into the traps waylaying bad actors. If you know all the words and never really think about the reasons that have made your character say what he or she does, you fall into that trap. It was a perfect illustration justifying the phrase already quoted: "Heavens, you must have a marvelous memory."

I don't mean to say that I didn't have ideas about the character of Lady M., nor do I mean to say that I hadn't come to understand her as I read my six different texts. I'd even go so far as to say that I psychoanalyzed her, followed her scent, and took her apart and put her back together again. Only, you see, the important thing was "knowing the lines." There'd be time enough later to find out why she said them.

Our director, William Gatskill, Alec Guinness, and the whole cast did everything they could to help me during those two months of rehearsal. They tried to rid me of the bad habits I had firmly contracted while I thought I was preparing myself piously to serve Shakespeare. I've often thought since that they must have been utterly nonplused after that first read-through. Maybe they met in the pub next door and told each other that it would turn out all right; I'd get the hang of that lovely language. After all, there were still two months. . . .

At the end of the first week I thought I had improved. They thought so too; at least that's what they said. It's probably at that moment (when it still wasn't too late) that less kindly people would have politely asked me to go home. It would have been easy to find an excuse for the press and the booking office. There are always those strange viruses that actors catch while waiting in the wings, which prevent them from honoring their contracts. I think I would have been perfectly capable of finding answers to the questions that would have been asked if they had decided to drop me. "No," I would have said, "I'm not capable of doing Lady Macbeth. Please excuse me; anyone can make a mistake."

When these things happen to a beginner, they're cruel. But when they happen to someone who, as they say, has a reputation, they're bitter but you get over them.

But since my friends were kind, if the idea of booting me out had ever crossed their minds, they suppressed it. Or perhaps they got so used to my flaws that they stopped noticing them—or possibly they even liked them? That's what's called a collective aberration. It's the great invisible monster curled up in the dress circle of the empty theater in which one rehearses in a euphoric condition. In order to tack down the monster and kill him, often the eye and ear of an outsider is sufficient, but one who has real affection for the cast—a family friend. It has to be someone who isn't afraid of being unpopular when he tells the truth.

"Whoa, there! Stop this massacre, friends! You've goofed badly."

But no one came to stop the massacre while there was still time. Those who saw our last rehearsals probably thought that it was too late to pull the alarm cord. Montand came for two days while there was still time—it was two weeks before opening night. His criticism was pertinent, but I decided to ignore it, sure as I was of my Anglo-Saxon accomplishments.

It was a Lady M. frozen stiff with stage fright but sure that she had been right to persist who made her entry onstage that first night. By the next day she was a poor creature who would have given millions to be elsewhere. With one or two exceptions, the entire press detested the whole production. The critics were cruel to Gatskill, whose nonconformist courage had shocked them. They were not gentle with Alec, whose interpretations had often surprised them. And as far as I was concerned, they were the worst one could dream of. They weren't cruel, they weren't hurtful, they were clearly miserable. They were terribly sorry. They were sorry, they said, because they liked me so much. But honestly...! I was impossible, inaudible, unbearable. Yet some of them must have understood me. They were the ones who said they had suffered intensely listening to me suffer with those words. They had pitied me. But that's generally not the purpose in the mind of an actress lady out to amaze people by the force of her cold determination.

The day after the opening I was faced with thirty evenings, a century, during which I was to appear and be judged every evening, since the theater had been sold clean out since the announcement of the good news of Shakespeare at the Royal Court.

I have said that I would have given millions to be elsewhere. This is probably the moment for me to point out that Alec and I were paid, during the run of that play, at the popular-theater rate: seven pounds a day. But I know I would have tried to find those millions the next day, and the day after that, and all those thirty days, in order not to have to set foot on that stage in front of all those people who already knew that I wouldn't be able to make it, but who were there because they had reserved their tickets in advance. They were there, and I could see them mouthing my lines along with me, and better than I could. Sometimes, though, there were some Japanese doing "London by Night." I didn't seem to bother them.

The cast was marvelously kind to me. They would see me each evening trembling with fear before my first entrance onstage, letter in hand. That letter, which Lady Macbeth reads to the audience because it's a résumé of the preceding action and a premonition of the crimes to come, should be read with the contained passion and icy-cold calm of a totally resolute woman. That's difficult when the paper is shaking in your hand as though it were a morning newspaper held on a bumpy bus.

On the third evening the last reviews had fallen before mine eyes—or rather on my head—just before I went onstage. There wasn't a reason in the world, I thought, that everyone in the audience hadn't read them too. And so it happened that during my first scene with Alec Guinness, during my third or fourth speech, I suddenly stopped. He caught on and saved me. He slid in, "If we should fail . . ." which comes much later in the scene. He used it to save his friend, who was in the process of drowning, having "dried up." It helped me to go on, and since we were playing to an audience of connoisseurs, they applauded. When the time came for him to repeat "If we should fail," this time in context, they applauded again.

I must have made some improvement during those four weeks. And, as it sometimes happens when the thrashing is unmerciful, we even had our defenders—and our fans.

But still, Will Shakespeare, I swear I'll never do it again.

I've kept a keen memory of that month of October 1966, a memory of great cold, the cold chill to the marrow caused by fear.

It's accompanied by a memory of great warmth. The warmth of my workmates, and the warmth of my pals in real life. Jack Clayton, Haya Harareet, Betsy Blair, Karel Reisz, Gordon Jackson, Michael Truman, Sean Connery, Dirk Bogarde, the Loseys. They comforted me, fed me in their homes, and made me laugh.

I also see myself back in my little apartment in the Savoy. The staff had noticed that Lady M. was less joyful than Alice Aisgill had been. They, too, read the newspapers.

And as I see that hotel apartment, I also see my cousin from Bratislava....

Chapter 14

IT was the questions Maurice Pons asked me over that six-day interrogation that awoke my memory. And it was in reading through the typescripts of those recorded tapes a few weeks later that I realized how often my answers had come out too pat, too fast, as they do in the normal flow of conversation, and how often I'd neglected replying to the essential. That's why, rightly or wrongly, I installed myself at my desk; why, alone and with time for thought, I tried to speak onto paper.

To think deeply or reflect doesn't imply you're going to pay extra attention to what you're about to say as a measure of prudence or diplomacy. Reflection is the exact opposite of conversation. It's directing the question to yourself, and sometimes adding other questions—those Maurice Pons didn't ask because he's not an inquisitor.

To speak about *The Confession (L'Aveu)* I don't need that sort of reflection, so I'd like to go back to the taped conversation. Come back, Maurice; I'm a bit lonely. Even if I seem to be covering already familiar ground, I'd still like to keep some of the freshness of those answers as they came out, and as I think they would come out again if the same questions were asked.

Question: As we talk about your films, I have the feeling that you always exercise a choice. You say you like to be the one who is chosen, maintaining, however, the right of refusal. But your films seem to follow along a line of "commitment."

Simone Signoret: I would be incapable of lending my face, my eyes, my voice—in other words, myself—to an enterprise that's contrary to my most profound convictions. I'm quite capable of playing a Gestapo spy in an antifascist film. But I would be incapable of playing an admirable mother or a delightful lover in a fascist film. I can't do it and I've never done it.

Question: You mean that you choose the enterprise rather than the character?

Simone Signoret: I'll say it again: I don't choose anything; I am chosen. There are many parts I would have loved to accept, but they weren't offered to me. I've simply always been free *not* to do things, *not* to accept. Prévert taught me that.

Question: There are the films you made that imply commitment on your part; I'm thinking of *The Confession*, which you made in 1969.

Simone Signoret: Yes, that was a problem for all of us. *L'Aveu*, the book by Artur London, had just been published. For many Communists and people of the left in our generation it represented an overwhelming and chilling moment. The book first appeared in Czechoslovakia. The Czech Communist party allowed the book to be published; it wanted it to be published. So in the beginning, the film was planned as a Franco-Czechoslovak coproduction. But that didn't last long; not only were the Czechs unable to make the film, but it became impossible for them to read London's book.

It was a heavy responsibility for us to make the film, and we almost abandoned the project. But there are things that happened that you have to know in order to understand the problem: London was rehabilitated in 1967. They gave him back his decorations and everything they had taken away from him at the time of his trial—his rigged trial. But one thing they never gave back to him was his lungs; all he had left was one-sixteenth of a lung. They didn't give him back his ability to sleep, either. So what they gave back to him was a kind of restricted life....

And then suddenly, in 1969, they started taking everything away once again. They decided that he couldn't be a Czech citizen anymore, and they began writing about him again, in Czechoslovakia, with the same lies and calumnies that they had used during his rigged trial. We really thought it was too much, and the whole thing touched us closely because we had lived that whole period and we were, to a certain extent, caught up in it. You may remember that famous sentence of Éluard's: "I've got too much to do with the innocent proclaiming their innocence to spend time on the guilty asserting their guilt." He was talking about the Slansky trial, and we both signed that declaration. I can still see that hotel room in Angers—Montand was there on tour—when Jaeger phoned us from Paris and asked us to sign. That's one of the things that became very hard to live with afterward.

The Confession is an anti-Stalinist film. At the end of the film you see tanks in the streets of Prague. They are not the fruit of the director's imagination; they're newsreel extracts. At one point you read on the screen: "Lenin, wake up! They have gone mad!" That isn't an inspiration the scriptwriter had one day; it's the translation of an inscription seen in the streets of Prague.

Montand talks very well about *The Confession*; much better than I do. I can't think of anyone who could have played the character of London as he did. You had to be absolutely torn apart, internally, as he was. He, too, had signed Éluard's text at the time. You had to feel a very strong measure of guilt in yourself in order to act the part as he did. He lost twenty-five pounds in six weeks so that he would literally be a skeleton. You had to be moved by feelings that are much stronger than those that generally move an actor. You had to know what it really was all about, and be crushed by the thought of all you hadn't known at the time of those crimes.

That's not the case with Costa, who is much younger than we are. But it is the case for Semprun, who spent months in a Nazi concentration camp, and who was the militant in *La Guerre Est Finie*, by Resnais, as played by Montand. He knows exactly what it's all about.

Question: Still, that film had a lot of very differing repercussions. At the time, wasn't there an attempt to bring you back to the fold?

Simone Signoret: Some of the people who speak ill of us may have said, for example, that after *The Confession* our problems with America were over; that they gave us our visas in exchange for that film. Well, I'd like it known that we still don't have American visas. We get temporary visas for a limited stay. If I want to go see friends in Los Angeles, I can't just get up and go, because I have to ask for permission to enter United States territory, which I won't do! Or if my daughter should fall sick there, I can't just go to Orly and take a plane—although any mafioso can take a plane at Kennedy airport and get off in Paris; Americans don't need a visa to come to France.

But to go back to *The Confession*; the film has more impact than the book, I know. It's terrible to see for yourself a dossier growing fatter—on nothing. It's terrible to be there during repeated interrogations that end up fattening that dossier—with no real evidence. It's terrible to see an accused man learning his speeches by heart, speeches he must make during a trial that will end up finding him guilty. That's what the film shows. It was very important to really *show* a rigged trial, wherever it may happen. In *The Crucible* they ask Proctor to sign a paper saying that he's guilty, that he's had relations with the devil, and he signs it. But he tears up his confession at the last moment, saying, "I don't want my children to be the children of a traitor and a renegade." Why can we tell that story, why can we tell how Lambrakis was assassinated because he was an honest man of the left, and not tell how they hanged eleven honest men of the left? Why? Why can we always only denounce in one direction?

In Costa's trilogy, the answer is given. In *State of Siege* he turns a spotlight on how the CIA functions in Latin America. With the help of Allende, the film was made in Chile, before the Allende government fell. Without Allende's help Costa could never have made this film, and no film documentary ever showed the CIA in such a severe and terrifying light. I think one has every right to say exactly what one wants as soon as one is absolutely convinced that the facts one is denouncing are true.

The story of *The Confession* didn't end between us and the Communists. They were the first to see the film. No journalist, no one, saw the film before they did. A private screening was organized one afternoon at the Boulogne studios just for them: Andrieu, Aragon, Daix...I don't know who else came. In *Les Lettres Françaises* the film wasn't panned; far from it. I must add that its editor in chief, Daix, is also London's son-in-law. He married the little girl you see in the film, who has just begun to understand that her father's in prison. François London lived that tragedy as a child, and children have excellent memories. She remembers that she had to be taken out of school because her classmates called her father a traitor. And Daix isn't precisely what you would call a reactionary! He, too, served his time in the Nazi concentration camps because he was a Communist. In that whole group, only Montand and I were never imprisoned in a camp and weren't Communists.

Question: And how did your Communist guests react to that first screening?

Simone Signoret: They didn't tell us. We showed them

the film, and then they left. But Montand got extraordinary mail from militants thanking him: "Thank you; someone had to make this film."

This conversation took place about three years ago. A lot has happened since. There have been revisions in the minds of certain people, apparently. I have no idea how the French Communist party would react today to a film like *The Confession*.

The French Communist party was out to get the people who made *The Confession* at the time they made it. *The Confession*, made in 1969 and shown in 1970, should carry a date, like a painting. Just as what I said to Maurice over three years ago should keep its rather heavy style and its repetitions....

There's the apartment in the Savoy Hotel that made me think of my cousin from Bratislava. And my cousin from Bratislava makes me think of the month of August 1968. While she was crossing the Czech frontier behind the wheel of a car her husband bought "with the price of [his] blood, the money ... of his rehabilitation," I and several others were living a few glorious weeks in the Swedish countryside. In other words, we, the people of *The Seagull*.

I spoke a long while back in this book that goes on forever about the affection that flowed through and around the filming of *Casque d'Or*. I can't go on again in the same vein or people will think it's a routine; yet it was like that. Once upon a time, during the months of August and September 1968, there was a big family living in 1896 with a dacha set at the edge of a lake with real seagulls flying over it. It had a tutor in blue jeans named Sidney Lumet, and a father called Anton Chekhov, who wore our costumes.

There are people who take LSD in order to go on trips. We took Chekhov, and after we had, the world could collapse. We were on vacation from our real world. And we were in the process of telling how the world whose story we were telling would collapse. In *The Seagull* we were telling about how no one loved the person who loved him; what happened if you abandoned your lands and were bored far from Moscow; how you took notes if you were a writer; how to commit suicide and miss, and finally not miss; how you could believe yourself an actress, and how to be an "actress"; and how to let time go by while you did nothing—that is, how to live in czarist Russia in 1896.

The world could collapse. And it was collapsing. In 1968, in Stockholm, we saw on the television screen young Chekhovians inside stationary tanks, visibly unable to understand why girls—and they, too, were characters out of Chekhov—were trying to explain to them that they had no business being in Prague.

There were groups of young black and white Americans wandering around Stockholm. There were American deserters. They, too, appeared on television.

We watched the TV news and listened to the Swedish commentators. It was before dinner. We remarked a bit on the pictures, in English. Not for very long. We wanted to return quickly to our own world; we didn't want to be disturbed. Absolutely chaste passions had come to make us indispensable to one another. We had all lived under the same roof; we had all shared the same bread and salt at every meal for two months. As the countdown approached, toward the end of the filming, we were in the process of going completely mad with shared tenderness and mutual comprehension. We didn't make love together, but we kissed, we held hands, we were becoming Russified as fast as we could. We never wanted to leave one another. And actually, we never had. We, the people of *The Seagull*, can call one another at any hour of the day or night, from one continent to another, and get a reply.

Our beloved *Seagull* took only a trial flight in Paris in a little art cinema (as if the names of Sidney Lumet, Vanessa Redgrave, James Mason, David Warner, and myself, playing Checkhov, weren't worth a tiny bit of publicity to tell people that this was going on, not far from the Pantheon). But our *Seagull* has been flying valiantly from one university to another, over the entire American continent, since 1969.

But that isn't my point. It's said that landing after an LSD trip can be painful. Coming back from a Chekhov trip was agonizing. I may not have been the best Arkadina there ever was, but—contrary to what happens when I think of Lady Macbeth—there are mornings when I wake up thinking: How sad! I'm not filming *The Seagull* today.

It was after I'd come back, once I'd landed from my trip, that I found the letter from my cousin from Bratislava. It was written on pink flimsy paper with that improbable return address already a month old. When I came back, I was politely asked to please start living in 1968 again, to read newspapers written in my language, and to hear in my language how the spring had died in Prague and how "normalization" was achieved there; and how for the first time dissident Soviet citizens had been arrested in the middle of Red Square—the news had crossed the borders.

While we were Chekhoving under the tall trees beside the lake, sipping our *chai*, which the prop man had boiled up between takes so the steam would "match" for each take, Montand, on the contrary, hadn't Chekhoved at all. He had been right in the middle of the twentieth century. He had been Lambrakis in Z while I was Arkadina. I was still Arkadina when he had made his comeback singing at the Olympia in September. For the first time in my life as a groupie, I wasn't there on opening night. Because of Chekhov. Catherine replaced me; she had learned all about it when she was very small; she's an excellent groupie. I wept copiously the day Sidney asked me not to take the Stockholm-Paris-Stockholm plane he had promised I could take. But he was surely right. It's Arkadina who would have been in Montand's dressing room that evening before and after the performance, not me.

That time it was Catherine who was there for the rehearsals, the previews, the anguish, and the doubt. She went out to get the tea and ham sandwiches in the bistro next door. It was she who kept quiet when it was required, and answered questions when she was asked. If Sidney had let me go for that one evening, I would have been a stranger passing through, there just long enough to be photographed between planes. And perhaps it would have been a stranger to *The Seagull* who would have landed the next day at the edge of the lake.

But it was certainly me and not Arkadina who slipped into the audience of the Olympia, accompanied by Vanessa, who was no longer Nina. It was an evening in October, and we hadn't told anyone we were coming. The film was finished; Arkadina and Nina were dead. But Vanessa and I were alive, and we were having great trouble separating. So she decided to stop by Paris on her way to London, and to come with me and see the show, which for the first time in twenty years was something I was going to see fresh.

It was a superb recital. I was furiously jealous that I had been deprived of its preparation. On the other hand, I was deeply proud that the myth had finally been broken: "He sings... but she's backstage." I hadn't been backstage. I was madly proud to be the wife of this man who dazzled me, and who dazzled my friend and, visibly, the three thousand people in the audience. And for the first time in nearly twenty years, it wasn't me who opened the dressing-room door from the inside; I knocked on the outside. The artist opened the door; he had heard that we were in the audience.... I was back home.

Naturally, a few days later I renewed my old habits, abandoned for two months, and I found myself in 1968 like everyone else. That was when all of us sent a telegram to the Soviet ambassador. I've kept the text. It is dated October 16, 1968. It wasn't to Mr. Vinogradov, as in 1956; it was to Mr. Zorin. It wasn't about Budapest; it was about Prague:

> We are all gathered together today, and we wish to send you this telegram. Mr. Ambassador, we ask you please to transmit our warmest congratulations to the Soviet people, whom you represent. It is with great relief that we realize that there are still people in the Soviet Union with the courage to carry on those traditions which have dazzled the world since 1905.* They have formed legions of men and women, in opposition to flocks of sheep, across the entire world. We are speaking, of course, of Pavel Litvinov, Larisa Daniel, Konstantin Babitsky, Vadim Deloney, Vladimir Dremlyuga. Happily for the peoples of the Soviet Union these five† exist and they are Soviet citizens. By the same token, it is wonderful for the American people that the Baltimore Nine—Daniel Berrigan, Philip Berrigan, David Darst, John Hogan, Thomas Lewis, Marjorie Melville, Thomas Melville, George Mische, Mary Moylan—and also, Dr. Benjamin Spock were born on American soil. Just as it is wonderful for France that Gabriel Péri, d'Estienne d'Orves, Manouchian the Armenian, Henri Martin, and Maurice Audin were French.‡
>
> We have sent a copy of this telegram to the newspapers, who will publish it; for good reasons or bad, they will publish it, and that's all that matters to us.
>
> [Signed:]   Yves Montand, Alain Resnais, Jorge Semprun, Vanessa Redgrave, Simone Signoret.

All the newspapers did reproduce this telegram, except the newspapers of the French Communist party.

*The year of the first, aborted, Russian revolution.
†The five Soviet intellectuals condemned in Moscow for having attempted to demonstrate in Red Square against the invasion of Czechoslovakia by Soviet troops.
‡The first three were heroes of the Resistance; all were executed. Martin was jailed for refusing to fight in Indochina. Audin, who denounced the methods of torture used by the French during the Algerian War, was killed—in circumstances that remain unclearly defined—after being imprisoned.

400

The *Herald Tribune*, under the headline "Celebrities Protest," reproduced only the first third. We, the celebrities, had stopped thinking after the phrase: "Happily for the peoples of the Soviet Union, these five exist and are Soviet citizens." I called the *Tribune* and asked to speak to the editor in chief. I didn't know him. I still don't know him. I mean, I've never met him. But I got to know him that day. I don't know if he's still on the same job, but by way of being a good American, he's good.

At first he was very disagreeable. The text he had published was as it had been in the dispatch that had been filed in his office; he didn't know what we were complaining about. I suggested that he read *Le Monde*, *Combat*, *France-Soir*, or *Figaro* and compare the information he was offering his readers with what was offered in those papers. He said that would take a moment. I replied that I had all the time in the world. He said okay. He didn't like me at all; I was lousing up his day.

He came back on the line five minutes later. During that time I imagined him sending someone to rummage through the wastepaper baskets of the newsroom to find the remains of the previous evening's French press. I worked for a newspaper only eight months, but I remember those wastebaskets full of information someone thought was unimportant or inopportune.

He came back on the line. Or rather a different man came back on the line. He liked me a lot; he thanked me. I hadn't loused up his day; he had read the text; I had been right to call him. To enable him to repair the error, would we please write him a letter asking for rectification. As press time was approaching, he and I composed it together on the telephone, and the next morning, under the heading "Amputation," our telegram reappeared, intact. It was preceded by our letter, signed Montand, Resnais, Semprun, Redgrave, and Signoret. The letter was followed by a little text I reproduce here: "The *Herald Tribune* agrees and apologizes. The report of the telegram was from United Press International, as the article indicated. The 'amputation' was done by UPI. The text of the telegram had not been made available to the *Herald Tribune*."

I called to thank him for having been so quick and efficient. "It's for me to thank you," he said. "You've introduced me to some names I didn't know. I've had my guys do some research. Now I know who Gabriel Péri, d'Estienne d'Orves, Manouchian, Maurice Audin, and Henri Martin were. I've had a good lesson in French history. And as for UPI—from now on I'll be keeping an eye on them."

We never did find out what use Tass made of our telegram.

Nor did we ever find out whether Monsieur Zorin transmitted our congratulations to Moscow. I can only hope that an echo did get as far as some of the old audience from the Tchaikovsky Theater, and perhaps the five prisoners were among them.

We did hear that the Baltimore Nine and Dr. Spock got our message.

We never found out into which of the *L'Humanité* wastepaper baskets the report circulated by the Agence France-Presse was dropped.

But I realize only today, on rereading the text of that telegram, where we picked up the "flocks of sheep" in it. I think we picked it up subconsciously, and it was probably because Montand opened his recital with Nâzim Hikmet's poem "Like the Scorpion, My Brother," the second line of which is "Like the sheep, my brother." As I say, I just noticed that today.

Nâzim Hikmet. The picture that comes to mind is the Alkron Hotel's dining room. The letter on pink flimsy paper is my cousin from Bratislava. Though I don't know this yet, as I shall only discover it later, but maybe my cousin was in the lobby of the Alkron that evening when we met Hikmet in the dining room. Hikmet, who was on his way to Moscow to lodge some complaint in the name of liberty. Even if she saw us from a distance, she couldn't have heard what we said. And she couldn't get near us.

It was Nâzim Hikmet who said: "In 1917 we were happy, gay—we were poor but we were handsome and well dressed in our rags," and when he said "we" he meant Mayakovski and Esenin. Vanessa's film before *The Seagull* was the one in which she played Isadora Duncan and married Esenin.... Semprun wrote *La Seconde Mort de Ramon Mercader*. Resnais had directed *La Guerre Est Finie* by Semprun. Montand sang Hikmet and Éluard, Prévert and Desnos, as well as Aragon. All the ghosts of flouted liberty, which makes fine songs, no doubt hovered over us that day. The day the theater was closed. Which is probably what made us want to compose the text of that telegram together. It was certainly closely connected with the bombing over Vietnam; it was certainly connected with Z, which Costa was editing (which explains his absence that day); it was certainly slightly because of Chekhov. Certainly it was not done to embarrass the French Communist party....

During that autumn of 1968 we wanted to show our solidarity with those who had the courage not to agree with what was being done in their names, in the West as well as in the East. That's all.

We began filming *L'Aveu* (*The Confession*) in autumn 1969. That wasn't meant to embarrass the French Communist party, either. There were Communists among us. All their names are on the list of credits, with the exception of one technician, who decided at the last moment—just before the film was released—that she preferred to remain incognito (after picking up her salary check for thirty weeks).

The only socialist country that showed *L'Aveu* is Yugoslavia. They had no objection to someone telling how you could be hung for "Titoism" in 1953.

I understand that there is a copy of *L'Aveu* in Moscow, and that it's sometimes shown to the happy few. I suppose it's languishing on the same shelf as *The Crucible*, *Z*, *State of Siege*, *Casque d'Or*, and the good old *Salt of the Earth*

403

(we never discovered whether the dubbing was ever finished), none of which have ever been shown to a Soviet audience.

And as I write this today, it's not my intention to embarrass the French Communist party.

I'm heading back to the original and now slightly ancient talks with Maurice Pons. We did not know one another when we began conversing. Nor did I know Dominique, who recorded the conversation. It would indeed have been surprising had the three of us maintained the awkward, overrespectful attitude we began with, after having made a six-day plunge into the past.

I'm the oldest of the three. When I talked to you about the occupation, Maurice, no doubt you saw yourself as a very young man, and you, Dominique—that is, if you were born—could not have been more than a babbling baby. I stuck my nose into the transcript because of *L'Aveu*.

I realize now that what at the time seemed like personal and original answers to intelligent questions seem, so many months later, rather down-at-heel answers to questions that are on their way to becoming old hat.

Things change fast, I've said—at interminable length—which comes to about the same thing as saying that records no longer revolve at 78 rpm and everybody has television, that information isn't the same anymore....Everyone knows that! And to avoid appearing like one of Claire Bretécher's heroines,* I'm telling both of you, Maurice and Dominique, that I don't intend to reproduce my colorful verbiage concerning several subjects which, though I firmly believed in them, and continue to believe in them, have become thoroughly square.

Probably all that tends to prove that commonplaces start off as original thoughts, and precisely if they are good

---

*Claire Bretécher is a well-known cartoonist with a weekly full-page strip in the weekly *Nouvel Observateur;* her work is also published in albums.

ideas, they forge ahead until they've become banalities, or simply subjects of conversation.

So here it is, all pellmell: pollution, women's liberation, psychoanalysis, drugs, abortion, and racism. Turn on your television sets; constantly there are "talking-head" round-tables and animated conversations on the topics.

Did I say new thoughts? I should have said very old ones. Not even thoughts: some notions I acquired when I was very young, which means they're old now.

Pollution: It begins if you don't have the good fortune to have a mother who makes you pick up your orange peels and eggshells after a picnic. Whether it's in the Bois de Boulogne or on the beach at Saint-Gildas.

Women's liberation: It begins the moment you consciously assume your condition as an unwed mother and tell the patronizing lady who is willing to allocate ration tickets for khaki wool only, making it clear that you're nothing socially, to get stuffed. But nothing is gained preaching anti-male racism.

Psychoanalysis: It has replaced the priest for Christians, the rabbi for Jews, and the pal you can call when things don't go right, with the difference that these give you their services for free.

Drugs: I talked about that during my report on Synanon.

Abortion: The militants of the Laissez-les-Vivre (Right to Life) movement are also generally in favor of the death penalty.

Racism: It's like pollution. It starts if your mother didn't forbid you to use works like Kike, Wop, Frog, Wog, Chink, Polack, Commie, and even Kraut, and the like, when you were four years old; in other words, at the same time you were taught to look right and left before crossing the street and not to snitch, to share your toys and candy and brush your teeth. If it didn't start then, you'll have trouble.

And now, let's go on!

Question: Did you feel "mobilized" in May 1968?

Simone Signoret: In May 1968 I wasn't in Paris. I was in

Saint-Paul. But I was in Paris when May '68 really began, with the Langlois Cinémathèque affair.° I was in front of the Palais de Chaillot with a few other film professionals when Godard lost his glasses in the first fight of what was later to become May '68. I think that was in April. I was in the Festival Hall in Cannes the morning that the winds of revolution began to blow on Paris. That evening I was back in Saint-Paul and I heard confirmation of what had been announced in the morning: The film festival had come to a standstill. That morning François Truffaut, Louis Malle, Jean-Luc Godard, and Roman Polanski had gotten up on the podium and explained to the audience why it would be indecent to go on celebrating the cinema, given what was happening in Paris. The next morning La Colombe was empty of all its guests. It was like June 1940. . . .

But I hadn't gone south for the festival. I had gone to Saint-Paul; and I stayed in Saint-Paul. I'm sure I missed things by staying there. I missed a certain number of emotional happenings. People in Paris apparently began to "communicate." As I've always "communicated," I probably would have been happy to see that old habit of mine, which goes back to the time when it was called talking together, suddenly spread through the streets. But if I missed some things, I'm pretty certain I also avoided some of the stupidities I surely would have committed. I wrote myself a letter at the time and kept it. It explains better than I could do today what I felt in May 1968.

SAINT-PAUL,
JUNE 2, 1968

I didn't go back. I lived out the whole thing here. So because I need to answer to myself, and prepare my answers to others, I'm sitting here this Sunday afternoon doing my homework. I didn't go back. I have all sorts of good reasons to excuse myself. But I know I could have gone back; one can always go back when that's the only

°Henri Langlois was the creator of the French Cinémathèque. He saved countless priceless prints from destruction. A Ministry of Culture decision to replace him was withdrawn after public outcry. He died in 1977.

thing to do. At moments of high passion, and I've known them, no transport strike in the world can keep you where you are. So I took advantage of the circumstances to stay where I was, and now I would like to know why. That's what bothers me most.

The Desire to Go Back

The two desires alternated at high speed, like spasms or gusts of wind. There's the old desire to participate, to be there, to see for myself. And also the fear of being accused of indifference when I've made so much noise about no one having the right to be indifferent. There's my terror of the "Where were you?" asked by the future veterans of May 1968. They will undoubtedly take the same attitude that I do myself when I ask people where they were between 1940 and 1944. I have a sense of shame when I spread the suntan cream because there's a hot sun on the pool, as I play a game of Scrabble with François, whereas there are barricades across Paris, and surely a lot of things could be done there....

The Desire Not to Go Back

Things to be done. Where, and with whom?

There's the Sorbonne. I would have gone there only once, I know. I would have gotten mixed up with the old people who'd want to jump on the youngsters' bandwagon, with the worldly left-wing ladies, with certain actresses who like to see their photographs in the papers, with the fervent fire-eaters. I would have been rejected by the kids. I would probably have been shocked by some of their statements at the same time I attempted to justify them. Well, so much for the Sorbonne; but after all I've seen and read about it, I would have gone there only once, and then returned home.

Join my own people, the actors? Why? By what sudden sense of responsibility should this particular social group have a voice in the revolution? At every occasion in the past, when they might have expressed themselves on matters as clear and simple as little political assassinations, or colonial wars, with certain well-known exceptions they always took refuge behind: "Me, I'm an actor; I don't get mixed up in politics." I've read the newspapers; there are some surprising names quoted playing the parts of Saint-Just and Robespierre. But I didn't read the names of Paul Crauchet or Jacques Rispal. They had been politically active, long before they ever were jailed for having been politically active.

So if I went back, I would without a shadow of a doubt fall into one trap or another. It would be in the passion of the moment following some bit of information. Or caused by an irrepressible indignation....

So with the help of the climate, the strike, good or bad excuses, I didn't go back. But fundamentally, it's because I wanted to be able to consider a profound revision of everything, alone, without a lot of talk, without people's opinions, without pressure. I wanted to take a good look at the things that would argue our case if we, my generation, were to be put on trial by this youthful judging generation. But pretty soon I had passed that stage. I think I understand them quite well, those kids. All those proofs of good faith, honesty, and courage are related to a past that means nothing to them, and if we were to list our various claims to those virtues, it would seem like a procession of wounded war veterans. They've got good reason to pile us all onto the same heap, even though they know there may be some good people on that heap. Finally, I began to realize that, without knowing it, I was saying just about the same things they were. For example, when I deplore the fact that when we take the highway that now joins Paris to Autheuil we no longer say, "Oh, Rosny, that's where Marie passed the *bac*° when she was young"—to which José always added, "And it's the only *bac* Marie's ever passed." Or, "There's Bonnières, Catherine; what do the Singer people make at Bonnières?" "Songbirds, of course." People no longer talk the way they used to on a highway because there are no landmarks for the memory. You have to be one hell of a Proustian to build a novel around an electronic toll gate.

°*Bac* means "ferryboat" and is also an abbreviation of *bachot*, itself an abbreviation of *baccalauréat*; a college exam.

De Gaulle

I've finally done with the sentimentality I've none-theless secretly held onto since 1940. De Gaulle has become what he said he was, or maybe he always was what his enemies said he was. It is inconceivable to me that at no moment did he utter a word of Victor Hugoesque pride in favor of this youthful generation, in whom he could not but recognize the National Genius. I'm capitalizing on purpose.

The Others

The old trade-union people, communists and social-ists alike, also seem exactly like the portraits their enemies have painted of them. Too bad. Even the old reactionaries are true to themselves, and consequently consistent.

It's sad to be excluded from what one would surely be if one were twenty. And it's frustrating not to be able to tell them. But it's extraordinary and horrifying to see from here, under the sun and at a distance, how they have been duped in just a few days.

I discover that at Saint-Paul no one has ever seen a CRS° and still less a platoon of CRS in combat formation. And they don't know the key points of Parisian geography, and consequently they don't have that innate instinct for the areas one chooses to stage a demonstration.

Listening to the radio, one recognizes all those old slogans from before the war. Suddenly you hear "France for the French" again, and you can shed a tear for poor Malraux, who thanks to a series of absolutely foreseeable circumstances, leads that procession....

I find it terribly important that the sons of the bourgeoisie are marching up the Boulevard Saint-Germain, shouting: "We all are German Jews." They

°Member of Compagnies Républicaines de Securité, mobile shock police stationed at key points throughout France. A popular taunt of 1968 was: "CRS = SS."

don't realize that it shocks some people, who are persuaded it's an expression of anti-Semitism. I heard Pierrot, the barman, announcing, in a bar empty of all tourists, that Mitterrand has been appointed Minister of Health (Santé) because he has just heard students shouting: "Mitterrand à la Santé" (the Santé prison) on his transistor. Shortly thereafter two Italian tourists explain that the red flags and the black flags side by side means the communists and fascists have joined forces. . . .

And then there's the painter Hans Hartung. He is German, but not a German Jew. He was put into a camp in France in 1939, then volunteered for the Foreign Legion in order to make war on Hitler. Hartung is young at sixty. I can see him out the window. He's leaning on the crutch that has served him as a leg since 1945 in Alsace, and he's trying to save a ladybird from drowning in the pool—it was his wife who first saw the ladybird. They were happy a little while ago. Now they're less so; all the paintings for the exhibition Malraux was to inaugurate are stuck somewhere between Tokyo and Paris. They're beginning to be tired of it all. . . . They've been fighting these wars since 1933. This is Saint-Paul at the beginning of June 1968.

Question: During that month, before you began writing to yourself, were you contacted by people who asked you why you hadn't come back?

Simone Signoret: Of course; but they were precisely the people who had never, but never, taken a stand before; and I practically keeled over when I discovered that they had suddenly become revolutionaries. Montand was in Paris, and he called me whenever the telephone worked. In fact, the only thing that really bothered me was not to be able to share with him the emotion that was abroad in the streets. He was actually living them, all those vivid stereotyped scenes. I wasn't. But at the Sorbonne or the Odéon or the meetings of the États Généreaux du Cinéma, organized by the film folk, he didn't take a really active part. He looked and listened. One evening he called and read me a text by Mendès-France. He told me about discussions he had had on the Pont-Neuf with the kids. That evening, when I hung up, I was almost ready to leave Saint-Paul on foot. Actually, that's what bothered me most about my period of inactivity. Not being able to share those moments with him. It's the only thing I missed. I never had the impression, which some tried to give me, that I was deserting. So much for my nonmobilization in 1968.

Question: When you returned to Paris, did you find that things had changed?

Simone Signoret: The Lion of Belfort statue had been painted red. All the graffiti hadn't yet been washed off, and there were still holes in the Rue Gay-Lussac where cobblestones had been ripped out. Thus my trip from Orly. But people had changed. Some of them irreversibly.

Question: Did you know any of the young people who became famous in 1968?

Simone Signoret: Not one. I discovered them on television. There were two evenings when they were invited to discuss their views, first with Georges Séguy, the CGT spokesman, then with the journalist Jean Ferniot. On one of the programs they were hounded, and on the other they were serenaded. If my memory serves me right, there was Cohn-Bendit, Sauvageot, Geismar, and Castro. A little later Séguy was to say, "Cohn-Bendit? Never heard of him."

Question: When you went back, did you meet them?

Simone Signoret: Absolutely not. I met people who told me how those days had changed them forever, kids who were still all excited by the first adventure of their lives. There were mothers who had cared for the eyes of their tear-gassed sons. Some had a bitter nostalgia; some were people who had been very scared for a few days, and were now heaving sighs of relief. Then Montand left to make Z, and I left to make *The Seagull*. Actually, we only met the people implicated by May 1968 much later, when they were no longer in the news; in fact, several of them had been in jail for months. Their trials, and those of Jean-

Pierre Le Dantec and Le Bris, and Geismar, and Christian Riss, took place while we were in America. We didn't follow them at all.

Question: How did you meet them?

Simone Signoret: About four years ago there was a hunger strike at the Sorbonne, and at the same time there was another in the chapel of Montparnasse station. There were two or three lines about those two strikes somewhere in the papers, but the reasons for those twin hunger strikes were not given, nor was it stated who the people were who were on strike. One Sunday morning, at breakfast, Montand said, "You must admit it's revolting—there are people who've been on a hunger strike for sixteen days now just around the corner from us, and we don't even know why." So we called Costa and the three of us went to the Sorbonne. We felt slightly ridiculous when we arrived there, so we said to them, "We know we're about as welcome as a hair in a bowl of soup, but . . . tell us about it." Then we realized that they were very happy to see us there, surprised, but happy. They didn't have a lot of visitors, and they were a good bunch of people. They explained that they were trying to instigate prison reforms. Not just for political prisoners, but for all prisoners. We asked them, "What can we do? We can't share your fast, but how can we be useful?" "You can be useful by unblocking the press. Some papers have mentioned us, but not the big papers." We promised them we'd try, and then we went off to lunch. Afterward we called Lazareff, as, incidentally, we have done quite often.

Question: What was your relationship with Pierre Lazareff?

Simone Signoret: Lazareff goes back to my childhood, because he was a friend of my father's. I met him again after the war, and I knew him the way all French actors knew him—a little better perhaps, due to the fact that I knew him when I was little. I've always used Lazareff; he was the boss of a press that isn't always blameless, but on a personal level he was one of the most fundamentally generous men I've ever met.

Question: Did he have real power?

Simone Signoret: He had enormous power. We never used our friendship with Lazareff for ourselves; it was sometimes even a little ridiculous, because something professionally important would happen to us, and only one paper wouldn't mention it, or would barely mention it, and that would be *France-Soir.* But I've never caught Lazareff evasive in a matter which didn't concern us personally, but which forced him to take a stand. When we asked him to cover the book that Georges Arnaud and Vergès had written about the torture of Djamila Bouhired during the Algerian War, the next day he himself wrote an editorial. When we asked him to help the film called *Loin du Vietnam (Far from Vietnam),* made by a group of film people working under the hidden direction of Chris Marker, he even lent them an office. The day before Grimau was to be executed by Franco, and there was still a chance of saving him, he gave it enormous space in his paper, and had Madame Grimau interviewed in an important TV current-affairs program, of which he was a coproducer.

I think I served as an escape valve for his conscience. We had a kind of ritual, he and I; I would call him and say, "Listen, Pierrot, I've got something for you." He would laugh, knowing it was a dare to take an unexpected stand. He never tried to wriggle out.

Lazareff was a man who always kept his friends, and I don't think there's a single person in Paris who can say, "Lazareff revenged himself on me," or "Lazareff did me dirt." On the other hand, he was also the boss of the paper called *France-Dimanche.* Once we even had to sue him because of an article in *France-Dimanche;* we won. That's the unfortunate side of that personality, the side he himself was not very proud of.

(I just said that we won the suit against *France-*

Dimanche. That's not really the correct way of putting it. If Georges weren't our friend, I would say that Maître Georges Kiejman won that suit. If we had gone to law many times in our lives, Montand and I, the name of our lawyer, Georges Kiejman, would have come up often in the course of this book. But as it happens, the lawsuit I've just mentioned is the only one there ever was. It didn't make a pennysworth of difference in the career of Maître Georges Kiejman. What did make all the difference to our lives, and Georges's, are all those years when there were no lawsuits, no articles in the press, and no fees; when he was just our friend. I might have mentioned the young law apprentice who dug out a minute flaw in the end of the scenario of *Ombres et Lumiéres* in 1950; and the young, fully fledged lawyer who helped at the time when it looked as though the "121 group" might be indicted; in fact, I might have mentioned him every time things were difficult. But the idea didn't occur to me. It's obvious that he was there. Today it would seem like bragging if I said that the admirable defender of Pierre Goldman* in Amiens is one of my oldest young friends.)

But to get back to the professors and their hunger strike: The next Sunday in Louveciennes, in a corner of Lazareff's living room, which was as crowded as always, I murmured to Pierrot, "I have a news story for you." That very evening he sent a reporter and a photographer to the Sorbonne and to the Saint-Bernard chapel. The next day, under a banner headline, they were written about from the first edition of *France-Soir* on. At one o'clock Montand, Costa, and I went to the chapel. It was full of press and radio people. Clavel, Foucault, Claude Mauriac, and Joris Ivens, who had been visiting and supporting them from the beginning, were there too. Among the strikers were Michèle Vian and Geneviève Clancy. They were sickly pale, they trembled

---

*A well-known recent criminal case. Goldman, accused of a double killing, was sentenced without proof to life imprisonment; as the result of public outcry and the efforts of Georges Kiejman, he was given a retrial and declared innocent.

and had difficulty talking; I think their health never totally recovered from those long days of fasting. In fact, those people were dying. Foucault asked them to stop. It was this first hunger strike, undertaken by these law-abiding, unconvicted people, similar to a species of dedicated early Christians, that marks the beginning of what is called the "prison reform." When Montand decided during that Sunday breakfast that we should go and see what was happening in that library at the Sorbonne, he had a very good idea.

Question: Would you have gone if you had been invited?

Simone Signoret: I really don't know. It would probably have depended on the day, the time, whether or not we were free—or rather how free we were at the time. Also, probably, on the way we were asked, and who asked us. But I do know that had we not gone after being asked, we would have felt very uncomfortable if a man or a woman had died—which was quite possible. I remember that someone from television asked us what we were doing there, and we answered that we'd rather be there while it was happening than receive a very fine script a little while later dealing with what had happened there, in case someone died. After all, when Gabrielle Russier was in jail, one can't honestly say that the whole of France rose up nobly to do something for her, but all of France went to see her as acted by Annie Girardot in the movies, and they cried a lot. . . . I, personally, have never forgiven myself for not writing to her when she was in Baumettes jail. I thought about it for a morning, but I didn't get to do it.

Question: Why?

Simone Signoret: For fear of being ridiculous, being indiscreet. For fear of thinking myself too important. After all, that young philosophy professor didn't necessarily know who I was. But the day I heard on the radio that she had committed suicide I was very annoyed with myself for not having stretched out a hand. I would have written her a cheering letter, and maybe it would have arrived in time.

The banner headline in *France-Soir* gave us a very good reputation as people who could rouse the press among the young people of 1968, who by now were four years older. So a little while later, when Montand was in Saint-Paul, I was very pointedly asked whether I wouldn't visit three hunger strikers who were workers in the Renault factory. I didn't want to because I'm not a worker at Renault. The problems of factory workers is a domain in which I don't have a right to intrude, because I don't know what I'm talking about. There's really no chance that I may someday be a worker at Renault, whereas we all run the risk of being in prison someday, which is why one can say that prison conditions concern us all.

Question: Who asked you to go?

Simone Signoret: Jean-Pierre Le Dantec. Sartre had sent him. I explained all that to him. He knew, but he wasn't interested in me as a pseudo proletarian; what he wanted was to attract the attention of the press. Nobody, but nobody, had talked about them. They had good reasons for this strike, which had already been going on for ten days. In any case, they had *their* reasons, and they wanted to be heard. So I went off in Jean-Pierre's old car (I hadn't known him before he came, but he has since become our friend), and we stopped in a small street in Billancourt in front of a modern chapel. There were banners up, saying: "Come in and we'll tell you why we're on a hunger strike." But the little street was hardly a thronged thoroughfare, and you had to be either a devout Catholic or a devout Maoist to find the place.

In the chapel's sacristy we found three camp beds, and on them three guys who didn't yet look as I remembered the people at the Sorbonne, but who were already not as lively as they must have been a week earlier. When they saw me, they were less surprised than the others had been, since they had sent for me. They were delighted, and were now sure that the next day *France-Soir*, *Aurore*, the *Express,* and maybe even *Match* would talk only about them. I told them not to count on it; sometimes it worked, sometimes it didn't.

Question: Why were they on that hunger strike?

Simone Signoret: Two of them had been fired: S. ben M., a Moroccan national, and J.D., a Portuguese. Both were skilled workers. I won't give their names in full, as they might not care for that kind of publicity, wherever they are today. The third was Christian Riss—not in the same category at all: a college professor. I don't think I'll be endangering him by giving his name. I left them, saying I would do my best, and I went home with a clean conscience. I thought I'd only gone to that chapel to visit. But I went back every day.

When you begin to get interested in the people who do that very difficult thing—not eating at all—there begins to exist between the hunger striker and the visitor a kind of current. The visitor goes home to his usual life, where he eats, but suddenly he begins to think every day, at mealtimes, about those people who aren't eating. Suddenly there's a relationship that has nothing to do with politics or a social conscience—it's an almost organic relationship. I went to see them once, and the next day I said to myself: "At this very moment, they're not eating...." So I went back. At the end I got used to going to see them, and they got used to seeing me. I'm not quite sure whether that's what's meant by purity in human relationships.... I went to see them nearly every day for a week and a half. And I never arrived with good news, because their hunger strike didn't really interest anyone. Oh, there were a few lines in the weekly *Nouvel Observateur*, but in the large-circulation daily press there was nothing. There was really nothing in the Communist papers—maybe a line or two in *Combat*, a bit in *Le Monde*, but nothing that really drew attention. Once again, I was very egotistical; I learned from it.

It allowed me once again to try to define myself vis-à-vis these people—which was very good for me. Like

Khrushchev, those hunger-striking workers had never really met actors, and they had a false vision of us. If one went to them, one had to take the precaution of flying one's true colors. It was my duty to tell them that I was not a revolutionary, that I earned a very good living—which they knew—that I understood their grievances but didn't share them because they weren't the same as mine; that I respected them because they were making a huge effort for things that wouldn't change my life but that I still wanted to know about. I didn't want to pretend that I was one of them. I think it must be possible to help people in their struggle and at the same time tell them honestly that one is not like them, that one doesn't live their life.

I watched those three men grow weaker day by day, and see fewer and fewer people. There are hunger strikes that work and others that are fiascos. Little by little, there was hardly anyone with them except me, and I was akin to those Russian ladies who took revolutionaries into their châteaux before 1905. I was both slightly ridiculous and at the same time not ridiculous at all: I would do numbers for them in which I poked fun at myself because it was a completely false situation. After a while there was no one around their cots except a few workers from Renault, Joris Ivens, who showed them some films, and Sartre. All that was completely incongruous and useless. I would take a taxi to the chapel, and when we got there, the driver would see the banners, which had become bedraggled in the rain, and twice a cabby said to me, "I'll go in with you; I want to see why they're on a hunger strike." I brought some people; I brought Régis Debray, and Costa-Gavras, and Michel Drach and Chris Marker.... I went to visit my hunger strikers the way charitable ladies in old-fashioned novels went to see their poor.

One day I was joking with them—since they couldn't eat, I thought they might as well laugh—and I said, "When you come to think of it, one of the three of you really should get very, very sick, and even maybe make the effort of trying to die. Because then the press would pay attention. . . ." I didn't know how right I was. They stopped their hunger strike at the end of the nineteenth day. I saw them pack up their bundles and go off to the hospital. The curé was there; he was fantastic, that curé. And the next day Pierrot Overney, who was not one of the hunger strikers, was shot dead by a Monsieur Tramoni, one of the Renault factory's armed guards. Then, at last, the papers talked about the hunger strikers.

As François Mitterrand said in his book, French television reporters crowded in to see the family of a Monsieur Nogrette, who was kidnapped shortly thereafter (I don't approve of kidnapping), but the television people never went to see Pierrot Overney's family.

Pierrot Overney became a "poster." I, having lived day to day with people's total lack of interest in those grievances, had suddenly realized that someone had to die in order to rouse the press—and the idea terrified me. And then there was Pierrot Overney's funeral. I'm not a funeral fan unless it means a great deal to the family; I don't go to the funerals of people I've loved. But some funerals take on the character of a demonstration, and they become the occasion for something other than just being seen there. So I went to that funeral, still with the feeling that I was a ridiculous actress lady intruding into some kind of street activity. Furthermore, I did it in a most luxurious fashion: I had gone down to Saint-Paul, and so I did a one-day return trip by plane. My day's outing must have cost approximately what a Renault worker earns in a month. I can understand being jeered at for this, and as it so happens, I'm jeering at myself.

Young Overney had been severely criticized by the French Communist party, which accused him of being an *agent provocateur*. This young *provocateur* had managed to get himself killed, and it was of vital importance not to attend the funeral; I haven't made this up, I read it. Even the curé was accused of not doing his job as a curé, and was soundly reprimanded for having given asylum to those hunger strikers. I'm certain that there must have been some agonizing scenes in kitchens in the workers' quarters around Paris among certain families of old-time Communist militants the morning of Pierrot Overney's funeral: It's the first time in my life that I've seen groups of unaccompanied women at this kind of a demonstration. At the funeral for the Charonne victims° I had seen a lot of couples, a lot of people who came two by two; but here I saw groups of women of my age and even older—they didn't seem to be all widows—who banded together on the Place Clichy. They weren't bourgeoises, they weren't elderly Maoists; they were proletarian women. They formed little groups with a kind of defiant look; they were women who must have said, "All right, I'll go alone." Marie-José Nat, Michel Drach, Maurice Clavel, and I listened to them talk as we walked to Père Lachaise cemetery.

In a strange way, that was one of the first tangible demonstrations of the change in the lives of proletarian women. A kid of twenty had been shot down. He was surely noisy and violent, he had had an iron rod in his hands when he was shot, but he wasn't about to bash Tramoni on the head when Tramoni shot him down. It was a murder, like many others. Visibly, those women weren't following orders; they had come to bury the kid. Even if he had been a Maoist. . . .

I saw meetings among old militants who had tears in their eyes and a kind of sad and gay smile: "Oh, you came too!" I saw someone go by who seemed very familiar. He waved a kind of salute, and I answered. A few minutes later I realized that I had never met him; he was the Communist-resistance FTP commander who is interviewed at length in the film *The Sorrow and the Pity*. He'd disappeared from sight when I realized who he was.

°During an anti-Algerian War demonstration in February 1962, police forces, in an "uncontrolled" action, charged a crowd and drove it into the entrance of the Charonne métro station, causing seven fatalities.

Question: Do you really think your presence was useful in any of these events?

Simone Signoret: Honestly, no. But while we're on the subject of usefulness, let me tell you a little story. . . .

About three years ago Alain Krivine was arrested and jailed for having called a demonstration against a meeting organized by a movement called Ordre Nouveau.* I am not a "child of May '68" and I'm not a Trotskyite; I know nothing about the schisms that divide the various Trotskyite movements, and I'd even go so far as to say I couldn't care less. I had never met the young man they had just thrown into jail, but I really didn't see why he should be in prison.

A delegation of personalities "of different beliefs, backgrounds, confessions, and tendencies" asked Montand to join them to go and request the Minister of Justice to release the prisoner at once.

My husband was in London at the time, and that's how I came to agree to replace him, along with my pals Reggiani and Piccoli, among a few professors, one or two Companions of the Liberation, representatives of the League of the Rights of Man, philosophy Ph.D.s, ministers of different sects, and representatives of the trade-union movement.

The gathering was to take place at four o'clock on the Place Vendôme in front of the Ministry of Justice. It was to be a small but highly select delegation.

At about 3:55, a taxi brought me and Serge to the door of the Ministry of Justice. We had lunched together chez Paul, and a gentleman who probably didn't realize that we could hear him recognized us and said, "Manda and Casque d'Or! I can't bear it when people age."

But that's not the point. It was 3:55, as I've already said. I've also already told you that it was to be a small, select

---

*A group of neofascist activists, which disbanded, then re-formed as Front National, with identical objectives.

delegation. It was so small and select that it wasn't there at all. There were two guards in front of the great door, but theirs were the only shadows on the elegant cobbles of that splendid square.

Then we heard a familiar whistle. A tall man dressed all in black was leaning against the railing that surrounds the Vendôme column. Alpaca suit, cravat—superb. It was Piccoli.

It was marvelously funny and comforting to tell ourselves that the only people who were prompt for this particular appointment were the mountebanks.

At about 4:07, there still wasn't the faintest shadow of a university professor or an antiracist cleric on the horizon. We began to wonder. At about 4:10, a few arched windows on the mezzanine floor of the Ministry of Justice opened, and we saw clusters of heads with curly or long hair hanging out to gawk at us. Piccoli appointed himself as chief of operations. He asked one of the guards, "Are they expecting a delegation inside?" The guard came back; his immediate superior knew nothing about it, but would we be kind enough to give him some autographs for his daughter?

At about 4:15, a man dressed in the morning coat and striped pants of a future receptionist of a grand hotel came running out of the Ritz, which is, as everyone who has read Proust or Hemingway knows, right next door to the Ministry of Justice. He had a handful of their splendid embossed stationery; he, too, wanted autographs.

At 4:18, we compared our memories. Maybe we had made a mistake about the time or got the date wrong? We would wait till five, and then go home. But what to do in the meantime?

Our Marx Brothers routine in the superb empty square, under the eyes of all the typists on the mezzanine—who were waving to us and bringing along more and more of their friends to come look out of the window—was becoming a little tedious. What to do? Have a drink while we waited for it to be five o'clock, when we would know if we had made a mistake.

To go for a drink when you're "mobilized with marching orders" on the Place Vendôme, and you can't risk leaving your combat post without "endangering the action"—that creates problems.

So, after brief consultation, my pals and I decided to go to the nearest place.

The young man in his morning coat had returned to his station, his hands full of autographs for his sisters, his cousins, and his mama. Courageously we walked up to him. Was there a bar in the Hotel Ritz where we could have a drink and wait for it to be five o'clock?

Since he was very nice and obviously fresh out of a hotel school, he told us that the bar on the "Rue Cambon side" of the building would certainly be open. But since he was very nice and fresh out of hotel school and far from stupid, he added that if he could in any way be useful to us, he would be happy . . . .

Piccoli, still in charge of his commando operation, asked him whether he would keep an eye on the square and let us know if a group—small but dignified—gathered in front of the door of the ministry. He said he would be glad to fulfill this mission, adding that he had plenty of time to keep an eye on the Place Vendôme, since this wasn't the season for the kind of tourists who fill grand hotels but the season for the kind of tourists who come in buses.

He told us which corridors to take in order to get to the bar on the Rue Cambon side. Striding over the thick-pile carpets, the three of us marched off. The bar on the Rue Cambon side was not quite next door. Along those long, narrow corridors, showcases belonging to our usual suppliers—Hermès, Lanvin, Cartier—glared down upon us. They would never have stared so defiantly in another grand hotel on a day we went to visit an American friend passing through Paris. But as we had not come to the Place Vendôme to greet the passage of some dear old friend from Hollywood, but for the reason you know, those meters of corridor soon lengthened into kilometers due to our frequent stops for fits of giggles.

The barman let us in. However, we visibly disturbed him. The hour was abnormal, not to say shocking. He was in the process of setting out olives and little bites to eat in the saucers he would later serve to his usual clients. They would turn up at about six. I'm not sure that he recognized the three "great dramatic artists" the typists on the Place Vendôme side had identified. In any case, the tone in which he asked us what we would like to drink made us want to answer, "Three beers," just to see his reaction.

I should add that our giggles were still undiluted—as evidenced by the "three beers"—since we'd begun the journey down the long corridor that had faced us with the realities and contradictions of the situation. Therefore, our entry into that deserted sanctuary of hallowed Cambon tradition must have appeared somewhat out of place to the barman.

Piccoli once again took things in hand, and with the elegance of an old friend of Mademoiselle Chanel—whom he had never met—he ordered three Fernet-Brancas. No beers; he was for a distinguished liqueur—distinguished, that is, to anyone who has ever traveled in Italy. The barman brought them and went back to his olives.

We were starting on our Fernet-Brancas when our friend the young graduate from hotel school made a breathless entrance, looking like one of the messengers in a pseudo-antique tragedy: "Monsieur le Directeur awaits you," he announced.

The barman looked up from his olives an instant. A rapid thought must have crossed his mind: That must be it, they must be salespeople, he should have known; who else would have come to the bar on the Cambon side at four-thirty but a salesman or a peasant—or three of them—from the backwaters of the provinces?

"We didn't ask to see the manager of the Ritz," Piccoli rapped out. The young man explained: No, he meant the director of the cabinet of the Minister of Justice. Our presence had been reported inside. The guards, the typists, the chief guard, must have talked inside the building. So Monsieur le Directeur de Cabinet had sent a guard, who had seen us go into the Ritz. The guard had asked the young man in the morning coat to ask us if we desired an audience—visibly we had not come to the Place Vendôme as tourists. He was awaiting us.

We had found no delegation in the midst of which we were to be intelligent "extras." We had no manifesto to read, nor did we have explicit facts that we could run down point by point. We had come because it displeased us that a young man had been thrown into jail because he couldn't accept a return to racism, something we had been protesting about since before that young man was born. That was a far cry from being a delegation of three. So we asked our messenger to reply that we would think about it.

He left, running. The barman reconsidered; we were obviously not salespeople, nor were we peasants, but we still weren't his regular clientele.

We decided that we would really be foolish not to take this chance, which was being offered on a silver platter, to tell our truth as we had just defined it among ourselves. For once, our pictures wouldn't be in the papers, with good or ill intent, and for once we could carry the real message that we wanted to carry; we could carry it ourselves, notwithstanding the statements that weren't necessarily exactly what we thought or wanted, statements that could be expounded by our more official partners who had asked us to be there, and who weren't there.

So Serge, Michel, and I said good-bye to the barman and went back along those corridors, this time trying not to look at the showcases; we found our new friend the messenger, and asked him to transmit the news that we were on our way.

Our friend ran with the news. The typists were still at the windows, the guards saluted us, and the attendant conducted us to a door where a very handsome man awaited us on the threshold and said, "Please come in."

He was smiling. It was clear that he didn't have the least idea of what had brought us to his doorstep, but he knew perfectly well who we were, and most courteously he exclaimed, "What a cast!"

He took us over to a kind of living-room corner of his enormous office, which looked out on a pretty garden. We were in the office of the director of the cabinet of the Minister of Justice, but he wanted to give us the impression that we were there on a friendly visit. "What's the problem?" he asked.

We hadn't had much rehearsal time in the rush from the bar in the Ritz to this luxurious sitting room; but we had decided that Piccoli should start the ball rolling, and that the first thing he should say was that we had made a mistake about time and date, so as to cast no doubt on a possible mistake made by the distinguished organizers of the delegation. We must do nothing to add to the legend that leftists are always messy.

So Piccoli explained that we were artists and thus absentminded like all artists, that we had undoubtedly misheard what had been said to us, but in any case, the delegation we were to be a part of would certainly appear within the next few days, and then, even if we were absent, we should be considered present. The director listened to him, smiling, and said, "Naturally."

Then we three told the director all we had told each other in the bar on the Rue Cambon side. We were the carriers of no text, we had been mandated by no organization, we probably wouldn't have gone to the demonstration Krivine had organized, but we didn't like it that Krivine had been put in jail because he didn't like Ordre Nouveau, because in that case maybe Monsieur le Directeur should put us in jail, too, for not liking Ordre Nouveau.

That was probably oversimplifying things, but simplicity sometimes has its advantages, and no doubt it was a change from the tone the director was accustomed to. In any case, he didn't seem to be bored.

When we thanked him for having taken the initiative of receiving us without an appointment, he thanked us in turn for not having hesitated to come and speak to him in all honesty, and he even made some excellent remarks on the validity of the spontaneous gesture and improvisation, compared with the harangue much rehearsed in advance.

We were in the process of having a little chat on the subject of Diderot's *Paradoxe sur le Comédien,*[*] and I could see the drawing room–office becoming simply a drawing room, period, when one of us—Serge, if I recall—using the time-honored formula "We don't wish to intrude on your time," got up to leave.

The director accompanied us to the door. He promised he would transmit our message to his minister, everybody thanked everybody else, and it almost came to the point of "Be seeing you soon."

If you're a Nobel Prize winner, the head of a hospital in which quantities of human lives are saved, a Companion of the Liberation, or a Sorbonne professor, and you find yourself alone in front of the Vendôme column (with two friends, one fine afternoon) because someone has forgotten to tell you that the delegation has been postponed for forty-eight hours, there's little chance that the typists will hang out the window to gape at you or someone from the Ritz staff will offer his services. It may even happen that after a few minutes the guards will ask you to please move along. So you would never have the opportunity of stepping into the Ministry of Justice and opening your heart to Monsieur le Directeur de Cabinet. Eternally condemned to official speeches—that's what you'd be. The answer: Be a movie actor . . . or actress.

[*]A dialogue by the eighteenth-century philosopher who founded the *Encyclopedia*.

And if you are a movie actor or actress, and you're asked to be an "extra" at a demonstration for or against something or other, don't get any grand ideas; rather get it stuck firmly in your head that most people will say that you have come to be photographed and get yourself a bit of free publicity.

Finally, if you are a movie actor and you leave the Hotel Ritz to go and ask the Minister of Justice to free a young revolutionary named Alain Krivine, and you are not framed by the camera of a photographer from *Minute*,° you're damned lucky. End of fable.

Question: Did May '68 change anything in your artistic choices?

Simone Signoret: Absolutely not. Both Montand and I have continued to take on or decline things on the same basis as before. Montand didn't remodel his recitals in order to be in post-'68 fashion. He did go back and include some songs he had sung before. If Nâzim Hikmet or Desnos or Prévert were suitable after '68, so much the better, because he had sung them well before then....

We would have made *L'Aveu* even without May '68 in Paris—because of August '68 in Prague. They began *Z* after May '68; they had been trying to get the picture off the ground for a year. When Montand made *La Guerre Est Finie*, by Resnais and Semprun, it was 1965. And if you think back to that film, the future kids of May '68 were already in it. No, May '68 didn't change anything in our artistic choices, nor in our behavior. May '68 revealed a certain number of astounding things, things that amazed us, that were healthy and insolent. Those things were done by the youngsters. The people of our generation who until then hadn't taken the time to see or listen often went off the rails when they embarked on their first space flight, wearing the hairdos and costumes they'd copied from the kids. If that's what's meant by being "in," we weren't in. No, we just went on doing what we've always done. We've

°An extreme right-wing newspaper known for its biased reporting.

gone on telling stories which do no harm because they are beautiful stories, but they don't "demobilize," either. I know why I'm using a fashionable word here, like "communicate" or "gross" today; it is because what I'm talking about is a certain vocabulary that's already out of date, although it's still used by a number of fifty-year-olds in show business or just plain business. . . .

If you move people, or make them laugh, that doesn't mean you're "demobilizing" them. I've never been a great one for making people laugh . . . though Solange Sicard once promised me a career as a comic because of my flaws of pronunciation.

It's difficult to make people laugh.

Montand is very good at it, as he's also very good at making them cry. He was learning the ropes in his music-hall days, before he had made any films. And that reminds me of those days in La Moutière, with Clouzot and Véra, when Montand was working on his scene from Anouilh. . . . He sweated, he cursed, he learned the words by heart . . . and then he recited them. He would say, "I'll never make it! I don't know why I'm sweating out this stuff when I can do exactly what I want with my own work." I was very sorry for him during those afternoons; he was as maladroit as I had been when I was with Solange Sicard. He knew it, and I knew it too. But then I'd stand in the wings of the Étoile—and there once again I'd feel the thrill. Today it thrills me when I see him act. I'm amazed and thrilled when I see him go from *The Devil by the Tail* to *Z*, from *César and Rosalie* to *The Confession*, from *State of Siege* to *Vincent, François, Paul, and the Others*; from *The Savage* to *Police Python*. He's amazing; he can play *Thousands of Clowns* in the theater and then—when the occasion warrants it—get up on a music-hall stage and give a two-hour recital, as he did in 1974 for the benefit of the Chilean refugees.

Question: When he sang for the Chileans, was that a militant act?

Simone Signoret: No. A militant is someone who acts by

reason of his profound convictions, but who also occasionally receives orders that are not to be discussed. If he discusses or refuses them, then he's no longer a militant. We take no orders or instructions. We move when the heart is stirred.

One morning in February Montand woke up and announced, "I'm going to sing." He hadn't sung for five years, he had just finished a film and was about to begin another, but instead of going off to read a poem for the benefit of some organization, he simply decided he would give a one-man recital for one evening at the Olympia, and that all the money taken at the box office, absolutely every franc of it, would go to the Chilean refugees. He had ten days in which to prepare; he went to work, he made up a program, rehearsed like a demon, practiced on the barre, and he filled the Olympia to the brim; people paid ten thousand, fifty thousand old francs° for a seat. Because Montand's heart was stirred; there's no other reason. Those aren't the actions of a militant!

Costa-Gavras and Montand made *State of Siege* in Chile. Without Allende, they wouldn't have been able to make that film. They stayed there for three and a half months, so they had time to see, absorb, and understand. When the end of that Chile came, with the death of Allende and the reign of Pinochet, it had already become unacceptable to a lot of people who had never set foot there. But for those who had lived there it was unbearable. Montand cried the day Allende died. Something had to be done. But what? What one is gifted for: one's work. One makes a present of one's work and one's talent, and that brings in money. Money is very important in such a situation; it can't bring back the people who've been assassinated, but it can do a little to help those who are living in exile.

The Chileans are the latest in a long list of exiles we've met. The list begins with the Spaniards, then came the

---

°That is, approximately five to twenty-five dollars.

Americans of the fifties, and then the Hungarians, the Greeks, the Czechs, and the Brazilians—and I'm not counting the very first, the German Jews of my childhood. And even before that there were the White Russians living around the Ternes neighborhood, whose mamas had their goodies delivered from the fancy pastry shops. And a little while ago I was visited by an American Indian; he wasn't an exile but he was traveling around Europe telling people about the American Indian liberation movement. He came to the Place Dauphine; he wore a feather in his hair and his name is Vernon Bellecourt, but he also has an Indian name I can't pronounce. The poor man came to Paris at the wrong time; the whole of France was passionately concentrating on the first Lip factory conflict, and no one cared about Indian problems at that moment. I gave him money . . . and I gave him a couple of pieces of advice: to go and see Gilbert Bécaud, who no doubt would be concerned with the problem, judging from his very fine song describing New York when it was still "the prairie." I don't know whether they met. I also advised him to pass the hat around among the manufacturers of redskin outfits for children, which sell so well at Christmas time. I don't know whether he did that, either.

So you see, it's quite normal for people to come to see us. When I was little they told me that tramps would leave mysterious signs on the doors of farms. They were intended for other tramps, their pals, following the same itinerary. They meant: "These people give," or "These people are mean," or "Here they give if you work." It was said in a sign language of crosses, lines, and circles cut into the door with a penknife. The door of the "caravan" undoubtedly bears some invisible symbols. It's fine when somebody comes along at the right moment. It's cruel when they come at the wrong moment. The day they come at the wrong moment you lose your reputation as a generous altruist. You lose it because you're swamped. There are too many of them. Too many asking for your signature or for money or for attention to their personal case—too many who are unhappy. Generally, the last arrival pays for the others. He's not necessarily the least interesting. But he came too late. He is liable to mark your door with the bad sign, and he's right. The same is true for the exiles. And it's true for our fellow citizens in trouble. . . . Speaking of trouble, the one who really meets trouble is the individual who happens along the day before the first day of a new film! He or she will really mark your door with a giant hex sign, because there you are trying to figure out whether you should limp with your right foot or your left foot to play *Le Chat*; there you are trying to practice limping all by yourself as though you'd limped for years when you're going to do it for the first time in your life the following day for a limited run of eight weeks. . . .

Question: With *Le Chat* (*The Cat*) and *La Veuve Couderc* (*The Widow Couderc*) you were interpreting Simenon. . . .

Simone Signoret: They're adaptations of two Simenon novels. You must ask Simenon whether he recognized his stories and characters in those films. Simenon has always sold the rights to his novels to the movies with the understanding that the film-maker has a free hand with his subjects and heroes. He's not one of those authors who scream that they've been betrayed. The adaptations are rarely betrayals. They're arrangements that end up serving Simenon's world. Because there is a definite Simenon world, and it doesn't evaporate. In *Le Chat*, the wife's name may be changed to Clemence because Florence is the name of one of Gabin's daughters and it bothered him; or she may have a different past—Granier-Deferre wanted her to be an ex-acrobat because he knows all about the circus—or she may talk about going back to work (I wanted to fit in the Signoret-Montand scene when I was in danger of not playing *Thérèse Raquin*). Still, that woman is a Simenon woman. Even if La Veuve Couderc isn't an old countrywoman running after younger men to prove her power of seduction, but is a peasant woman with graying hair, in love with a kind of son she never had—she's still a Simenon woman. At least I think so, I hope so. At least that's what we hoped when we played those tailor-made characters by Pascal Jardin and Granier-Deferre, Gabin and I in *Le Chat*; and Delon and I in *La Veuve*.

Question: Do you get along well with Gabin?*

Simone Signoret: Admirably. Gabin's everyday interests are the opposite of mine: I don't run trotting horses in Vincennes and I don't raise cattle; and we don't agree on a great many things. But we agree on one thing and that's vital: how you act in a film together. We loved acting the hatred for each other in the film. During the breaks he would tell me about his Hollywood and about the time spent with his Jean Renoir and his Jacques Prévert, and it was beautiful to look at him and catch in his eye the deserter in *Quai des Brumes* and in his smile the smile of Captain Maréchal in *La Grande Illusion*.

Question: And with Alain Delon?

Simone Signoret: Admirably too. I detest firearms; my choices and opinions are at the other end of the scale from his; his friends are not my friends. He's crazy, but he's a gentle madman trying to seem tough, and he's a generous madman. We're happy when we work together because we work very well together. I don't know that other Delon, the one with race horses and the big business projects. I only know the one who during the breaks tells how he was forced to enlist in the army at seventeen.

Question: I see there's a book lying on that small table—*Les Mémoires d'un Révolutionnaire*, by Victor Serge. A bedside book, or a film project?

Simone Signoret: "Although this book is lent by Jean-Pierre Melville, that doesn't in any way imply that he no longer owns it." That's what is written on the flyleaf of this book salvaged from a fire, the one that destroyed his Rue Jenner studio. The reason it's on that table is because we'd set it aside to give back to Melville one day when he was due for lunch here to discuss with Montand a film they

*Jean Gabin died in 1976.

intended making together. He never came to lunch; he died the previous night. The date was August 2, 1973. We've never changed the book's place.

Question: Montand made *Le Cercle Rouge* with him and you *L'Armée des Ombres*. What did playing Mathilde, the Resistance heroine, represent for you?

Simone Signoret: It didn't stir up any memories, because I had done nothing fabulous or heroic. I never experienced the sort of things that happened to her. I could only correlate my references to what I'd been told. I'd come into contact with women like Mathilde, but at the time I knew nothing of what they really were. On the other hand, I can say that she seemed to me "manifest," that woman, during the entire time I played her; the more so as on the set we had a real "Mathilde." Maud Begon had put in nineteen months' captivity, from fort to camps. She made us up—that is, she improved me and she disfigured those who'd supposedly been subjected to torture.

For the latter, she undoubtedly called on her memories to do her job well. She didn't relate her memories; still, now, she keeps them to herself. Maud is frail and gay. She only wears her Legion of Honor rosette when the traffic is likely to be particularly dense. The police are more lenient on illicitly parked cars driven by people with decorations.

I could tell you peripheral stories about the film, as I could about Melville and about Lino Ventura, who was on bad terms with Melville right from the first day's shooting. They didn't speak to each other for three months. I believe this was wonderfully beneficial: One completely believes in the utter loneliness of the character played by Lino, faced with his responsibilities, precisely because on the set he was an isolated man.

Melville was a director who didn't give actors any hard and fast instructions; you were directed by him without realizing it. At the end of the film, Mathilde is gunned down in the Avenue Hoche. We had a technical run-through of this fairly complicated sequence. Under my raincoat I was loaded with little bags of stage blood, designed to burst as the bullets hit me. It was an incredible session; we were on location, and there must have been well nigh four hundred onlookers gawking while the plumbing operations proceeded, the tubes being coiled all over me so the blood would spurt from the holes provided for the purpose. I was ashamed at taking part in this public preparation of a sauce recipe. I was to come out of Gestapo headquarters and walk up the avenue. We rehearsed. I exited, walked with eyes glued firmly to the ground. Melville came toward me, saying: "That was fine. Don't change a thing. Your walk's great." And I, who never want to explain anything, somehow felt compelled to add: "Well, maybe . . . still, she's just betrayed her pals." "Who told you she's betrayed them?" "I've read the script." "So what! I wasn't there! I don't know if she gave them away!" "Nonetheless, they're going to kill her!" "Yes, they will kill her, but that doesn't prove that it was she who talked too much. . . ." That's a fantastic indication, full of ambiguity. When the camera pans on those four guys in the car, for a fraction of a second there's this look exchanged between Mathilde and her pals: She realizes they are going to kill her. If Melville hadn't talked to me the way he did just before the take, that look would never have existed: a mingling of surprise, terror, and complete understanding. That's the way Melville directed: a word or two tossed into the conversation. Indications like these work wonders!

That's also the way René Clément directs. In 1962, a week or so before we began filming *Le Jour et l'Heure*—in which the action also takes place during the occupation— René came to the Flore for a chat with me around 7 P.M. The script was finished, my costumes were ready, I had tried on but not yet worn Thérèse's shoes, my "satchel" was prepared for the journey to Rethel, where she'd wear her shoes for the first time. I knew all about the adventures awaiting her which for the next three months would take her from the Belgian border to the Spanish border. . . . René sat looking at me. And then, out of the blue, he said: "Just an idea . . . I'm not sure, mind you, but maybe, ages

435

ago, when she was in her teens, Thérèse had to bear some enormous grief; perhaps she had an illegitimate child, or perhaps she loved her father more than her mother, or maybe she wasn't allowed to marry someone she really loved. . . . Who knows? Whatever it is, forget everything I've just said." My foot! Those few words didn't drop into deaf ears.

Question: Do directors making their first film know how to talk to actors that way?

Simone Signoret: Yes, when they're gifted.

Question: How many "first" films have you made?

Simone Signoret: Room at the Top, directed by Jack Clayton; *Les Mauvais Coups*, by François Leterrier; *Compartiment Tueurs*, by Costa-Gavras; *La Chair de l'Orchidée*, by Patrice Chéreau. There have also been one or two benevolent appearances: I've no regrets for having helped Marcel Bozzufi make *L'Americain*, and Roger Pigaut, *Compte a Rebours*.

Question: Because you've made so many successful films, do you sometimes have the impression of having become an official person? Did success bring you to personal contact with those in power?

Simone Signoret: We've never had any personal relations in that area.

Question: Not even during the time of General de Gaulle?

Simone Signoret: The only contact we ever had with him was an official letter we once sent to help our friend Louis Lecoin, the little imp we'd known for ages. He was over seventy years old and he had just begun his umpteenth hunger strike because he wanted a law passed in favor of conscientious objectors. Louis Lecoin had spent many years in prison—fourteen, I think—for having refused to wear a uniform for a single day of his long life. He was a utopian pacifist. He had the eyes of a child. When he died, in 1972, the crematorium of Père Lachaise cemetery was too small for all the people who came, and who were pleased with each other for being there. We never got a reply from General de Gaulle, but since at the time a great many of us wrote to him, I suppose it was impossible to reply to everyone. However, he did have the law for conscientious objectors passed, and that's the only thing that counts.

No, we've never been to the Élysée.° Marcel Carné invited us one day: The President of the Republic, Giscard d'Estaing, had invited him for lunch and had asked him to make up the table. So Carné invited people he had worked with. I suspect we hurt his feelings when we refused his invitation. We wrote a letter explaining why we were refusing. We hadn't gone to the Élysée when de Gaulle invited us, we didn't go when Pompidou invited us, and we wouldn't even go should Mitterrand† invite us. It's a kind of rule we made for ourselves on returning from trips to the East and West. It's not an aggressive attitude; it's simply that we want to maintain a distance between ourselves and the people in power. Whatever the power. Which doesn't mean that if a President of the Republic were to turn up on our set one day—that is, if he came to us and not the other way round—we would refuse to have a chat with him over a snack and a drink in the cafeteria. At our own expense!

We don't go to the Russian Embassy to celebrate the October Revolution, or to the American Embassy for the Fourth of July celebration. We feel better that way.

Our rule could hit snags. But I think that after an event which took place one day in the Lazareffs' home at Louveciennes, just outside Paris, there won't be any danger of snags....

One day General de Gaulle invited a whole crowd of French artists to a big party at the Élysée. It must have been in 1967. We sent back our "Absent from Paris" note politely. The party was on a Friday. It so happened that the next Sunday I was invited to lunch at Louveciennes. You might say that there's a certain hypocrisy involved in

---

°That is, the Élysée Palace, the president's official town residence.
†François Mitterrand, secretary general of the Socialist party, leader of the opposition and a potential future president.

refusing to go to the Élysée and then going to lunch at the Lazareffs'. But I've always been invited to the Lazareffs', even when I was officially punished for having signed the Manifesto of 121. (I particularly remember a Sunday in 1961. Françoise Sagan was there too, and she was in quarantine also. I think Monsieur Pompidou and his wife were there. I know Maître Floriot was there. He spoke aggressively to me and to Françoise Sagan, something like: "Well, well—the two Arab-lovers." He was a distinguished lawyer, but the level of his wit notably lacked distinction.)

Well, on that particular Sunday there was nobody else especially important around the table. It was intimate and fun. There was Françoise Arnoul, the Gall brothers, and Gérard Lebovici, then still a very young man and not yet the important impresario he is today. I don't remember exactly who the other guests were, but I know that at about five in the afternoon those I've named were the only people left, besides, of course, Hélène* and Pierrot. Suddenly the dining-room door opened, and there was André Malraux, stopping in as a neighbor, without having telephoned. He was with his wife and his son-in-law. At the time he was Minister of Culture, so he had been co-host of the splendid party the previous Friday, to which we had politely answered "Absent from Paris." Of course, having been caught in Louveciennes, I could legitimately have claimed not to be in Paris. . . .

So here I was, caught in the act by my guardian minister. I had only met André Malraux once before in my life; it was in Cannes the evening he had handed me my prize for *Room at the Top*. My reply had been short and to the point: I'd said, "Thank you," and that was the sum total of our contact. Hélène introduced us. As it happened, I knew Madame Malraux, having met her a few days after her marriage to Roland Malraux, shortly before he was arrested by the Germans. He died later in a concentration camp. I had never again met the young widow, who later

*Hélène Lazareff, the director of *Elle* magazine.

438

married her brother-in-law. But she clearly remembered that evening, which must have been in spring 1944.

For about ten minutes Malraux acted as though he didn't know who I was. He talked with Pierrot and Hélène, but then he turned abruptly toward me and said, "By the way, we didn't see you Friday at the Élysée."

Hélène had that rigid smile of a hostess who fears that one of her guests is about to commit a colossal gaffe. Pierrot sank into his chair like a Ping-Pong fan waiting for the tournament to begin.

"No, no; finally we couldn't make it. You know how it is: I had a pile of laundry this high, it builds up and up, and when at last I got to do it, I didn't keep track of time, and when I looked at the clock it was too late; there wasn't time to get dressed. . . ." It wasn't the funniest joke of the year, but delivered with appropriate gestures and timing, it was funny enough. Malraux laughed; everyone laughed— especially Hélène. A relieved Hélène!

"Oh, we gave them lots to eat and drink after I'd slapped a Legion of Honor on five or six of 'em. They left quite content," Malraux said, with the superb disdain he can manage like no one else.

"Well, listening to you talk like that, Monsieur le Ministre, I'm glad it was laundry day."

We knew from those who went there (under the banner of being able to express their feelings and do something for culture) that it was carefully arranged so that no one had been able to talk to de Gaulle or Malraux; they remained in a little antechamber where the guests were led one by one from the big salon, and the conversation was limited to "Delighted to see you," which did strictly nothing for the Maisons de la Culture budget, or for the film industry.

But here we weren't in a little antechamber, and we talked. Malraux made a few remarks about some of the stands we had taken, and since the level of his humor was different from that of Maître Floriot, it was very funny. I ended up telling him that if I thought as I did about some things, it was probably because I had read his book La

Condition Humaine (Man's Fate) when I was very young. He was as fascinating as he was on some of his big television interviews, as overwhelming as he had been about Jean Moulin. It was before 1968, so I didn't have to ask him how he felt about shouting: "France for the French." That was yet to come.

The Malrauxes stayed a long time. Finally they left. Hélène and Pierrot took them to the veranda. I stayed alone in the dining room for a moment; Françoise and the others had gone to get their coats. I was ruminating over those last two hours. Suddenly Malraux reappeared at the door, came to me, tapped my shoulder, and said, "I got you, didn't I?" He laughed, I laughed, and I said, "Yes."

He whirled out. A meeting like that is worth ten official meetings, and it confirmed us in our decision to make no exceptions to our rule to refuse any of those decorations they "slap" on you.

A little while back someone proposed to Montand that he "propose" him for the Legion of Honor. It was a very kind letter from the Centre du Cinéma* and was accompanied by a printed questionnaire. All you had to do was sit down at a desk for a few hours and try to remember all the admirable things you had accomplished in the course of your exemplary life: acts of courage, services rendered to the Nation and Art, foreign successes that contributed to France's renown, etc. You had to write those things down after each printed question. It was a little like a visa form, if you see what I mean! After that you sign your name, but you sign it after a statement that says in effect that because of all the things you have enumerated *you* solicit the honor of being raised to the rank of Chevalier of the Legion of Honor.

About fifteen years ago, our friend François Périer suddenly said to me, "I'm very pleased; I wrote my letter this morning." "What letter?" "My letter refusing the Legion of Honor." "Did they offer it to you?" "Not yet, but

---

*The National Film Center, the professional organization for the entire film industry, run by civil servants.

given my splendid career, they're bound to offer it to me someday or other, so I might as well have my letter ready. This morning I had the time." "Will you show it to me?" "No; I'll show it to you the day they offer it to me." Years passed. One fine morning there's François on the telephone. "I hope I'm not waking you up, *ma chérie*, but I thought you might like to hear my letter. It came this morning, my offer from the Legion of Honor."

His letter had great courtesy and dignity. It said that he had been active in a profession he loved, that he hoped he had served the theater, but he didn't feel himself worthy of a decoration that had always seemed to him to be for those who had served the nation.

Composing Montand's letter was a slightly more delicate matter. He explained that as the son of naturalized immigrants, he was all the more touched by the honor that was offered. If his parents were still alive, he would run the risk of shocking them if he refused. Unfortunately, however, they had died, and thus were no longer shockable. The letter ended with somewhat the same remarks as François had written in his letter—in fact, the three of us composed it together. We had a good time that afternoon, and I wish we had kept some of the drafts, because they were funny.

Question: Did they ever offer it to you?

Simone Signoret: No.

Question: When did all this happen?

Simone Signoret: About three years ago.

Question: Suppose they offered it to you today?

Simone Signoret: We would sit down again, Montand, François, and I, and write another letter....

Question: During this interview you keep saying "we," rarely "I." In twenty-seven years, you've never disagreed with Montand?

Simone Signoret: We've squabbled a lot—thank goodness, or it would be tragic. It would indicate that we no longer talk. It would indicate that we no longer see the world around us or see each other. Things may change, but we'll go on squabbling—and loving.

Question: What might change?

Simone Signoret: I've never thought that any couple was safe from a possible separation. I've never had that kind of certainty. I've always been wildly astonished, every day, that things go on.

We're just the same age, Montand and I. He's lived beside me while I aged, and I've lived beside him while he matured. That's one of the differences between men and women. *They* mature; their white hair is called "silvery temples," the lines on their faces are "chiseled," and sometimes they trot their fifties around like my Professor Vantieghem at Neuilly when I was seventeen. If they happen to be good actors, and on top of everything sing well, and if they're funny and tender and strong and famous and rich, it would be quite abnormal for girls not to notice them, and for them not to notice girls. It would be quite presumptuous to set aside the possibility that they might fall in love for keeps and that the girl involved wouldn't necessarily be a bitch.

I hope I can honestly say that if Montand were to fall in love with a beautiful young creature and suddenly wanted to remake his life with her—that is, to wake up in a bed that wasn't hers but was theirs, in a house that belonged to both of them—I wouldn't reply with: "You can't do this to me after everything we've been through together." I think I'd be up to it. Maybe I'm lying; maybe I'm lying to myself. I may be a thorough hypocrite when I say that, but say it I do. Maybe I'm being a little like François with his letter for the Legion of Honor. I'm taking precautions . . . just in case.

If it were to happen, I think that cutie would occasionally run into me around the house . . . even if I never went there. It wouldn't be fair to her; not fair to weigh on the present and the future in the name of the past . . . but it would probably be like that.

I'm doing my grandiloquent number . . . I'd rather it didn't happen, but if it were to happen, I hope I'd be up to the level of today's grand statements.

No more questions, Maurice?

Epilogue

I will never know what person, thing, or place provoked nostalgia for the writer of that New York graffiti. He obviously felt an urge to write on that wall that it "isn't what it used to be." Maybe the spirit that moved him was that he was glad to get it out of his system. Or perhaps he was sad to find nothing around that reawakened it.

It took a good memory to take my dive back into time. That's really no accomplishment: I have a good memory. What I don't have is nostalgia.

To check on my memory I went from Autheuil to the Place Dauphine via the old road that we haven't taken for years. It has no tollbooths, and yet it's called the "Route de Quarante Sous."

To my great satisfaction, I saw that they still make songbirds in Bonnières, that in Rosny there's still a main street that the schoolchildren cross at about eleven-thirty. I didn't check to see whether the only *bac* that Marie ever passed is still there, but I did observe that the statue of Sully hasn't been replaced by a skyscraper. If you go through Mantes-la-Jolie, instead of going around it on the

autoroute, you still see the Normandie cinema, where
Montand sang one evening in 1953 or 1954 and where his
posters were daubed with tar. And Rolleboise still rhymes
with *framboise*.

At the end of the trip there's a Science Fiction City.
That's Puteaux and Courbevoie. That was the beginning or
the end of the Fête de Neuilly. There was once a crossroads
there, and a statue: La Défense. Today it's a complex, a
section of the city, a group of tall buildings with all that
goes with them. "Our offices are at La Défense," announce
the young organizers of symposia and colloquia. They
don't know that their air-conditioned, honeycomb-like
cells on the thirty-third floor have sprung from roots dug
far below in small cellars and humble two-rooms-with-
kitchen.

And from those lodgings forever came early in the
morning the Madame Albertines to do the cleaning in
Neuilly, and to those two-rooms-with-kitchen their
daughters returned in the afternoon, after we said good-
bye at the door of our school. They had gotten their
certificates from the local elementary school, and arrived
in our secondary school with a perfect knowledge of math,
geography, grammar, and spelling. They worked like mad
to catch up with the rest of us in Latin. And they did catch
up. They never went out with the rest of us on Thursday
afternoon; they didn't come to the teas, nor, later, did they
come to the dancing parties. They were the Puteaux or
Courbevoie group. They were serious, hard-working, and
proud. And they probably folded out a cot in the dining
room once the dishes had been wiped and the neatly
written essay on Lamartine had been carefully put into
their schoolbag for the next morning. That neat, well-
written essay, well-punctuated and cleanly copied out,
honored the elementary-school teacher who had explained
to one Madame Albertine that it was surely worthwhile for
la petite to continue her schooling.

I have no memory of Puteaux or Courbevoie. We never
ventured there. Those were the poor suburbs. But the other

morning I saw them, my schoolmates, as I drove through their section of town, which now looks like the constructions my Benjamin builds with his Lego set. There weren't many of them; I saw three. Their sweaters weren't cashmere; their stockings were cotton. Their textbooks were obviously secondhand, carefully patched with Scotch tape, and protected by midnight-blue covers. A label showed that one was a Latin grammar and the other selections from nineteenth-century literature. Those little girls never drew mustaches or imperial tufts on the faces of Caesar or Brutus. When the midnight-blue paper was torn and scuffed, the books reappeared with fresh covers. They never had yo-yos. Being half-day boarders, they had their lunches in and never ran up any debts with Gladys, the concierge. They knew how to do without a croissant or a chocolate roll at recreation time. After class, they rushed to get their bus while we walked quietly home through our well-tended streets. Neither in the junior nor in the senior class did they ever go near the Sabot Bleu. They had Christian names like Véronique, Caroline, Mathilde. Old-fashioned names now borrowed by the hostesses in the thirty-three air-conditioned stories at La Défense. But in the thirties, being named Véronique and living in Puteaux, or worse still, in the damp and grimy Ile de la Jatte, wasn't easy for an adolescent confronted with the Michelines, Claudines, Simones, and Annies living in Neuilly-sur-Seine. Even less easy was the papa in overalls waiting for you on the sidewalk across the street. That was after the *pré-bac*, the rehearsal for the real *bachot* exam. In the solid bourgeois families, when you come home you're greeted with a knowing "Well, what were the exam questions?" and in working families it's "Did you know the answers?"

It was those skyscrapers that made me think about those girls. I've never really thought about them since we were separated, without ever having really met. I must have involuntarily "computerized" them.

Our island will never have a skyscraper. There aren't

445

many of us living on it, the little triangle called Place Dauphine. We all know one another by sight. We aren't neighborly in the sense that we visit one another. But we smile when we meet chez Paul. Our kind of collusion is like what we used to see in the sly eyes of the Bretons when they watched the tourists arrive, back in my childhood; an attitude that would be revised a little later when the "tourists" began to build.

But no one's going to build here. And no one's going to demolish here. It's not really an island; it's really more a tiny islet. The new high-rise buildings are all around. They're coming closer. But there's a frontier they'll never cross. Not unless they can climb, or jump, over the Pont-Neuf.

The chestnut trees have been replanted on our triangle, and they're in foliage. Maybe one day they'll no longer be standing because of the parking garage that was hollowed out underneath us. But for us islanders nothing appears to have changed, and nothing appears to be changeable, and we have a kind of stupid pride about it like the inhabitants of a fortified city under siege who know it will never capitulate.

We have our history, and our stories. Our history includes Henri IV, Louis XIII, the French Revolution, and the Liberation of Paris. That's our history, the history of France. We have three layers of cellars, our walls are more than a meter thick, and our houses often have two exits.

But our stories—our own history—concern events like the arm exercises of the old lady in No. 14 who's just had her cast removed; a tearoom opening in the little store that used to house a chaste and timid seamstress; a long or short stay by a new tramp on the Place benches; a second child born to someone who used to ring doorbells at the time our Catherine rang doorbells; the memory of Georgette and Hubert, the two tramps who, forced off the banks of the Seine by the 1954 floods, came up to cohabit with us, the islanders, on our benches and in our cellars, depending on the weather, for so long. The flood had made emigrants of them, and they liked it better in their new location. Georgette had a degree in literature and Hubert was a lawyer. Her bereavements and his return from deportation had made tramps of them. The police picked them up regularly, to the great disapproval of the islanders. They would get into the paddy wagon with the sandwiches that had been thrust upon them, among good wishes for a speedy return. The same paddy wagon would bring them back a few days later. They were sobered up, deloused, and thirsty, and they would take up their habitation on our benches again. Our children would come down off the two huge stone lions and the steps of the Palace of Justice, which were their playground—unless they happened to be going around ringing doorbells—and announce the good news: "Hubert and Georgette are back!"

Hubert and Georgette are dead. We still talk about them. We've forgotten how they were sometimes noisy and smelly; all we remember is that they were intelligent and cultivated and very funny. Then there was big Simone with her pirate's hat. She wasn't a boozer! She would drink her daily glass of milk at our kitchen window, and wash herself early in the morning in the clean, cool water in the gutter. One morning at five-thirty when I left to film on location for *Casque d'Or*, there she was in the middle of the square, stark naked. Her bundles and the 1930-model pram that was her suitcase and closet were strewn around her bench. She said, "Bonjour, Simone," and I said, "Bonjour, Simone." That same week I met her on the Champs Élysées, and I said, "Bonjour, Simone," but she refused to recognize me; we weren't in our territory. Big Simone has disappeared, but we still talk about her. We'll talk about her more and more. We cling to them, our legendary characters, and our little island legends. We're sorry for the newcomers, or rather we look at them with a certain condescension. Oh, you live on the Place Dauphine! Did you know Georgette, Hubert, Simone?

Catherine, my daughter, whatever fine residential quarter you'll live in, I know that Benjamin, my grandson, will never rub shoulders with the descendants of the Court of Miracles, those precursors of the hippies, the way you did when you were a child, daily, naturally.

It takes the big trial days to remind us that we live in the shadow of that palace, the Palace of Justice, which we really consider an accessory to our environment. When a taxi driver confuses the Porte Dauphine with the Place Dauphine, we generally say, "Place Dauphine, near the Palais de Justice." When we pronounce those two sonorous words, *Palais* and *Justice*, we're making sounds the way we did when we were children and sang: *"Dansons la Capucine, y a pas de pain chez nous, y en a chez la voisine, mais ce n'est pas pour nous. You, les petits cailloux!"*°

That is, one isn't really thinking about the meaning of the words one's sowing in the sky.

Palaisdejustice—that's one word. The steps of the Palais, the stone lions, all that very quickly becomes a ritual language used by the island mothers to denote the place where they're certain of finding their sons and daughters to round them up for their baths or showers or sponge baths in the kitchen sink at about seven in the evening.

But a "palace" is a castle, a habitation, a dwelling, a residence, a kingdom. It's a solemn word. As solemn as the words "there's no bread in our larder, the neighbor has some" seem trite.

It takes the big trials, however, for the restaurants on the Place to hang out their "Full" placards, and remind us that every day inside that edifice there are accused, accusors, the guilty, the innocent, the witnesses, the false witnesses, the judges, the juries, the Peeping Toms, the clerks, and the policemen. Every day just up the road from us. That gentleman taking three turns around the Place, looking worried and talking to himself, may be the widower of that murdered woman, or the thief's brother, or the future divorcee, or the careless accountant. He comes and goes in

°"Dance like Capuchin nuns, there's no bread in our larder, the neighbor has some, but it's not for the likes of us. O ho, the little pebbles."

front of windows whose curtains are discreetly inched aside by a finger, the way it's done by provincial busybodies. We're used to it. Strangers in the Place always seem to be strangely troubled. We don't even notice them anymore. We know they're only there in transit. In a little while, they'll go up that great stone staircase. Now they're rehearsing the truths or lies they've decided to tell or that they've been counseled to tell under oath, and someone's liberty or nonliberty, or sometimes life or death—voted, computerized, desired—will depend upon it.

Without those trials we'd forget that the steps of the Palais are more than a playground. It's all played out right next to us. But we rarely think about it.

On the second floor of the Palais, two or three windows often remain lit up till a late hour of the night. We look up at them when we come home very late. We don't know what's being hatched behind those glass panes, but we know it isn't gay; never.

But by morning we've forgotten. We aren't even able to recognize which windows were illuminated in the night. When day breaks, they're all the same. And daytimes, on the Place, everything's gay; always. When it rains we say, "What weather!" and if it's fine we say, "What weather!"

I've brought myself home. I was beginning to run the danger of becoming a chronicler. I would never have come to a stop. There'd be no reason not to go on till I die. . . .

I've played on the words "memory" and "nostalgia" with a certain hypocrisy. I couldn't swear that I've been totally sincere when I say I have no nostalgia. I may have a nostalgia for the unshared memory. . . .

But one's recollections are never entirely shared. When one puts them to the test of a confrontation, it's often as hopeless as a witness for the defense who says in all good faith that the dress was blue when it was green.

It was green for me.

It was colorless for another.

It was blue for a third person.

449

All of us liked one another. We didn't see the same things. Or rather we saw the same things together at the same moment, and we saw them differently.

When one tells a story one usurps the memory of others. Because of the simple fact that they were there, one has stolen their memories, their recollections, their nostalgia, their truths.

When I said "we," I took possession. But that was to tell the tale. My memory or my nostalgia have made me weave threads. Not forge chains.

Index

Annabella, 46
Antonioni, Michelangelo, 75
Aragon, Louis, 175–177, 181, 204, 245–248, 395
Aragon, Mrs. Louis, 175, 176, 177, 248
Arletty (actress), 69, 74
Arnhem battle, 92
Arnoul, Françoise, 386, 438
Arrighi, Madame, 17, 18
Artur, José, 143
Astaire, Fred, 265, 327
Aubrac, Lucie, 40
Audin, Maurice, 280
Aujourd 'hui, 52
Aunt Claire, 39, 87
Autheuil, 141–143, 262
Avedon, Richard, 336
Averty, Jean-Christophe, 105
Aymé, Marcel, 144, 153–154, 162

Bacall, Lauren, 279, 301
Balachova (actress), 75
Baldwin, James, 283, 367
Barbie, 40
Barrault, Jean-Louis, 61
Bates, Alan, 379
Baudouin, Madame, 50–52
Beaume, Georges, 265
Becker, Jacques, 85, 126–135, 146, 178
Begon, Maude, 434
Bellon, Loleh, 130
Beloyannis (Greek hero), 380–383

Benassy, Monsieur, 268
Ben-Gurion, David, 272, 273
Ben-Gurion, Madame, 272, 273
Ben-Hur, 327, 328
Bergman, Ingrid, 367
Bernes (Russian Sinatra), 190, 204
Bernstein, Leonard, 301
Bernstein, Mrs. Leonard, 301
Berry, John, 143
Berry, Jules, 74
Bert, Liliane, 70
Besse, Jacques, 35
Beverly Hills Hotel, 308, 309, 312, 324
Biberman, Herbert, 186
Billancourt studios, 131
Birch Society, 354
Blanchard, Claude, 52
Blier, Bernard, 98, 155, 156, 159, 160
Blin, Roger, 36, 56, 61, 62, 127
Bodne family, 285, 286
Bogarde, Dirk, 366
Boléro, 69
Bolshoi Ballet, 192, 193
Borderie (producer), 162, 163, 167, 169, 170
Borderie-DEFA coproduction, 162
Boussinot, Roger, 216
Bouvier, Jacqueline, 78, 79, 137
Braine, John, 256–258

457